UNCOMMON MEN

The Sergeants Major
of the
Marine Corps

D0988773

JOHN C. CHAPIN
Captain, USMCR, Retired

Foreword
by
Alfred M. Gray
General, USMC, Retired

 White Mane Publishing Company, Inc.

This Burd Street Press publication
was printed by
Beidel Printing House, Inc.
63 West Burd Street
Shippensburg, PA 17257-0152 USA

In respect for the scholarship contained herein, the acid-free paper used in this book meets the guidelines for permanence and durability of the Committee on Production Guidelines for Book Longevity of the Council on Library Resources.

For a complete list of available publications
please write
Burd Street Press
Division of White Mane Publishing Company, Inc.
P.O. Box 152
Shippensburg, PA 17257-0152 USA

Library of Congress Cataloging-in-Publication Data
Chapin, John C.
        Uncommon men : the sergeants major of the Marine Corps / John C.
    Chapin : foreword by Alfred M. Gray.
            p.   cm.
        Includes bibliographical references and index.
        ISBN 0-942597-45-1. -- ISBN 1-57249-154-X (pbk.)
            1. United States.   Marine Corps—Non-commissioned officers.
    I. Title.
    VE23.C43   1992
    359.9'6338'0973--dc20   92-32620
                                                                CIP

CONTENTS

FOREWORD

This is a book which strikes a responsive chord in me. Having served as a sergeant myself, preceding my 37 years as a commissioned officer, I have had over all these years a strong personal feeling about the crucial role of the noncommissioned officer in the Marine Corps. When I was commanding general of the 2d Marine Division and then of the Fleet Marine Force, Atlantic, I saw on a daily basis how much my sergeants major there contributed to our operations. Going back through the years, I have known the various Sergeants Major of the Marine Corps and always had great respect for them. Now, as Commandant, I have an even greater appreciation for both the billet and its current occupant. Through his frequent contact and frank communication with me, this sergeant major has proven to be an invaluable representative in decisions affecting all the enlisted personnel of our Corps.

He is, I well realize, the successor to a line of ten superb men who, for more than 30 years, have similarly worked with the Commandant. I have previously emphasized the critical need for "enhancing within ourselves what we call the warrior virtues: courage, integrity, intelligence, and concerned leadership." The men in this book personify those virtues to a pre-eminent degree, and their careers, told herein, add lustre to the title, "The Sergeant Major of the Marine Corps."

Alfred M. Gray
General, U.S. Marine Corps
Commandant of the Marine Corps, 1987-91

AUTHOR'S PREFACE

This book began as a result of a logical analysis and ended up as a labor of love. Originally, I was struck by the wide variety of books published by and about senior officers of the Marine Corps (as well as the other military services), while there was next to nothing in print about outstanding enlisted men. And who could be more outstanding than the talented men who have filled the top-most post of Sergeant Major of the Marine Corps?

As I moved from this self-evident fact to the research, interviews, and writing, my motivation changed from the pure rationality of filling a void to one of respect and admiration for those men who are portrayed in this book. They came alive for me as dedicated, distinctive individuals, rather than as a succession of stereotyped, faceless automatons following the same career path. Rising from the simplest of backgrounds, often with no financial resources and a minimal education, they struck a chord in my heart because they exemplify a basic conviction on which our country is built: If you work hard enough to learn your profession and serve others, no matter where you started, you can go all the way to the top! So it developed that the years I spent immersed in the lives of these men gave me a deep sense of humility, and this book became, in fact, a labor of love.

Given the range of time and personalities herein, it is obvious that the cooperation and willing help of a good many people and organizations were essential. I wish to thank, first and foremost, the men who have served as Sergeant Major of the Marine Corps. Every one of them gave me information that was a critical supplement to the bare-bones outline of the official file biographies. (Although one overly modest individual took several months of persuading, and another was hidden away in the Arctic wilderness and didn't answer his mail for months!)

In several cases, the wives and/or children of these men added considerably to their stories. Then, too, the Commandants with whom they served so intimately supplied their special insights. Fortunately, five of those retired four-star generals were still alive, and each gave me a generous allotment of his time and his memories. I am grateful to General Alfred Gray for the foreword he contributed from his knowledgeable perspective.

There are other retired generals and colonels who shared with me their recollections of the billet (office) of Sergeant Major of the Marine Corps, as well as comments on some of the occupants. In addition, there is an interlocking blood brotherhood of retired sergeants major spread all over the United States. They all know each other; they all have served on active duty with each other; they all keep in touch with each other at organizational reunions, Marine Corps birthday balls, by visits and phone calls—or at least it seems this way. They had lots of "sea stories" to relate about the eleven men in this book.

Because all the retired individuals I mentioned had personal, first-hand knowledge of what happened and what the man was really like, I chose to quote them directly and extensively. This gives a more accurate, incisive picture than any second-hand paraphrase I could substitute.

Within the present Marine Corps, there were many sources of assistance. The Public Affairs office at Headquarters combed its files; the eleventh Sergeant Major of the Marine Corps gave me access to his correspondence, as well as two thoughtful and informative interviews. (Curiously, there is no file whatsoever at Headquarters or elsewhere with the work papers of past Sergeants Major of the Marine Corps.)

The History and Museums Division of Headquarters is located in the Marine Corps Historical Center in the Washington Navy Yard. Closely connected to its mission is a separate legal entity, the Marine Corps Historical Foundation, located in Quantico, Virginia. I am very thankful for the exceptional support I have received from these two groups. The Division was helpful in my office logistics, thanks to the interest of its Director, Brigadier General Edwin Simmons, USMC, Retired. The various resources at the Historical Center proved invaluable: the Archives, the Library, the Art Collection, the Reference Section, and the Photography Section. The Foundation made a generous grant which greatly facilitated the research travel and the typing of this book. The latter was superbly handled by my Wizard of the Word Processor, Mrs. Meredith Hartley, whose magic fingers produced accurate, orderly printouts from my chaotic, scrambled original drafts. William S. Birdseye and Martin K. Gordon, White Mane's editors, performed well those editorial tasks that prepared my manuscript for publication.

I owe acknowledgement to Major Hubert G. Duncan, USMC, Retired, for permission to use those wonderfully apt quotations in the Dedication and Chapter 2 of this book.

In Quantico, Virginia, the Marine Corps Association publishes two magazines which currently circulate throughout the Corps: *Leatherneck* and *Marine Corps Gazette*. The editors of these were kind to me in making available photographs and granting permission for quotations.

To one and all, I say again, "Thank you for helping tell the stories of these remarkable men."

John C. Chapin
Captain, USMCR, Retired
Washington, D.C.

The author as a lieutenant.
Author's Collection

DEDICATION

This book is dedicated to those first eleven "uncommon men" who have faithfully served as Sergeant Major of the Marine Corps, as well as to the other noncommissioned officers they have represented so superbly. In the final analysis, however, it is dedicated to *all* the enlisted men of the Corps, who have stood for something unique that has touched the very fiber of our nation for over 200 years. Their quintessence is well depicted in this profile by Hubert G. Duncan, a retired Marine major:

> "He must have been in his early sixties. He had the weathered look of a retired Marine. I saw a lifetime of dedication and loyalty. I saw the deep love he felt for the Marine Corps. I saw the blind obedience of a young recruit for the mere utterances of his NCOs. I saw the pride of a young Marine on his first leave as he strutted about in his uniform. I saw the fear of battle well controlled by the discipline seemingly inherent in him. I saw the sorrow of lost comrades. I saw the bravery which caused him to wade ashore on countless beaches in the face of murderous fire. I saw the humanity which precluded rage and long-lasting hate for the enemy who had tried to kill him in so many wars...I saw the love for his family and the hope for his children...But through it all I saw the overwhelming love for the Marine Corps and all it stood for."

Chapter 1

HOW IT ALL STARTED

Sergeant Major! The words have come down through the years with a unique mystique, symbolic of a small elite group of professional military men. It's a title that evokes a cluster of different images. Some will see in their mind's eye the traditional British sergeant major leading his regiment into hand to hand combat. Some will think of the private who sees from afar a sergeant major as the remote, all-powerful embodiment and voice of the colonel who commands his regiment. Others will envision a grizzled veteran in stiffly starched khaki managing an endless flow of administrative papers across his desk. However, there is one additional and special vignette in the mind of every U.S. Marine: the single man who stands at the apex of all noncommissioned officers, the "uncommon man" who is Sergeant Major of the Marine Corps.

How did this happen? How did it all start? Like many traditions in the military, the roots reach a long way into history. Sergeant was a well-known rank in the feudal foot soldiers of the 13th century, and the English army of the 16th century had sergeants major. Reintroduced in the 18th century, in the succeeding years and wars the rank of sergeant major came to occupy an almost legendary senior position of prestige and power in the regiments of the

British army. The long years of experience, serving in all parts of the globe and moving up the promotion ladder, the command presence they projected, the leadership in battle—all these contributed to an aura of authority that gave them enormous influence over the lives of the enlisted men under them. Serving in direct command of the troops, they oversaw the drill, discipline, and administration of their regiments.

These then, were some of the historical precedents when Congress passed the Act of July 11, 1798, making a Marine Corps a part of the naval establishment of the new United States government. However, the Corps has for many years marked as its birthday November 10, the day in 1775 when the Continental Congress established the United States Marines Corps.

The 1798 Act allowed for the appointment of a sergeant major, and it was not long before the Commandant of the Marine Corps seized this opportunity. On January 1, 1801, Archibald Summers became the first sergeant major in the Marine Corps. He was succeeded in 1803 by Alexander Forrest, who served until his death at age seventy in 1832, drawing down a basic pay of $10.00 a month. (Although there were additional perquisites, such as pay for rations, wood, and hay.) Privates of that period received $6.00 a month as basic compensation. In spite of the impressive title of 'sergeant major,' those men were really just clerks at Headquarters, assistants to the adjutant. Their uniforms gave the impression of authority and they did have a key role in administration, but in reality they had no function in relation to the other enlisted men of the Marine Corps. In fact, they viewed their enlistment papers merely as articles of employment.

After the two pioneers, the Marine Corps finally moved, in 1833, to establish the sergeant major as a permanent position. Legislation enacted in 1834 confirmed the right of the Marine Corps to issue warrants (certificates of appointment) for sergeant major. Accordingly, Venerando Pulizzi served in the position from 1836 to 1852 and saw his monthly pay climb to $17.00.

By 1865 the sergeant major's base pay had risen, as a result of the Civil War, to $348 a year. In the peacetime era that followed it gradually fell to $276 a year in 1893. After continuing with one man in that rank for the rest of the 19th century, the Marine Corps was authorized five sergeants major in 1899 as a result of the War with Spain. Base pay was $388 a month. Since then, an expanding Corps with growing responsibilities in the 20th century has necessitated a corresponding increase in the number and pay of sergeants major. No longer recruited from young men on the Civil List, as in the earliest years, but rising through the ranks, the modern senior NCOs have the professional skills that earn them their authority. While there have been episodes of those men in combat, their principal responsibility has remained administrative, burdened by the explosive growth of the complex and technical requirements of modern warfare.

Two of the most famous sergeants major in Marine Corps history were awarded the Medal of Honor for exploits in their younger days. Dan Daly, as a private in China in 1900 during the Boxer Rebellion and as a gunnery sergeant in Haiti in 1915, became the only enlisted Marine ever to receive two Medals of Honor. It was he who leaped forward into the teeth of heavy German fire at Belleau Wood in World War I, and then reputedly yelled at his men, "Come on, you sons of bitches, do you want to live forever?"

John Quick was awarded his Medal of Honor for conspicuous bravery during the War with Spain in 1898. When a U.S. Navy ship misdirected its shells on a detachment of U.S. Marines, Sergeant Quick mounted a hilltop under furious Spanish rifle fire and coolly semaphored the ship to shift its fire. His dramatic career continued afterwards with more medals for heroic achievements in the Philippines, Mexico, and France.

All through the years of the 20th century, until the end of World War II, the Marine Corps tinkered constantly with the nomenclature, pay, and organization of its enlisted ranks. The sergeant major always remained at the top of the hierarchy and pay scale, but various other ranks moved in and out of his pay level. Further, promotion policies to the rank of sergeant major changed often. At one time, first sergeants were chagrined to see sergeants and even corporals who had limited line experience jumped over them to sergeant major. That was corrected in a later policy restricting promotion to sergeant major to first sergeants only. The increasing specialization of military skills was illustrated when Headquarters Marine Corps instituted the rank of sergeant major (aviation) in 1945.

By 1946, there were a myriad of noncommissioned officer titles, and with machine record accounting replacing hand processing, a radical restructuring took place. After nearly 150 years of prestige and tradition, the sergeants major of 1946 were dismayed to find their historic title abolished. They were now to be thrown in with seven other senior enlisted grades and designated master sergeants.

The eclipse lasted eight long years, but finally, in December, 1954, an official Marine Corps Memorandum recognized that the role of the most senior enlisted leader was too important to be lumped together with specialists such as cooks and paymasters. The new edict resurrected the rank of sergeant major and gave it precedence as the senior noncommissioned officer (NCO), although the pay level was the same as that for first sergeants and master sergeants.

The Marine Corps had now arrived at an important juncture. With the Korean War and the advent of more and more technical and mechanical equipment requirements, the number of noncommissioned officers—including senior levels—had grown to an unprecedented 58 percent of total enlisted strength (compared to 25 percent in 1941). This presented the Commandant of the Marine Corps with a critical question: how best to create a channel for the unfettered flow of information to and from this large and crucial group of noncommissioned officers? And how to give proper recognition to the very best men? The story of how those questions were answered is an interesting example of how change can sometimes be accomplished—even in a compartmentalized bureaucracy like the headquarters of any military service.

General Randolph Pate, who instituted the present position and picked the first individual for the position of Sergeant Major of the Marine Corps.

General Randolph Pate was Commandant in 1957. Two of his key assistants were Colonel Ormond Simpson, the military secretary to the Commandant, and Colonel DeWolf Schatzel, the secretary of the general staff. As in most organizations, there were relaxed "bull sessions" after the office had formally closed. During one of the late afternoon sessions, early in 1957, the idea surfaced that the communication and recognition problems might be reduced by creating a new, prestigious position for an individual who would be the senior enlisted person in the Marine Corps, with the rank of "Sergeant Major of the Marine Corps." The vision called for someone of a different order than the men who had filled the familiar billet of Headquarters Sergeant Major, a function that went back to Archibald Summers. The idea was broached informally to General Pate and his chief of staff, Lieutenant General Vernon Megee, and soon the word came through, "We'll do it!"

Both the records of Headquarters Marine Corps and General Pate's personal papers have no details of that fundamental policy decision, but there are two uncorroborated stories that may help explain what led up to it. There are those (including General Louis Wilson, a later Commandant) who believe that an "Anglophile Mafia" at Headquarters influenced the Commandant. Certainly, the post-Korean War mood there was one which would lead to reinstating traditional ranks such as Marine gunner (a senior NCO who has received a warrant to the status of officer), gunnery sergeant, and lance corporal. Moreover, there was then in the Plans Branch of Headquarters a redoubtable colonel who had just returned from a tour of duty at the British Amphibious Warfare Center in Fremington, England. Robert Heinl, quirky with his swagger stick and old-fashioned Sam Browne belt, was devoted to British military lore with its dramatic role for the sergeant major, and he had become the leading Marine writer on historical traditions of the Corps. The Commandant was sympathetic and Heinl had his ear.

The other story suggests a much more mundane factor in General Pate's decision. The general had seen first-hand the value of a senior sergeant major when he had commanded the 1st Division in Korea and had had a sergeant major there who had worked very closely with him. Now, as Commandant, the question may well have gone through his mind, "If a sergeant major was so helpful to me then, why don't I have one now?"

Whatever the influences, the decision was made. This was an historic first, unique in the annals of American military history, for there was no similar billet in any other branch of the United States Armed Forces.

Next came the need to implement the policy decision. There was quick agreement that the new sergeant major would be placed in the Office of the Chief of Staff, which funneled all appropriate matters to the Commandant. There he would serve as principal advisor on issues affecting the enlisted men and women of the Marine Corps.

With that general, all-inclusive function established, the next step was to pinpoint the right man to launch the new concept. Outstanding administrative skills were clearly a priority, to help deal with the excessive 58% proportion of noncommissioned officers in the Marine Corps. To find the best man to fill such a demanding billet, the search naturally turned to the senior NCOs of the Corps. There were some 240 sergeants major on active duty at that time. Who should be selected? As before, an informal process produced an answer. When the Commandant asked for suggestions, the Secretary of the General Staff, Colonel Schatzel, commented, "We've got a very good man right here who runs the 'back room' where all the correspondence for you and Chief of Staff is processed." General Pate accepted this recommendation, and so it was that the first in a series of remarkable men took up the office of Sergeant Major of the Marine Corps.

That was the beginning of a pioneering relationship between the most senior of the Marine Corps' commissioned and noncommissioned officers. It was a combination that would undergo many changes as diverse personalities served together in the decades ahead.

Chapter 2

THE PIONEER

Sergeant Major Wilbur Bestwick

Wilbur Bestwick was the man in the "back room." In June, 1956, the Administration Division of Headquarters had specifically requested him for duty as a sergeant major. In spite of the fact that he was a master sergeant at the time, he came to the headquarters battalion to serve as administrative chief to the secretary of the general staff. It was a prestigious, demanding job, but one for which twenty years of active duty service had well prepared him.

Acting, as he had in previous billets, as a sergeant major, but without an actual warrant for that rank, Bestwick initiated his own paperwork in January, 1957, titled "Verification of desire for appointment to the rank of first sergeant/sergeant major." That formal request was enthusiastically endorsed by the assistant commandant, Lieutenant General Vernon Megee. He wrote:

> I have made a careful examination of Bestwick's entire service record, and I am greatly impressed with what I have seen. The record shows 20 years of service, characterized by consistently exemplary performance in positions of increasing responsibility. Honest, faithful per-

formance of duty is, of course, a characteristic of a number of fine Marines. Master Sergeant Bestwick's record goes far beyond this. Without exception, his commanding officers have given him superior fitness reports and service record book markings.

He has earned the confidence and respect of all. His high professional qualifications for all duties—in garrison and in the field—have been remarked upon with regularity. He has performed first sergeant/ sergeant major duties in a wide variety of assignments, always with distinction. Included in his service is a period as sergeant major of the 1st Marine Division during the Korean conflict. This assignment, I think, is an adequate testimonial to his qualities.

In his present job, Master Sergeant Bestwick is performing duties as Sergeant Major, Headquarters Marine Corps. Quite apart from his professional abilities, Bestwick shows the tact, dignity, and bearing needed for such an important assignment. In my opinion, his selection for designation as first sergeant/sergeant major would bring to that most important rank a Marine who possesses, to a preeminent degree, the qualities traditionally associated with it. I recommend him without reservation.

Nevertheless, the wheels of promotion moved slowly, and in early May, 1957, he was still a master sergeant. Then came the Commandant's selection of him to be the pioneer Sergeant Major of the Marine Corps, and overnight his warrant for that rank came through. In an historic ceremony on May 23 he took office, and General Pate (whom Bestwick had served with in Korea four years earlier) had the pleasure of personally welcoming him to the new position.

In true Marine tradition, there had to be a badge of office. Marine noncommissioned officers had for many years carried a sword, originally in war and then on ceremonial occasions. The NCO sword of 1957 was directly based on a style originally adopted by the War Department in 1850 for foot officers of the infantry and was slightly modified in 1934. Aside from the Marine officer's sword, it is the oldest weapon in American arms still in use. Thus it had been for over a century a special symbol of the rank and authority of a Marine noncommissioned officer. Accordingly, as an appropriate emblem of the new office, a sword was selected and engraved "Sergeant Major of the Marine Corps." The Commandant presented it to Bestwick in the fall of 1957 with the following order:

I hereby give into your charge the Sword of Office of the Sergeant Major of the Marine Corps, symbolizing the proud traditions which distinguish the Sergeants Major of the Corps.

Take this sword and wear it honorably. Guard and cherish it as you guard and cherish the things for which it stands. Deliver it untarnished to your successors, and let your successors deliver it to theirs, and let it thus remain the bright emblem of your office.

Bestwick's official portrait taken in September, 1958.

In his new position, Bestwick had to find his way with no precedents on which to rely. In fact, it was not until he had been in his new billet for five months that a Headquarters order was issued to give some official (albeit generalized) definition to his work: "The Sergeant Major of the Marine Corps assists the Chief of Staff, the Deputy Chiefs of Staff, and the Secretary of the General Staff in the performance of their duties." His wide-ranging experience and a gift for diplomacy stood him in good stead. Working at one moment with senior generals and in the next with new privates or with salty old senior noncommissioned officers, he developed a pattern of what it meant to "assist." Always, there was the inexorable flow of paperwork which had to be referred, answered, or amended.

During that breaking-in period, there were bound to have been many at Headquarters, both commissioned and noncommissioned officers, who were curious about the new man in the new billet. Some, one can surmise, were skeptical of the innovation, while others may have been concerned about the range of the sergeant major's responsibility. Doing his job doggedly, day by day, week by week, and month by month, Bestwick began to crystalize and personify the specifics of what it meant to fill that billet in an exemplary way. General Megee later noted, "His office was tucked away in a corner, but he was very much respected. His style was persuasive rather than dictatorial. In this way he became an advisor on a wide range of issues, far beyond his purely administrative functions."

Those administrative functions focussed on handling the steady flux of paperwork in and out of the chief of staff's office. Beyond this, he was called on for advice on many decisions affecting enlisted personnel. These included such sensitive matters as promotion, pay, and transfers—each an area that called for balanced judgment based on wide experience, as well as a personal style which could achieve consensus agreement, rather than cause confrontation when differing opinions surfaced, as they often did.

Besides these internal responsibilities at Headquarters, there were the visits to the field commands. General Pate established a new custom: his sergeant major would accompany him on all his official trips. Senior noncommissioned officers would then hold a reception for Bestwick at the various posts being inspected to provide frequent opportunities to exchange frank comments and

Inspection trip with the Commandant in October, 1957. Carrying his swagger stick, Bestwick meets with a sergeant major at Camp Lejeune.

learn the latest news on Headquarters policies. It was a new and valuable pipeline for the field NCOs, to make sure that their views and recommendations reached the proper ears at the most senior levels of Headquarters Marine Corps.

In October, 1957, the two men covered Camp Lejeune, the infantry base in North Carolina; Parris Island, the East Coast Recruit Depot in South Carolina; the Marine Corps Supply Center, Albany, Georgia; and seven Marine bases in California, including San Diego, the West Coast Recruit Depot, and the infantry units at Camp Pendleton. The next month they were off again on an even longer trip: Hawaii, Wake Island, the Philippines, Hong Kong, Okinawa, Japan, Korea, Japan again, and finally home via Midway Island.

The talent that had been evident when Bestwick was originally the Headquarters Sergeant Major had led to his selection as Sergeant Major of the Marine Corps. Now his service in that billet, both at his desk and on trips, impressed his superior officers, and their ultimate judgments were evident in Bestwick's fitness reports. Those rendered a unanimous, favorable verdict, sprinkled with such phrases as: "thorough concern over what is good for the Corps and each individual Marine"—"diligence in execution"—"highest order of professional competence"—"untiring attention to his duties and highly efficient"—"discretion"—"dependable"—"dignity"—and on and on.

A major change took place in the status of senior enlisted men late in 1958. Congress created two new top pay grades, with the rank of sergeant major at the peak (the "E-9" grade) as the senior noncommissioned officer (although master gunnery sergeants were to receive the same pay). Those two ranks were also authorized to add another "rocker" stripe to their chevrons, making an impressive total of four. Those perquisites were given to only a select few, for sergeants major in 1958 composed only $3/_{10}$ of 1% of the Corps' enlisted strength. In addition, Congress had allocated to the Sergeant Major of the Marine Corps an extra pay bonus above the other 500 sergeants major then on active duty.

A later sergeant major, George Rogers, remembered:

> [Bestwick] smoothed out some of the real problems we had in getting the Marine Corps sergeant major/first sergeant program back on track. For instance, you had people in the Marine Corps who were "O1s" [the personnel code for enlisted administrative chiefs] who had been calling themselves sergeant major and first sergeant since before World War II. Many of those people didn't make the new, official sergeant major/first sergeant's list, and they were quite bitter about it. It was rough! There were a lot of in-the-ranks problems. It was tough on those guys to lose that title, and then for us, who really were now sergeants major, to come along.
>
> I had one of those cynical kind approach me in the Staff NCO club one night and say, "What does it mean? I don't get any money for that rank. What does that sergeant major stripe mean? It don't mean anything. Just get promotions quick that's all." I answered, "Well, George, it don't

mean anything 'til you get into my outfit!"

There's another side to the story of these times, however. A lot of troops at that time had what I call a "civil service attitude." But when the sergeant major/first sergeant program came along, with a man like Bestwick as Sergeant Major of the Corps, then these other people we're talking about, they said, "Man, it's time to stand up and look tall!"

I know guys that kept an extra pair of trousers at work, and when they got to work they'd take off the ones they had sat on coming from home, and they would press those rascals and then spit-shine those shoes. They had Marine Corps emblems in their eyeballs!

Rogers went on to describe an episode at the Marine Air Base at Iwakuni in Japan in 1958. Bestwick arrived embodying his convictions about proper NCO appearance: spit-shined shoes, swagger stick in position, gloves in hand, proper to the smallest detail. His impact was immediate: "It didn't take Bestwick long to get those staff NCOs there squared away: 'There will be *no* raincoats over your uniform. You do *not* carry an umbrella during the monsoon season. You *do* shine your shoes; you *don't* wear gators. You *do* carry your swagger stick. You *do* look like a leading NCO.' "

Amidst those problems of morale and appearance, the travel always continued: Cherry Point, North Carolina, Lejeune again, back out to the Pacific, including that time Guam and Formosa (today called Taiwan), and California again. It never seemed to stop. His wife, Florence, spent a lot of time alone in their apartment in Arlington, Virginia, near Headquarters. It was more of the same in 1959. The leadership visited the West Coast, the East Coast, and in a switch the overseas trip went to Morocco, Spain, Italy, and France for a frenetic nineteen days.

By 1959, the pioneering work had been done. Bestwick had set a smooth pattern for the administrative procedures of his office, as he kept an eagle eye on the chief of staff's correspondence. Productive lines of communication to and from enlisted personnel had been opened through letters, phone calls, and visits. Thoughtful advice on enlisted concerns had been given to senior officers and well received, and the new custom of travel with the Commandant had been firmly established.

In May, he knew his time at Headquarters was soon coming to an end. With twenty-five years of service, he set a goal of thirty. Accordingly, General Pate arranged to send Bestwick, when that tour of duty would end, to Headquarters, Fleet Marine Force, Pacific, (FMFPac) in Hawaii, the senior echelon of all Marine units in the Pacific Ocean area. The Commandant had selected the sergeant major there, Francis Rauber, to come to Washington as the new Sergeant Major of the Corps, so the two men would simply switch jobs. Bestwick's final weeks were crowded. There were visits to Camp Lejeune and Cherry Point, a staff NCO symposium at the latter, and a return visit eleven days later, showing his successor the procedures he had established.

On August 31, 1959, an impressive ceremony was held as part of the evening parade at the historic Marine Barracks in Washington, D.C. The sergeant major and the Commandant shared the honor of reviewing the parade. Bestwick passed the Sergeant Major's Sword to Rauber, the new incumbent, and a letter of commendation from General Pate was made part of Bestwick's official record:

> I take this opportunity to express my sincere appreciation for your meritorious service as Sergeant Major of the Marine Corps from 23 May, 1957, to 1 September, 1959.
>
> Because of your experience, professional ability, and military bearing, you were selected from an outstanding group of top ranking noncommissioned officers for the assignment as the first Sergeant Major of the Marine Corps. You have successfully fulfilled all the requisites of this highly essential position.
>
> You brought to this Headquarters an enviable record of service in a wide variety of assignments, including combat duty during the Korean conflict. Your service has been characterized by consistent exemplary performance of duty in positions of ever increasing responsibilities.
>
> In carrying out your duties as Sergeant Major of the Marine Corps you have worked in close harmony with civilians, as well as high ranking military personnel, demonstrating at all times the utmost tact and dignity. By your professional competence and administrative ability, you have capably assisted me and my staff on numerous field inspection trips throughout your tour of duty. Your primary concern, the good of the Marine Corps and each individual Marine, has been exemplified by your guidance and counseling of our most senior noncommissioned officers, and has earned for you the genuine respect of the officers and men of the Marine Corps.
>
> Be assured of my deep appreciation of your loyalty and devotion to duty, which reflect the highest credit upon you and the United States Marine Corps. I wish you continued success in your career as a Marine.

So it ended that August 31, and he and Florence moved on to the final phase of his pioneering career. Arriving in Oahu, they found a place to live in Pearl City, and Bestwick took on his last sergeant major's assignment, FMFPac. Early in October, he was again presented with a sergeant major's sword of office in another ceremony. As in Washington, he would keep it during his tenure of office, and then pass it on to his successor. When not in use, he kept it in a special mount in his office, adjoining a series of metal plaques listing the names and dates of those who had held the post.

Slipping easily into his new position, Bestwick soon had well in hand the varied duties which were his responsibilities in the far-ranging command. These duties were similar to the ones he had in Washington: administrative control of the chief of staff's correspondence; communication to and from enlisted personnel scattered around the far-flung Pacific bases; and advice at Headquarters, FMFPac, on a wide range of policies affecting enlisted personnel. Bestwick realized, however, that permanent retirement loomed in the future. In preparation for that, he enrolled in his off-duty hours in Jackson College and earned a degree in business administration.

This same year there was another staff NCO symposium with advice required from all over the Corps. At the preliminary meeting in Hawaii, Bestwick presided and his style made a deep impression on an up-and-coming first sergeant who represented the Marine Barracks at Pearl Harbor. He was Clinton Puckett, who would reach the summit himself some thirteen years later. As he later recalled, "I was very, very impressed with his professionalism, his knowledge, his skill in mediation, that type of thing. He was very accomplished, smooth, intelligent, controlled; seemingly without effort, he kept things on track to address logical issues, and he could divert attention from things that were obviously not headed for presentation as an item for action."

In July, 1962, Bestwick requested retirement from active duty and transfer to the Fleet Marine Corps Reserve to take effect on September 30. Two days before that termination date there was a parade, with his wife and friends watching in the stands. As a tribute to Bestwick and his position, the drum and bugle team and marching troops passed in precise array before the reviewing officer, Lieutenant General Carson Roberts, Commanding General, Fleet Marine Force, Pacific. An unseen narrator read over the loudspeaker the sergeant major's official retirement orders, and for the last time he reported to his commanding officer. Taking a position of honor alongside General Roberts, Bestwick watched with emotions one can well imagine as the troops passed in review before him. It was the end of a remarkable active duty career.

Just how remarkable is clearly demonstrated by the fitness report marks that he had consistently received from a succession of commanding officers. There were six levels of quality on the report form, ranging from "Unsatisfactory" to "Outstanding." Then there were six areas to rate under "Performance of Duty," including a particularly revealing one, "Handling of Enlisted Personnel." In addition, there was a questionnaire which asked "To What Degree Has He Exhibited The Following?" This category was an exhaustive listing of twelve characteristics such as "Leadership," "Judgment," and "Force."

As if these weren't enough to lay bare a man's soul, there were two final summary sentences requiring rating. His commanding officer had to select an answer to this question, "Considering the possible requirements of service in war, indicate your attitude toward having this noncommissioned officer under your command. Would you: 'Prefer Not to Have?'—'Be Willing to Have?'— 'Be Glad to Have?'—'Particularly Desire to Have?' " Lastly, an overall estimate of the NCO's "General Value to the Service" was required. Bestwick through the years unfailingly received from his superiors markings of "Particularly Desire to Have" and "Outstanding" in both categories.

Having finished his active duty with such accolades, he added three months of reserve time, and this, together with his earlier time in the Marine Reserve and National Guard, gave him his magic total of thirty years' service to his country when he finally retired on December 31, 1962.

The retirement came after he and Florence (whom he had married twenty-two years earlier) had moved back to the mainland from Hawaii, and had settled into a house in Sunnyvale, California, to make the major transition to civilian life. Early in 1963 he was back at work, only now it was for the Air Force

Systems Command in Mira Loma, California. After a spell there, he felt that he wanted something of a non-military nature, so he became a partner in a local wholesale tool company. Retiring from that, he went with his wife on a final move to a home in Palo Alto.

Their lives there brought them very close together, and so it was a crushing blow to Florence when her husband died on July 10, 1972, at the Stanford University Hospital. He was buried in his Marine uniform at the Alta Mesa Memorial Park in Palo Alto. With no children to comfort her and with her indispensable man gone, Florence took it hard, and eight months later she was dead.

And what sort of man was he who had carved out such a superb Marine career as a pioneer? Thin, and seemingly taller than his six feet, he winced at being called "Wilbur," preferring "Bill." Nearly bald, with strong, dark eyes heavily circled underneath, he had, when needed, a look that could stare right through a man. While firm in style, he was still very quiet in his demeanor, a gentleman who never cursed or raised his voice and hardly drank at all (a rarity in the Marine Corps of his time—especially for a sergeant major!). He even gave up the cigarettes that he had smoked in his earlier years.

He kept himself in top athletic shape, and, wherever he went in the Marine Corps, he always saw to it that there was a baseball team in his unit, a team on which he himself played with great enthusiasm. Equally devoted to golf, that became his passion in retirement, along with an active participation in the Freemasons. Totally loyal to "his general," he would not listen to any criticism of Pate. With the steady self-control and air of great dignity he had, respect seemed to flow naturally toward him. Holding himself always in an erect military carriage, Bill Bestwick was a special man. As one of his officer friends summarized him, "You could have put him in the uniform of a full Marine colonel, and he would have looked and acted the part perfectly."

His memory lived on. Just fifty years after Bestwick had enlisted and some twenty-two years after he had retired, the then-Commandant, General Paul X. Kelley, proposed the Enlisted Awards Program, with the Sergeant Major Wilbur Bestwick Award as the senior prize. Kelley had served, as a junior officer, at Headquarters during Bestwick's tour of duty, so he had seen at first hand the remarkable work he had done as a pioneer. Now he insured Bestwick's memory by instituting an annual award, carried on today under the auspices of the Marine Corps League. Nominations are solicited from the field commands of the Corps. Then a special board at Headquarters, with the Sergeant Major of the Marine Corps as chairman, makes the final selection. The definitive criterion for the award is that it goes to "an enlisted Marine in a ground combat element of any FMF unit who has made an outstanding contribution to increased combat readiness within the organization." The honored recipient receives a handsome pewter replica of the U.S. Marine Corps War Memorial (the Iwo Jima Monument) from the Commandant.

Since that tribute is taking place more than half a century after the start of Bestwick's career, it is obvious that it is due not only to his performance as Sergeant Major of the Marine Corps, but, in fact, to his achievements throughout his entire career. And what was that service that had prepared him so well for the highest rank?

His beginnings were modest in the extreme. There is an obscure little town of less than 2,000 people, tucked in a remote corner of northeast Kansas. It is called Sabetha, and there Bestwick was born on November 27, 1911. His father, Albert, had come from Kentucky originally, while his mother, Bertha, had been born in Ireland. They sent their two sons, Wilbur and Charles, to a tiny neighboring village, Oneida, for grade schooling. That was followed by a start in high school in Sabetha, but, after two years, Wilbur had had enough. He left in 1931. Those were desperate years in the Great Depression, especially for someone with no skills and little education, and any offer of regular pay was attractive. Accordingly, he joined the Kansas National Guard as a private in the Field Artillery. His two years in the Guard convinced Bestwick that he would be happy making a career of military service.

So it was that the die was cast, and on October 16, 1934, he enlisted in Portland, Oregon, as a private in the Marine Corps. At that time he had black hair (a severe casualty in later years), brown eyes, and 176 pounds spread thinly over his 5 foot, 11 inch frame. Sent to the recruit depot in San Diego, he received the standard shock treatment from his drill instructor (DI). He survived, however, and when he finished in December, 1934, he was awarded sea duty, a choice assignment. The Marine Corps was and is careful about the men it sends to serve on the Navy's capital ships. Those men must operate successfully as an independent command, yet the ship's captain is in frequent contact with them. Rigid discipline, meticulous uniform appearance, and correct military bearing are essentials.

It must have been a strange feeling for the young man from land-locked Kansas as he went aboard the U.S.S. *Louisville*, a heavy cruiser, in January, 1935, and saw the sights of the cruises that followed: Alaska and Pearl Harbor, Hawaii, in 1935; "good will" calls at Latin American ports in 1936-7; and for a grand finale in 1938, visits to Hawaii, Samoa, Australia, and Tahiti. During those three and a half years of sea duty, Bestwick became an expert at manning the 5 inch anti-aircraft guns of the cruiser, and found time to continue his schooling by taking correspondence courses from the Marine Corps Institute. His application to duty and drive for self-improvement resulted in corporal's stripes for him in June, 1938.

The following month he received orders for guard duty ashore at the Marine Barracks at Bremerton, Washington. It was a different Corps then. When Bestwick was on the *Louisville*, for instance, the entire strength of the Corps numbered only 16,000 men (and no women, of course). A good man took nearly four years to earn his corporal's stripes. There were many World War I

Bestwick as a 31-year-old first sergeant with the 9th Regiment at Camp Pendleton in November, 1942.

veterans still around, and during those long nights aboard ship, Bestwick undoubtedly heard many "sea stories" about the *real* "Old Corps"—"Now when I was at Belleau Wood"—"I remember when Sergeant Major Dan Daly (or John Quick) said or did so and so."

That, then, was the atmosphere in which Bestwick was immersed during his four-year enlistment. When it expired in October, 1938, he decided to see how civilian life compared with the military, and so he enlisted in the Volunteer Marine Corps Reserve as a sergeant on inactive duty. Settling in the Los Angeles area, he found work first as a postal clerk and then as a street car operator. It was during this time that he met the right girl, Florence Peterson, who had found her way there from Cripple Creek, Colorado. She was a little, blue-eyed lady, just 5 feet, 5 inches tall, and three years older than Bestwick. They were married November 20, 1940, at Riverside, California.

His lifestyle as a married man with a new bride was rudely interrupted when the Marine Corps recalled him to active duty on July 15, 1941. With the Nazi war machine in control of most of Europe, there was great apprehension in Washington. The size of the Marine Corps had already increased by over 10,000 men from Bestwick's sea-going days, and now it wanted him back at work.

After reporting in at the Marine Barracks, San Diego, he was immediately sent back to his old post, the Marine Barracks at Bremerton. Leaving Florence in Los Angeles, he began his assignment as an instructor in infantry weapons. With the attack on Pearl Harbor and the United States' entry into the war, the Corps started an explosive growth, which meant a crying need for experienced NCOs to train and lead the flood of raw recruits. Promotions accelerated for those with previous active duty. Thus Bestwick was given a warrant as a "Temporary" platoon sergeant in April, 1942.

Anxious to further his career skills (and, of course, open the door for further promotions) he applied for and was accepted in the First Sergeants School in San Diego. There he successfully negotiated the two months' course in administration, graduating with a 92.5 average in July, 1942. Capitalizing on that asset, he immediately requested a transfer from his reserve status to the regular Marine Corps with a rank of first sergeant.

October, 1942, saw the expiration of his second "cruise" (enlistment), and by "shipping over" (reenlisting) he was able to become a first sergeant in the regulars. Now based at Camp Pendleton, with Florence finally nearby in Los Angeles, he began a new phase in his service: duty with the Headquarters Company, 9th Regiment, 3d Division. It was a different atmosphere from the old days. As his regiment trained for combat, Bestwick had daily opportunities to put into practice what he had learned in the First Sergeants School. Never one to rest content, he applied in December for his further promotion to marine gunner, the tradition-encrusted name usually given to the rank of warrant officer. Nothing came of that, but there were now more important events brewing.

The division sailed in February, 1943, for New Zealand. In the front of every man's mind was the knowledge of the 1st Division's recent desperate battle on Guadalcanal, and premonitions of similar struggles which the 3d Division would probably have to endure. Those conjectures lent a serious tone to the men's intensive training in New Zealand. As a first sergeant in a headquarters company, Bestwick was heavily engaged in administrative responsibilities, keeping track of the message traffic, personnel changes, and correspondence. In June, 1943, he received a promotion to "Temporary" sergeant major (line duty). It was quite a contrast: he had leapt from sergeant to sergeant major in just over one year, while on his first cruise it had taken nearly four years to make corporal.

The division moved from New Zealand to now-pacified Guadalcanal. From July to October there was a final drive to perfect combat readiness. Then came the payoff, and Bestwick was there with his company for the Battle of Cape Torokina on Bougainville November 1-6, 1943. Leaving there at the end of December, they returned to Guadalcanal for six months to replace their casualties and prepare for the next landing. Another abortive recommendation for promoting Bestwick to warrant officer was sent up through command echelons at this time.

July 21, 1944, was D-day at Guam for Bestwick and his division. He remained there through the fighting until November, and after a return to the rear base at Guadalcanal, he received a transfer stateside in March, 1945. This sent him to comfortable duty as acting post sergeant major at the Marine Barracks, Navy Yard, Mare Island.

The fall of 1945 brought service as the sergeant major of the Depot of Supplies in San Francisco. Wartime demands had ballooned the Corps' strength to 485,000 men and women by that time. The depot was a major supply center for western United States and Pacific Marine operations, and Bestwick was in charge of a large number of clerks and the inevitable reams of forms ordering and disbursing supplies, accompanied by a high rate of personnel turnover.

His October end of enlistment date rolled around again in 1946. He had completed twelve years in the Corps and was clearly on a career path, so he shipped over for another four-year cruise. Florence and he then took off for eighty-five days back in Kansas for a relaxed time together.

Still focussed on professional advancement (and sensitive, no doubt, to his limited early schooling), he took the U.S. Armed Forces Institute tests on his return to San Francisco. He did well, and in December of 1946, he was selected for the rank of "Temporary" master sergeant. A few months later, he again applied for selection as a warrant officer. His commander, Brigadier General Andrew Creesy, gave a strong endorsement in which he noted the current postwar "rapid demobilization" and the "innumerable assignments" Bestwick had to make. He praised Bestwick's "outstanding ability and adaptability in coping with the numerous personnel matters under his supervision." Again, nothing came of the application.

A year later, in February, 1948, the indefatigable Bestwick tried again for promotion. This time he requested a transfer to limited duty officer status with the rank of second lieutenant, and again Brigadier General Creesy recommended favorable action by Headquarters Marine Corps. This request was denied, because Bestwick could not complete thirty years of active duty before reaching age fifty-five.

It's not hard to understand why his superiors always supported his requests. In those days, the individual service record book for each man (which always accompanied the man wherever he moved) contained six categories for evaluating his personal and professional characteristics. Those categories were searching and covered a wide range: military efficiency, neatness and military bearing, intelligence, obedience, sobriety, and conduct. Every enlisted Marine would be graded in each of the six to the decimal point: 3.6 or 4.2, or, the best of the best, 5.0. Bestwick routinely received 5.0 across the board.

After almost four years at the Depot of Supplies, Headquarters Marine Corps sent him, in September, 1949, to Parris Island to be the recruit depot sergeant major. There he went to work on his education once more, completing the Officers Basic Extension Course of the Marine Corps Schools with a grade of "Excellent." He used it and his 5.0 marks as a springboard for yet another application for warrant officer in February, 1952. As usual, his commander, Brigadier General Matthew Horner, knew a good man when he saw one, and his recommendation made clear that Bestwick's principal virtue, beyond the average senior NCO, was to carry the execution of his duties to a higher degree of "smoothness and efficiency," demonstrating "outstanding management ability." These qualities impressed Brigadier General Horner because of the situation then at Parris Island:

> Since August, 1950, this depot had been in a continuous state of flux. Recruit loads and resulting workloads have fluctuated widely and unpredictably. Many problems, unforeseen prior to the receipt of inductees and the effecting of reduced enlistment standards, have more than doubled the administrative load that would have been anticipated.
>
> During this entire period, Master Sergeant Bestwick has remained his serene, efficient, and industrious self. No problem is ever too formidable for him to tackle. Work hours mean nothing as long as there is a job for him to do.

The problems the general referred to were real. The Korean War was now on, and recruits flooded into the Parris Island boot camp. The resulting administrative burdens fell directly on Bestwick. Three years at the recruit depot was enough, so he welcomed a switch in August, 1952, sending him out to the field.

One old-timer, Hubert G. Duncan, used some pungent phrases to describe life in the Corps as Bestwick then encountered it:

> Everyone was issued dress blues. You kept your rifle in the barracks.... Everyone was a Marine, and his ethnic background was unimportant. We had heroes....
>
> We starched our khaki, and looked like hell after sitting down the first time. We wore the short green jacket with the winter uniform.... We kept our packs made up and hanging on the edge of the rack [bed]....
>
> UA [unauthorized absence] meant being a few minutes late from a great liberty [weekend leave from duty], and only happened once per career. Brigs were truly "correctional facilities." Sergeants were gods....
>
> You did your own laundry, including ironing. You aired bedding. Daily police [straightening up] of outside areas was held, although they were always clean.... A tour as Duty NCO was an honor.
>
> We had bugle calls.... Parking was the least of problems. Troops couldn't afford cars. You weren't married unless you could afford it.... We wore leggings and herringbone utilities.... We had to take and pass promotion tests....
>
> We had unit parties overseas with warm beer and no drugs.... Marines wore dog tags all the time. We spit-shined shoes and brushed boots. We wore boondockers [heavy field boots]. We starched field scarves [ties]. We worked a five and one-half day work week....
>
> Greater privileges for NCOs were not a "right." EM [Enlisted Men's] Clubs were where you felt at home...and safe. We sailed on troop ships. We rode on troop trains. Sentries had some authority.... Marines went to chapel on Sundays. Weekend liberty to a distant place was a rarity. The color of a Marine's skin was of no consequence. The Marine Corps was a big team made up of thousands of little teams.

Bestwick was originally scheduled to join the 2d Division at Camp Lejeune, but revised orders sent him to Camp Pendleton for further assignment to a replacement draft headed for the 1st Division and combat with the Chinese in Korea.

Florence was left in Los Angeles, and he headed overseas, but the start of his Korean tour of duty looked like a career dead end. He was initially assigned, in one of those curious title juxtapositions he was by now so familiar with, as a master sergeant serving as a sergeant major of a battalion. It was, unfortunately, a motor transport battalion, not a billet that promised much of a future for a highly motivated man like Bestwick. However, there were probably senior officers who knew his track record and senior NCOs who respected his professional expertise, and they were experienced at putting an unofficial word in the right ear at the right place. Within a month he was transferred out of motor transport and to the most envied—and most senior—NCO position in the division: Division Sergeant Major!

It only lasted nine months, but that tour of duty was to have a profound effect on Bestwick's subsequent career. Running the headquarters company of the division brought him into intimate, daily contact with the commanding general, Major General Randolph Pate. General Pate was impressed, too; he signed off on an official Letter of Recommendation.

It opened with recognition of Bestwick's "outstanding ability...professional skill...adept administrative...maximum efficiency." In addition, it went on to specify the high degree of Bestwick's individual achievements:

> His keen sense of duty and desire to achieve the highest standards of administrative proficiency were manifested in the extremely long hours of conscientious effort put forth by him. He continuously attempted to advise, cooperate with, and assist the forward administrative elements of the division. His meticulous attention to detail, outstanding attention to duty, and knowledge of details involved in the division's administrative procedures enabled him to effectively coordinate the elements of his section.

Such was the indelible impression that Bestwick left in Pate's mind. The general would well remember it only four years later when he had to pick the pioneer to become the first Sergeant Major of the Marine Corps.

Other officers there with the 1st Division also carried away vivid memories of Bestwick. One of them remembered, "He would stand there on the corner of the sand box on which stood the stove for the tent. He'd listen thoughtfully to you, take his eyeglasses off, put them back on, contemplate the matter carefully, and then slowly—never rashly—give you his comment. Tall, thin, nearly bald, he was exceptionally hard working and so, although somewhat introverted, he was well respected."

In September, 1953, he headed home. Back in California, reunited once again with Florence, he took on a radically different assignment. He was named as the staff sergeant major for the inspector-instructor of the 1st Air Delivery Company in San Jose. Working with reserve Marines there didn't diminish by one iota Bestwick's plans to further his career. Twenty years after he had first enlisted, he was still sending his personal requests through the channels of command.

Thus, in September of 1954 he requested a change in his military occupational specialty (MOS) from "01" to "03—combat field," and nine months later it came through: "Approved." This set the stage for the next move; in the summer and fall of 1955, he mounted a double-barrelled offensive. First, one more application for warrant officer, and, immediately thereafter, an application for appointment to the rank of first sergeant/sergeant major. (Those senior NCO billets had only been revived a few months earlier.)

As usual, his commanding officer went to bat. The inspector-instructor of the 1st Air Delivery Company, First Lieutenant Donald Anderson, sent to the Commandant through the proper channels the following comments, as part of a much longer recommendation:

> His handling and training of the enlisted personnel of this unit is outstanding. His endurance, military bearing, neatness, attention to duty, cooperation, and initiative is paralleled by none.... His force, leadership, economy, and loyalty have been the dominating factor in a smooth running organization.

From this initial effort, nothing happened. Or so it seemed, but a year and a half later, all the hard preparation, all the long years of 5.0 service, all the straining for personal, professional advancement came together in a rush of events, and Bill Bestwick showed everyone how to serve superbly as the pioneer Sergeant Major of the Marine Corps.

Chapter 3

A MAN OF DIGNITY

Sergeant Major Francis D. Rauber

Bestwick's successor as Sergeant Major of the Marine Corps was Francis Rauber. He had had a long career leading up to that billet, but his life had been unusual because a sixteen-year period as a civilian had interrupted his military service.

It all began in Rochester, New York, where he was born on July 10, 1901, and attended the local high school. He came to know some Marines on duty at the Naval Arsenal nearby, and, as he later recalled, "they made a great impression on me that I never forgot. I felt that I'd never be satisfied with anything else. I only wanted to be in the Marines."

Acting on a teen-age impulse, he slipped away from high school one day to join the Corps. Unfortunately he was under the legal age, and his mother came—to his great embarrassment—and took him back home.

Graduation came in 1918, while America was caught up in the patriotic fervor of World War I. Accordingly, Rauber joined an Army National Guard unit for a two-year stint of weekend duty in Rochester during 1919-20. The emotional tug of the Marines continued, however, and on December 9, 1921, he enlisted in the Corps. Even then, he knew enough to realize that this would not be a parade ground, dress blues life. As he later commented, "I knew what I was in for before I went in. I could see nothing ahead but a hard way to go." Sent to boot camp in Parris Island, Rauber looked on himself as just another recruit who had to pay the price of admission, "I went in a civilian; I came out a Marine."

Still, nothing had prepared him for assignment to Haiti after his graduation. The Marines had been sent to Haiti in 1915, and there had been some gruelling experiences there. The year 1918 had seen arduous, sustained combat with the native revolutionaries under their charismatic leader, Charlemagne Peralte. By 1922, when Rauber arrived in Haiti, a tenuous peace had been restored, but the Marines stayed on to assure law and order, "justices of the peace" in Rauber's words, as well as to try to help build a viable life for the Haitian people.

Assigned to the 1st Brigade, which was headquartered in the capital of Port-au-Prince, Rauber later admitted that his first thought was, "What the hell kind of a place is this?" He was soon sent to even more primitive locales, serving with small detachments in remote villages with strange sounding names: Carecochan, Belladére, and Savanette. All around him were poverty, illiteracy, and an allegiance to voodoo magic. One bright spot was the Haitian runner who carried his messages. Originally bearing the elegant name of Antoinne Louis, he was so devoted to Rauber's Marine predecessor that he insisted on being called "Applegate."

Completing his tour of duty after fifteen months, Rauber was transferred back to the United States. There, he served in a succession of more prosaic assignments: the 5th Marines (5th Regiment), a part of the Marine Expeditionary Force based in Quantico (the ready brigade for emergencies, and a forerunner of today's Fleet Marine Force combat units); the Marine Barracks in Norfolk, Virginia; and finally in the 4th Marines at the Marine Corps Base, San Diego, California. Even with the slow promotions in the tiny, peace-time Corps of 15,500 men, he had worked his way up to sergeant when his enlistment expired.

In February, 1926, came the interruption in his military career. He requested and received an honorable discharge to marry Remigia Kane, a hospital nurse from his home town. Rauber, called Frank by his friends, was twenty-five, vigorous, tall, and handsome, and he set out to support his bride. He went to work for a Cadillac dealership in Rochester, New York. Very quickly, his dignified, articulate style and ability made him the top salesman. The owner of the dealership was a difficult man who continually put more and more pressure on his salesmen. But Rauber solved that problem in his own way. When he felt that he had sold enough cars in a week, he went home to his wife and enjoyed an uninterrupted personal life because he had taken care to have his phone number unlisted.

Two daughters joined the family and for sixteen years it was a good life. Then came the hard-to-believe news that Pearl Harbor had been bombed, and Rauber contacted the Marine Corps about returning to duty. His explanation was simple: "I was a Marine and I answered the bell." He was warmly welcomed, for the Corps saw the urgent need for old hands to shape the mass of untrained volunteers. Thus Rauber was able to reenlist as a sergeant on May 1, 1942. With his previous experience and demonstrated talent, and with wartime pressures, he had an opportunity for quick advancement. He was soon sent to the First Sergeants School at the Philadelphia Navy Yard.

Graduating in January, 1943, the following month he became the post sergeant major at the New York Naval Shipyard in Brooklyn. One can guess that he may have looked at his astonishing ascent from sergeant to sergeant major in less than a year, and then contrasted that meteoric rise with the painfully slow crawl that characterized promotion in his old days in Haiti, so long ago and so different from a Marine Corps that was now expanding exponentially to prepare for its massive Pacific campaigns.

As always happens, after a couple of years Rauber was transferred to be the sergeant major of the 3d Marine Corps Reserve District in New York City. There he sat during those crucial years of World War II, as Marines he knew blasted their bloody way through the islands of the Pacific, while his orders kept him chained to the security and comfort of stateside duty.

Finally, after the action was over and the victory won, in March, 1948, he was transferred to the west coast for assignment to FMFPac as sergeant major of the 9th Marines of the 1st Provisional Marine Brigade. Arriving in Guam in May, Rauber served there, as well as in Tsingtao, Peking, and Shanghai, China.

His stay in China was brief, for in April, 1949, he returned to Camp Witek, the Marine base in Guam. A two-year tour with the brigade ended when he returned in March, 1950, to the states. His new post was a pleasant one, filled with reunions with friends from his youth, as he took over the sergeant major's billet on the staff of the inspector-instructor of the 19th Infantry Battalion (Reserves) in his home town of Rochester. Once again, the good life there did not last, and in nine months he was gone.

The new job was a radical change of pace: an air base. Rauber's succinct reaction was, "I was not ready for aviation; I just went along with the assignment." Reporting in to the Marine Air Station at Cherry Point, North Carolina, in January, 1951, Rauber served consecutively as squadron sergeant major of Marine Corps Ground Control Intercept Squadron 5 and then Marine Air Control Group 1. Those units were given the mission of controlling the fighter-bomber elements of the 2d Marine Aircraft Wing, which was trained to provide close air support to the 2d Division at nearby Camp Lejeune. (The Marines call this their Air-Ground Team.)

That two-year tour ended with a move to another aviation billet. In March, 1952, he took over as Operations Squadron 3 Sergeant Major at the air station in Miami, Florida. The following year, in June, he became the headquarters sergeant major of the base. Meanwhile, his wife and their two young girls were living in nearby Opa Locka.

As regularly as clockwork, a transfer came through after two years in Florida. In April, 1954, Rauber received dramatic new orders: report to Headquarters Marine Corps for duty as personnel sergeant major. To an outsider that may seem like just another routine administrative post, but in the reality of life in the Corps it was (and is) a position of immense power, affecting the lives of every enlisted person in the sensitive areas of promotions and transfers to new billets. Furthermore, in a subtle way, that position could have an influence on the future career of the occupant, for he would be in frequent contact with the senior leadership of the Corps. If he did his job in a superior manner, it would be noted by general officers for future assignments to the most senior billets.

While Rauber's professional career was going well, his personal life suffered a great loss when his wife, Remigia, died in November, 1955. Still he found some consolation in his work. He was in a key position of prominence at Headquarters when General Randolph Pate instituted the new billet of Sergeant Major of the Marine Corps in May, 1957. Naturally, Rauber worked closely with Bill Bestwick, the first occupant. They were two "old pros" who knew their business, and they spent a year together in meetings and discussions of correspondence from enlisted personnel in the field. The watchful eye of the chief of staff, Lieutenant General Vernon McGee, must have taken all this in and seen clearly that Rauber was unusually serious in his work, an excellent administrator, and a man who achieved results with a low-key personality which nevertheless radiated dignity.

When four years had passed and it was time for Rauber's relief, the quality of his work paid off; he was given the plum assignment of sergeant major of FMFPac. Upon arriving in Hawaii in May, 1958, he reported in to the commanding general, Lieutenant General Megee. Accepting the sword and swagger stick that symbolized the authority of his new billet, Rauber went to work.

There was, of course, a huge concentration of senior military personnel at Pearl Harbor. Commander in Chief, Pacific (CinCPac) was a joint headquarters there, with staff from all branches of the U.S. Armed Forces. That staff included a pretty woman, an Air Force master sergeant named Kathleen Benton. She was working as secretary to a Navy admiral who was chief of staff at CinCPac. Rauber was stationed not far away at Camp Holland M. Smith, the Marine base in Honolulu, and official business often took him to CinCPac. Soon there were unofficial trips, and in January, 1959, the master sergeant married the sergeant major, followed by a wonderful party at the Pearl Harbor NCO Club. Kay, with her alert mind, military savvy, and charming personality would be a vital force in Rauber's life from then on. (She had come a long way from McCook, Nebraska.)

The island of Oahu is, of course, studded with other Marine bases, which facilitated a broad range of contacts for Rauber. On one occasion, there was a gathering of nine sergeants major, totally 183 years of service to the Corps.

Among those present was Thomas McHugh, a "youngster" who was station-ed at Kaneohe and had "only" twenty years of service. Rauber knew him from joint service together back in his Guam days, and he would see more of him later in special circumstances at Headquarters in Washington.

The years of training, however, had also taught Rauber the crucial value of keeping in close touch with *all* ranks. He was just as often in contact with privates as he was with staff NCOs. A fellow sergeant major, Floyd Stocks, later commented on this widespread range of involvement, "Frank was sergeant major of Fleet Marine Force, Pacific at that time. I've seen it myself, and I've heard it from young Marines and old Marines around the world: a lot of peo-ple going to and from WestPac [the Western Pacific] would go through Hickam [Air Force Base], and Frank and Kay would go down and just walk through the terminal there and say hello to these youngsters. It really was important to them. It was great!"

During Rauber's months in Hawaii, changes were afoot in Washington. Bestwick's term as Sergeant Major of the Marine Corps was drawing to a close in 1959. A special board of twenty-five colonels had begun combing the file jackets of fifty sergeants major who had both seniority and outstanding service records. Their recommendations went on to another board of five generals,

On August 28, 1959: General Pate presents the Sword of Office to Rauber as the new Sergeant Major of the Marine Corps, while Bestwick (left) smiles.

chaired by the assistant commandant, Lieutenant General Verne McCaul. One of the names drew strong support from overseas; MeGee made his feelings about Rauber quite clear. Pate chose Rauber over three more senior men to be Sergeant Major of the Marine Corps, and his travel orders were issued: Washington! Rauber's reaction was typically modest when he said afterwards, "I think they hung names up on the wall and threw darts."

As is customary in a major change of command, there were formal ceremonies to mark the transition. A contemporary newspaper account gave an outline which recreated the events for anyone who had never attended the famous Marine Sunset Parade:

> Ordinarily this would just be another Friday evening Sunset Parade for the men stationed at Marine Barracks, but this night, August 28, 1959, would be more than just routine; it was something special—extra special to the enlisted men—for it was the relief and installation of the Sergeant Major of the Marine Corps.

The reporter then went on to describe the sequence of events: the bugler's call, the sudden burst of floodlights, the Marine Band sounding forth, the precise drill of the troops. The account then continued:

> Visitors were awed with the music and drill when, suddenly, there came over the loud speaker the words..."Sergeant Major of the Marine Corps...front and center." With that command, Sergeant Major Wilbur Bestwick, the first Sergeant Major of the Marine Corps...marched smartly across the parade field to relinquish his "badge of office," the Staff NCO Sword, to General Randolph McC. Pate, Commandant of the Marine Corps....
>
> "Sergeant Major Rauber...front and center." As the command "front and center" was issued for the second time during the Sunset Parade ceremonies, Sergeant Major Francis D. Rauber marched proudly across the parade ground to his post directly in front of the Commandant and to the left of Sergeant Major Bestwick. At this point the public address system was once again utilized to carry the orders of transfer for Sergeant Major Rauber who would replace Sergeant Major Bestwick in the Marine Corps' top enlisted billet....
>
> After the orders had been read, the Commandant then received the Staff NCO Sword from Sergeant Major Bestwick and passed it to Rauber, thus completing the ceremony of transferring and installing a new Sergeant Major of the Marine Corps.

After the ceremony, there was a big official party, with Rauber and Kay and daughter Rosemary heading a receiving line which included Bestwick and his wife. The first person down the line was the Commandant, telling Rauber he looked forward to his coming aboard and wishing Bestwick well in his new post as Sergeant Major, FMFPac. Then old friends crowded around, senior generals from Headquarters shook hands, and staff NCOs relived memories of "remember when we...."

Rauber was an impressive sight in the receiving line, the epitome of dignity. Resplendent in his dress blues, with its ribbons and service stripes, he stood six feet one inch tall, erect and well-built with strong brown eyes, and typical close-cropped hair, which had turned white by this time. When asked about his new appointment, his reply was soft-spoken. He admitted he was "highly elated" and expressed appreciation to the generals who had selected him. Looking ahead, he said, "I will do everything within my power to do the fine job that my predecessor has done, and will strive to accomplish even more if that's possible. This new billet is an inspiration to enlisted men of the Marine Corps, especially in the administration field, and one we definitely want to retain with pride and honor."

The big day came on September 1, 1959, when he formally assumed office. He was fifty-eight years old and had almost twenty-two years of active Marine service, with over sixteen of that as a sergeant major.

Trips with the Commandant began quickly. Kay Rauber, probably reflecting comments from her husband, observed, "Pate had a lot of flair and drive, and seemed to know just what he wanted to do for the Marine Corps. Every official trip they took, stateside or abroad, commenced, as soon as they boarded the plane, with a martini cocktail and a toast 'for the success of the trip.' "

One such trip was to WestPac in October, 1959. Stopping in Okinawa and other Marine locations for inspections, Rauber concentrated on meeting a wide variety of NCOs in the field and familiarizing himself with their problems. Whether it was a formal reception, or chow in the mess hall, or a late night beer at the NCO Club, he asked and he listened. "You can learn a great deal that way," was his terse commentary.

While Rauber was flying to far-away places, family life was going along nicely back home. Kay had a challenging job in the office of the deputy chief of staff for Air Force personnel, surrounded by old acquaintances. Rosemary had married Daniel Malay, a Marine gunnery sergeant at Parris Island. Mimi, Rauber's younger daughter, was now the wife of Captain Waldemar Riley, in a U.S. Army Reserve unit in Williamsburg, Virginia.

Back at Headquarters, Rauber had the same busy daily life that Bestwick had had (and their successors would have)—phone calls, letters (which he could take direct to the Branch chiefs), and a regular round of staff meetings. He made it a practice that any enlisted person could use his "open door" policy to come directly to his office, at any time, without making a request for an appointment through official channels. This was an innovation which received an enthusiastic response. The billet was still so new that many Marines were not sure of its meaning, and they were certainly not used to walking into a senior office in Headquarters without going through channels. Thus Rauber's initiative established a receptivity to free and easy communication which enlisted Marines put to good use.

The end of 1959 marked the conclusion of Pate's tenure as Commandant. His successor, promoted over nine generals more senior, was the redoubtable General David Shoup, who took over on January 1, 1960. A cigar-chewing,

Medal of Honor winner, Shoup was a strong-minded leader, and he moved quickly to put his stamp on the Corps. Three days after taking office, he issued a famous "manifesto." He condemned the negative attitude of some Marines who were giving the Corps a "minority group" complex; he abolished the swagger stick, that traditional symbol of authority; he warned officers that promotions and transfers would be made solely "with the best interests of the Corps in mind"; and he reduced the Headquarters staff to move more personnel out into the field. A writer of this time put it in a pithy capsule, "Marines are inclined to operate their best under a 'top Marine' who is stronger, profaner, braver, gutsier, more cantankerous, prouder, and who has a sharper crease in his trousers than any of them. In Shoup they had found their man."

Now this was a boss of distinctive hue, and one with whom the Sergeant Major of the Marine Corps would necessarily have to work intimately. Rauber never batted an eye; the years of experience had taught him well how to work effectively with all manner of men, and he carried on without missing a beat. As Kay noted, "Frank thought that the Marine Corps finally had the best man for the job it had had in a very long time."

Asked at that time about his job and their relationship, Rauber replied, "I am a member of the staff. I advise and assist the Commandant in the performance of his duties, those officially concerning enlisted promotions, welfare, and morale. I am the enlisted viewpoint he wants to hear." As to Shoup, he answered, "He's one hundred percent as a Commandant, a Marine, and a human being." Shoup, in his "manifesto," had made his feelings clear about his staff, "Either I believe or I relieve." Rauber stayed on.

In his innermost heart, this probably wasn't what he wanted most. Many years later, he recalled, "After my tour as personnel sergeant major, I wanted to stay away from Washington; I wanted to get out of Washington. I'd been there before, and I never liked that duty. But Dave Shoup became Commandant, and I said to myself, 'Oh, God, I'll never get out of Washington now. He'll keep me here.' So I stayed in Washington with him. Nevertheless, he was the greatest guy I ever knew."

As a Marine veteran whose service went back to Haitian expeditionary days, Rauber was in a good position to evaluate the Corps of 1960. He was convinced that it really hadn't changed in its basic values, but merely "evolved." At that time he felt, "We're more modern in our viewpoint and approach. We have newer tactics, better and more modern weapons. But one thing, and make no mistake about it, will never change. Every Marine is basically a rifleman, no matter what his specialty is. He can be called to act as one at any time."

There were always the letters from mothers showing up on his desk top, letters complaining that "my boy is down there [at boot camp or an infantry base], and they're teaching him how to be a killer." Rauber's reaction to the letters would always be the same, "This is unfortunate and unpleasant," and his reply would always be the same, "When the chips are down, if that training will save people's lives, then it is a necessity. We thrive only on our training and spirit. Our spirit and leadership set us apart. We have a wonderful thing here. No other service has it. It will always be tough training, and there will never be a markdown on the price tag attached to becoming a Marine."

Even more persistent in demanding Rauber's attention was the need for continuous communication to all enlisted personnel on the vital subject of transfers of duty station. Every visit to every base brought a discussion of this. Rauber also tried to disseminate the policy on those transfers by writing an article summarizing the ground rules in one of the professional Marine magazines:

> On visits to various posts and stations of the Corps I find considerable misunderstanding of the enlisted assignment policies....
>
> Personnel are not detailed by "cards flying out of a machine," or "darts thrown against map boards." The careers of sergeants and above are monitored individually. The purpose is to make appropriate assignments which will provide as broad and varied a career as possible, within the limitations of the individual's capabilities and the requirements of the Marine Corps. The Marine Corps is the only Armed Force which provides this service from the highest Headquarters level.
>
> Corporals and below are normally transferred by quotas from field commands. However, when reported and transferred by name, they also receive the same personalized and individual scrutiny afforded our senior noncommissioned officers. In no case is an individual enlisted Marine assigned by name without his personnel file being thoroughly screened.

Rauber went on in his article to add many further explanatory details. Since he seldom wrote for publication, it seems logical to assume that he felt the issue of transfers was so critical, with so much misunderstanding in the minds of the enlisted Marines he met on field trips, that he had to explain the policies personally. He was, after all, the senior NCO who had made his recommendations in the personnel staff meetings at Headquarters and had given the Commandant his views, so he was heavily involved in determining the final regulations.

An additional channel of communication was the staff NCO symposium, with sergeants major in the majority, although there were also master gunnery sergeants and first sergeants. General Pate had earlier agreed that this should be an annual affair with the Sergeant Major of the Marine Corps as chairman. This gave Rauber a direct pipeline to the feelings and recommendations of the senior enlisted personnel in the field. For instance, the August, 1960, symposium was held at Pendleton, and Rauber was there to listen, to evaluate, and to relay their suggestions and concerns to the proper policy decision-maker in Washington.

He also had his own regular methods to keep information flowing both ways all the time. The fundamental one was a policy of corresponding with sergeants major throughout the Marine Corps. This was complemented by a pattern of meticulous response to any letters sent to him. In addition, as Sergeant Major Stocks remembered:

He had a little message system of his own. If there was something going on, and the inspector general [IG] was in the field, Frank would send messages with the inspector general's sergeant major. Between such visits (of course, we only got them about once a year from the IG at a given station or post), Frank would correspond with us routinely and keep us up on what was going on.

Rauber played a key role when staff NCOs had individual personal problems. As Sergeant Major of the Marine Corps, he was a regular member of the Personnel Review Board, and this gave him a direct look at the records of any borderline person. Stocks observed:

General Shoup (left) hears from his sergeant major.

Rauber photo

Maybe they had had some bad fitness reports; maybe things seemed too good for those guys; maybe they had learned to drink a little too much; these things. When that review board would meet there were about three categories. You were either in; you were told to shape up within a given time; or you were told that you wouldn't be allowed to reenlist. Now this was getting tough out there in the ranks, where these guys had been leaning on the work of their friends and their fellow staff NCOs for years in some cases.

But when a situation like this occurred, Frank would write to the local sergeant major, at the wing, or the division, or the base, and he would tell him the situation. It was effective. It put us in the system. A lot of guys in Frank's position might have contacted the man directly and by-passed his senior NCOs. Frank was not like that. He communicated through his sergeants major and first sergeants. He didn't jump past them; he didn't go down into the ranks. It was good. It was great.

As he had done with Pate, Rauber went with Shoup on an intensive three-week inspection tour of WestPac. In October, 1960, they made a circuit of Tokyo and the Marine Corps Air Station at Iwakuni in Japan; Seoul, Korea; Okinawa; Taiwan; the Philippines; Guam; and Hawaii; along with brief stops at Kodiak and Adak in Alaska; as well as Wake Island, a tiny dot of land isolated in the vast reaches of the Pacific.

Those visits were marked by a certain set of rituals that reoccurred at each stop. The senior Marine at the location would greet the Commandant; there would often be a parade of the local Marine detachment; the Commandant would meet with the officers to assess the condition of the command; the sergeant major would take soundings with the enlisted personnel; where there were foreign Marine Corps in existence, there would be exchanges with their Commandants; and, besides the working sessions, there would be the requirement for attendance at the inevitable receptions, teas, luncheons, and dinners given by the military of the host country.

In Taiwan, for example, they were met on arrival at the airport by Colonel Angus Fraser, Senior U.S. Marine Advisor to the Nationalist Chinese Marines, and senior Chinese Marine officers. Then, as a part of the total schedule of events, Shoup gave a lunch for the Chinese Commandant. Later in the day, Rauber and Shoup were given the place of honor at a formal drill-parade by Chinese Marines and then inspected their facilities, finishing just in time to prepare for dinners given for them that evening: one for Shoup and his wife by the Chinese Commandant, and a separate one for Rauber and his wife by the staff NCOs of the U.S. Marine Advisory Group.

The happiest note for Rauber, of course, was the fact that Kay was able to accompany him. She had been given special Air Force orders to join the delegation. As a highly trained secretary, she was able to help with the unavoidable paper work, the thank you letters, and the notes that were always made on the trip to bring back for action upon return to Headquarters. In addition, she and Mrs. Shoup would go shopping when their husbands were in meetings. Taking a list the men had given them, the ladies would look for what was needed for the delegation.

Every now and then their VIP status would bring a nice surprise. One that no woman would ever forget occurred when their plane landed in Taiwan. Kay described it:

> Madame Chiang-Kai Shek's tailor met us right on the airport tarmac and he started measuring us, this way and that way. He was going to make a Chinese gown for each of us to wear to a dinner with Admiral Li of the Chinese Navy in Taiwan. That evening, before the dinner, they came with these fabulous gowns, beautifully made with little tucks and snaps, with a high Chinese collar and slit to the hip on the side. We went to this dinner and there were all kinds of high Chinese officials present. Mrs. Shoup and I were the only Americans there!

The Marine Corps entered a new era in January, 1961. The first Sergeant Major of Women Marines took office, Bertha Peters. (Subsequently, she would marry another sergeant major, and they would both retire with thirty years' service—she being the first woman Marine to achieve that.) To a Marine trained in the days of "men only," that came as something of a shock. Kay was blunt, "Frank could not imagine such a thing at first, maybe he was thinking of combat. But he came around when more and more women joined the Corps and proved themselves. He eventually had a devoted group of Women Marines in his own office, so that, when the position of Sergeant Major of Women Marines evolved, we met several sharp and personable women who filled these positions, and he finally had to agree that the Corps couldn't do without them. One of them, in fact, served as his right-hand assistant for a long time."

On the WestPac circuit with General Shoup in October, 1961, Rauber received the full welcoming treatment in Hawaii. It started with leis, wives, and uniforms, as Bestwick (left) and his wife (right) greet the Raubers (center).

Rauber photo

On the domestic front, Rauber and his wife had found a place to live near Headquarters, and he would walk to and from work each day. Kay would usually get home first, and when Rauber returned, he liked to read the paper or perhaps watch a little TV. Sometimes he would go over to the Staff NCO Club to swap sea stories and knock off a few beers with old friends. At home, however, there was never any talk of what went on in either of their offices. It seemed better to leave the problems and pressures of the day behind them. With his innate dignity, "he was generally pretty even-tempered," Kay recollected, "but every now and then he'd get fired up about something and blow off steam. Mostly, though, he kept his worries under wraps."

The trips with the Commandant continued apace in 1961. In April Rauber accompanied him to Norfolk, Virginia, where Shoup spoke to the Armed Forces Staff College. Rauber had the pleasure of reviewing a formal parade in his honor by the Marines at the Naval Station. As was his custom, he probably seized the opportunity to take a few soundings with the local staff NCOs afterwards.

October found Shoup and Rauber back in WestPac, covering the familiar ground of Alaska, Japan, Korea, Okinawa, Taiwan (where the Commandant of the Republic of China Marines gave a tea party for Rauber), the Philippines, and Guam, ending with a four-day tour of Marine facilities on Oahu, Hawaii. Kay was again able to make the trip, and Rauber's opening comment in Hawaii was, "This is like coming home to us, since we were stationed here previously." Speaking to an assemblage of staff NCOs of FMFPac, he began with two fundamentals, "You can rest assured that this Commandant of ours is concerned with the welfare of the individual Marine...Our prime purpose in the Marine Corps is to be ready to go whenever a match is lit." Moving to more specific issues, he gave his audience the latest information on promotions, pay, and changes in uniform regulations. When this speech was over, he moved to Kaneohe and repeated it with the Marines there.

Those trips gave Shoup, with his demanding standards, many chances to see Rauber in a full range of circumstances—with generals and privates, with other branches of the U.S. Armed Forces, with civilians, and with foreign VIPs. He liked what he saw, and summed up the value of the billet thusly:

> Noncommissioned officers provide the strong, tough enlisted framework upon which a combat-ready Marine Corps is built. Traditionally, the officers of the Marine Corps have always worked closely with their non-coms. That is why the Commandant has the Sergeant Major of the Marine Corps as one of his principal assistants. The sergeant major is the senior NCO of the Marine Corps with many years of enlisted experience. The Commandant turns to him for advice in any problems affecting the welfare, efficiency, or fighting spirit of the men of the Marine Corps.

The last full-scale trip abroad for Rauber and his wife came in May of 1962. The Commandant led his group on an exhaustive (and exhausting) tour of Port Lyautey and Rabat, Morocco; Corsica; Naples; Rota, Spain; Paris; and London and Plymouth, England. The training center for the Royal Marines was at Lympstone near Plymouth, and a visit there was a must. Kay later recalled:

> Those Marines took him to their club, and all they wanted to do was try to drink someone under the table. That's what they tried, anyway. But I was not with him, for I was with the wives of some of the NCOs there. So they had a wild night of drinking and eating and so forth. The next morning Frank woke up fine (he could always hold his liquor), and he went around looking for all of them. The Royal Marine sergeant major was out like a light. None of them could come out. It must have been some night! I was glad Frank was alright, because we had to go on then with our trip.

That trip proved to be the last one for Rauber. Shoup wanted him to stay a year past the normal end of his term, and then have a joint retirement ceremony in 1963 for him and Kay. The deciding voice was hers, "I just couldn't stay there any longer. I wanted to go back to Hawaii." Being a sensible husband, Rauber said, "Okay, we'll go back to Hawaii."

When the Commandant had to select his new sergeant major, he asked Rauber, "Whom should we pick up?" And Rauber replied, "I'll tell you what, I won't answer that question. But I'll put a name on a piece of paper and put it in an envelope, and you keep it until after you've selected." Shoup later opened the envelope and it said, "Tom McHugh." And, by coincidence, that was the man Shoup chose.

For Rauber's departure there was a garden party at the Commandant's House, a Sunset Parade with a passing of the Sword of Office to his old friend McHugh, many gifts and farewells, and on June 28, 1962, he was off to retirement.

Afterwards there was a nice summary written of some of the subtle actions that had characterized his tenure:

> Still retaining a strong administrative background, Rauber brought to the office, and to all enlisted Marines, a level of distinction new to the Corps— and to the times. The enlisted Marine became recognized for what he was and how well he functioned, rather than in the broad category of enlisted Marine. During Rauber's tour, the refinement in the sorting process was tuned and the Corps greatly expanded its approach to get the right man in the slot.
>
> Although dictated by modern and complicated weapons systems, it was Rauber who now had the ear of the Commandant on behalf of all enlisted Marines and was able to give that final reassurance—"this is the best way to do it." Rauber also became a regular member of the Commandant's party on inspection trips and visits to Marine Corps commands. The enlisted ear to the ground and a voice at the top was now firmly established.

Arriving in Hawaii, they built a house in the Pacific Heights section of Honolulu. There they were close to the Punchbowl, the Pacific National Cemetery where so many Marines from the island assaults of World War II lie buried beneath geometrically aligned rows of crosses. While Rauber was now a civilian—and what memories must have continually surged through his mind when he looked back over the decades from 1962 to when he had first enlisted in the National Guard in 1918—Kay was still to be on active duty for the Air Force for another six months until her retirement. Friends in Washington had seen to it that a transfer for her to Hickam Air Force Base in Honolulu was arranged to coincide with their move to Hawaii.

They were in their new home for nine years, and, not surprisingly, they were busy years. Rauber, looking ahead to his retirement, had obtained employment with Dean Van Lines on Oahu. Dean moved many service personnel who needed shipments when they were reassigned, and Rauber handled all the relations with the military. He would find out who was moving in any of the branches of the Armed Forces, and then make arrangements for the transfer of their belongings.

It was a change of pace to switch from a military lifetime of pressure to perform at maximum capacity to a relaxed retirement as a civilian. There were many pleasant evenings after he would return from work. Kay later recalled:

> We had lots of parties there; we had a lanai [porch] that leaned outward, and when you went out there, you actually leaned out over kind of a jungle area, because we were way up high, back in the hills. So when we had a party, if anyone would take their drink out there, they would always feel like they were going to fall overboard because of the way it was built. Down below it was truly a jungle. There were mongoose and everything running around down there!

Sadness entered Rauber's life again in 1965; his eldest daughter, Rosemary, died.

With the wide range of friendships which Rauber and his wife had both developed in their long years of military service, it was natural that there would be some great reunions in a crossroads like Hawaii. Late in 1962, for instance, Shoup flew in again, this time with the new Sergeant Major of the Corps, Tom McHugh. On hand to greet them were both Rauber and Bill Bestwick (who was just finishing his last tour of duty as the Sergeant Major of FMFPac).

Unfortunately, there was another side to a life set in a crossroads location. Visitors came in a steady stream, and it seemed that there was an endless succession of taking people out to dinner, or to the airport, or sight-seeing. Kay admitted, "We got a little stir crazy finally. After years of this, I said, 'I can't stand this another minute.' "

That was that! Still the sensible husband, Rauber again acceded to his wife's wishes, and they said their goodbyes, sold their house, and packed up for departure. In May, 1971, just before Rauber turned 70, they were back in the States, looking over Arizona and California for a new home. The choice fell on Sun City, inland and halfway between Los Angeles and San Diego, California. It was a modest retirement town with streets laid out in perfectly aligned grids. Using their attractive new house as a base, they bought a motor home and toured the U.S.A., camping and seeing the parts of the country that they had never before visited.

One of the aspects which had lured them to Sun City was its proximity to a variety of Marine and Air Force bases. This enabled them to make frequent visits to see old friends in places like Camp Pendleton. At home, Rauber was active in the Sun City Civic Association and the local branch of the American Legion. There were periodic visits from his daughter, Mimi, who would fly in from her home in Williamsburg, Virginia. (It was Mimi who somehow coined the loving nickname of "Tubby" for her lean, well-muscled father, and now Kay used it, too.)

The years rolled by pleasantly, but advancing age brought health problems for Rauber. In 1983 Kay and he were in their motor home, headed for Las Vegas when Rauber was overtaken by a dizzy spell. That was the end of the motor home trips, for he then had a series of small strokes and finally Parkinson's Disease took hold. Confined to his home, Rauber kept his dignity and struggled bravely, but his indomitable spirit was of no avail. Kay was always at his side, supportive and cheerful as she saw him worsen. The end came in 1991; he died on February 19 in Sun City. Services were held at Arlington National Cemetery six days later, and he was buried there with full military honors.

He left vivid memories in the minds of those who knew him. His niece, a nun called Sister Remigia (after Rauber's first wife), commented:

> He maintained a balanced perspective—could be serious, could laugh at the proper time, and could be supportive. He was a man of integrity, justice, and high ethics. As a father, husband, and uncle, he was protective and loving.

Rauber's funeral at Arlington Cemetery.

As a Marine, he could be stern and demand what the situation required. He protected his country as he did his loved ones. He worked hard and did so because he loved what the Corps stood for—what it did and the people who made it up.

During the years of World War II, Francis never talked about what he did himself. From others I heard sketchy hints about two dramatic episodes. One was that he rode the train with some parts of the atomic bomb, guarding the secret cargo the whole way until it arrived where it was to be assembled. The other was that, as a Marine who understood German, he was on the beach at Long Island, New York, when they caught the German spies who landed there.

Rauber also had a strong impact on the men with whom he worked. They kept a vivid picture in their minds of the sergeant major they had known and greatly respected as a dedicated, highly principled leader. A former Commandant, General Paul X. Kelley, reflected, "He was a very interesting fellow, extremely dignified, very articulate, and very capable. If you had put him in a cowboy hat and boots, you'd have said that he was the epitome of a Texas oil millionaire—a tall, handsome man with a shock of grey-white hair."

One of his successors as Sergeant Major of the Marine Corps, Clinton Puckett, carried a life-long impression of one meeting with Rauber,

I stood in for the barracks sergeant major at Frank Rauber's reception, when he was leaving FMFPac to assume the position of Sergeant Major of the Corps. Most distinguished Marine I think I've ever met, both in appearance and in demeanor. Later, when I went back to Camp Smith, Frank Rauber was retired from the Corps, of course, and working in Hawaii. So I saw him on a number of occasions.

I don't think I've ever met a Marine that I respect more than I do Frank Rauber. Just an absolute prince of a gentleman. He showed dignity in appearance, stature. He made general officers seem to be PFCs by comparison. His contribution to the Corps and to the position of Sergeant Major of the Corps was that of dignity.

He lived that way; he died that way; Frank Rauber will always be remembered as a Man of Dignity.

Chapter 4

THE QUIET ONE
Sergeant Major Thomas J. McHugh

When Francis Rauber had put the name "Tom McHugh" in that envelope as his choice for a successor, it was not because they were old friends. He had many of those amongst the sergeants major whom he had known over his long years of service. It was because he had seen something special in Thomas McHugh when they had worked together. That critical ingredient had been a particular temperament and personality that convinced Rauber that McHugh was the best man to take over as Sergeant Major of the Marine Corps.

Effective leadership and unusual ability are mysterious things. Speaking broadly, there are two styles or types, each able to achieve major accomplishments and motivate those around and under them to give their best efforts to the cause (read: organization, or effort, or battle, or sacrifice).

The first type will often be colorful (sometimes flamboyant), dramatic, gregarious, out-going in personality, loquacious (frequently salted with four-letter words), overt in thoughts and actions, probably well-known to his peers (and perhaps the public), exuding authority, charisma, and self confidence (maybe even, occasionally, arrogance). What you see is what you get. When that person walks in a room, you know it. When that person speaks, you listen. When that person leads, you follow.

However, the second type has proven equally effective and talented in a radically different and much more subtle way. Their style is quiet, often dignified. Their words are few and their personal demeanor is calm and modest (with very little ego calling for attention). They may seem to be lost in the crowd, keeping their own counsel and often appearing to work alone. Their personality is hidden under a cloak of professionalism. A casual observer might think at first glance, "Nothing special in this person."

And yet, they too have proven themselves over the long haul. For what you see is not what you really get. Beneath the placid, prosaic surface lie determination, dedication, devotion and dependability—precious assets anywhere and doubly so in the military. They, too, in their quiet way, have found their way into the hearts and minds of the troops, have shown the leadership and ability to earn their way to the top, and have produced the results which their fellow professionals have seen and felt and come to admire.

In the Marine Corps, both Bestwick and Rauber were generally of this latter type, but the best example was their successor, Tom McHugh, the quiet, modest man who let his superb career achievements speak for him.

Standing six feet four inches tall, erect of carriage, solid and well muscled at 200 pounds, he had a build that would lend itself to a dramatic extrovert. His style, however, was low-key, with steady blue eyes and a low, even voice, underneath which were hints of the innate authority of a man who had seen much combat and led Marines under great pressure. In later years his brown hair had turned a steely gray, close cropped as always, and there were eye glasses, but the stamp of competence was still there upon him, as he spoke with modesty and reluctance about his life.

He was New York City Irish. His father, Peter, had come from Ireland, while his mother, Bridget, was Scotch. On December 23, 1919, Thomas John McHugh was born. Family life was brief and soon disrupted when his father died and he was taken, at the age of three, with his sister Mary to Philadelphia, where there were aunts and uncles.

After grammar school there, he enrolled in a vocational school, getting an auto mechanic's training. Two and a half years of that was enough for him and he left. Starting in 1936, he worked as an arc welder on ships in the Philadelphia Navy Yard for $43 a week. Away from his job, he enjoyed playing baseball, and he was talented enough to earn a tryout with a semi-pro team.

The dividing line in his life came on October 3, 1938. Since he "had just about always wanted to be a Marine," he marched into the Philadelphia Recruiting Office and enlisted in the Organized Reserves. Duty at weekend drills and summer training camps brought promotions to private first class (PFC) in February, 1940, and to corporal another four months later.

With Hitler on the rampage in Europe, the Marine Corps started to shift from its restricted peacetime pattern. Orders came through calling McHugh to active duty on November 7, 1940. For ten months he served with the Marine detachment in his old location, the Navy Yard. Then it was off to Quantico, Virginia, in September, 1941. There he was assigned to a special readiness battalion. Scuttlebutt (a grapevine rumor) was rife. Some Marines might be going to Europe; some to Iceland (where a Marine Brigade had gone four months earlier to counter the threat of German invasion).

Instead, McHugh's company was sent to Camp Lejeune, North Carolina, for further infantry training. The Japanese attack on Pearl Harbor on December 7, 1941, sent an electric shock throughout the Marine Corps. It meant that heavy combat in the Pacific lay ahead. It must have been a let-down

A 21-year-old corporal McHugh goes on active duty in November, 1940.

for McHugh, then, when he was sent, two days later, to a routine, boring job on the sidelines. Some twenty-five to thirty men were plucked out of the company and sent to be a guard detachment at the nearby base at Cherry Point. A Marine air station was under construction there, and his action consisted of watching over trucks and bulldozers.

McHugh was not cut out for that. In February, 1942, he requested a transfer to the newly-formed 1st Division at Camp Lejeune. It was sure to be headed where the real action was. The following month was an exciting one for McHugh. His promotion to "Temporary Sergeant-Line" came through, along with orders to the 1st Regiment in the 1st Division. Expectations were fulfilled when the unit sailed in June, 1942.

Arriving in New Zealand, the division began a training cycle which was soon interrupted by an emergency speedup of plans. That was caused by the news of Japanese construction of a strategic airfield on an island no one had even heard of before. It was called Guadalcanal, and the division was now given the task of assaulting and capturing it—an assignment that called for defeating an enemy who had thus far rolled invincibly to an unbroken string of island victories in the Pacific.

With that sobering job ahead, the men of the division were caught up in one of those ludicrous distractions that characterize war. The cargo on their transport and supply ships had been incorrectly stowed, and now the ships had to be wholly emptied, and then everything had to be put back in combat loaded priorities. This meant that, when the assault came, the first items needed (ammunition, food, medical supplies) would be on top, ready at hand. Thus McHugh and the others there would never forget "24 hours a day, six or seven days a week" sweating at the docks in Wellington.

Finally the miserable job was completed, and the division headed for a landing rehearsal in the Fiji Islands, and then for the assault on Guadalcanal, and an historic clash of two tough fighting forces. McHugh, now acting platoon sergeant, went in with the assault waves on D-day, August 7. The tempo of the battle soon increased, and an important fight took place at Alligator Creek (mistakenly called the Tenaru River). There McHugh's battalion, in an encircling maneuver, was able to pin a reinforced battalion of Imperial Japanese Marines in the crossfire from another U.S. Marine battalion. When the fight was over, there were piles of Japanese bodies everywhere, 600-700 of them. Still the struggle for the island ground on, while the ravages of malaria, the shortages of supplies, and the wounds and deaths of endless weeks of combat sapped the weary Marines.

Eventually it came time for McHugh to rotate back to Australia, and, in January, 1943, he was sent to Melbourne. It was not a pleasant stay. He was hospitalized four times with recurring sieges of malaria. Back with his old company, there was the pressing need to train replacements for the division's next operation. In May, 1943, McHugh took a step which foreshadowed his probable future as a "lifer": he transferred from the Reserves to the regulars, and then in October, received his warrant as a "Temporary Platoon Sergeant" (with one "rocker" added underneath the three chevrons he had as a "buck" sergeant).

Leaving Australia in September, the division went to an obscure, isolated base called Goodenough Island for a final shake-down. In December, 1943, McHugh went in again on a D-day landing at Cape Gloucester, New Britain. Briefly, there was bitter fighting, but the Japanese fled and in a month it was all over. McHugh remembered it as "a matter of a lot of patrolling and wet and swampy land." As usual, he understated conditions. The land and climate were ghastly with 200-foot trees and huge vines forming a nearly impenetrable jungle, mud up to your waist, knife-edged kunai grass, and enormous, stinking swamps. Everywhere there were mosquitoes and ticks to transmit dysentery, scurvy, beri-beri, and malaria. Add the swarms of giant spiders, centipedes, snakes, scorpions, and wicked wasps, and it's clear why the division was anxious to leave.

The "rest camp" to which they returned in April, 1944, was not much better. Called Pavuvu, in the Russell Islands, it featured more swamps, interminable rain, poor food, sickness, and low morale. It was a miserable setting in which to get ready for the next—and far bloodier—landing, now planned for Peleliu in the Palau Islands. During his four months on Pavuvu, McHugh took one more step forward in his career when he made "Temporary Gunnery Sergeant" in August.

So it was that, when the assault on deadly Peleliu Island began on September 15, McHugh was in the thick of it as the "company gunny." The landing was a brutal, violent, and costly slugging match from the start. The Japanese looked down on every move from their fortified, camouflaged caves on what soon came to be called "Bloody Nose Ridge." Mortar rounds poured

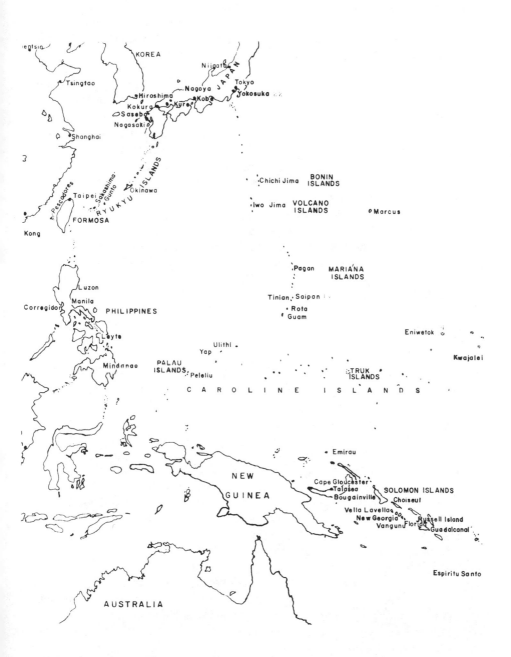

down in a hail on the Marines, and, on the third day, shrapnel tore into McHugh's right arm. He wanted to remain with his company, but his first sergeant was blunt in his order, "You're going for medical treatment!" Since there was no safe area in the landing zone, this meant a move out to a hospital ship. There McHugh had a chance to recuperate—and look back on one Purple Heart and three D-Day landings in a two-year span.

The respite did not last long. In a few weeks he was back at Pavuvu, but then came welcome orders sending him back to the United States in November.

After a month's leave of absence—long dreamed of in the Pacific—in January, 1945, he reported for duty at Cherry Point, a familiar location. It was quite a change for him: comfortable living quarters and a pleasant climate instead of the miseries of Pavuvu or an edge-of-death foxhole. The base had been transformed, too, in the three years since he had been there. The rumble of construction trucks had been replaced by the roar of fighter plane engines, and, instead of a few Marines guarding bare foundations in the ground, there was now an impressive array of barracks and hangars all teeming with aviators on their way to, or just back from, combat.

As a highly trained infantryman, McHugh was assigned to be the NCO in charge of the rifle range. Six months later he was back at Camp Lejeune, at home in an infantry training regiment. Still a gunnery sergeant, he nevertheless was acting as a company first sergeant.

Life, however, was more than just work. Camp Lejeune was by now well-supplied with women Marines, including a 21-year-old corporal named Doris Riffel from South Bend, Indiana. One thing led to another, and on September 10, 1945, she and McHugh were married.

With the war now ended, they settled into the peace-time routine of a Marine base with continuous training and time for family and relaxation. He was transferred to the 1st Marine Special Brigade in January, 1946, and that April Doris became the mother of Patricia (affectionately called "Patty Ann" by the family). Another transfer, in mid-1946, brought McHugh to the 8th Marines, part of the 2d Division, which was now at Camp Lejeune as its new permanent base. As an acting first sergeant, he also served as a platoon leader of machine guns and mortars (usually a lieutenant's assignment). There was also added duty as NCO in charge of the rifle range. The end of 1946 brought his warrant as "Temporary Technical Sergeant," not a promotion, just a change of title.

Doris added another daughter, Margaret ("Peggy"), to the family in January, 1948. McHugh, meanwhile, had settled into a steady routine in his billet, so these years brought forth a typically reticent evaluation later on, "I can't really think of any special experiences during that time." Yet there were training exercises near Norfolk, Virginia, in the Caribbean, in Newfoundland, and in the Mediterranean, events that would lead to a string of "sea stories" from most Marines, but not from McHugh.

By September, 1948, McHugh felt that it was time for a change. He had been at Lejeune for over three years, and the urge to move along took precedence over the joys of family living. Accordingly, he requested overseas duty. Doris moved back to South Bend with the two girls; he packed his foot locker (trunk) and his sea (duffel) bag. When his orders came through, he proceeded to San Francisco, and thence by slow ship to Pearl Harbor and finally to Guam. There he joined the 5th Marines of the 1st Provisional Brigade in September, 1948, serving as a company gunnery sergeant/first sergeant, although his actual rank remained technical sergeant. (Due to severe peacetime budgetary restrictions on the Corps, the 5th Marines at this time were actually a reinforced battalion rather than the traditional regimental-sized unit.) The focus was, as usual, on infantry training exercises run as a battalion landing team. A little over a year later, in January, 1950, the 5th Marines moved to California. There it joined two other battalions at Camp Pendleton to make a full-fledged regiment in the 1st Division.

Suddenly the invasion of South Korea on June 25, 1950, shattered his training routine. The desperate need for highly-trained U.S. infantrymen there was soon painfully obvious, and the Marine Corps, with its long history of combat readiness and expeditionary capability, was the obvious stop-gap solution. Orders to activate and prepare to ship out a fully-equipped 1st Provisional Brigade came early in July. Marines from active duty stations everywhere were pulled in to beef up the brigade to the maximum strength. From ships' detachments, from the East Coast, from recruiting stations, from supply depots, and from fighter plane cockpits, they came in droves around the clock. Meanwhile the wives and children of the men moved to their home bases, with McHugh's family going to Philadelphia, while he and his regiment at Camp Pendleton dealt with the influx of new men.

McHugh later described the scene, "We worked pretty well around the clock, night and day, six or seven days a week, joining replacements, fitting people in, and getting gear [equipment] issued." Again, the calmly understated summary, "Just a busy time." But his conclusion then gave the triumphant outcome, "We did make our deadline and sailed when we were scheduled to." It was a memorable achievement. In one short week the Corps had built a peace-time skeleton unit into a 6500-man brigade, fully equipped and on board its transport ships, en route to war!

Since it was obvious that the brigade would need to be expanded into a full-scale division, the President, on July 19, authorized the calling up of Marine reserves to flesh out an additional regimental combat team. Now a second torrent, civilians ordered to report for active duty, poured into Camp Pendleton. By August 10 the gigantic organizational job was well along, and the first of the division's ships had sailed for the Far East.

McHugh and the rest of the 5th Marines, who formed the basis of the brigade, were hard at work on board ship. As he later recalled:

> Most of the new people were sort of professional. The NCOs and most of these people who were brought in had a background in infantry, but they may have been away from it for a while. So it didn't take too much of the good leadership provided by the staff NCOs I had in my company

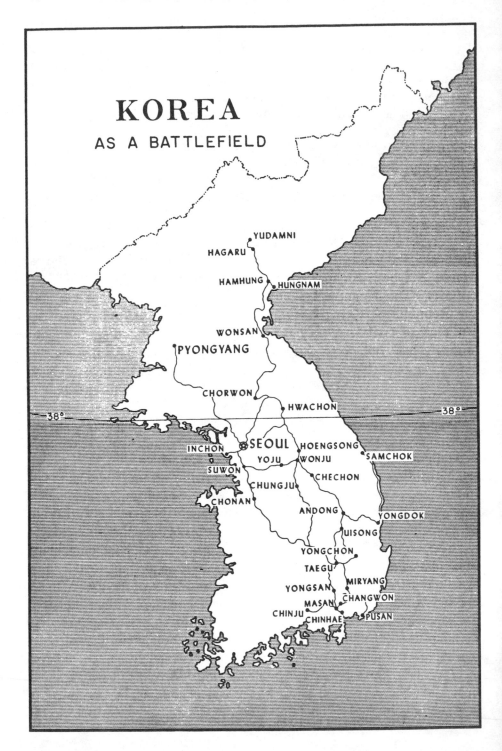

KOREA
AS A BATTLEFIELD

and the commanding officers, and we soon had a real spirited organization. I think we spent a lot of time, on the way over to Korea, talking about training. Some of the people may have forgotten some of the things from World War II: what the enemy would be like, or what to expect. So we got a lot done in that period.

Early in August the regiment landed at Pusan, the last United Nations toehold on the Korean peninsula, and, as the first Marine ground unit to arrive, its shipboard refresher courses were put to immediate combat testing. Following successful repulses of the North Korean invaders in the Naktong River battles and the stabilization of the defense perimeter, the regiment pulled back to Pusan. There McHugh and the other Marines prepared for their next operation. That was to be the famous Inchon amphibious landing in September that struck far behind the enemy front lines. It was a huge gamble, with treacherous tides dictating the precise date. Nevertheless, the 1st Division, with its veterans of World War II assault landings in the Pacific, successfully fought its way ashore. A hard drive inland took it into bitter hand-to-hand fighting in the streets of the capital, Seoul. The capture of this city marked a turning point in the Korean War.

During these critical days, McHugh's superb performance brought him a Navy Commendation Medal with Combat "V." The citation by the commanding general of the division, Major General Oliver Smith, praised his "great skill, courage, and confidence...under the most adverse conditions." McHugh had heavy responsibilities in the rapidly moving combat actions of his infantry company during September 15 to November 2, 1950. He was in charge of all administrative functions such as supplies of food and ammunition, personnel problems with replacements for casualties, and reports to the battalion commander. The citation went on to commend him, "On one occasion, when his company was engaged in attacking strong enemy positions near Seoul, Korea, he courageously refused to submit to evacuation even though he was suffering from a serious stomach ailment. Unable to sleep or eat for a four-day period, and suffering from a considerable loss of weight, his initiative and actions constantly set an example to all who worked with him."

McHugh's company commander, who had assumed command back on Guam and continued during this period of heavy Korean combat, was Captain Joseph Fegan, an officer who recognized the value of a NCO with ten years' service and World War II assaults under his belt. He is reported to have admitted, half seriously and half in jest, "I just did what Gunny McHugh told me to do, and everything turned out fine! He was the model staff NCO for all others to emulate."

With the Inchon-Seoul operation successfully over, McHugh and his men (and, in fact, the entire 1st Division) got ready for the next assignment. The division was moved to the opposite side of the Korean Peninsula and ordered to attack towards the Chosin Reservoir close to the Chinese border. Meanwhile, moving secretly by night, some thirteen select Chinese Army divisions surrounded the Marine division, and then, confident of annihilating the Marines with their apparently overwhelming numbers, they struck viciously in December, 1950.

Again, McHugh was in the center of the crisis, for his battalion was at the reservoir. Amidst the violent, close-in fighting he had to keep the supplies, manpower, and communications functioning for his company to survive in the freezing weather. There ensued an epic struggle that saw the division finally slug its way out of the trap in brutal, sub-zero temperatures, and come back to the coast with all its equipment and personnel. They left the Chinese divisions shattered as organized fighting units.

McHugh's memories modestly focus on what others did, rather than his own exploits, "It was COLD, but once again the positive leadership of our NCOs, platoon leaders, and company commander was how we got our guys in to our objective and then how we got them out (as best we could). There were fire fights with the Chinese all along the way: night attacks by them with their bugles blowing madly."

There was still more combat for McHugh after the grueling experiences of "Frozen Chosin." After making "Temporary Master Sergeant" in December, 1950, he was back in the division's fighting on the Central Korean Front early the next year. While his administrative duties continued their previous diversity, there was a particular emphasis on rotating combat veterans out and training new men who came in as replacements. In addition, McHugh was a frequent member of his company's combat patrols.

March, 1951, was a very good month, for orders came through sending him back to the United States. Thus he passed through Pusan one last time, headed for San Francisco and a well-earned leave and reunion with Doris and his two daughters. All too soon the relaxation ended, and it was back to work: a brief assignment as an assistant battalion sergeant major with the Officers Candidate Class at Parris Island.

Then, in July, he was sent to Norfolk, Virginia, for a three-week training course to prepare him for his next tour of duty. And what a change of pace the new orders brought. The combat veteran, with all those battle stars on his World War II and Korean ribbons, was headed for Yale University. There he would serve in the Naval ROTC program as the Assistant Marine Officer-Instructor. He had serious doubts about this assignment:

> I said to myself, "What am I doing here?" But about a week later, I saw the reason I was sent there. A gent by the name of Major Fegan walked in, my old company commander whom I'd had for Guam, Korea, and everything else. When I saw the major walk in I felt much, much more relieved and much more at home. He was the new Marine Officer-Instructor (and, of course, he later went on to become a lieutenant general).
>
> In addition, I was sort of surprised a little bit about Yale. The young people we had in our program were all well motivated. They were conscientious; they were sincere in learning. A lot of times, if I'd be holding a lecture on something and they wanted some more information, they would come back to the office in their free time and ask more about it. Then maybe they'd ask permission to take a weapon apart...that sort of thing. So I was impressed by them.

Besides the NROTC students, we also had additional duties: the procurement for Officer Candidate Classes and Platoon Leaders Classes. Those people were independent from the NROTC program. Marines would come in and ask for information about those classes and fill out their applications; then we'd take them down and get them physical exams and stuff like that required for the programs. We stayed busy!

McHugh's focus on youngsters took on a personal priority in January, 1952, when his first son, Thomas, arrived to add to his growing family.

His sojourn in academia came to an end in August, 1954, with a return to the harsh realities of infantry life at Camp Lejeune. McHugh started out acting as the sergeant major of an engineer battalion in the 2d Division there. In January, 1955, however, he got a chance to spread his wings, for he took on broader responsibilities. Not long before, the 2d Division had pioneered a new concept in how best to employ its most senior NCOs. McHugh later explained:

> The division had started this program about two years earlier, and I was probably the second man in the job. You had the admin-type sergeant major, who was pretty well tied up in those days in paperwork, paperwork, and more paperwork. However, the division commander at that time felt that he liked a sergeant major to see what was going on out in the field. So I was made a "field sergeant major," and I worked directly for the commanding general and through the chief of staff [while another senior NCO handled the administrative chores]. I set up the ceremonies, the parades, kept track of the marksmanship progress of the unit, and checked the daily training schedules that the troops were supposed to be carrying out. In general, I just roamed through the area...

One of the senior officers who saw McHugh in this free-wheeling position of responsibility was the assistant division commander, Brigadier General Wallace Greene. Their paths would cross again nine years later when Greene became Commandant.

When the Corps resurrected the rank of sergeant major, McHugh quickly made application for consideration by the selection board. That was accompanied by a ringing endorsement from the division chief of staff, "Master Sergeant McHugh has repeatedly demonstrated, in the performance of his duties as field sergeant major, a capability for greatly increased responsibilities. He has been exceptionally effective in his relationship with both officers and senior noncommissioned officers of the division staff and division units. His professional skill, force, consistent attention to duty, leadership, wholehearted cooperation and loyalty mark him as being highly qualified for appointment to the rank of sergeant major." Apparently, some other people felt the same way, and thus McHugh was among the very first to be given a sergeant major's warrant in December, 1955.

The three-year tour at Lejeune came to an end in July, 1957, with McHugh going overseas for duty with the 1st Brigade at Kaneohe Bay, Hawaii. There he served as a sergeant major at three different levels: brigade, regiment, and

As sergeant major of the 4th Regiment in Kaneohe, Hawaii, in 1960, McHugh (center, top) checks out an Ontos with its six 106 mm guns.

McHugh photo

battalion. Watching McHugh at work was a hard-charging young staff sergeant, Leland Crawford; their natures were diametrically opposed, but there was a mutual respect, and their paths would cross again. Kaneohe was also the place where McHugh's family expanded once again, for his fourth and last child, another daughter, Kathleen ("Kathy"), was born in June of 1959.

An officer, Second Lieutenant (later Colonel) Ernest Baulch, who knew him then, remembered his style well:

> McHugh was a big help to the junior officers. Always respectful, he never failed to stand up from his desk chair when a young officer entered his office. When asked for advice, he would never offer "the solution," but would instead suggest various options. He always seemed to have time to listen.
>
> With the troops, he would stand 6' 4" tall in front of them and talk to them like a father. Sober looking, seldom smiling, always calm, he never had to raise his voice; his method was "admonish in private and a pat on the back in public." So you could always feel his hand in running things, but it was never overt.
>
> Modest to the point of shyness, he seemed to stand in awe of the billet of Sergeant Major of the Marine Corps. Perhaps he didn't think he was good enough, for his feeling seemed to be, "I'll never get that job."

Two short years later, he would have it!

A year later, it was time to move again, and, over a farewell cup of coffee, McHugh's administrative chief, Warrant Officer James Chance, made a prescient prediction, "Sergeant Major, some day you'll be the Sergeant Major of the Marine Corps." His orders took him to the Landing Force Development Center at Quantico. There he worked on preparing revised Tables of Organization for infantry units, weapons changes, and modifications to the Corps' infrastructure.

Moving sideways, in May, 1961, he transferred to the air station in Quantico. One of the young NCOs in the headquarters building there, Corporal David Hugel, later recollected:

> The sergeant major always appeared to me to be a very professional gentleman, very polite, just the kind of person you would envision as the stern but caring kind of older uncle or someone like that in your family. I always found him to be quite dignified and proper in his appearance, but certainly cordial and friendly. He certainly was one where, even if he didn't say a lot, you could tell that he recognized who you were from having even brief dealings with you. He was always courteous and greeted you, usually, by name.
>
> If you ever met him you would never forget it. He was a very imposing figure, very tall and very trim, about 200 pounds of muscle. He had, at that time, a very close-cropped, somewhat of a flat-top, haircut, sandy to possibly turning a little whiter grey. If you ever heard the sergeant major speak, you would remember him. He always treated you with respect and dignity in whatever rank you were. He was professional, businesslike, yet he was respected and well liked by those around him. All in all, he was the kind of person that you just don't forget. Of all the people I served with, he's one that sticks out very vividly in my mind.

A sergeant major who knew him then gave another glimpse into the very private personal life of McHugh. He noted that he (McHugh) was "a very devout Catholic. It seemed that he went to church seven days a week in Quantico."

Again it was time for overseas duty, and in April, 1962, McHugh received orders to report to the 3d Division on Okinawa. He would never forget what happened shortly thereafter:

> I was getting ready to ship my foot locker one day. I was sitting in the office at the air station, and the CO [commanding officer] got a call from Headquarters Marine Corps on his phone. He asked me to come into his office and use his phone; it was the general who was the personnel director, and he said I was being considered for the Sergeant Major of the Marine Corps position; would I accept if this was the outcome? I answered, "Well, sure I would!" He went on, "This is a conversation just between you and me right now. We're not going to say anything about this to anybody, just wait." The next thing I know, the commanding general of Quantico came over in his car and congratulated me on being the next Sergeant Major of the Marine Corps. It was a matter of about half an hour!

June 29, 1962: McHugh (right) accepts the Sword of Office of the Sergeant Major of the Marine Corps from the Commandant, General David Shoup, as his predecessor, Frank Rauber (center) stands at attention.

A board of general officers, headed by the assistant commandant, Lieutenant General John Munn, had looked carefully at the records of the top 100 sergeants major. Although McHugh was 85th in seniority, he was selected as one of six finalists recommended to the Commandant, General David Shoup, winner of the Medal of Honor at Tarawa. Shoup picked McHugh. Thus it was that the sergeant major changed the shipping label on his foot locker from Okinawa to Washington, D.C.

Upon arrival, he reported in at Headquarters and was greeted by retiring Sergeant Major Frank Rauber. They were old friends from duty fourteen years earlier in Guam, when Rauber had used his superior administrative skills to help out McHugh with the paperwork he faced there. As McHugh admitted:

> He was an expert in administration, while I was more or less an infantry type then, so I was learning as I was going along. He'd been in it for years. During that time there was a General Order when we shifted over to unit diaries. Frank was available and I went over to his office, and he explained quite a few things on how it should be done. So he guided me quite a bit in the administrative field.

Rauber was again able to show McHugh the ropes—that time in a new location. He took McHugh around Headquarters, introduced him to the key people he would be working with, and listed the staff meetings he would be attending. It didn't take long; "we were professionals." On June 29, 1962, in a formal parade and review at the Washington Barracks, McHugh took over as the third Sergeant Major of the Marine Corps. He had spent over twenty-three years of his forty-two-year life span in the Corps, six of it as a sergeant major.

When he had his first meeting with the Commandant, it was brief and surprisingly vague. Shoup said, "Welcome aboard. I'm sure you're going to do the job that's expected of you." He must have had a lot of confidence in McHugh, for there were no "marching orders" or details of what he expected. McHugh would have to find his own way and set his own style in the billet.

One pattern continued: when Shoup made a trip that would involve enlisted personnel, and this was 90 percent of the time, McHugh would accompany him. On arrival at a base, they would split up, with the sergeant major going around, as he said, to "see what the troops were doing and check this and check that—any place the Commandant wasn't going to go."

A crucial time came on the plane returning to Headquarters, for then McHugh would relay his observations to Shoup. Sometimes there were problems to be discussed—lack of leadership, or low morale, or poor uniform appearance, or below standard barracks. Similarly, there was an opportunity for praise for an outstanding unit. They were hard-working trips for McHugh, since Doris could not come along due to the responsibilities for their young children at home.

Stiff and formal as always, the official portrait of McHugh as Sergeant Major of the Marine Corps: July, 1962.

Thus there were many separations. In September, 1962, there was a fifteen-day trip to Hawaii, Japan, Okinawa, Vietnam, Thailand, and Guam. Then back out to FMFPac in February, 1963. Two months later, it was London (and a visit to the Royal Marines), a checkout of Marine Embassy Guards at Port Lyautey in Morocco, Rota in Spain, Naples, Paris, and Bermuda. Next came Lejeune for a NCO symposium. In the same month of August, 1963, they were off again, this time to the Cold Weather Training Center at Bridgeport, California, and on to the air station in Yuma, Arizona, the 1st Division at Pendleton, the air station at El Toro, the Barstow Supply Center, and Twentynine Palms in California. Then there were trips to Newfoundland and Iceland, as well as the Caribbean—an exhausting schedule.

Back in the office, he would see Shoup daily at the Commandant's briefing, but their actual meetings for discussion were less frequent. The sergeant major would make an appointment through Shoup's aide and they would sit down together, "once or twice a week and sometimes less than that." More frequently, there would be a memo, or a trip report, from McHugh to the Commandant.

In addition, there were regular, scheduled Headquarters staff meetings to be attended. Every day the mail came pouring in, and this required a close, diplomatic, working relationship with the sergeants major monitor and the personnel sergeant major. These were men in commanding positions, and his years of experience served McHugh well in dealing with them. As he described it:

> Well, what really happened, I would get a lot of letters from people asking about promotions, asking about transfers, asking about everything else. Any time I would get a letter, I would go to the persons involved—say the monitor or the personnel sergeant major—with a 25 MOS or a 35 or

any other MOS. I would go down and say, "Here's what I got from so-and-so. He'd like to know the chances of being transferred to so-and-so. Take this and give me an answer. What can I tell him?" That's just the way I worked with them. I would not make the decisions. If this man was entitled to his transfer or not, those people would make the decisions.

However, when McHugh did find someone who was not really doing his job, he would take the initiative in these joint discussions. As he summarized the procedure:

> Of course we always went through a man's record, what he had there in his file jacket. I may have run across something on a trip that I picked up on. When I got back I'd go to Personnel and say, "Look, we've got this guy in this position, and he's just not doing it." Then we'd try to work it out together. They would move him to a different billet, or move him towards retirement, whatever the case called for. Then there was the good side too. I would encounter some individual where I felt, "This guy really should be promoted. He's terrific!" Generally, we were able to help him.

Then there were the phone calls—lots of them. McHugh winced as he recalled:

> [They came in] 24 hours a day, believe it or not. You're called at home; you're called on weekends; you're called at 2:00 in the morning. Maybe it was only 11:00 pm out at Pendleton or somewhere, but the phone would wake you up and some guy would ask, "Hey, is the promotion list out?" or "How about so-and-so?" It went on seven days a week, all hours of the day and night.

No wonder that McHugh would summarize his job as "to feel the pulse of an organization!"

With all those activities, and with the propensity of Marine Commandants to press for "my policy" or "my priority program," one might suppose that some special focus dominated McHugh's time and efforts. But not so; in his typically restrained manner he later denied any "particular policy" or "specific problem" in which he would represent his chief's personal goals to the enlisted personnel throughout the Corps.

One principle held fast: the drive to tap experienced NCOs for improvements in the Corps continued unabated. Each year Headquarters held a staff NCO symposium at widely different locations. The senior leadership from Headquarters, including McHugh, always attended. Each meeting would result in recommendations for the better functioning of the Corps, but, as McHugh later observed, "some of those submitted were things that we could not possibly do within the Corps, such as pay increases. They were out of our hands, but problems within the Corps we could correct. We got some worthwhile input, and we did make some changes."

The end of 1963 found McHugh operating smoothly in his critical position, but it brought a major change in the Corps' leadership. General Wallace Greene replaced Shoup as Commandant. That was a fortuitous occurrence for McHugh, in view of his earlier association with Greene in the 2d Division in

1955. Furthermore, Greene had been serving as chief of staff at Headquarters, so he had had frequent opportunities to work with McHugh there and evaluate his abilities. Finally, McHugh had served only a year and a half in the billet. Thus the transition went smoothly, for Greene asked McHugh to stay on in January, 1964.

Because all relationships vary when two men are working in close concert, there was a slightly different empathy between McHugh and the new Commandant; McHugh felt "because I had done a lot of work for General Greene earlier, I guess I felt personally closer to him." Greene's attitude was equally positive:

> I had a great deal of contact with McHugh because I admired him as a Marine; I knew what he had done in the past. He was a fine-looking, outstanding noncommissioned officer, and I knew that he was going to be a great deal of help to me. So, at every opportunity that I had, I asked McHugh to either travel with me on a trip, or to advise me on matters in particular relating to enlisted problems that we had, I'd say several times a week. I actually used him. He wasn't just a figurehead; he was a very useful member of my staff.
>
> Then there was his style of operating. He was a very personable individual to start off with, and very cooperative. He never had any difficulty in establishing a good relationship with officers or enlisted men on any problem that might come up. That was one of his main values as a Marine Corps sergeant major: the ability to get along with a wide range of people.
>
> He was a tall, strong-looking, erect Marine—just the sort of person that you would be glad to have with you in the field within the setting of a Marine division, or at any headquarters.

General Greene went on to speak enthusiastically about McHugh's role when they made trips together, both in the United States and throughout the world:

> He was the sort of individual that you could take with you and, while you might be involved in liaison with the civilian public possibly, or some local Marine Corps units, you could always call on him to go out and make special contacts and get special information that you might need. I could sum it up by saying that McHugh was very useful in getting the "straight scoop" on any problems that might exist in the area in which you were visiting.
>
> Sometimes I would give him a problem assignment before we left Headquarters for him to look into while we were on the trip. There were a number of concerns that he could look into. One was problems with families, wives and children with their husband or father away, and they would be having difficulties—financial and other family difficulties—and he was able to talk with them and then we could help them. I think that was a very important part of his trips.

One of the first trips that they took together was to Vietnam in January, 1964. There the Marines already had a small contingent, a few men in Saigon

A trip to England in 1965 brought McHugh to a handshake with the berobed Lord Mayor of London (above, left) and talks with his foreign counterparts (above, right). In full dress blues with medals, swords, and white gloves are (left to right) the Sergeant Major of the Netherlands Marine Corps, the Sergeant Major of the Royal Marines, and McHugh.

A visit to a Montagnard tribe in the Central Highlands of Vietnam in January, 1964, finds McHugh sampling who knows what. Greene (far left) discreetly walks away.

Another inspection trip in April, 1965, takes McHugh (right) to Okinawa. Here he is welcomed by Herbert Sweet, sergeant major of the 3d Division and later to be the next Sergeant Major of the Marine Corps (left).

En route home from WestPac, McHugh (right) and Greene (left) stop off in Hawaii in April, 1965. The sergeant major holds a Chinese "burp gun," while the Commandant describes its capture to a press conference.

and a handful down in the Delta, assigned to the Vietnamese Marine Corps. When Greene and McHugh arrived in Saigon, by coincidence the same young Corporal Hugel, who had served under the sergeant major in Quantico, was there, assigned to accompany them. Their reunion remained etched in his memory ever afterward:

> I looked and there was a familiar face. It was Sergeant Major McHugh. He was a very imposing figure. You couldn't miss him. He got off the plane and he looked around, and then he looked at me and he said, "Well, Hugel, we're a long way from Quantico." And all I could reply was, "Yes, sir, Sergeant Major, we sure are." That was one day I will never forget because here I was, at that time a corporal, and certainly I had made it clear that I was doing a tour in the Marine Corps and enjoyed it, but that was not going to be my career. Now here was the Sergeant Major of the Marine Corps, whom I had served with a year or more before, greeting me personally by name.

Later, at a luncheon for the visitors, the two men shared a few reminiscences of their Quantico days, and Hugel found McHugh, despite the separation in their ranks, "very cordial and accommodating, a real gentleman, extremely professional, and extremely courteous."

From Saigon, McHugh went on with Greene for a whirlwind tour of United States and Vietnamese military facilities throughout the country. Then they went on to other Marine units in the Far East, and finally home again.

The next year and a half held more of the same long and short trips, interspersed with ceaseless work at Headquarters. (The year 1964, for instance, saw the sergeant major log over 150,000 miles in travel.) As the spring of 1965 began, McHugh took a careful look at his own future: "I felt that three years in that billet would be enough. General Greene did ask me if I would like to stay on until he left office. I said, of course, that I appreciated it and everything else, but I felt that, after three years, it was time to get new blood in the job. I saw that the Vietnam War was starting to be a little bit hot at that time, so I wanted to get back into the field with the troops." In addition, he decided that he wanted to be a "30-year man," and he still needed five more years of service to achieve that goal.

Accordingly, the usual selection board nominated his successor in April, 1965, and McHugh cleaned up the final papers on his desk. The final ceremony—by now a tradition—of posting the new Sergeant Major of the Marine Corps and relieving his predecessor took place with pomp and martial splendor at the Washington Barracks on July 16, 1965. McHugh passed along the Sword of Office to Sergeant Major Herbert Sweet, and Greene pinned on his dress blues the Navy Achievement Medal "for outstanding achievement in the superior performance of his duties as Sergeant Major of the Marine Corps." The citation from the Secretary of the Navy filled in the specifics:

> As the senior enlisted Marine in a position of great trust and responsibility, Sergeant Major McHugh devised ways of improving efficiency, morale and esprit de corps of such caliber that he brought distinction upon

himself and enhanced the prestige of the position of Sergeant Major of the Marine Corps. Through his professional competence and administrative ability, he rendered outstanding assistance to the Commandant and his staff on numerous field inspection trips to Marine Corps commands throughout the United States and foreign countries.

His primary concern, the good of the Marine Corps and each individual Marine, was characterized by his guidance and wise counselling of the Marine Corps' most senior noncommissioned officers, and earned for him the genuine respect of both officers and men of the entire Corps. His tact, diligent and conscientious attention to the many detailed duties assigned him were a credit to himself and the Marine Corps, and were in keeping with the highest traditions of the United States Naval Service.

His new orders took him to Okinawa where he served as the sergeant major of Camp Butler. He was back where he wanted to be, "in the field with the troops." (Doris, however, stayed behind in Alexandria, Virginia, since this was to be what the Marine Corps terms "an unaccompanied tour of duty.")

Camp Butler was a busy staging point for Marines coming from and going to Vietnam. McHugh's many duties included supervision of meeting the arrivals, loading the planes for departures, seeing to it that men from combat received fresh, clean uniforms, indoctrinating those headed for Vietnam, and making sure that they had the equipment they needed.

Policy at that time called for tours in the Far East to be of one-year duration, so a transfer came through and McHugh headed back in September, 1966, to familiar territory at Quantico. There he was attached to the Development and Education Command, and Doris rejoined him once more. By now, McHugh was an "old pro" able to provide superb guidance for younger Marines, and his commanding general recognized this in an official Certificate of Commendation in April, 1968, noting his:

...outstanding achievement in the superior performance of his duties in the field of leadership. While serving as Sergeant Major, Marine Corps Schools, and upon redesignation of this command, as Sergeant Major, Marine Corps Development and Education Command, Sergeant Major McHugh performed his duties with exemplary dedication and professionalism.

Exhibiting outstanding leadership and initiative, he contributed significantly to the morale of the men, he maintained close personal contact with each subordinate echelon, and worked tirelessly in advising and counselling Marines. Throughout his tenure, his dedicated efforts and exceptional administrative abilities contributed significantly to the accomplishment of the mission of this command.

The next month the Corps transferred McHugh to Lejeune to serve as sergeant major of force troops, Fleet Marine Force, Atlantic (FMFLant) there. An old acquaintance from Kaneohe days, Sergeant Major Leland Crawford, who was a reconnaissance specialist, reported in that fall, expecting to be assigned to force reconnaissance. McHugh had other ideas and abruptly sent him to a communications battalion to improve discipline there. (Crawford later became Sergeant Major of the Marine Corps and never lost his "boundless admiration" for McHugh, perhaps because he also believed that McHugh was responsible for his later transfer to the prestigious post of sergeant major of the Washington Barracks.)

It was time for overseas duty again. In May, 1969, in a radical change of duty, McHugh was sent to be sergeant major of the 1st Marine Aircraft Wing at Da Nang in Vietnam. There he flew regularly with the wing commander, Major General William Thrash, and his assistants to visit the Marine air groups at places like Phu Bai and Quang Tri. McHugh later recollected:

> I'd go and spend three or four days at a place. I would be checking on how they were doing, any problems they had, such as how their messes were running, if they were getting their quarters, how the building program was coming, etc. We were doing the best we could for them under the circumstances, and seeing if there were any big problems—mail problems, for instance, were important to the troops. I would make these contacts, and if we had any major problems I would take them up with the wing commander and say, "We've got a problem with so and so." Then action would be taken and the problem corrected as fast as we possibly could. Communication was a crucial function.

With his teeth into that demanding combat job, McHugh made two efforts, in December, 1969, and the following month, to secure an extension of his active duty service beyond the normal 30-year deadline. Although vigorously endorsed by Major General Thrash, his appeals were denied by Headquarters in Washington. Apparently the feeling there was, "We've got a lot of good, combat-proven, senior men coming along, and, by drawing the line at 30, we give them a shot at the top billets."

Thus, in the spring of 1970, McHugh prepared for one last move back to the States. His fitness report from Major General Thrash left no doubt about the contributions he had made:

> Sergeant Major McHugh has been an outstanding sergeant major for the 1st Marine Aircraft Wing. He is quiet in his demeanor, but is intelligent, forceful, and possesses sound and mature judgement.
>
> During the period of this report, Sergeant Major McHugh has worked closely with all of the senior staff NCOs of the 1st Wing. He instilled a greater sense of responsibility throughout the staff NCO ranks of the wing which manifested itself in many ways. The morale of the command, military presence, and discipline all improved under his leadership. The success of his programs can be measured by the small number of problems that were encountered. The increasing importance of the human relations program was fully understood by Sergeant Major McHugh, and he was outstanding in its progressive development.
>
> He was a distinct asset to this command and a credit to the sergeant major rank.

His transfer came through in April, 1970, to his final tour at Camp Lejeune. There he served at the air station as the sergeant major of a squadron of helicopters. The end came with a formal retirement ceremony there on December 1, 1970. With his normal understatement, McHugh later admitted, "a few nice words were said about me then." The Commandant at that juncture, General Leonard Chapman, had more to say. In a personal letter to McHugh, he wrote:

> I am pleased to note your record of service, including your participation in armed conflict against enemy forces at Guadalcanal, Cape Gloucester, and Peleliu during World War II, later in Korea, and again in Vietnam.
>
> I also note that you were awarded the Navy Commendation Medal with Combat "V" for excellent service, while serving with a Marine infantry company during operations in Korea from 15

In full regalia, McHugh (left) smiles as he greets Lieutenant General James Masters (right), his former commanding general in Quantico in April, 1968.

> September to 2 November, 1950; the Navy Achievement Medal for your outstanding achievement in the superior performance of duties as Sergeant Major of the Marine Corps from 29 June, 1962, to 16 July, 1965; the Purple Heart Medal for wounds received on Peleliu on 17 September, 1944; several letters of commendation and numerous campaign and service awards.
>
> Your record further reflects one of the finest documented records of consistently outstanding performance of duty throughout one's career that I have ever seen.

It was a fitting close for a notable career. As one of his friends who knew him well observed, "He was a man who lived for God, for Country, and for the Corps."

After retirement, McHugh typically set about the task of civilian living in an industrious fashion. Aware of his limited formal schooling, he enrolled at Coastal Carolina College, a community college in Jacksonville, North Carolina, near the gates of Camp Lejeune. Among the courses he took there during a two-year span was one in electrical work. This led him to employment with an electrical contractor doing jobs at the barracks on his old base.

In 1974 he shifted over to the Marine Corps Exchange (PX) there, repairing vending machines. This must have seemed a far cry from the past years he had known of power and prestige, but McHugh took it calmly in stride, befitting his solid, steady temperament. Besides, he was, in a way, still with "his Corps," and many old friends had also retired in Jacksonville to keep him company in lighter moments of relaxation.

In the fall of 1988 he entered real retirement, and his focus shifted wholly to Doris, his home, his children, and his friends. This gave him, for the first time in 69 years, a chance truly to relax and find other outlets for his energy. "I played golf as much as I possibly could, and when I wasn't playing golf, I'd do some work around the house. I liked to get out and trim and take care of the lawn and stuff like that, do the home repairs as far as a little painting here and a little fixing there, if it needed it."

Like so many wives of career Marines, Doris had had to bear the burdens of raising their children, shifting their residences, and the long periods when he was overseas. They hadn't even been able to own their own house until McHugh went to Washington as Sergeant Major of the Marine Corps in 1962. Finally, in 1969, with retirement looming, they had bought their permanent home in Jacksonville.

How can one properly evaluate a complex man like McHugh? What sort of inner person was hidden beneath the paradox, what you see is not what you really get? One clue is the way the Marine Corps made its judgments. Year after year, under a variety of commanding officers in a variety of assignments, he consistently received "outstanding" marks on his fitness reports. Furthermore, the Corps looks very closely at its staff NCOs who want to serve beyond the 20-year mark. The superior men stay on, and the lesser ones go "out." McHugh was a "30-year man." Even more discerning were the men who served with him, both his peers in senior positions and able young NCOs on their way up. They saw the solid, quiet, undemonstrative, sober, almost somber, exterior, but in war and peace across the globe, they also saw the inner strengths and resources that made McHugh a strong and effective human being, as well as a skilled professional.

During his long years of active duty, McHugh worked with many of the men who also saw service as the Sergeant Major of the Marine Corps. Reporting in to Parris Island in 1951 as a master sergeant, he came under the watchful eye of the Post Sergeant Major, Bill Bestwick, and those contacts were repeated in the late 1950s when Bestwick visited McHugh's duty stations on inspection trips as Sergeant Major of the Marine Corps.

McHugh saw a lot of Frank Rauber when they served together on Guam during 1948-50. Then they worked together at Headquarters in 1962, when he took over as Rauber's successor in the top job.

In 1957, he helped train the man who was to follow him as field sergeant major of the 2d Division at Camp Lejeune, Herbert Sweet. They duplicated that process in Washington in 1965, when Sweet succeeded him as Sergeant Major of the Marine Corps. As McHugh said later, "I just told him what the job was all about and the way I approached it, what I did and everything else that might be helpful. I thought he was a sergeant major; he knew what command policy was and how to carry it out. So I felt he was well capable of carrying on. Of course, he was a little more talkative, I guess, than I was. But, outside of that, I guess he got the job done as well as I did."

Henry Black, who would later rise to the peak, served with McHugh in Quantico in 1967. They came to know each other as only men can who have shared together the multiple tribulations and occasional successes of a golf course.

When asked if he had any comments to sum up all of his years of action and personal relationships, McHugh replied in typically reticent fashion, "I don't believe so." Others, however, were eager to comment on him. Edward Pullen, a sergeant major who twice served with him, characterized him as "hard, but fair—strictly a good leader. Most of his service was in units of the Fleet Marine Force—the Corps' infantry—where leadership is of paramount importance and a very personal thing between a rifleman and his sergeant." Another spoke of him as "hard working, dedicated, sincere, and compassionate. He might have a mean look sometimes, but he never raised his voice."

Sergeant Major John Carson, who lived near him in Jacksonville and had known him since their days together in Korea, put it this way, "As the Sergeant Major of the Corps, he was smooth as silk, yet totally sincere. He had an air that caused retired generals to address him as 'Sir.' "

Indeed, all three of the first Sergeants Major of the Marine Corps were held in a special light by those who knew them. As one man reflected, "Bill Bestwick, Frank Rauber, and Tom McHugh all had something *extra*, and they had it all the time."

Clinton Puckett, their successor some years later as Sergeant Major of the Marine Corps, was equally convinced about the special impact of these three pioneers in the post. He first felt McHugh's impact when he had a reconnaissance battalion at Camp Pendleton and received an eagle-eyed inspection by the sergeant major, "I was very impressed by him." Then, when he himself rose to that billet and traveled the world, he recalled, "Each of those three men, in his way, made a definite contribution to the Corps. When I visited Korea with the Commandant, I met the Sergeant Major of the ROK Army who had eight years in grade. Then there was the Sergeant Major of the Philippine Marines, and the Sergeant Major of the Chinese Marines. What I'm saying is that there are senior enlisted now in any number of countries around the world, but it all stems from three gentlemen: Bill Bestwick, Frank Rauber, and Tom McHugh."

From a somewhat different perspective, Rauber's wife, Kay, commented:

> He was an excellent man; he was all Marine. Tom was really involved in the job he was doing, but he was always very quiet. He wouldn't say too much unless you were talking to him. He was built like Frank was. He was a tall fellow, six foot three, I think. When they were trying out material for new uniforms, he had seven or eight of them, I guess.
>
> But as far as being the life of the party or making a speech, I don't remember that he ever made a speech in front of any group that I saw.
>
> I think he was probably excellent in paperwork; in the studies they did, Tom was probably very good at that sort of thing. He sort of was working on his own in a sense. I think that, with anything he tried to do, he didn't

bring a lot of people into it. He sat down alone—sort of operated by himself—and worked out what he was supposed to do, and then he was very quiet in explaining what he had done.

McHugh's low-key style worked in subtle ways. One of those who followed him as Sergeant Major of the Marine Corps, Leland Crawford, was undoubtedly his total opposite in temperament and style. Raucous, ebullient, and extroverted, he still came to see McHugh, the quiet man, as one of the three most important men who had influenced his whole life, "I really admired him." He had served under McHugh in Hawaii, and, in his typically earthy language, summarized him as "a no-bull-shit type of person. He was a hands-on guy; he did his job and he expected you to do your job."

Crawford also had memories outside of duty assignments:

> Tom loved to play golf, and he loved to drink beer, and he didn't say much. I'd go down and play golf with Tom and another first sergeant every Saturday and Sunday. Saturday night at Camp Lejeune, what do you want to do as a bachelor first sergeant? Where would I be? I'd be in the clubhouse drinking beer with the sergeant major. Next morning at 8:01 we'd be right on that tee again. He'd get that ball out of bounds, and he'd cuss like hell. Oh, yes, a hot-tempered Irishman—but in a quiet way. I really felt that his only interests were golf and the Marine Corps.

(Needless to say, McHugh denied any memory of such colorful episodes.)

These, then, were some of the insights and memories of his fellow Marines. There remains one more special point of view, one that probes deeply into the inner man, one that expresses the love his children felt for their father— the private family man that his daughters saw. Peggy, for instance, recalled that "he was not around a lot due to his military commitments, but his presence was always felt." Home life was centered on the family, not his work. "At the dinner table, my Mom would ask, 'What's new?' and he would answer, 'I don't want to talk about it.' This happened frequently when he was the Sergeant Major of the Marine Corps." Referring to McHugh's passion for golf, she noted that "he really enjoyed it—especially the 19th hole with his buddies!"

One family story Doris handed down to Peggy was a description of her mother's first meeting with McHugh. They were both on active duty at Camp Lejeune. In the Enlisted Club there "he walked up to her and said, 'What's a pretty girl like you doing in a place like this?' She replied, 'It's none of your business.' I'm glad he decided to make it his business!"

Kathy commented on the broad responsibilities that inevitably fell on Doris and the family when the husband and father was gone so much of the time, "My father taught us all to be independent. My mother was responsible for the household. It was from her that I learned how to change the electric plug on a lamp or fix a vacuum cleaner. We all felt Daddy was a valuable asset to our family, which we were forced to live without for extended periods. Mother, being an ex-Marine herself, was well aware of this, and took all of it on, including the day-to-day challenges of raising a family."

Kathy went on to describe the standards that McHugh set, "Over the years my father maintained a professional attitude. We were always expected to abide by the rules. Despite our regimented upbringing, Dad was a kind, generous man. He was also a proud man, yet did not share his accomplishments freely."

Lastly, there were the feelings and memories of Peggy—an outpouring from her heart:

> This is my perception of "life with father." Dad loved God, country, and family. He had a deep faith. Many of my memories of him were on his knees praying, or reading a well-worn, small prayer book, or saying the Rosary. He was a "good Catholic." First Fridays, novenas, Stations of the Cross during Lent, and meatless Fridays were a great part of his life.
>
> He was a U.S. Marine through and through. There was usually a mild undercurrent of urgency when it came to making sure the uniform, ribbons, etc. were in order. And, when there was an occasion for "blues," there was a flurry of activity as white things were made white, brass was shined up, uniforms were cleaned! My father took his job as a U.S. Marine seriously. He was dedicated, conscientious, disciplined, committed.
>
> As I was growing up, I don't recall ever hearing a curse or swear word from my father. He was a man with high moral standards, honest, and upright. He modeled these ideals for us. We did not spend time discussing "right" or "wrong"; things just were! Nor did we spend time discussing our feelings—if there was something to be done, you just did it!

"You just did it" was an apt summary of McHugh himself. A remarkable strain of consistency marked his life, whether at home or during all the years of his service in the Corps. He held fast to his basic convictions and faithfully carried out his responsibilities in a low-key, quiet way that was the hallmark of his nature.

Chapter 5

"SHIFTY"
THE PURPLE HEART MAN
Sergeant Major Herbert J. Sweet

Thomas McHugh's successor was Herbert Sweet, and if you had paid him a visit in retirement, you would have found your way to a typical, small suburban home of an older couple. You turned left into a short, dead-end lane. The first thing you noticed was the flagpole with the American flag strategically centered on the axis of the little street. You parked in front and received a warm, enthusiastic welcome from the solidly-built, crew-cut man and his good-looking wife. In two minutes you found out that this was a man of far different temperament than his predecessors. While the setting was characteristic of an average American, the story of the man that unfolded was exceptional—thirty-two years in an outstanding Marine career.

Sweet was born October 8, 1919, in Hartford, Connecticut, in harsh circumstances. His mother, Clara, died in giving birth to him, and his father,

Robert, promptly abandoned the baby and disappeared. Taken to Troy, New York, he was raised at first by the nuns of St. Joseph's Orphan Home. An aunt and uncle then took him in and started him in school. That didn't last long. As he remembered, "I was raised in a very good but strict home. I loved my aunt and uncle, but I just got disenchanted with school and with life in general and I said, 'I need a change.'" So he left school in the middle of the tenth grade, and with the written permission of his aunt and uncle to enlist (he was only seventeen), he headed for New York City.

There he went to see the Marine recruiting sergeant and asked him what he had to offer. Sweet never forgot his reply, "Blood, sweat, tears, and the privilege to serve!" That was a compelling answer for the young man, and he took his oath on February 26, 1937. Sweet then went by steamship from New York City to Savannah, Georgia, from there to Yemassee, South Carolina by bus, and then by tug boat to the famous Parris Island Recruit Depot.

He learned basic truths there that would stay with him throughout his Marine Corps career. He recalled, "You really had to study and work, and be loyal to your superiors, and you would be rewarded accordingly. I found out that 'first aboard, last ashore' was something I would always believe in. From then on I was first in in the morning in my unit, and the last out at night."

From the rigors of recruit training, he moved briefly to Quantico, Virginia, and then to a crack drill unit of ceremonial troops which represented the Marine Corps at the World's Fair in New York City in 1939. After a layover in Quantico during the winter, they returned for a repeat performance in 1940.

In true Marine Corps fashion, his glamorous life then rotated to the opposite extreme. He was sent to a security unit at a naval seaplane base in Trinidad, British West Indies. There he contracted a case of malaria and so was returned to Quantico.

The Japanese bombing of Pearl Harbor changed every Marine career. Sweet later sketched his reaction, "I was an assistant instructor at the Officers Candidate School in Quantico. I was a hard-charging, newly-made platoon sergeant at the time, and I wanted to join the 3d Division, which was forming at Camp Lejeune. Repeatedly, I requested transfer, and repeatedly the request was denied. 'Your time will come,' I was told, and it finally did." Orders came through sending him to the 21st Regiment in the 3d Division, and, after hard training in North Carolina, it shipped out to polish its combat readiness in New Zealand and then Guadalcanal.

Sweet, now a gunnery sergeant, saw his first combat in the division's assault on Bougainville in December, 1943. He was wounded in the arm and received his first Purple Heart Medal. That campaign was only a stepping stone, and the division returned to Guadalcanal to prepare for its next strike. Sweet was promoted to first sergeant, and he set about training his rifle company to a fine edge for the forthcoming operation in July, 1944, to recapture Guam. His company commander was killed soon after the initial landing, which put a heavy responsibility for leadership on Sweet. However, he himself was hit shortly thereafter. As he later described it, "I was hit by an artillery shell next to me and dazed with shrapnel in my head, so I fell down into a foxhole. When I woke up I observed the enemy, a Japanese soldier, aiming his rifle at me. He was successful in hitting me, but only in the arm. I didn't think that was very soldierly of him!"

Evacuated to a Navy hospital in the New Hebrides Islands, Sweet was awarded his second Purple Heart. When the arm had healed, he returned to his old regiment, and once more trained intensively for his next assault. In February, 1945, they went ashore on the bloody beaches of Iwo Jima. His bravery there brought him a Bronze Star Medal with Combat "V." The citation from the Commanding General of the Fleet Marine Force, Pacific, read:

> For heroic achievement in connection with operations against the enemy while serving with a Marine infantry battalion in Iwo Jima, Volcano Islands, on 24 Feb, 1945. First Sergeant Sweet, fully aware of the extreme danger involved, led two volunteers across an area swept by enemy fire, and succeeded in evacuating to safety his company commander and two other men who had been wounded. He then led a stretcher team to another area where a platoon was pinned down by enemy fire, and, although held up for a short time by enemy fire, finally succeeded in reaching his objective and evacuating the wounded to safety.
>
> On still another occasion, he went to the aid of a wounded man in a danger area, and succeeded in carrying him to a place from which he was evacuated to safety. His courage and leadership, together with his insistence that the wounded be evacuated as soon as possible, were instrumental in saving many lives. First Sergeant Sweet was later wounded and evacuated. His heroic actions were in keeping with the highest traditions of the United States Naval Service.

Slightly wounded soon afterwards, Sweet was evacuated for medical treatment on a hospital ship offshore. He immediately talked the doctors into allowing him to return to his company, which was going through the worst of the battle for Iwo.

Once back with his men, Sweet was wounded still again, this time seriously. As he recounted it, "I got hit by a phosphorus shell, and I don't even recall being hit by it, but when I woke up there were about four or five Marines digging me out of this volcanic sand. I was coughing and this was the result of a white phosphorus shell. It got all over my legs and my back, and burned me badly."

He had been in the Corps barely eight years, and he already had three Purple Heart Medals. Those were scant consolation for the grim year of hospitalization that followed. It was a painful progression of treatment from Hawaii to San Francisco to Quantico. At long last he was declared fit for duty, and, in spite of a permanently crippled finger on his right hand, he was sent in 1946 to Parris Island. Now he was the combat-seasoned, well-decorated first sergeant of a recruit training battalion, turning new recruits into Marines.

A year there brought a transfer to the Marine detachment at the naval ordnance plant in Macon, Georgia. Soon he was given new orders for sea duty.

The high standards required for that assignment called for a senior NCO who could really take charge of his men and give them the demanding type of leadership needed aboard ship. Sweet was selected as the right man to be first sergeant for a sea-going detachment of sixty-six Marines, and he reported aboard the U.S.S. *Missouri* in 1948. It was the only battleship then on active duty in the U.S. Navy, and it was taking midshipmen from the Naval Academy for their summer cruise to European ports.

Those were difficult days for the Marine Corps ashore. There had been bruising political battles after World War II. Powerful voices had been raised to decimate the Corps and abolish its traditional functions. It was saved by the National Security Act of 1947, but civilian budget makers wielded sharp knives, slashing the authorized strength of the Corps to the bone. By 1950 there were fewer than 3,000 sea-going billets for enlisted men, and the total number of Marines was due to drop to 67,000 by June 30, 1950. In that atmosphere, Sweet finished his two years of sea duty in early 1950 and transferred to Camp Lejeune as an infantry chief in the School Battalion there. He found a melange of skeleton structures, versus the full-sized combat units he had been part of in the Pacific. The 2d Division's "regiments" were little more than reinforced battalions. It could muster only one-third of its proper war-time strength.

Nevertheless, Sweet plunged into his new assignment, which involved him deeply in drilling and training the men in infantry tactics. It was the right kind of a billet to prepare for what came next. The Korean War broke out on June 25, 1950, and the reduced personnel limits of peacetime were immediately jettisoned for feverish expansion. Sweet immediately requested combat duty. In 1951 he got his wish, and was sent out as a master sergeant to serve as first sergeant of a rifle company in the 5th Marines.

The 1st Marine Division was then in the central highlands of Korea, a key part of the United Nations battle line that extended across the whole peninsula. By September 20, the division had advanced well north of the 38th Parallel to seize a group of commanding hills in hard fighting against Chinese and North Korean forces. The 5th Marines were in an area around Hill 812 when the orders came through to revert to a defensive posture. However, there continued to be small local actions to protect the Marine vantage points. In one of these, Sweet again demonstrated his leadership abilities. He was awarded the Navy Commendation Medal with Combat "V" by Major General Gerald Thomas, commanding general of the 1st Division:

> For excellent service in the line of his profession while serving with a Marine infantry company during operations against the enemy in Korea on 22 September, 1951. Master Sergeant Sweet, serving as company first sergeant, performed his duties in a highly professional manner. When the company was in the attack of a heavily fortified and defended position, he maintained a steady flow of supplies to the attacking units of the company, and organized and directed the stretcher parties in the evacuation of the wounded.
>
> Through his untiring efforts, the wounded were evacuated swiftly and safely from the scene of the battle, thereby contributing materially to their

Korea, 1951: As a master sergeant, Sweet served as first sergeant of D Company, 5th Marines. It was his prerogative to mark the time of day by ringing their ship's bell.

While serving as sergeant major of the 3d Division on Okinawa in December, 1964, Sweet had a chance to hear a few jokes from Bob Hope.

Sweet photo

recovery. His disregard for his personal safety and his determined devotion to duty served as an inspiration to all who observed him. Master Sergeant Sweet's conduct throughout was in keeping with the highest traditions of the United States Naval Service.

It was during these days and nights of heavy fighting in Korea that Sweet earned the nickname by which he would be known ever after, "Shifty." Instead of the usual negative connotation normally associated with this word, it was a name given lovingly and respectfully for his actions on behalf of his men. As he explained it:

> I was in the habit of getting to every foxhole during the day, talking to the men, and making sure that they had the proper rations and the proper amount of ammunition. I had to make sure that the rations were distributed fairly for everybody, so that no one would get fat and another person would stay hungry. That's the reason I got that nickname, because I would shift from one foxhole to another and cover the complete line, sometimes twice a day, and sometimes it was under fire.

In the course of this intense combat duty, he was wounded one more time. So he became "Shifty" Sweet, the man with four Purple Heart medals.

May, 1952, brought a return to Camp Lejeune to serve with the 2d Marines. Here again his performance caught the eye of his superior officers. He remembered the occasion:

> The commanding general of the 2d Division [Major General Edwin Pollock] said that he wanted to see me. I talked to the general and he said that he wanted me to act as his sergeant major, but in the field; he didn't want me to be an eight-to-four sergeant major. They had one there who never seemed to...well, he was inside all the time. (He worked for the division adjutant.) So, consequently, I took on the duties of a field sergeant major for the division. I worked out of the chief of staff's office, and went to the various regiments: the 2d Marines, the 10th Marines, the 6th Marines, and the 8th Marines, and all our supporting units.

The next change of duty was a major break in the pattern of Sweet's career. From rugged infantry duty in the hills of Korea and the woods of North Carolina, he was sent to Columbia University in New York City. There he labored from 1953-5 as an assistant military instructor in the Naval ROTC program, with the formal title of Assistant to the Professor of Naval Science. The work was somewhat more pedestrian than the title implied. He had to take young men who were immersed in Plato or organic chemistry or French verbs and, in the limited time available for NROTC, indoctrinate them into another world of close-order drills, rifles, and hand grenades. The rifle range was in the gymnasium; target practice was with .22s. Any time a VIP showed up, Sweet had to muster his midshipmen and parade them in honor of the visiting dignitary.

Yet there were rewards, sometimes reaped years later. One midshipman, Roy Lynch, became a Marine student and retired finally as a brigadier general. Other men later became Navy captains who, upon meeting Sweet, would say, "Hey, Sergeant Major, remember me? I was one of your students at Columbia and I had two left feet then."

As he looked at his career, Sweet was in a quandary: stay in or get out of the Corps? There had been massive changes since the lean days of 1950. In 1952 Congress had mandated a Corps of three combat divisions with their three supporting air wings. The Korean War had swollen the Corps to 261,000 in 1953, but the armistice came in July of that year. Another period of radical reductions in authorized strength inevitably took place. Promotion slowed to a near halt.

Nearing the end of his tour of duty at Columbia, Sweet faced a major career decision:

> When I was completing my tour in the Columbia University NROTC, I was thinking about getting out because I would soon have twenty years in, and I was a master sergeant, E-7 pay grade, and I guess I had about ten years seniority. A commander on duty there with me was the one who persuaded me to stay in. He said, "Don't you know that they're going to come up with two more pay grades?" I replied, "I've heard about it." He urged, "Well, if you stay, you may stand a good chance of getting it."

Sweet decided to go for it, and accepted orders for a two-year tour back at Camp Lejeune.

Then the time for another overseas tour arrived, and Sweet was off in 1958 to an exotic locale at Subic Bay, Philippine Islands. Here his patience paid off. In one day he was jumped from the E-7 pay level to the new, top-most E-9 grade, the first one to make this in all the military branches of the Philippine Command. So the ex-master sergeant was now formally the first-ever sergeant major of the Marine Barracks at Subic Bay, the largest barracks in the Corps at that time.

His two-year tour there ended with a return to Georgia for duty as sergeant major of the 6th Reserve and Recruitment District in Atlanta. As usual, that was followed by another overseas assignment. Reporting in on Okinawa, in July, 1964, Sweet became the sergeant major of the 3d Division—the same unit he had served with twenty years earlier as a young platoon sergeant in the Pacific campaigns.

Early in 1965, the tension level in the division was raised several notches when Washington began to send American combat units to Vietnam. Sweet had just seen the 9th Marines off to the battle zone in Vietnam in March when his own life took an equally dramatic turn. Years later the moment was still fresh in his mind:

> The commanding general of the 3d Division [Major General William Collins] was my reporting senior. Every morning I would report to him and we'd talk things over, usually after his staff had left. Then one morning he casually mentioned, as I was walking out, "Oh, by the way, Sergeant Major, I've got a little dispatch here. You've been nominated to be the next Sergeant Major of the Marine Corps, and, the Commandant, General Greene, wants to know if you will accept." I quickly answered, "Of course I will! I will be honored to." He shook my hand and added, "I'll get a dispatch back right away." So he sent a dispatch back indicating I'd accepted the nomination.

Back at Headquarters, the usual screening process had been taking place just as it had previously for Tom McHugh. The individual records of all the sergeants major in the Corps had been carefully reviewed by a special board comprised of five general officers, headed by the chief of staff, Lieutenant General Leonard Chapman, and the Sergeant Major of the Marine Corps, Tom McHugh. A small number of finalists were nominated, and these names were presented to the chief of staff and to General Greene, who together picked Herbert ("Shifty") Sweet on April 2, 1965, to be the new Sergeant Major of the Marine Corps.

On July 16, Sweet took over his new post from Tom McHugh. He summarized his work as being "in an advisory status on General Greene's staff. I didn't have any command responsibility. I was sort of his eyes and ears, but at the same time I tried not to be a Sneaky Pete." Sweet described his function when the two men would go on a tour:

> I'd establish close liaison with the sergeant major of the base or the division or the unit we were at. I'd prepare my reports and give them to the Commandant, and he, in turn, would take it from there. Most of the time he would say, "Well, what did you do about this, Sergeant Major?" and I'd tell him, "I have already talked to the sergeant major out there about it, and he said that it would be taken care of, and he would let me know accordingly."
>
> We got along very well. General Greene was very, very good to work with. He required the best, and hopefully, I gave him the best. I always admired him. I liked to smoke cigars and he didn't smoke, but he never did complain about my smoking cigars. However, I made sure that I didn't smoke in his presence or any area where he would breathe in that smoke.

Greene, for his part, found Sweet to be "very outstanding" in his performance:

> He was always with me whenever I could take him on a trip. He rendered invaluable service to me and to the Marine Corps. For example, he also was of great use to me at Headquarters when we had some problem that had to do with enlisted men in particular. I could always refer that to Sweet and he would get a logical and good answer. I would say that Sweet was something of an intellectual type, but the interesting thing was that he also had the talent of establishing a close liaison with other Marines.
>
> On probably eight out of every ten trips I took, my sergeant major would accompany me, and once in a great while his wife would come along.

Commenting on these trips, Sweet observed:

> Of course, everybody was in apple pie order. They knew we were coming! Let's face it, they all had their best foot forward. One time in Camp Lejeune, I was visiting the new brig and a couple of the prisoners demanded to see the Commandant. I asked them, "Have you talked to your first sergeant, or have you talked to the warden about this, or gone to a Request Mast [hearing before a commanding officer]?" They answered, "No."

Official—and atypical—picture of Sweet as Sergeant Major of the Marine Corps in 1965. A Legion of Merit was later added to the Bronze Star atop his ribbons.

So I closed out the discussion, "Then I'm not going to bring this up to General Greene." Then they started to raise cain. This was one of the embarrassing situations that I was in at the time.

On other bases a Marine would come up and say, "I want to see the Commandant; I want to talk to him." Again I would ask, "Did you talk to the inspector general about this? Or did you talk to your first sergeant? Did you talk to your sergeant major? And if you didn't get satisfaction, did you talk to your commanding officer about this?" If it was in the negative, than I would say, "Then I can't do anything about that." That's a command function there at that base.

Ever since the disastrous Ribbon Creek episode at the Parris Island Recruit Depot, when a drill instructor had caused the drowning of some recruits on a night march some years earlier, the Marine Corps had been concerned about dealing with the worries of parents of recruits during their training. It had become increasingly clear that some kind of organized, regular procedure would be helpful to welcome and inform parents when they came to Parris Island to see how their son was doing in the rigorous training there. Greene had been president of the Court of Inquiry after the debacle and then commanding general of the Recruit Training Center in the shakeup that followed. With this grim experience in mind, Greene took Sweet and his wife (whom he had married in 1952) with him when he flew down to Parris Island for a Commandant's Inspection. Upon their arrival, the Sweets were directed to check out a successful visitors program at the nearby Marine air base in Cherry Point, North Carolina.

A few years earlier a joint reception center had been organized there. Spurred by a base sergeant major, the NCOs there had put together a group they called the Career Wives Organization, which operated the Center. Sweet and his wife took a look at this model, returned to Parris Island and laid the groundwork for a similar program there. Now when concerned mothers and fathers would arrive to check up on their young recruit, there was a system in place to ease their uncertainties. The career wives at Parris Island would welcome them, put them up in the Hostess House (an on-base guest house), escort them around the recruit depot, and then invite them to the wives' homes to eat dinner with the family of a drill instructor, thus putting a humane face on the boot camp experience.

Back at his desk, Sweet was well aware of the value of written communication as a vital adjunct to the verbal interchanges in his many face-to-face and telephonic conversations and speeches. To this end, he supplemented his steady outpouring of letters with a faithful commitment to a regular column in the enlisted Marines' *Leatherneck* magazine. As he viewed it, "the column was from my past experience, and I put that together with my trips, what I had observed when I talked to these general officers and senior staff NCOs, as well as the sergeants and the corporals and the privates. I put this all together and then wrote my column."

A typical one would include some simple example from Marine Corps life to illustrate a homily which Sweet wanted to impress upon his enlisted readers. In one column, he made his point this way:

> Today's young men in the Corps have an opportunity to learn a skill. As our Corps has increased in numbers and has become more specialized in its technology, the men who are the backbone of the Corps have had to become more specialized and proficient in their jobs.
>
> For example, a young corporal I met recently is a radar technician. He has a little more than two years as a Marine and is only 20 years old, but there he is, working on highly complicated and expensive electronic equipment. The maze of tubes, transistors, and wires he was involved with really snowed me, but he did his job as easily as a drill instructor does the manual of arms.
>
> In talking with this man, I found that he spends many hours over and above his normal working day studying and reviewing technical manuals so he can be good at his job. You have to give this man, and the many others like him, credit. There were the days when, at the sound of recall, Marines headed for the barracks to shower, change, and head for a beer joint on liberty. Not so today. The Marine's job, no matter what it may be, requires extra hours of study and work if he wants to keep climbing the promotion ladder....

Leatherneck, for its part, realized that there was a big question mark out there in the field amongst both enlisted and commissioned Marines, about what the Sergeant Major of the Marine Corps actually did. To answer this, the magazine ran a detailed profile of a typical, busy day in Sweet's life at Headquarters. The article touched on many of his diverse activities, such as the Enlisted Performance Board, the Meritorious Promotion Board, correspondence with Marines in the field, the Personnel Programs Branch, and the Permanent Uniform Board. (See Appendix C for a full account.)

The responsibility to work closely with the Commandant had been recognized (in varying degrees) ever since the days of Bill Bestwick, a decade earlier. The Office of the Sergeant Major of the Marine Corps had, however, always been listed organizationally as a part of the chief of staff's office. It was during Sweet's tenure that it was moved to a more logical listing: the Immediate Office of the Commandant.

The senior noncommissioned officers of the four Armed Services: Left to Right, the first Chief Master Sergeant of the Air Force, Paul Airey; the second Sergeant Major of the Army, George Dunaway; the fourth Sergeant Major of the Marine Corps, Herbert Sweet; and the first Master Chief Petty Officer of the Navy, Delbert Black.

U.S. Department of Defense photo

It was also during Sweet's tour that there was another, and different, recognition of the unique role and proven functional value of the most senior enlisted man. For nearly ten years the Marine Corps had stood alone among the U.S. military branches in having such a position. Now the other services caught up by authorizing a Chief Master Sergeant of the Air Force, a Sergeant Major of the Army, and a Master Chief Petty Officer of the Navy. Sweet knew that that development reflected not primarily his achievements, but the cumulative productiveness of all of his predecessors as *the* Sergeant Major of the Marine Corps. There was a cliche which, naturally, did escape a few Marine lips, "Imitation is the sincerest form of flattery."

With this focus on the billet, a formal paper was prepared in Headquarters to codify officially the role of Sergeant Major of the Marine Corps, as it had evolved over the first ten years. In the usual frozen, bureaucratic language the paper covered responsibilities, duties, selection, tour of duty, and pay. (See Appendix D for full text.)

At the end of 1967, Greene's term as Commandant came to an end. Before leaving office, however, he made sure that there was official recognition of Sweet's contributions. There was an award of a Navy Achievement Medal from the Secretary of the Navy; it cited Sweet for a wide range of achievements, such as "improving efficiency, raising morale, and instilling esprit de corps." It went on to praise "his guidance and wise counseling...his tact, diligence, and...outstanding leadership, judgment, and inspiring devotion to duty."

The exit of the man who had chosen him for the job put Sweet's future in grave doubt. He confessed:

> When he left, I thought that I was going to be relieved because General Chapman was coming in as Commandant. General Greene gave me a good recommendation. When he left after his term was up, all the officers on his staff had to scramble for a billet. General Chapman came in with his own officers and I was asked by the military secretary, Colonel Foster LaHue, "Where are you going to go for your next tour of duty?" I said, "Well, Colonel, I can't go any place. If I go any place, I would go downward. I'll have to go out of the Corps. But I'd prefer to stay put."
>
> It was the custom to put your letter of resignation in, but I didn't do anything, and then General Chapman called me in, after a meeting with all the generals. He said, "I want you to stick around, Sergeant Major; I'd like to have you stay with me as my sergeant major." I answered, "I certainly would really appreciate that, General." He went on, "I want you to carry on just like you did when you were working for General Greene." I replied, "I sure will." He added, "If there are any changes, I'll let you know."

That transition, and the decision to retain Sweet, was made easier for Chapman because, as the previous chief of staff and then assistant commandant, he had seen the sergeant major in action and, as he later said, "held an extremely high opinion of him." So it was that Sweet began the second half of his tour as Sergeant Major of the Marine Corps under a new Commandant in January, 1968. The revolving pattern of the past continued—in Headquarters, out on a trip, then back to his office, and then out again. When they were at Headquarters, Chapman set a pattern in which he and Sweet would see each other daily "for a few moments at least" and then for "lengthy conferences on other occasions." There was one minor, but delightful, change from Greene's time. Chapman was also a cigar smoker, so the two of them puffed away together.

Representative of their stateside trips was one that they took in 1969 to the Marine Corps Air Station in Beaufort, South Carolina. As always, Sweet's schedule was jam-packed. He started at 7:00 am with a breakfast at the Staff NCO Club and then addressed the sergeants major and other senior staff NCOs. The talk dealt with the inevitable issues of promotions, pay, housing, and fitness reports. It also included a strong appeal to encourage Marines with two or three years' service to make a career in the Corps. There were questions, of course, and Sweet handled them with practiced ease. Then the staff NCOs presented a plaque to him as a token of appreciation for a "job well done" as Sergeant Major of the Marine Corps. (As might be expected, his trips over the years generated a considerable number of plaques!)

Next on the schedule was a review of an honor guard by Chapman and Sweet, and then a tour of the air station. After this Sweet moved to the theater for a speech similar to his earlier one, but this time directed to the remaining staff NCOs. He concluded with an offer of a personal review of their record, if any of them had a question about promotion. An hour later Sweet was on his feet again, speaking in front of a large assembly of sergeants and junior enlisted personnel. He could not resist mentioning that on that exact day, 32 years earlier, he had started his boot training. When he finished, it was time to go to the mess hall, and, as was his custom, Sweet made sure he talked individually with the men working there on mess duty before he ate. He had a conviction that "the best place to get an instant 'feel' of a Marine unit was in the mess hall. You just get a sense of how it smells, what the men's faces are like, their general attitudes and morale." After lunch, Chapman and Sweet were off to another near-by Marine base to repeat their exhausting schedule all over again.

Overseas trips were similarly a regular part of the work pattern for the two of them. Chapman remembered:

> When I went to Vietnam, he was always with me. When we arrived, I'd branch off on my schedule and then he had his own schedule. This encompassed the staff NCOs principally. He took soundings. He discussed Marine Corps problems and Marine Corps actions as well as their own problems. He talked and he listened, and then he'd write a report when we got back to Headquarters. That report came to me. Of course, we'd talk about it, also, when we were flying along in the airplane. In the office, I'd send it to the Chief of Staff, and get him to take whatever action he and the staff thought appropriate.

In Vietnam there was always the critical need for Sweet to be in close contact with the men serving there. A sergeant major in the 7th Marines recounted many years later, "I'll never forget his act at the Staff NCO Club in Da Nang, where his theme was 'We Care About You.' It was a very, very colorful, enjoyable, yet enlightening talk. Herb just turned them on." (That particular sergeant major would go on to the top himself; he was Clinton Puckett.) Speeches like this were, in fact, vital factors in dealing with a major issue facing the Corps during these tense years. As Chapman pointed out, "We had big problems in Vietnam with manning the force, keeping our foxhole strength up, what with the one-year rotation and all of its complexities. So when we went to Vietnam, which we did twice a year (and Okinawa too), those were the subjects that Sweet would focus on."

Sweet's superior performance of duty across the board led to a prestigious award. The Navy League of the United States annually honors a Marine by presenting the General Gerald C. Thomas Award for Inspirational Leadership. (Some call it informally "The Marine of the Year.") In May, 1969, it was awarded to Sweet with glowing praise for his "inspirational leadership and professional competence...dedication to duty...32 years of service...accompanying the Commandant on visits...efforts to communicate with the enlisted Marines...superb example..."

A trip to Vietnam with the Commandant in August, 1967. A Chinese field telephone captured from the North Vietnamese Army was presented to him by a South Vietnamese master sergeant. In the background is a military map showing the symbols for unit positions.

Perhaps a better look at Sweet's style, temperament, and actions can be seen in the comments of two of the other staff NCOs who knew him and would be his successors as Sergeant Major of the Marine Corps.

Henry Black said: "My God, the visitors you had at Headquarters! Herb was into everything, as he should have been, and was, I think, very well-liked. He was really a fine representative of enlisted Marines, and he did a hell of a job as far as I'm concerned."

Clinton Puckett observed: "Herb's reputation preceded him. I'd heard of him for years and years. "Shifty" Sweet was kind of a throw-back, the colorful staff NCO. What is a staff NCO's first rule? Look out for the troops, and I may as well say, look out for the troops was Herb Sweet's theme. He was a colorful character, but I found he was a staff NCO every inch of the way when I'd met him on several occasions, before I got to Headquarters Marine Corps."

A couple of his peers noted, with a chuckle, that there was a rumor floating around about how he *really* got the nickname of "Shifty." The story goes that a bunch of old staff NCOs would sit around a table with "Shifty," having a few rounds of beer. But, whenever the check arrived, Sweet was very quick to shift his position to avoid being hit by the bill!

A future Commandant, General Paul X. Kelley, when he was a more junior officer, knew him and never forgot him: "Sergeant Major Sweet, now he's not one that you would ever call a shrinking violet; very much extroverted, outgoing, but always had the best interest of the troops at heart."

These evaluations matched Chapman's own words, "very forthright, aggressive, articulate, active, energetic. He could listen and he could tell you how it really was."

The media found it easy to write about him; a newspaper saw him "puffing on stogies...Shifty is a tall, tough Marine with a weathered face and a sleeve full of hash marks. Five rows of decorations, including four Purple Hearts, brighten his blouse.... As he strode to the podium, they hung a mike around Shifty's neck. His boot camp bellow shook the light bulbs and someone hurried up to remove his mike. He had been to Vietnam three times and prefaces many of his remarks with, 'Everything is not peaches and cream in the Marine Corps....' Rubbing his pear-bald head, Shifty pronounced it 'sort of shaggy. Time for me to go to the barber and tell him to cut off a dollars' worth....' "

A magazine encapsulated his character:

> As an extremely personable, competent, and pleasant Marine, he was a friend to everyone—private and general alike. Completely disarming, if there were a problem, he had an uncanny knack of introducing the solution as if it were the original idea of the one who brought up the problem. He is best characterized as humanizing the office, and he brought a degree of color that lets all enlisted Marines know that this epitome of success is within reach of anyone willing to aspire to it. Sergeant Major Sweet to this day has the enlisted man at heart.

When January, 1969, arrived, Sweet was right around the 32-year mark in service, and he realized that "it was time for me to go," but he asked Chapman if he could stay on until July 31, "because of the ten percent anticipated pay raise we were going to have." Being the kind of man he was, and taking into account what Sweet had done for him and for the Corps, the general replied, "That's a very good reason, Sergeant Major; I'll arrange it." And he did.

There was a comfortable period of winding down. He could tally some formidable statistics from his tour of duty: seven trips to Vietnam, two to Europe, and forty-nine to Marine posts and stations throughout the United States with two different Commandants, speaking to many thousands of Marines. In addition, there were the thousands of letters, and the special feeling that came when he had helped someone. He thought back, for instance, to one such letter from a staff sergeant who had been inadvertently overlooked by the Promotion Board for two years. When he wrote to Sweet he got action. His case was put before the Remedial Promotion Board, and, on the morning they were to meet, the hopeful staff sergeant received a letter which assured him, "The Sergeant Major of the Marine Corps lit a candle for you at the 10:30 a.m. church service." The results: the Marine was promoted and received two years' back pay. "It's results like this that make the job worthwhile, but they aren't all as fortunate," was Sweet's summary.

In his nearly a third of a century of service, he had seen fundamental modifications in the Corps. Although the training and discipline hadn't changed much, the men (and now women) had. He could say that the average Marine now was:

> ...better educated, better motivated, and knows where he is headed and why. Career opportunities in the Marine Corps have never been better. We've got the best promotion system of any service, the pay picture looks good, and living conditions, both on and off post, are improving tremendously....
>
> The rapid expansion of the Marine Corps has had telling effects. Big holes were left in our senior staff NCO ranks, because so many of them were commissioned. But we were able to fill their shoes by outstanding young staff NCOs, who in turn were replaced by even younger but experienced NCOs. The Marine Corps will face another transition period in July, when thousands of staff NCOs start to transfer to the Fleet Reserve. When this 'brain drain' starts, I believe we will be in a good position to fill their ranks with the young staff NCOs who moved up recently.

With his retirement looming ever closer, Sweet had some parting words of advice for the NCOs whose lives and careers had been so deeply and emotionally intertwined with his own career:

> To sergeants major and first sergeants: You are going to be replaced soon. Go out and shake the bushes and get more of your better corporals and sergeants to reenlist. The Corps needs them.
>
> To staff NCOs: Don't lose touch with your men by being an 8:00 to 4:30 car-pool Marine. Spend more time with your men than you do commuting. Get to know them in the barracks where they live. Lead them. Advise them. Motivate them.
>
> To corporals and sergeants: Be easy to find. Study. Strive for a billet two ranks above you; but most of all, be loyal to your commander.

In a more subjective personal way, he admitted, "It is going to be a sad day when I have to take my saber off my office wall and hang it on my den wall at home—but I'll always be a Marine!"

There was one very consoling thought about retirement. A couple of years earlier, after the other services had appointed their most senior NCOs, there was an organized effort to obtain legislation putting the financial reimbursement for the four top billets in a special category. In 1967 that effort had been successful, and an extra pay bonus of $150 a month was authorized. Furthermore, the four men would have their retirement income based on their special individual pay rate. Thus Sweet looked forward to being the first Sergeant Major of the Marine Corps to enjoy this bonus.

The final day came on July 31, 1969. A top-level group, including the Secretary of Defense, assembled for the retirement ceremony. Chapman presented Sweet with the Legion of Merit. The citation by the Secretary of the Navy began by noting Sweet's "exceptional professionalism, executive and organizational skills...sound judgement...wise guidance and counseling of enlisted personnel." The award then went on to say:

Now it was Sweet's turn to retire and turn over the office of Sergeant Major of the Marine Corps to his successor on July 31, 1969. Reviewing the parade are General Chapman, Commandant (on left); Herbert Sweet; his successor, Joseph Dailey; and the commanding officer of the Washington Barracks, Colonel Paul Graham.

His enthusiasm for perfection served as an example for both junior and seniors alike, and contributed immeasurably in maintaining the prestige of the position of Sergeant Major of the Marine Corps. One of the outstanding Marines of all times, he was of inestimable value to the Marine Corps and to the Commandant of the Marine Corps.

Sensitive to the needs and problems of all enlisted Marines, Sergeant Major Sweet worked indefatigably in their support, while keeping the Commandant informed of the morale of the men. He combined helpfulness, undivided attention, and leadership in the performance of duty, and made these practices an inherent part of his daily life. He accompanied the Commandant on numerous long and arduous trips, appearing many times before the news media, and always comported himself in a way to bring credit to the Corps....

The Sword of Office of the Sergeant Major of the Marine Corps was passed to his successor; there was martial music, close order drill, precision marching, lots of saluting, dress blues and whites, long rows of hash marks, masses of medals, and then it was all over; a lifetime career was finished.

Yet, in another sense, it was only a prelude to a new beginning. "Shifty" Sweet was not a man to slide into idleness at age forty-nine. Speaking of the start of his "retirement," he recalled, "It really wasn't a letdown because, living so close to Headquarters Marine Corps and with military all around you, it wasn't that bad. I did go back to Headquarters a couple of times, but I found that I was better off not going up there. I mean with all those people up there, the new sergeant major has got enough people telling him what to do without me telling him."

Sweet then took the Civil Service test. His results were good, and within three weeks he was at work in the Veterans Administration—a transition which he pioneered and which would be followed by several of his successor sergeants major. Eight months of learning the details of the VA programs prepared him for one last overseas tour of duty. In March, 1970, he volunteered to go back to Vietnam. "I wanted to work with the young Marines, and this was the best place," he explained. "There was a big job to do over there." His old boss, General Chapman, issued a set of invitational orders, and he was on his way as a veteran's benefits counselor.

Once there, he operated in typical Sweet fashion. It was no secret when he would visit a unit: old Marine NCO friends would call out, "Here comes Shifty!" And his jeep would roll to a stop; the familiar figure would ease out— six feet tall, 160 pounds, bright brown eyes, brown hair cut to his scalp—clad in Marine khaki (without the insignia), cigar always in mouth, flaming red socks always serving as a trademark. His pitch to the unit would soon follow, accompanied, as one observer noted, "with some shouting and much hand waving." While his main job was to explain the VA benefits available to them, he never failed to include a plug for making a career out of their Marine service. Sweet was not a man to let an opportunity with a captive audience slip away without giving them the full treatment!

He described his work this way, "I spent three to four days weekly traveling and visiting various units. We spoke wherever we were invited, to groups of any size. We wanted to inform the young people of what they had earned." He covered every part of the Marines' assigned zone of operations in Vietnam, and as the time neared for his return to the States, he summarized:

> I gave over 100 unit presentations, and I like to feel that I accomplished something through them. I addressed more than 8300 men during those unit presentations. They often took me into unsecure areas, out into the "bush." But any unit requesting my services could expect me. I logged over 5500 miles in my jeep. I also conducted more than 3000 personal interviews in places ranging from the shower to my office. Many hitch-hikers received my lecture when I picked them up. I even gave interviews in the surf of the South China Sea!
>
> When I conducted departure briefings for Marines and Navy personnel about to leave Vietnam for the U.S., there really wasn't too much I could tell them. They were too excited to listen to me for more than about five seconds. My unit presentations, of course, were much more in depth, but I did brief well over 24,000 departing servicemen during my tour there.

At the end of six months, he felt "that was enough; I'd paid my dues," and he headed home to his family.

Back stateside, Sweet stayed with the VA until 1977 when he left the Civil Service, and then went to work for the Fleet Reserve Association. Still devoted to veterans' benefits, he continued that until June of 1986 when he really, finally, absolutely retired.

Now, of course, his focus was on family, home, and old friends. Over thirty-five years earlier he had found just the right young lady from his old home town of Troy, New York. On May 24, 1952, immediately after his return from Korea, he had married Dorthea Martin. They had moved around as the winds of the Corps blew him from one assignment to the next. Finally settled in a Washington billet, he bought a permanent home for them in suburban Alexandria, Virginia, in 1968.

While he was absorbed in the demanding duties of the Sergeant Major of the Marine Corps, his home life was necessarily curtailed. It was a routine of "out of the house at 6:15 a.m. and maybe return at 6:15 p.m." Dot, as he called her, quickly learned not to wait dinner for him—he might get home at any hour of the night. When he did make it, the first priority was a beer, then a cigar, next the financial pages of the newspaper, and perhaps a TV news program. When that was over, it was a signal for their two young children, Kathleen and Michael, to start their homework. Kathleen had joined the family in March, 1953, while Sweet was on duty with the Columbia University NROTC. Two and a half years later, while Sweet was serving at Camp Lejeune, Michael was born in November, 1955.

When he could find the time, Sweet was active in Boy Scouts and Little League programs, along with family camping, swimming, and fishing. With his out-going nature, he was soon well-known to the neighborhood children; they called him "Uncle Shifty."

His final retirement brought a special bonus: a chance at long last for them to have some real time together. Dot exclaimed, "I loved it! We did everything that we'd always wanted to do, when we wanted to do it, and that was it. For one thing, we did a lot of walking which was good for both of us, and then we had a trailer down at the beach, and we spent the whole summer at Fenwick Island in Delaware. In addition, we've had some wonderful trips abroad."

Besides his home and family, old friends continued to play an important part in Sweet's life. He was, for instance, part of a colorful crew named the "Gang of 30" who gathered for convivial luncheons from time to time. The members ranged from a former lance corporal through a batch of sergeants major to a lieutenant general. One of them commented,

> Shifty probably did more than anyone else to bring out the necessity and the value of the sergeant major's position at the top level in the Marine Corps. He was probably the greatest PR guy in the whole bunch. Herb was never bashful! And he was always there at our luncheons. When the Marine Corps birthday came in November, he recited the Commandant's message, and he did it with such emotion. And, of course at the end of it, he always raised his arms up in the air and yelled out, "Glory to the Corps!" and everybody stood up and applauded. He was a tremendous guy; the guy

loved the Marine Corps; ate, lived it. I don't know anybody in my life whom I've run into who loved the Corps as much as Herb Sweet did. He was just a tremendous guy in that area. Did anything and everything for the Marine Corps.... What an all-around good guy!

"All-around good guy" was not a bad label to hang on "Shifty" Sweet. He had shown his stuff in combat with those four Purple Hearts. He had risen to the absolute top of his chosen profession. He had helped thousands for the VA. He had pitched in willingly as a family man. And he didn't lose touch with his old friends.

This, then, was the extrovert with all those extraordinary achievements in an unusual life who was the real story behind the ordinary-looking man in the ordinary-looking house in the ordinary-looking suburb.

Chapter 6

THE OUTDOORSMAN
Sergeant Major Joseph W. Dailey

With Herbert Sweet's retirement, the temperament of the next Sergeant Major of the Marine Corps once more represented a radical change. Joseph Dailey was not the gregarious, extroverted type, perfectly at ease in a Headquarters office. His youth, Marine Corps service, family life, and the pattern of his retirement were all focussed on one priority, an overriding love of the out-of-doors. This unwavering focus meshed completely with his low-key, unvarnished, down-to-earth style, extending even to a love of solitude (when that was possible). That last characteristic was necessarily sublimated during his years of immersion in the Corps, but it became the dominant feature of his retirement years. These deeply ingrained traits clearly stemmed from an early life that molded him forever after.

It began in the Ozark Mountains of Arkansas in the village of Black Mountain near the western edge of the state. There, at Spirits Creek, Joseph Dailey was born on February 17, 1917. (Years later, the Marine Corps would foul up

Dailey's records and list him for a time as born in 1918 in Mason City, Iowa.)
His father, Ruesso, a sawmill foreman, had come there from Ohio, while his
mother, Ona, was originally from Missouri. Dailey had a childhood with a clear
set of ground rules. As he put it:

> I was near the last of fourteen children. My folks were very strict. They
> had high moral values. We were not allowed to drink liquor, or smoke,
> or even drink coffee. Pa wouldn't let us date until we were at least 21. He
> taught us to treat a girl friend like we would our sister—and to find a good
> woman like our mother to marry. My father and mother were not church-
> goers, but we read the Bible in our home. We had to make our own recrea-
> tion. We were good ball players and would always beat the city-slickers.
> Pa taught us never to lose at anything. We were always to be winners.

Dailey's formal education in those years was very limited: he finished grammar school in nearby Jethro, and that was it—no high school. His practical
education, however, broadened when he turned eighteen. His father had just
died, and, following the inherent bent of his nature, the young man signed
up for an outdoor job with the Civilian Conservation Corps (CCC) in February,
1935. Dailey later described how the CCC, working with the Army and the
Forest Service, helped in building trails, roads, bridges, and planting trees. He
recalled:

> The CCC paid $30.00 a month; $25.00 of that was sent to my folks.
> This helped my mother a great deal because I had a younger brother at
> home. It helped get him through school and my older sister to get through
> college.
> The Arkansas boys were sent west in 1936. My company was right out
> of the heart of the Ozarks and had never been on a train before—or away
> from home. We were loaded on Army troop trains. My company went
> into Oregon. This brought a great change in my life—being on my own
> and away from home and friends.

Those years in the CCC would prove useful to Dailey in his later life. He
learned strong lessons in discipline, military organization, leadership, and the
values of hard outdoor work, and he did well, already showing the qualities
which would permeate his whole life. As he later explained,

> The camps, in those days, had what they called a first sergeant; he was
> a leader. They had the Forest Service people we worked for, and they had
> Army officers in there as our company commanders. Then we had leaders
> that went out in the field, and I was one of those, next in line to the Forest
> Service ranger. They had a "36-dollar man" and then they had a "45-dollar
> man." Remember, the standard pay was only 30 dollars a month, and 25
> of that had to go home to my parents. You couldn't be married. I worked
> hard. I got to be a "36-dollar man" and then a "45-dollar man." That was
> the top, for us enlisted, in the CCC. So they made me first sergeant of the
> Arkansas boys.

It was during the Oregon days, as Dailey was widening his Ozark horizons, that he took the first steps to further his abbreviated schooling, enrolling in some correspondence courses.

By 1939 he felt that he wanted to be out on his own, so he left the CCC. This step led him to some very rough times out of doors. He ran out of money, slept on park benches, lived in hobo "jungles," moved around from town to town in the Northwest, barely surviving on any odd jobs he could get. There was apple picking and then a sawmill job, but "the man who hired us couldn't get paid for his lumber, so he couldn't pay us. I never did get paid for the work I did there, but I wouldn't ask him for money. Many times I went to saw wood on an empty stomach. I guess I would have starved that winter if it hadn't been for generous neighbors who shared their farm produce with me. That was a long hard winter. It taught me to appreciate a good job and comfortable living."

There were two new developments, however, which were destined to play crucial, intertwining roles in the rest of his life. First, while working in Washington state, he had decided that his life of bare subsistence had to change. His thoughts came to focus on the military and particularly on the Marine Corps. His family remembers that he had always said, "If we ever have a war, I'm going to join the Marine Corps before they take me into the Army." Several earlier attempts to enlist in the Marines had all been rejected because there were no openings, just a waiting list. Dailey, however, was a determined man, and his accomplishments in the semi-military life of the CCC had convinced him that he could have a real career in the Marine Corps. Accordingly, when a friend offered him a ride to California to try again for the Marines, he accepted.

They only went as far as Hillsboro, Oregon, where other friends asked them to spend the Christmas of 1939. It was there that the second critical development occurred. His friends invited him to go to the little local church of the Latter Day Saints (LDS) to help decorate a Christmas tree, and besides, they added, there would be girls there on their missionary assignment. Dailey, after due consideration, finally agreed to go despite his reservations, " 'What use do I have for girls? I don't even have a car—besides the good ones won't have anything to do with me, and I sure don't want the other kind.' I was informed that these girls were different—they were from Utah, 'You can't date them during the eighteen months they are on their mission—you have to keep them at arm's length.' I answered that if they weren't any different than those Oregon or Washington girls, I'd stay 10 arm lengths away."

That's not how it turned out. One of the girls, Leone Paul, smiled at him when he was working on the tree, and that changed his solitary life forever: "I was shy and a loner, and it surprised me that anyone would smile at me. Something told me that she was a different type of girl than I'd seen before. You might say that it was love at first sight. I never could figure out why I softened towards girls that night, when I'd been so bitter against them. It had to be God's plan for Leone and me to meet thus."

That meeting led Dailey to start regular attendance at the LDS church, and in March, 1940, he was baptized as a member of the Mormon Church. Leone stayed on her mission for 21 months, and he knew that it would be impossible to propose marriage until her time was finished. However, she returned to Salt Lake City when her mission was over, so he went back again to lumbering in Oregon and Washington.

Then came the attack on Pearl Harbor. Six days later, on December 13, 1941, he enlisted in the Marine Corps Reserve in Portland, Oregon. He was a likely looking recruit: six feet, two inches tall, blue eyes, brown hair, and 204 pounds of solid muscle. Ordered to boot camp in San Diego, he found:

> It was tough, but I had been a lumberjack and a log cutter. Anybody who worked in the lumber mills had to do real work. I was a very hard man and I took a lot of exercise. I hadn't been in the Marine Corps, but I knew a lot about military service. The only thing different from the CCC was that we didn't have any drill there.
>
> So, when I went through boot camp, my whole goal was to become a first sergeant or sergeant major later on. Of course it was tough there, but I was tough enough to take it. I never drank; I never smoked, so I never had to worry about giving out. I remember DIs thumping some other people around, but they never thumped me. I always tried to do my best, so they didn't bother me.

He started his long climb up the ladder of rank when he made PFC in March, 1942. That came as he was ordered to duty at the Marine Barracks which were then at an airfield on Terminal Island, near Los Angeles. It was an interesting tour, as he later remarked:

> We took over the old Terminal Island prison for a brig. They moved the former prisoners out of there; it had been a state prison. So we put a lot of Marines in there with a guard, naval prisoners and Marine prisoners.
>
> It was the beginning of the war. I remember a lot of movie stars used to come in and out the Marines' gate for USO shows. There were Mary Pickford and her husband, Buddy Rogers, Jack Benny, and many others. I rose to be a Sergeant of the Guard before I left.

The long arm of coincidence reached out at that time. A lady at the LDS church which Dailey attended knew, of all people, Leone Paul, and invited her (perhaps with a little urging?) to come for a visit. That was all the opening Dailey needed. In the few days of her stay there, they agreed to marry. The wedding took place in Los Angeles on June 18, 1942. She was a lovely lady, five feet, eight inches tall, with green eyes and brown hair...and seven years older than Dailey.

Naturally, Leone wanted him to meet her family, so their honeymoon was a Greyhound bus trip to Salt Lake City. It was quite a welcome there for the reformed bachelor: "Leone's relatives were so nice to me, but almost overwhelmed me with their kisses. I wasn't used to that. We were not a demonstrative family. Although I knew my mother loved me, I can only remember her kissing me once. I liked Leone's relatives very much, and they were such good cooks."

After that brief visit, it was back to work. More promotions followed, with "Temporary Corporal" coming in July, 1942, and "Temporary Sergeant" the following March. A transfer came through in August, 1943, sending Dailey to an infantry battalion at Camp Elliott in San Diego, and the next month to a replacement battalion. The 1st Division had finished its victorious struggle on Guadalcanal, suffering 3000 casualties, and it was easy to see what was coming next. Dailey and the other replacements were sent first to New Caledonia in the southwest Pacific in October, 1943. From there Dailey went in December to join the 1st Marines at Goodenough Island. Here he became acquainted with Tom McHugh, who was in the same battalion. The division was now preparing for its next operation, and Dailey was happy, "I had wanted to get out of Terminal Island a year before, but they wouldn't let me go. I wanted to get into combat so badly."

His first move (late in 1943) was to Finschhafen on the eastern shore of New Guinea, with fire fights and combat patrols there. Then it was on to the division's full-scale attack at Cape Gloucester on the western tip of New Britain on the day after Christmas, 1943. Dailey was now in his element:

> I well remember the landing there, and I liked it very much because we got into some pretty good battles. In the first one, we lost quite a few Marines, and they had to carry them out of there on stretchers. I got some good action in there because I was a sergeant squad leader, at that time.
>
> It rained every day at Cape Gloucester—how it rained! I recall that we went back one morning, and they said they had some coffee for us. I didn't drink coffee, but they said they had some hot chow and also some hot chocolate they'd brought up from the Navy. It was very hard for the trucks to get through the deep mud on the road, and when they did arrive, there were the bodies of these dead Marines stacked in there with our chow!

Finishing the main part of the battle in March, 1944, Dailey's unit next participated in mopping up the Japanese on Iboki Island, and from there he moved to the "rest camp" at Pavuvu in the Russell Islands northwest of Guadalcanal. As he later described it with a grimace:

> It was just a small island. They had the whole division there. We cleared the coconut trees out, some of them, and made camps. We were all very close together. I remember that we had these open heads [latrines], terrible things. They brought Red Cross women in there, and I'll never forget that the Marines, right away, had to put up target cloth around the toilets. One memory, I guess the best of all, was the USO show which came in there with Bob Hope and Jerry Colonna. They had a girl, Thomas, and Francis Langford. These were the first women we'd seen in a long time, except Navy women.

An event such as that was, of course, a temporary interlude. The division trained hard, because the men had been told plainly that the Japanese waiting for them on the next operation were very well equipped, healthy, and ready for an all-out slugging match; it was going to be tough. As the time for the land-

ing on Peleliu in the Palau Islands drew near there were intensive air strikes
to try to neutralize the defenders dug into their caves. Then came the assault
force—an imposing array of 600 warships, support ships, and transports with
the division's units on board. Approaching the island, the warships laid down
a thunderous barrage, with the battleships pouring in 2000-pound shells. For
three days and nights the barrage continued. It was an awe-inspiring sight, but
one that other Marines had seen before, and then found the enemy ready and
waiting when they came ashore. Such was the case at Peleliu; the caves with
their reinforced concrete protected the Japanese well, and comparatively few
were killed. They, too, were ready and waiting when H-hour on D-day arrived
at 0830 on September 15, 1944.

Dailey later recounted what followed:

> We were going in over the beaches that morning. We were one of the
> first waves (the platoon I was in), and we didn't get off the beach for two
> days. We just stayed on that beach! That was as far as we could get. They
> shelled us there all day long and into the next day, and we lost so many
> men. There were dead men laying all around, and it was so hot. The Navy
> thought they they'd shelled it well enough so that there weren't any Japanese
> living. But they were in those blockhouses, and they were shooting down
> at us from the mountain. Sometimes I thought there was no need for dig-
> ging a foxhole, because I wasn't going to live anyway. It was so tough. When
> we finally did get off the beach, it was about four or five days before we
> could even get to our objective. And we lost so many people!
>
> What I remember most was that we had camouflaged our faces before
> we went in there, and the Marines who got killed—and the Navy men who
> got killed—I remember today how they swelled up. They swelled up so
> big right after being killed in that hot weather, and they looked so terrible
> with their faces camouflaged. And we couldn't get them off the beach
> ...everybody had to be fighting. And the Japanese we killed were right there,
> too. We couldn't get the dead out of the way, and a lot of the amtracs
> [amphibious tractors] ran over them. That was the stinkingest, smelliest place
> I'd ever seen in my life. It was a terrible smell!
>
> I'll never forget those two days there; I just couldn't eat anything. And
> then the Navy sent in a bunch of the sailors with some sandwiches. It was
> about the second or third day: those sailors brought in those sandwiches
> in bags and gave them to the Marines, and we ate them. I remember how
> great those were. Otherwise I couldn't eat those C rations...You'd sit down
> beside either a dead Marine or a dead Japanese soldier.
>
> It was really tough; they had those big guns in those caves up in the
> mountain and in the blockhouses too. It was a long time before our tanks
> could knock out the blockhouses. From the mountain, they looked right
> down at us. It was like shooting fish in a rain barrel. And on that beach,
> the Marines couldn't move.

Finally, Dailey and the rest of the 1st Marines were able to fight their way
off the beach, and went from the frying pan into the fire. Literally fire, as it

poured forth in a deadly hail into the teeth of the Marines during their dogged, yard-by-yard grind against a series of crests on Bloody Nose Ridge, the backbone of the Japanese defense. Five days after the landing the 1st Marines had suffered a stunning 1700 casualties, and by the sixth day it had lost 56 percent of its men. When the battle was finally over, the division had suffered 6,000 casualties, but it had eliminated the Japanese. Their casualties were estimated at 10,695.

The Marine survivors then returned to the miserable camp on Pavuvu, and new replacements streamed in. The veterans of three campaigns took them in hand, and the training started all over again. A move to Guadalcanal was then made to practice night fighting, which would be essential on their next operation. Dailey was promoted to platoon sergeant in December, 1944, but was acting as a gunnery sergeant at this time, and he noted "how fouled up our Marines were in switching from fighting in the jungles in the day to night fighting. But it was a good thing we learned; we would make use of that practice."

Again there came the familiar sequence: pack up all the gear; go aboard ship; travel to the target; see the advance bombardment; load aboard the amtracs; and then hit the beach. It was April 1, 1945—Easter Day—and the place was Okinawa, the final bastion of the inner defensive line of the Japanese homeland. Dailey later recollected:

> We were one of the first waves that went in. When we hit the beaches we saw a lot of women and children there. We ran into some Japanese soldiers, but not too many the first day. Then we went south. The Army had landed down below us, and they ran into trouble. So we moved down near Shuri Castle, and that's where the battles really began. I think we had about forty days and forty nights of fighting there, and it rained every day. We lost tanks and more tanks; you couldn't even see them out in the mud.
>
> I remember our general telling us that we had to take Shuri Castle regardless of whether we got any tank or artillery support. But they did have artillery hub to hub across the island with the Marines and the Army, and they would support us when we couldn't get any tanks. (Because they were all bogged down on account of the rain.)
>
> As for my own self, I was never scared in combat. I felt like I had a job to do, and I wanted to fight so bad. It was a great experience for me because it was a different fight than in the jungle. We'd fought in the jungle a couple of years, I guess, but that was an all-together different war. Now we had tanks; we had artillery; we were able to see the enemy. But one thing that was bad about Okinawa: they had a lot of knee mortars, and the Japanese were well-prepared. This was their last stand, they were told...even their officers committed hari kari. So we really had to fight.
>
> But we were getting more firing from knee mortars; they were just zeroing in on top of us. I've seen so many Marines killed. I particularly remember one young man. I was an acting gunnery sergeant then, so I was up front with our company commander, and he had a radio operator who got hit with

one of those knee mortars right on top of his head. It still rings in my ears, but it killed him!

In this intensive fighting Dailey distinguished himself and was awarded the Silver Star Medal. He later sketched in the details:

> During the battle we fought so hard and we were trying to get our wounded out, but we were losing so many men.... The Japanese were getting ready to overrun our lines while we were getting some of those wounded out. But then I saw that we weren't going to be able to get all of them out. So I had to go and get some reserves from the rear. At that time, the radios weren't working very well, so I ran all the way back, got those guys, and then ran them up to our position to fight with us and help with the wounded. Our casualties were so heavy that, after the battle, I still had to go out for our wounded men.

Dailey's citation for the Silver Star from the Secretary of the Navy referred to his "conspicuous gallantry and intrepidity" on May 3, 1945, and went on to praise his dangerous rescue mission.

In June, 1945, the conquest of Okinawa was complete, and Dailey received a total change of duty. It had been almost two years of hectic combat duty in a rifle company, and now, in the fall of 1945, he was transferred to be the acting first sergeant of the headquarters company and then to—of all things—an anti-aircraft artillery battalion. But these were just temporary assignments; he was going home. Arriving in San Diego, he was discharged from the Corps on November 23, 1945.

Dailey later confessed why he made such an abrupt move to civilian life:

> I was going to stay in the Marine Corps after World War II, but I kind of got a dirty deal from a new company commander. At that time promotions weren't coming from Headquarters Marine Corps; they were being handed out in the field. I was doing a first sergeant's job in combat, after our first sergeant got hit. Our old company commander also had been hit; he had to leave and he never came back. So they sent another officer from headquarters company over, and he took over as our new company commander.
>
> I was never a drinker, and they started sending booze out right after World War II and let the platoons have it. He got to drinking; he and another platoon sergeant and another sergeant, they all got to drinking together. I wouldn't drink with them, so when the promotions came out he gave it to this other guy instead of me.

Once he was a civilian, Dailey made a beeline for Pleasant Grove, Utah, for a long-awaited reunion with Leone. It must have been a moment of high emotion, for she had naturally read of all the bloody battles and wondered if her man would ever come home alive.

For nearly five years, they had a quiet, normal family life. Moving to Oakland, California, Dailey worked as a yard clerk for the Southern Pacific Railroad. He also attended classes at two different business colleges, taking

Dailey as a first sergeant at Camp Pendleton in March, 1951.

courses in vocabulary building, salesmanship, and leadership, making up for some of the high school education he had never had as a teenager.

In June, 1948, despite his earlier raw deal, he re-enlisted in the Reserves as a "Permanent" staff sergeant. And their family began to grow; Connie was born in February, 1949, and Janis in September the next year.

Then the Korean War erupted. There was no doubt in Dailey's mind what he would do, "I never did like civilian life." On October 2, 1950, he went back on active duty as a staff sergeant, and was sent to the headquarters battalion at Camp Pendleton. Leone eventually followed and found a place to live in North Hollywood. He was assigned a first sergeant's duties in an infantry training regiment, but that was not what an outdoorsman had in mind.

First, orally, and then (in June, 1952) in writing, he requested a transfer to his old outfit, the 1st Division, now heavily engaged in Korea. Nothing seemed to happen because "they needed first sergeants who had experience in World War II, and they had so many people going through Camp Pendleton. So they kept me and some others. I thought that they would never let us go; but finally, I got over there. My orders came through at last in September, 'for duty and further transportation beyond the seas.' I was really pleased to see that!" Leone returned with the two girls to Salt Lake City, while Dailey went to join the 5th Marines in October.

The division was fighting in a strategic sector of the Central Front at this time. For the men in the rifle companies it was a life of ceaseless raids, night patrols, probing attacks, shelling, and ambushes—and the enemy responded in kind. Dailey wrote home about that in simple, homespun words that tell exactly what it was like at the most elemental level of war:

> October 16, 1952: I am on the front lines now. We do most of our work at night. The enemy is about two or three hundred yards in front of us. We are on one hill and they on another across from us. If we move around in the day time, they start shooting at us. After dark, patrols are sent out from our lines to try to find out about them. They have a lot of land mines in the area, so you have to watch out where you step, and that is hard to do in the dark. We had four boys get wounded about two nights ago from one that blew up.
>
> October 23: I'm so glad when morning comes and I can get into my warm sleeping bag. We have a place dug into the ground and covered over with sand bags—it is about six feet deep and room for four people to sleep

in. At night we stay out in the trenches, which are about six feet deep. A
patrol was out the other night and made contact with the enemy. Three boys
were injured and one killed. They couldn't bring in the one that was killed,
and when they went back the next night to get him, the enemy was waiting
with guns set up all around....

November 1: I go out on patrol every fourth night. There is one officer
and one platoon sergeant to each platoon, and there are three rifle platoons
in a company. We take 15 men on a patrol with a radio and telephone with
a roll of wire. We roll the telephone wire as we go out, and have the phone
hook on the wire so we can talk with the company commander about what
goes on around us. If the enemy gets in behind and cuts a wire, we always
have the radio to fall back on. We never start a fight with them. We have
good medical care. We have a hospital corpsman along with us. If a person
is wounded really bad, they call a hospital plane and they can have him
back in the division hospital within an hour. We have been on the front
lines one month and will stay about another six weeks, and then go back
for a month. We had another boy killed last night and one the night before....

In the hilly terrain there, elevated outposts with commanding views were
vital to tactical control of the area. Dailey drew a typical assignment in February,
1953:

We were tasked to take an outpost back. At that time they were short
on officers in the company. I was a platoon sergeant, but they didn't have
an officer, so I became platoon leader. Our whole company attacked up
to the top of the hill, but then they shoved all of us back down. I decided
that they couldn't shove us off, so I led my own platoon back up, and we
took that hill! We had lost so many men there before and had to leave them,
but I knew that we just had to get our casualties out.

Now, in spite of Dailey's low-key summary of his actions, that was a feat
of enormous daring and constant danger, calling for leadership of the highest
order under maximum combat pressure. The result was a Navy Cross for Dailey.
This was an award second only to the Medal of Honor, and, after review by
eight successive levels of command, the Secretary of the Navy made this citation:

For extraordinary heroism while serving as a platoon leader of Company
F, 2d Battalion, 5th Marines, 1st Marine Division (Reinforced), in action against
enemy aggressor forces in Korea on 25 February, 1953. While participating
in a company raid on an enemy outpost, Technical Sergeant Dailey
unhesitatingly volunteered to lead a rescue squad in an attempt to recover
four Marine casualties who were discovered lying a few feet from a strongly
fortified enemy-held trench.

Moving quickly to his objective, he skillfully maneuvered his squad into
a position from which he was able to rescue the casualties and, despite an
intense hail of enemy machine gun, grenade, and automatic weapons fire,
carried out a further search of the surrounding terrain until he located and
recovered two other wounded Marines.

As an enemy force advanced toward his position, he skillfully withdrew his men and all the recovered casualties to friendly lines. By his exceptional courage, outstanding leadership, and daring initiative in the face of continuous hostile fire, Technical Sergeant Dailey was directly instrumental in saving the lives of six wounded Marines and upheld the highest traditions of the United States Naval Service.

The Government of the Republic of (South) Korea also took note of Dailey's exploits, awarding him "The Order of Military Merit, Wharang with Gold Star."

There was intensive fighting again the next month. One pair of outpost hills above the Imjin River was named Jane Russell (after a famous movie star of the day who had a well-publicized bosom). On March 26, 1953, the enemy overran this important tactical location, and Dailey was among those ordered to recapture it. Later he outlined what happened, "We had to go back. So the whole company went, and my company commander was killed that night. We got up to the top, but they chased us down with mortars. We had to go back to the foot of the hill. While attacking up the hill, I got hit in my hip with a mortar fragment. They carried me out on a stretcher, but the next day our men took that outpost back!"

Again, Dailey's description was modest. Others saw his actions in another light, and he was awarded a Bronze Star Medal with Combat "V." The citation from the commanding general of the 1st Division, Major General Randolph Pate, called his actions a "heroic achievement" and lauded his "exceptional courage, initiative, and professional skill."

The wound proved to be a nasty one. Taken first to a field hospital, he was told that the shrapnel was too deeply imbedded to remove there. His most vivid memory of that stay was not medical, however. Forced to lie on his stomach, he encountered a woman movie star who came by and jokingly told him that he "must have been stealing watermelons." He was soon transferred to a Danish hospital ship offshore where a series of operations finally extracted the mortar fragments. In April he was finally able to rejoin his company.

With the Purple Heart that came with his wound, Dailey had now been decorated four times in one month. It was not surprising, therefore, that after a warrant for technical sergeant came through in June, he received a "Special Meritorious Promotion" to master sergeant in August, 1953. This promotion led to a switch in his actual function from company gunnery sergeant to company first sergeant, a role that was all inclusive in an infantry company in combat. Dailey's official file contained a nugget of condensation that well summarized his varied responsibilities:

> Assisted the company commander in formulating plans and with training the men in infantry tactics, discipline, physical fitness, and leadership for the noncommissioned officers. When in combat, set up command post, inspected company positions on line, took charge of rifle platoons when officers became casualties, during the shortage of officers in the company. Took charge of night patrols and a rifle platoon on a company-size raid....

Supervised the administrative details such as morning report, casual report, correspondence, rosters, personnel file cards, and company filing system.

At long last, in November, 1953, the magic orders to return to the States filtered down to him. Arriving in San Diego, he was joined by Leone and the girls for a wonderful time of leave. Then he returned to duty as the first sergeant of a company in the Communications and Electronics School Battalion there. Here there was an important distinction. Every Marine had a Military Occupational Specialty (MOS), with "O1" being administration and "O3" being infantry. Dailey later smiled as he explained, "I was an O3 master sergeant and they had a lot of O1 master sergeants. An O1 master sergeant was supposed to be a first sergeant because he could type. I never could type; I was too dumb. I was a *field* Marine. I was actually a 'field first sergeant'; that's what I wanted to call myself because that was a non-typist. So they brought an O1 in there, and they took me out. And I went over to handle all the students who were graduating from that battalion. There were problems there, so that's why I was put in charge of them."

This type of duty didn't fit in very well with Dailey's natural bent as an outdoorsman and an O3. Finally, in January, 1955, he requested a transfer back to the infantry in the 2d Division at Camp Lejeune, or, alternatively, to Inspector and Instructor (I and I) duty with a reserve training unit. Six months later, Headquarters Marine Corps prepared orders sending him to the I and I staff of the 33d Special Infantry Company, USMCR, in Beaumont, Texas. However, the orders were never sent. As Dailey later recounted the circumstances:

They had a major who was at the Electronics School. He knew me very well, and they had put him in charge of the Officers Club. Well, he wanted somebody over there to run that place, to oversee the civilian help and these Marines that they had over there at this Officers Club. So he came and told me that he was going to get me to go over there. I said, "Major, I'll do anything that you want me to in the Marine Corps, but I didn't come in this Marine Corps to work in an Officers Club. I don't drink!" "Well," he replied, "that's why I want you over there." I repeated, "I don't drink. I don't fool with liquor. I don't go to the other clubs. I don't do that." "Well," he stated, "I'm going to get you down there anyway."

What happened, fortunately, was that there was a captain who came aboard the base at that exact time, and he was looking for a first sergeant. He was the commanding officer of the Marine Detachment aboard the USS *Bremerton*, a heavy cruiser. So the sergeant major of our base called me up and advised me, "We've got a captain here looking...."

I told the sergeant major that I didn't want to go down to the club. Then he said, "He wants a first sergeant. Why don't you come up and be interviewed?" So I went up and I talked to the captain and he really wanted me. I told him my history, and he was able to arrange it so they sent a message to Headquarters Marine Corps, and that's how they assigned me aboard the USS *Bremerton*.

With Dailey going off to sea, Leone and the children moved to Santa Ana, California, once more to await the return of their traveling man.

Aboard ship, he served as first sergeant of the Marine Detachment. That, as usual, encompassed the administrative work and supervision of many activities: training in infantry tactics, discipline, physical fitness, drill, leadership of the other NCOs, and mustering honor guards—all directed towards one set of goals: "to uphold the tradition of the Corps, to maintain the sharpest military appearance, and to represent the Marine Corps to the Navy in an outstanding manner." Dailey enjoyed himself, fitting in easily to sea-going duty, "We went many different places in the Pacific. We also went on some good-will tours such as going up to Canada. We stayed in Bremerton, Washington, a while for upkeep; went into Yokosuka, Japan. The Navy was so good to me. They had a captain aboard that ship who trusted in me and asked me many things. He used to come and talk to me about a lot of things, because he knew that I was in World War II, and I was almost his age."

In the fall of 1955 the Marine Corps made a major overhaul of its most senior NCO ranks, reinstituting the formal titles of "First Sergeant" and "Sergeant Major." (For years men had been acting with those titles when they were officially master sergeants.) Dailey quickly submitted his application for sergeant major in September, with the enthusiastic endorsement of his commanding officer.

December, 1955, was a memorable time for Dailey. The *Bremerton* had gone to the western Pacific at a time of tension off the coast of China. The Nationalist government had two small but strategic islands, Quemoy and Matsu, guarding their stronghold on Formosa (as Taiwan was then called). The United States feared that those outposts might be the object of an attack by the Communist Chinese on the mainland. The *Bremerton* was sent, as part of a three-warship division, to stand watch in the waters adjoining the islands. Thus Dailey celebrated another memorable Christmas afloat, 12 years to the day since he had gone in on the assault at Cape Gloucester.

Far away in Westminster, California, near Long Beach, *Bremerton's* home port, Leone was buying the first house they had ever owned, and had settled in to make it their home.

The final major event of that December was a dramatic action by Headquarters Marine Corps which Dailey found out about later. He had been given his warrant as an official first sergeant, ranking from December 30, 1955, as well as a simultaneous second warrant, effective December 31, from the special board which had been convened to "select the master sergeant who was the most senior" to be a sergeant major. Because of his superb record, Dailey was now the senior sergeant major in the entire Corps. When he got the news it was an electric moment, the far-reaching dreams of his youth come true!

With that kind of recognition, Dailey came to feel that the scope of a thirty-nine-man ship's detachment was rather narrow, so, in June, 1956, he requested a transfer, pointing out that the "experience is limited." He realized that the Corps would want to utilize a sergeant major in billets with the larger FMF units.

The following month, Headquarters Marine Corps agreed to transfer him to the 1st Division at Camp Pendleton. After a delay in order to locate a proper replacement for him on the *Bremerton*, Dailey received orders in November, 1956, to the 7th Marines as a battalion sergeant major. It was like coming home for the outdoorsman:

> We'd been away from that in the Marine Corps for a long time, especially us O3s. We'd been waiting for something like this. I remember going into it; it was a good experience. I was getting back in the field, training with Marines again, continuous combat training. We went to many different places. We had desert training; we had aboard ship training; we had cold weather training at Bridgeport, California, everything.

Developments in Washington in the meantime had set Dailey to thinking about the value of rounding out his career profile. In May, 1957, Wilbur Bestwick was selected as the first Sergeant Major of the Marine Corps, and Dailey reflected, "I guess I was in the running for that. But anyway, they selected him, and he was a good man. I knew someday I wanted to be Sergeant Major of the Marine Corps." Accordingly, he requested duty in the Los Angeles area in December "to further my education." When this was denied, he thought, "Maybe I'd better go on I&I duty, get a little work with the Reserves for a while. So I put in for I&I, and they sent me to Houston, Texas, in February, 1959."

There he served on the staff of the 6th Infantry Battalion, part of the 23d Marines, 4th Division, USMCR. Leone and the children left California to be with him in a house outside town. To get out of doors from his office, Dailey walked the four miles every day to work in the morning and back again to the house in the evening. "I liked that Reserve duty because we almost had 1000 men in there. Houston was a big outfit!"

In October, 1959, Dailey got still another opportunity to round out his professional skills. He was able to take a short leave from Houston and completed the Sergeants Major Course at Parris Island: "It was a good course. I was glad they sent me there. There were a lot of things I didn't know that they brought up. It wasn't clerical work; it was other things that we needed to know as senior NCOs in the Marine Corps. We were all first sergeants and sergeants major, and it was one of the best schools I'd been to." In addition to this, Dailey added one other asset in his drive to reach the very top of his profession. Keenly aware of the fact that he had never even been to high school, he then enrolled in an intensive series of correspondence courses from the Marine Corps Institute between December, 1960, and July, 1962.

New orders arrived in August, 1962 moving him up the chain of command: he was sent to be the regimental sergeant major of the 2d Marines at Camp Lejeune. His family did not join him there, as Leone was a trained genealogist and wanted to use her time in the east to work in the National Archives in Washington, D.C. His family lived in a house in Cheverly, Maryland, while he supervised the training of the three battalions under him in North Carolina and commuted long-distance on the Lejeune-D.C. buses every other weekend.

At this time (fall, 1962) the Cuban Missile Crisis broke out. The 2d Marines had gone to Vieques in Puerto Rico for a routine training exercise at the Marine camp there. Dailey recalled:

> We never did get off the ship. We were going to unload and train on Vieques, then reload back on and offload again for training. We just got in there, and some of us started to get off, and they got word that the Cuban thing had come to a showdown. So they took us back out, and we joined the task force.
>
> We had been down there for about a week, and then they brought all the rest of the 2d Division down, loaded aboard ship. There was hardly anybody left at Camp Lejeune, only just a caretaker outfit. We were down there for over a month, until almost Christmas.

When that crisis passed, another emergency arose. A big tropical storm had caused a levee to break near the Navy base at Mayport, Florida, and serious floods were imminent. So Dailey and his men ended up filling countless sandbags there.

By now there was really only one element missing in his plan to be the completely well-rounded Marine, with experience at every level of the Corps. He had never served at Headquarters. This omission was rectified in August, 1963, when he was ordered to the G-3 (Plans and Operations) Division in Washington. Dailey made the changeover smoothly:

> General Cushman was the G-3 officer, and I worked for him. He brought me up there. Each Division, like G-3 and G-1, had a sergeant major working for it. I came to know a little bit more about operations, training, and things like that, but it wasn't a year that I was there.
>
> Tom McHugh was the Sergeant Major of the Corps then. That's when I served with him again for the first time since we'd been together in World War II. It certainly was different there. A lot of stuff that you had to handle was Top Secret. I worked with mostly officers. There weren't many enlisted there. When I worked with General Cushman, I was kind of his "top kick."
> So that was a learning experience for me.
>
> I didn't particularly like to be in Headquarters, but there I was, and I thought it was a good experience, although everybody I ever talked to from Headquarters didn't want to be there anyway.

Fortunately, the outdoorsman did not have to stay cooped up in an office. There were trips to the field sometimes, and the tour at Headquarters proved to be a short one—only ten months—just long enough for Dailey to make an impression on Cushman and other senior generals that would stand him in good stead in the future. A new opportunity now opened up. As he later explained:

> In June, 1964, they needed a new sergeant major at the Washington Barracks at 8th and I Streets. The guy there wanted to get out; he'd had too many parade seasons over there. So they were trying to find somebody that stood tall, had parade ground experience, and all that. They asked for some interviews, and Tom McHugh said that I should go over there.

I knew I would be glad if I could get out of Headquarters, because I wanted to get on the parade field over there. That was something that would be in your career record. It would help you. I'd done everything else. I'd been a company first sergeant; I'd been a battalion sergeant major; I'd been on I&I duty; I'd been in Headquarters at G-3, helping them; now I wanted to get on that drill field.

The colonel interviewed me, said he wanted me, and so the next day I went over there.

It was a whole new experience for Dailey. As he summarized it:

We'd have the parade every Friday night, and then they'd have it during the week when they'd put it on for dignitaries. That was a great thing, to be able to meet some of those people, people like the Secretary of the Navy....

There was something else that we had when I was there that they don't have today. I was the head of the flag pageant. We showed it all over the Virginia, Maryland, and Washington, D.C. area, and we went to many dignitaries to put it on for them. We had flags from the beginning days of Betsy Ross, all the way down through time, and we had a Marine rifle team that would march out on the stage with them. I'd narrate it, and then we had the Drum and Bugle Corps play the music of that time....

But the parades were also a great thing for me, coming out there in front of all those 5000 people. I'd march out there, as the sergeant major in front of that battalion, and do an about face. It was like being a movie star!

Satisfying as this tour of duty was, Dailey was keenly aware that, on the other side of the world, his kind of Marines were being killed doing his kind of job in infantry battalions in Vietnam. He had completed two parade seasons and part of a third. Even with a family, he couldn't stand to stay out of the Vietnam War any longer. And duty there would put him back in the field, where he felt most at home. In August, 1966, he volunteered and was sent to rejoin his old regiment, the 1st Marines, in Vietnam. It was altogether a different kind of war from the two in which Dailey had already fought. As he later contrasted the changes:

You came in and you didn't have any front lines in Vietnam! Everything around you was the front lines, where in the other wars you had a trench line or a front line, so that was very different. The water and the rations: before it had been hard to get rations; there were plenty of rations in Vietnam. People in the rear, they had their booze and their beer. You'd never seen that in the other wars. The only people who didn't get it were up at the front.

I have to say this: I was first put in as a sergeant major of a battalion, but it was a small-unit war. Officers did not get to have a lot of experience at handling troops. You put fire teams and squad leaders and platoons way out in the front area. We had them there and the battalion commander and I went to see them every day, most of them. We would have a fire team with a young corporal and four men way out there.... So it wasn't an officers' war; it was an enlisted man's war. Sometimes we got in a big battle, but most of the time it was that type of small-unit war.

When I first went there, in '66, the drugs and the liquor weren't as bad as later on. When I went back the second time in '68, that's when it was bad."

Dailey went directly into action, as his unit deployed in Operation Troy in the Da Nang area in September. The style of his commanding officer (CO) was be up front, with the troops, and Dailey went with him, earning his Combat Action Ribbon at the forward battalion CP for being "in direct contact with enemy ground forces." As he later described it, "Operation Troy...we went a long time on that. This was when they wanted to have a free election in the Da Nang area, and our battalion had the duty of making sure that the people had the right to go to the voting booths. That's when we had to go around and make sure that we cleared out all the area. We did run into a lot of Vietnamese guerrillas, the Viet Cong. We ran into them and many, many different civilians."

The following month of October was a grim one for Dailey. He was riding in the back of a jeep when a South Vietnamese Army truck rammed into them; his CO was killed and he himself suffered a severe compound fracture of his right leg. It was a traumatic experience, for Dailey had been a close friend of his CO back in Washington days, and regarded him as "one of the finest skippers I ever knew. It really did hurt me to see him killed." The fracture was so bad that it necessitated air evacuation to a series of hospitals, first in the Philippines, then to Guam, and finally, in November, 1966, to the Bethesda Naval Hospital outside Washington. There the doctors inserted two screws in the leg and did a skin graft. The good news was that Leone came to join him, finding a place to live in nearby Hyattsville.

Dailey's recuperation was a long, slow process, and it was not until March of 1968 that he was declared "fit for duty"—seventeen months after the crash. His new orders took him to the Inspection Division at Headquarters Marine Corps as the sergeant major for the inspector general. They were soon on the road for trips to check out the troops at various bases stateside, as well as one visit to Okinawa. Dailey later gave the results:

I found a lot of things. My duty was to go onto the posts, generally as a representative of the Commandant of the Marine Corps. So you've got to find out what's going on. I never let a sergeant major there lead me around. He told my general, for he probably had it all figured out where the general was to go when he got there. But he didn't tell me where to go!

If he told me to go to this barracks over here or go down there to the troops, I knew he'd already seen them and he had them prepared for me. I knew that from being a "top kick" myself. So I'd go a little separately to find out things. If I found something that he wasn't doing right, I'd tell him, and I also told my general that those things should be straightened out.

*"Let's get with the troops"—
Dailey moves quickly out of the
command helicopter during his
tour as sergeant major of the 3d
Division, Vietnam, early 1969.*
Dailey photo

**The Sword of the Post Sergeant Major of the Washington Barracks is presented to Dailey
(center) in June, 1964.**

> Otherwise, there wasn't a need for us to be there if everything was perfect. And there was nothing perfect.
>
> A lot of things I found out: I found fat people; I found people that weren't in the right MOS; might not be doing their job; might be too many down at the club; or too many over at the theater cleaning it up. I found such things as those, that shouldn't be going on. At that time they needed to be in Vietnam! So that was the reason for me to be out there on those visits.

The conviction gnawed inside Dailey, however, that he had not fully discharged his obligations in Vietnam; he had been there too short a time. As a result, he secured orders to return there in July, 1968, after only four months in the Inspection Division. Leone moved back once more to Salt Lake City, where their two girls were enrolled in Brigham Young University. Meanwhile he joined the 3d Division, back in the field as the sergeant major of an engineer battalion. Once again, he faced a different set of circumstances:

> Vietnam had changed a lot. For example, I went to a different area, up north next to the Demilitarized Zone [DMZ] in Quang Tri Province, well away from my former area near Da Nang. Up there the difference was that we were fighting in the mountains; we were using artillery fire; we were fighting on outposts; we were fighting all around. We had to land in there with helicopters, without built roads. The DMZ area was altogether different from the Da Nang area. And we'd moved further into civic action then. We were building hospitals; we were building schools; we were building roads; we were helping with their land and soil erosion. My engineers were doing a lot of this with the Seabees. It was a new experience for me.
>
> As I think about our enlisted man there, I believe that he was still fundamentally the same Marine. The Marines of World War II, however, were not as well educated as the Marines you found in Vietnam. Now you found high school graduates. In the enlisted ranks of World War II, it was hard to find one. They still were loyal, and they were still fighting men, but they'd been called into a war that nobody wanted. In World War II, when we went to war, everybody was behind you. That was the difference. In this war, even his folks back home didn't want him over there.
>
> Moreover, by this time there was racial friction and the drugs were bad.

After four months with the engineer battalion, Dailey was transferred. The sergeant major of the 3d Division had been killed, and, as the senior man, he was promoted to that choice billet. As he later defined the job:

> I went from riding around in a jeep to a helicopter, and I went all over our division area. Up there we had around 40,000 or 50,000 troops [counting all the attached reinforcing units and South Vietnamese troops] who were under the division commanding general. We'd land here; we'd land there...the general and I tried to see all the troops. I went with him every place since I was his "top kick." I went out and talked to the enlisted troops while he was talking to the officers.

I found a lot of problems. We had all these companies on these out-posts and in forward areas out there, and then we had casual companies behind. We also had a headquarters battalion that stayed behind. My big-gest job there was kicking some of those guys back out to the front lines; there were even staff NCOs that wanted to stay back. They had a NCO club in the rear, and they wanted to be there and get their booze. I'd find that they had come back to do a little duty behind the lines to pick up something.

You know, the lieutenant would say to his platoon sergeant, "Well, you can go back today," or there would be a company commander send-ing a gunnery sergeant back. Then I'd find some of these guys still back there. And I cleaned out a lot of those casual companies as well, because we had front line companies that were under strength.

That war in Vietnam sure was different! At the same time you had this big set-up in the rear—clubs and everything—you would fly these other guys, perhaps a whole company, in helicopters to those outposts.

Then there were some Marines in the rear casual companies who wanted to avoid combat; they would say that they had something wrong with them. I think that it came from this young people's problem back there in the States, where they wanted to change the world. We had a few Marines out there, not very many, who wanted to be like them.

I used to say, "Why did you join the Marine Corps if you didn't want to fight? That's the first thing we do. The reason they have a Marine Corps is to fight and to protect our country!" They would answer, "Well, I was drafted." Then I'd say, "Yes, drafted, but I didn't pass the draft law. That was passed by our Congress of the United States and signed by the Presi-dent. He's the Commander in Chief. I had nothing to do with it, but if we have to have that to get people to fight, then you're one of them. You hap-pened to be selected for the Marines. You should have volunteered!"

Then they'd object, "Well, Sergeant Major, you can't make us fight." I'd reply, "The Marine Corps can't make you fight, but it can take you up where the fighting is! And then you'll have to make up your mind whether you want to fight or not. You are going where those people up there are dying, and you may have to fight with them. You have that choice." So they went up and I never heard from them again.

Most of Dailey's time, of course, was spent with the men on the firing line, trying to make their grim life just a little bit easier:

The general and I were out there with the rifle units, going to visit them every day. If they needed something from the rear, if it wasn't getting out there to them, I'd go back and recommend it to the general and he'd call his G-4 or G-3 [logistics or operations staff officers] or someone, and he'd see if he could get it. I was out talking to those front line troopers when he was talking to the officers. And they'd give me the word. I'd try and find out the real situation. Even if they needed something small, like a newspaper or magazine up there, and if I could get it in the rear, I'd send it up to them.

Major General Ngo Quang Truong (right) awards Dailey (center) the Vietnamese Armed Forces Honor Medal, 2d Class, in June, 1969, shortly before Dailey left for Washington. His successor as division sergeant major (left) stands at attention.

Dailey (left) talks to Marines in the field. (Early 1969.)

Dailey photo

Besides constantly helping the men who directly bore the brunt of battle, Dailey also gave real assistance to the two commanding generals with whom he served, Major General Raymond Davis and Major General William Jones, "I worked closely with them, I tried to do my best; I tried to help them. They asked me for a lot of advice, and I gave it to them. A lot of times when we were out in those helicopters we got shot at by the machine guns of the enemy. So we took a chance as much as the front line troops, because we landed right on the front lines with the helicopter as the division sergeant major and the division commanding officer. I worked as hard as I could."

The medals rolled in. A Navy Commendation Medal with Combat Distinguishing Device, and a citation signed by the commanding general of FMFPac, Lieutenant General Henry Buse, detailed his achievements from August 16, 1968, to June 23, 1969:

> ...Constantly concerned with the welfare of his enlisted Marines, he was always readily available for consultation concerning personal and professional problems and, in addition, provided his commanding general with a source of insight into the level of morale within the division.
>
> On 15 March 1969, Fire Support Base Cunningham in Quang Tri Province came under intense mortar fire during the commanding general's visit, resulting in several casualties among Marines located near the landing zone. Completely disregarding his own safety, Sergeant Major Dailey unhesitatingly relinquished his place on the aircraft and directed that the wounded be placed aboard....

The South Vietnamese Army also recognized Dailey. On June 2, 1969, Major General Ngo Quang Truong, "C.G. 1st Infantry Division—Concurrently, C.G. 11th Division Tactical Area," awarded Dailey the Vietnamese Cross of Gallantry with Silver Star, citing him for:

> Professional noncommissioned officer, having great capabilities and experiences on the battlefield and unusually devoted to duty.
>
> Served as Sergeant Major of the 3d Marine Division during the period from August, 1968, to June, 1969. Sergeant Major Dailey has vividly participated in most of the desperate battles from the lowland areas of Quang Tri Province to the Ashau Valley.
>
> In spite of the difficulties of terrain in the operational areas, Sergeant Major Dailey bravely exposed himself under the enemy fire and was always present beside the division commanding general in order to visit and encourage the troops.
>
> Sergeant Major Dailey's courage, bravery, and esprit de corps have contributed greatly to the triumphant achievements of the 3d Marine Division in the mission to eliminate the invading Communists in the 11th Division Tactical Area of Operations.

Four days later, the action had moved to a higher echelon, and Lieutenant General Hoang Xuan Lam, "C.G. I Corps Tactical Zone," awarded a second Cross of Gallantry with Silver Star for a "courageous noncommissioned officer with high anti-communist spirit." The final award came a month later, when Hoang Xuan Lam added one final Vietnamese flourish for Dailey, the Armed Forces Service Honor Medal, Second Class. The citation began with a reference to his "outstanding moral fiber in sacrificing personal comforts in order to accomplish assigned missions," and continued:

> During his assignment as the senior enlisted man of the 3d Marine Division, Sergeant Major Dailey maintained the highest standards of this position, demonstrating true friendship and cooperation with his comrades in arms. He was of invaluable assistance during the operations of the 1st ARVN Infantry Division to destroy the Communists in the 11th Division Tactical Area. In spite of his many pressing duties, Sergeant Major Dailey found the time to assist the local populace and contributed to the betterment of their social, medical, and cultural facilities. His efforts contributed immeasurably to the success of the mission of the 1st ARVN Infantry Division.

All that recognition was gratifying to Dailey. In the twenty-eight years since he had first enlisted, he had seen heavy combat in three different wars, received an impressive array of medals, and was the senior sergeant major in the Corps—yet a question hung in the back of his mind, "What next?"

The answer came with stunning suddenness in May, 1969. Dailey later told the story:

> We'd come back off the front lines, and I went to my quarters, and the general went over to his. We were right close together in the CP. A few minutes after we'd come back, he called me over. He said (laughing), "I've got a surprise here for you." I didn't know what it was; I thought maybe he got me a transfer, or he might be sending me on R&R [Rest and Recreation], or something. He went on, "It just came in on the wires here that you've been selected as Sergeant Major of the Corps." I said, "General, I'm surprised! There were so many other people in the running."
>
> I ran the race with 500-600 others, so I was totally surprised. I had thought this was my last chance, because I knew that after the Vietnam War they'd probably ask me to retire. I prayed a lot about it, and I figured I'd worked as hard as I could, and I left it to the Lord if he was going to give me this job.
>
> But I did have a little hope because General Walt, the assistant commandant of the Marine Corps, had spoken to me when he was out there about a month before this happened. At that time, it had gone through the colonel's board. Then it had gone to the general's board and finally to the Commandant. General Walt had told me, "Three books have gone to the Commandant. You are one of them. I'm not supposed to tell you this, but it's true."
>
> I had served under General Walt in Korea where he was my regimental commander. He had called me in then when I got the Navy Cross. Now he predicted, "You're going to be the next Sergeant Major of the Marine Corps." I said, "General, there are all those other guys (I didn't even know who they were), and I certainly don't know who those other two guys were that went with my name over to the Commandant."

The announcement of Dailey's selection as Sergeant Major of the Marine Corps brought a reporter from the rear-echelon Da Nang Press Center up to the real war at Dong Ha in the I Corps area. In an interview there Dailey put the Marine Corps' best foot forward. Asked for his impression of "today's Marines," he replied:

I can describe them in one word, great! They are great in every sense of the word. Today's Marine believes in himself. He is dedicated, better educated, better trained, and in better physical condition than Marines of past generations. He has come here to serve his country and Corps, and does so with fierce pride in his work. He realizes this is a hard war, but a war with two aspects, fighting and pacification, and he devotes his efforts to both of them. He is not afraid of self-sacrifice. He gets dirty, tired, and hungry, but he carries on. He is proud and determined. He is a Marine!

Then, like so many of the military men of his day, he gave an up-beat assessment of the progress of the war:

My tour with the 3d Marine Division has been in I Corps, and I feel we've made great progress there. You only need to take a trip around this area of operation to see that Marines, Army, Air Force, and Navy personnel are able to go anywhere, any time, to set up bases and from these bases, seek, find, close with, and destroy the enemy.

Progress is also indicated by the success of the pacification effort in the area of operations. In villages like Cam Lo and Gia Dang you see people working in their fields and planting rice without fear. Refugees are moving back to their former homes without fear. Children are able to run up and down the beaches and swim in the surf believing and knowing that they are secure. This all adds up to great progress in the war....

Press interviews made his new appointment actually seem to be official, and Dailey took personal satisfaction in the fact that he had finally reached the absolute peak of an enlisted career, just as he had made that his ultimate objective all those years earlier.

His orders were to proceed to Washington, so he went down to Da Nang for his flight. While there, he encountered the regimental sergeant major of the 7th Marines (in the 1st Division), Clinton Puckett, who also held a Navy Cross, and would soon be working with him at Headquarters.

Upon arrival in Washington in July, 1969, Dailey was able to reassemble his family once more. Leone, who had always had his power of attorney, once more sold a house she had bought (this time in Salt Lake City), and once more packed, and once more moved, and once more bought a new house (this time in New Carrollton, Maryland), and once more unpacked. This was the most wrenching upheaval yet. On her earlier return to Salt Lake City and the LDS Church she loved there, she had told her husband, "This is where I want to retire, and I want this house here as my home." Little did she realize then that this dream would never come true in any permanent way in the future. Rather, the vagabond life she had been leading, constantly traveling from place to place as her husband's duty assignments dictated, would prove to be a foretaste of what would come later in Dailey's retirement years: she and her husband as rolling stones, always on the move, out-of-doors, seeking solitude.

Dailey's return brought Leone flying, since it was an exciting opportunity for her to be reunited with him after so many long absences overseas. He, on his part, was fully aware of what Leone's managerial skills meant to their marriage, "That's what made my Marine Corps life so easy; she was such a good provider, and she didn't ask me to do those things like buying and selling houses. I gave her power of attorney and she did them. So I could do my Marine Corps work; I didn't have to take off any days to go and handle personal business."

Reporting in at Headquarters, Dailey was taken in hand by the outgoing Sergeant Major of the Marine Corps, Herbert Sweet. There was a ten-day span with the normal routine of the "old hand" reviewing procedures, responsibilities, and activities for the benefit of the newcomer. The two men presented a clear contrast: "Shifty" the colorful, ebullient, out-going personality and Dailey with his quiet, reserved, thoughtful, soft-spoken temperament.

Then came July 31, 1969, and the Post and Relief Ceremony at the Washington Barracks. Dailey received the Sword of Office from the Commandant, General Leonard Chapman, who spoke of the significance of the occasion:

> This is an important day. This is the day the sword of the Sergeant Major of our Corps changes hands. As in the past, strong hands relinquish that hilt, and strong hands receive it. That is our custom. It is a source of our strength....
>
> We recognize the truth that the noncommissioned officer is the backbone of our Corps. It is a working fact that, no matter how brilliant the plan or holy the purpose, it is the noncommissioned officer who ensures the final steps of accomplishment.
>
> To the young enlisted Marine, the senior noncommissioned officer is an example of courage, self-discipline, dedication, and professional skills. To the officer, this man is a strong right arm, a source of wisdom, and a master of plain Marine know-how. To enlisted and commissioned Marines alike, the senior noncommissioned officer is both teacher and keeper of the tradition. And in this he binds together all of the energies of our Corps....
>
> To you, Sergeant Major Dailey, as you take the Sword of Office, congratulations and welcome. I look forward to serving with you.

Dailey's own words on this memorable day were simple and humble, "I look forward to this assignment. I will confer with enlisted men wherever they might be. I will hear their problems and do everything in my power to alleviate them."

Moving into his new office across the hallway from the Commandant and his aide, the new Sergeant Major of the Marine Corps was a figure to command attention: a devout Mormon, a nonsmoker, a non-drinker, trimmed down now to 180 rock-hard pounds, chiseled face, reading glasses, flecks of grey in his hair now, rugged and stern looking, but soft-spoken, with the rows of ribbons that vividly portrayed what he had achieved in his career.

Once again Dailey receives his emblematic sword of office at the Washington Barracks; this time it is for the Office of Sergeant Major of the Marine Corps. The Commandant, General Chapman, presents it to the new incumbent on July 31, 1969.

Dailey looks very formal in this 1970 picture of him as Sergeant Major of the Marine Corps.

Reflecting later on his selection of Dailey, Chapman summarized the factors which had caught his eye:

> He was very senior. He had a Navy Cross which always is good, and he had several other decorations, too. He'd served with distinction as a sergeant major and in his previous ranks. I had not known him personally, but I had met him at the 3d Marine Division when I visited them. He was the picture of a Marine: tall, broad-shouldered, erect, very military. I also remembered him at 8th and I [the Washington Barracks], where he was a model parade ground Marine.
>
> Another thing that commended him to me was that he never went to high school, never went to college. He just finished grammar school. I thought that was commendable: to start with that kind of base and make his way all the way to the top in the Marine Corps. It was kind of a beacon for future young Marines, that you don't have to graduate from college with honors to get to be the top sergeant major in the Marine Corps.

The first day of work for Dailey was August 1, and Chapman called him into his office. Surely the Commandant must have had at least a small question in the back of his mind: "Can this rough-hewn, plain spoken infantryman who has seen so much combat adjust to the sophisticated, intricate staff requirements of Headquarters activities?" There was only one way to get a definite answer to this crucial question, so Chapman gave him his marching orders:

> Sergeant Major, you've been out in the field all the time. You've hardly been back here in Headquarters. You've never had a job like this. Now you've come to be over the whole Marine Corps as the senior advisor to me for the enlisted. You're going to be working with me. You've got access to me any time you want to see me....
>
> I don't want you to write a lot of papers and bring them to me. I want you to come in here and sit down with me and tell me what you saw out there. I'll make a note of it, and if there are things that need to be done, I'll give them to my staff.
>
> And another thing, you're going to be making talks throughout the Marine Corps, and you're going to be making talks to civilians. That you haven't done before. When we go to a base, they've already got a plan for me. They know where they're going to take me. I know that. But you go and don't let anybody show you around. You go and see what's going on.
>
> Now, what do you think about the Corps?

Chapman had set a tone for straight-from-the-shoulder talk, and that's what he received when Dailey immediately replied to his question, "We've got a good Corps, General, but a lot of them had been in Vietnam too long. They booze it up; they're fat. We'd better start with the staff NCOs." Chapman agreed, "You take care of them, and I'll take care of the officers." The two men had a chance to start right away, because they left the very next day for a ten-day inspection trip to Vietnam. It was the first of seven such visits they would make together. Besides the "booze" and the "fat," there were serious problems with drugs and racial friction which they had to face head-on.

Dailey later recounted those tension-filled times, "That's when we were having fighting in the Marine Corps, the Navy, and all of the military. We were having them, before I left, in Vietnam. I saw fights we had to break up all day long. There were drugs, and blacks and whites fighting. It was so bad there; the drugs were so bad. So when I came and took over as the sergeant major, this is when the race problem was a high priority for us."

The trips to Vietnam also mirrored the deteriorating military situation as American troops were pulled out in stages. Dailey remembered:

> I was with the general when there weren't any Army troops left there. We went into the Da Nang area, the Quang Tri area, and the Saigon area. The only people we had left down there were a few Army and Marine State Department personnel, our Embassy Guard. And we also had a few Marines on these communication posts. I was in there shortly before Saigon was overrun.
>
> When we went up in the Quang Tri area we saw this Vietnamese general who had given me all those medals. He told General Chapman then that they'd be overrun. He said, "Our South Vietnamese Army isn't trained well enough yet to keep the Chinese and the North Vietnamese from coming down." It was sad....

There were also, of course, a plethora of stateside trips. As usual, promotions and enlisted housing were always central problems for discussion. It was at this time, however, that the Corps first began to get the money necessary to implement a changeover from its traditional squad bays in barracks to a new style of two- or four-man rooms—with air conditioning yet. The issue of overweight, out-of-condition Marines underwent intensive discussion. Dailey recalled:

> We found a fat sergeant major up there [in Philadelphia]. The commanding officer was also fat. I told General Chapman right then, "You see too many fat NCOs up here. You saw the sergeant major was fat too, didn't you? And the staff NCOs are overweight."
>
> We came back and that's when we started this fitness program for slimming down. That's when the Commandant decided, "We'll get rid of the ones who have over twenty years' service and don't want to be real Marines any longer." I commented, "The whole thing is that they stayed in Vietnam too long. A lot of them just want to put in their thirty years." And that's when he put the 30-year limit on [for enlisted active duty service]. We had to go to the Defense Department for authorization to do that.
>
> Another time we went to Vieques in Puerto Rico, and there were a fat sergeant major, fat staff NCOs, and a fat colonel. We came out of there, and I said, "General you can see what it was like in Vieques." He answered, "Yes. I put that colonel on an overweight program. I told him I'd be back down here in about two months." When we went back in two months, that guy had lost so much weight; he admitted, "I'm a little bit scared." And that sergeant major had lost weight too.

Dailey knew all the tricks of the trade practiced by his fellow senior NCOs. When he and the Commandant visited a unit, he knew that the fat Marines would be tucked away in some obscure back corner—and that's what he would sniff out and head for. Similarly, if the local sergeant major tried to steer him away from a certain barracks, that's the one he would inspect—and there would be the overweight Marines. Dailey was not a good man to try to steer around!

The steady recurrence of the weight problem led to a whole new Headquarters policy of individual evaluation. For a staff NCO to re-enlist, he had to write a letter to Headquarters requesting an extension. There was a loophole in this process, and Dailey promptly put his finger on it:

> At that time, the commanding officer would put an endorsement on the letter and send it in, and then they were reenlisted. But I said, "General, you don't know how that staff NCO looks. He may be fat. The commanding officers—a lot of them are overweight, you know that—let that guy get by. There's only one way we'll stop that. Officers have to send in pictures. Why can't you make staff NCOs do that? When they want to reenlist, they must send a picture in." And we started that, and a lot of big, fat pictures came in.
>
> I happened to be on the Commandant's Evaluation Board. We also had Sergeant Major Puckett, the personnel sergeant major, who sat on it all the time. Here would come in that picture, and you could tell whether he was fat and crummy.

The central issue that the Corps had to face at this time was much more pressing than the question of overweight, which was a surface manifestation of a deeper question. It was an issue that went to the very fiber of what it should mean to be a Marine. How could the Corps maintain high standards and retain enlisted personnel of superior quality while getting rid of the malcontents, drug users, racists, and those who simply were mediocre? Chapman was under the gun and had to face the challenge squarely. It was at this point that Dailey came to him with a decisive plan to bite the bullet. Chapman gave him full credit:

> Sergeant Major Dailey came up with the recommendation that the Enlisted Performance Board (now that we were coming out of Vietnam) curry-comb the records of all the staff NCOs in the Marine Corps, pick out the ones that hadn't measured up in the Vietnam War, and discharge them. It was his idea, and we did that. It was a hard, hard thing to do because we administratively discharged some staff NCOs ("for the convenience of the Government") in the middle of their enlistments or just short of the necessary time for them to get their twenty-year retirement pay.
>
> There were some very unhappy men, but each one had compiled a record that deserved it. He'd not succeeded in the war. He'd gotten poor fitness reports; he'd not been a good Marine staff NCO.... So we discharged them regardless of their time....
>
> The Marine Corps, at that time, was reducing from its war peak of 317,000 down to our permanent strength of just under 200,000. Thus we

were discharging the difference of 100 and some thousand Marines.... It was a tough time, but it left a Marine Corps of about 200,000 who were of really top quality, hard line, severely disciplined, and meeting all the standards of a parade-ground Marine ready for inspection.

Besides the winnowing out of sub-standard Marines, there was the complicated problem of maintaining high standards among those who stayed in. As Dailey ruefully remarked, "Our job was very difficult because outside young people were trying to change this country. That's where our young Marines came from, and that's what we had to deal with." Again, Chapman had to set a firm policy amid a complex web of social change in the civilian world and the resulting impact on the military. With Dailey's help, he acted decisively. As he later recollected:

> There was a lot of racial unrest in the Armed Forces. The Army changed their policies, relaxed their regulations, allowed beer in the barracks, long haircuts. The Navy did the same thing. So I had a conference with Sergeant Major Dailey, just the two of us, one day. I asked him, "What do you think we should do? I'm inclined to come out with a hard, tough Marine Corps stance on discipline and performance and appearance and all things like that." He said, "Do it! That's the best thing you could possibly do for the Corps!" So I did. That's when I came out with the hard-line Marine Corps policy.
>
> Then immediately after that, we made another one of our trips to Vietnam. On the way going out there, we stopped at Hawaii, Japan, Okinawa, and then Vietnam, and some other places on the way back. At each one of those places, I would assemble the officers and make them a speech on the new hard line of the Marine Corps. Meanwhile, Sergeant Major Dailey would assemble the staff NCOs at each of these places, and give them a hard, tough talk on the line the Marine Corps was going to take in all of this.
>
> It was going 180 degrees opposite from the Army and the Navy, and he got great pleasure out of assembling the staff NCOs at a luncheon or a conference or a meeting and giving them the line. He'd pound on the rostrum, and he'd say, "Shape up or ship out!" Which is just what I was saying.

Dailey would never forget the scenes that occurred when some young Marines would approach him. It was serious to them but ludicrous to him when they would vociferously argue, "Look at these pictures of the old Marines, back in 1775. They all had long hair!" His reply was always that "we just can't have it today. We can't be like the Army and the Navy. If we do, we're going to be all the same. We're going to have to stick to this short hair." Afterwards, looking back on those confrontations, he observed, "With the long hair rule, we won out on it, and I think the Marines appreciated it. I talked to a lot of young Marines later on, and they were glad that General Chapman took that stand, because I think it paid off in the long run. We saw that later on the Navy went back to it and the Army went back to it, so I think we stuck to our guns and kept the Marine Corps tradition."

As if these weren't enough major problems to wrestle with, the Corps was handed a new directive from the Department of Defense, which specified that there would be no more use of the term "Negroes"; instead all the military services would use the word "blacks." Chapman and Dailey were scheduled to leave the following day for the Marine air station at Cherry Point, North Carolina. This would be the first of many base visits during which they would team up to explain the new, official terminology. Dailey encountered an interesting reaction on this first trip:

> The idea had come in from the outside with the phrase, "Black is beautiful." When we went to Cherry Point, the Commandant made a speech that afternoon, and he told them there would be no more calling Marines "Negroes"; they would be called "blacks." I had a meeting and spoke to the staff NCOs that night. When the meeting broke up the blacks stayed there, the black staff NCOs. They were older, and they stated "We're not going to be blacks. We're going to be called Negroes." I said, "I can't help it."
>
> They answered back, "The whole thing is that you people are trying to please the young Negro Marine, and he's taking advantage of you. We Negro staff NCOs who built the Marine Corps to what it is today, you're kicking us aside and calling us blacks." We went through that and went through that time and again. I stayed up that night with old Sergeant Major Huff (it must have been 3:00 or 4:00 in the morning before I got in bed) trying to convince him that it wasn't the Marine Corps' idea, calling them blacks instead of Negroes; it was the Defense Department.

Dailey played a central role in still another area of policy. As soon as he came aboard, he went after Chapman on an issue he felt very strongly about: advanced schooling for staff NCOs. Contrasting the comprehensive programs which the Corps had for the continuing education of its officers with its neglect of key enlisted men, Dailey pointed out the need, "If an officer couldn't be there in any situation, the staff NCO had to be able to take over and do his job." The solution was clear to Dailey, and he "talked General Chapman into it—starting a Staff NCO School in Quantico. We needed to train a sergeant—a sergeant who was going to stay in the Marine Corps—or a staff sergeant so he would become a good gunnery sergeant, master sergeant, first sergeant, or sergeant major and master gunnery sergeant. I got the Commandant to agree, so that was the beginning. Later on, one was begun on the west coast."

Besides the major policy issues in which Dailey was so heavily involved, there were always the little episodes which equally illustrated his style. For instance, George Rogers, a first sergeant who was tucked away in charge of a small Marine education program for staff NCOs at Palomar College in California, recounted a revealing vignette of Dailey:

> I was at home on Saturday, and I got a phone call from a woman who identified herself as the staff sergeant who was the administrative chief for Sergeant Major Dailey, and she said that he wanted to talk to me. Well, I was about to tell her to quit kidding and identify who she really was,

because the Sergeant Major of the Marine Corps did not call first sergeants personally on Saturday mornings. I didn't think anybody even worked at Headquarters Marine Corps on Saturday!

But something told me to hang on and, sure enough, Sergeant Major Dailey himself came on the phone and told me that he was interested in the college program, and wanted to know if he could come out and visit us. I was really pleased because no one from anywhere in the Marine Corps had ever officially expressed any interest about coming out to visit us, and, as a matter of fact, no one else ever did in the two years that I was there.

There was a false start when Dailey was unable to make a planned visit—to the acute disappointment of Rogers and his waiting students. His account continued:

That night about 10:00 we were at home, and there was a knock on the door. I went to answer it and there, in all his glory—full uniform—stood Sergeant Major Joseph Dailey. You could have knocked me over with a feather because at this time, as a first sergeant, I didn't have much contact with the Sergeant Major of the Marine Corps. He was somebody who sat next to the throne as far as I was concerned. To have the Sergeant Major of the Marine Corps, at 10:00 at night, standing on my front doorstep was quite an experience! He came in and we sat down and had coffee. He really was genuinely sorry that he hadn't been able to make it. We talked for about an hour I guess. To me that was a real experience because he was a very impressive Marine.

The two men made plans that evening for a visit by Dailey in the following month, and Rogers applauded the successful outcome:

When you think of his impact you would have to be familiar with how he looked. He was probably just what you would imagine when you think of the Sergeant Major of the Marine Corps: a tall, immaculately groomed, erect, stern-looking individual, the type that you didn't argue with just by looking at him. Yet, when he talked, he was obviously very concerned about my Marines, and he was truly interested in what we were doing. He wanted us to be sure that we didn't forget that we were Marines while we were out there in that civilian environment.

Dailey made the same kind of strong impression on younger NCOs as well. A new staff sergeant named Robert Cleary (who would one day follow Dailey's footsteps to the top) always remembered a visit to his unit by the sergeant major: "He was a real believer in taking notes; and then, not only taking notes, he was also a doer. He would act on the notes. That impressed me an awful lot about the man. He looked like the tall, lean, well-set up individual that he was, but he was people-type sergeant major, and really concerned."

When not on trips, Dailey had, of course, the constant rush of normal Headquarters activities that always typified the billet of Sergeant Major of the Marine Corps. There were meetings with Chapman, "sometimes practically every day, other times every two or three days, and frequently two times a day after returning from a trip." Chapman was candid when he later described Dailey's forthright approach, "He'd say, 'General, you'd better do so and so.' I'd ask, 'Why?' and he'd reply, 'I'll tell you why,' and he'd tell me! If it was a written recommendation which came directly to me from him, and I agreed, then I'd farm it out to my chief of staff with a notation, 'I like it; let's do it,' with my initials."

The same forthrightness prevailed in the Commandant's staff meetings with all the senior generals present, as well as Dailey. As Chapman put it, "He had his finger on the pulse of the staff NCOs of the Corps. This was extremely valuable, so he was always asked to comment. Believe me, all those generals didn't intimidate Dailey one bit, and he would speak right out."

Then there were the meetings of the Enlisted Performance Board and other promotion boards. And the mail—always the mail. In one seven-month period 3100 letters were handled. This flood necessitated a tripling of Dailey's office staff (from one to three) and the creation of an additional administrative support section. In addition, there were the hundreds of phone calls, and a steady stream of visitors—most of whom wanted help with a personal problem.

The professional way in which Dailey handled these burdens, combined with the strong leadership he had shown on the major policy problems, more than answered the original question which may have been in Chapman's mind about whether a combat, field Marine had the ability to switch over effectively to a ticklish, complex Headquarters staff billet as the senior enlisted man of the Corps.

That billet was now given a distinctive insignia. Between the three upper chevrons and four bottom "rockers" of a sergeant major was a star, but at this time the single large star was replaced by the traditional Marine globe and anchor with a small star on either side, as the exclusive sign of the Sergeant Major of the Corps.

Dailey's way of working was characterized by a very low-key style. He would never have thought of himself as a deep intellectual, a profound philosopher, a dynamic public speaker, or a colorful personality. Instead, he went his way quietly, doggedly determined to do each job to the very best of his ability. Clinton Puckett saw the strength of his nature, "He was far and away the most dedicated Marine that I've ever known. Hard working, not the most brilliant perhaps, but I have never seen total dedication and hard work in anyone like I've seen in Joe Dailey."

Others of his peers naturally referred to "the best combat record of any Sergeant Major of the Corps," or called him "just a legend in his own time." The Commandant summarized his own feelings in a fitness report he made on Dailey, "One of the great all-time Marines. In all respects the top staff NCO of the Corps. Discerning, determined, demanding, devoted, strong—sets the example and demands the best. He has made major contributions to the quality of the Corps."

After these halcyon days with Chapman, the advent of a new Commandant pushed Dailey's life at Headquarters into a more complicated, different period. On January 1, 1972, General Robert Cushman took over the helm, and the two men, even though they had been together eight years earlier in Headquarters, now had to develop a new working relationship. It was a big change of pace from the way things had been under Chapman. Cushman had been an assistant to Vice President Nixon, and when Nixon became President he made Cushman Deputy Director of the Central Intelligence Agency. This caused subsequent problems in Dailey's mind:

> Since General Cushman had been away from the Marine Corps for long periods, totalling six and a half years, when he came in as Commandant, it was hard to get him to see some of the things that General Chapman had been right on all the time. It was very difficult to convince him of a lot of things that we needed to get done.
>
> His original direction to me was "Continue to march." But then there were things he didn't go along with, things which I recommended that General Chapman and I had done. We really had it on the move and then he relaxed on the overweight problem. That kind of upset me....
>
> I had a good relationship with the staff officers, and so I worked very closely with them and the enlisted in Headquarters Marine Corps on the things that had to go back out into the field. When I came back from a trip with General Chapman, I always brought up the things that had been requested in the field. I told him that we had to take care of them. General Cushman never used to work that way with me. Sometimes my recommendation would just die on his desk unless I got it to the staff.
>
> General Chapman, in contrast, would take my recommendations and personally put them directly into his staff with his signature added to mine. We always sat down and talked about them a long time. I hated to see him go because he was such a fine officer, an outstanding man. But General Cushman and I never had the same relationship. It seemed to me that, after those years in civilian life, it was hard for him to get back into the real life of the Corps; he seemed to have lost a lot of interest.

In spite of these disappointments, Dailey made one last effort. In May, 1972, even though he was then past the retirement age of 55, he requested a two-year extension of duty on the basis of a "desire to work for the new Commandant for at least one year." Cushman approved the request, and the two of them took off in June for a whirlwind eight-day trip—Washington, to Japan, to Okinawa, to the Philippines, to Saigon and Da Nang in Vietnam, back to the Philippines, back to Okinawa, to Hawaii, and finally (exhausted, no doubt) a return to Washington. Apparently, Cushman liked what he saw in Dailey, for he wrote on his June fitness report "an outstanding Marine in all respects."

Nevertheless, it just wasn't working out right, and Dailey decided that he'd had enough. The official word went out in July, 1972, "The Sergeant Major of the Marine Corps will retire on February 1, 1973." Dailey offered a few personal farewell comments: "It's time now to make room for another man.... I think my biggest accomplishments during my tour as Sergeant Major of the Marine Corps came from talking to the sergeants and below—getting their ideas and feelings on the Corps. I had the opportunity to travel throughout the Corps, and I spent over 50 percent of my time talking, but mostly listening, to our younger Marines. These are the men we've got to turn toward to make our Corps better."

The Post and Relief Ceremony took place on January 31, 1973, at the Washington Barracks. A high point was the award by Cushman of the Legion of Merit to Dailey, with a citation, signed by the Secretary of the Navy, which specified, among other attributes, his "high degree of professionalism, executive and organizational abilities, and perceptive judgment." That same day Dailey's status was changed to "Fleet Marine Corps Reserve with benefits of extraordinary heroism." That, coupled with the extra pay authorized for the Sergeant Major of the Marine Corps, gave him an added financial cushion for the years ahead. In August of 1974, he finally reached the magic total of 30 years of service, and full retirement as a civilian began.

At that point Dailey took a very different route from his predecessors and successors. A routine, nine-to-five job in some office or settling down to an inactive home life were the furthest things from his mind. Now he was finally able to give free rein to his fundamental nature as an outdoorsman and wanderer, and finally able to lose himself in true solitude. All those years of moving around in and after his CCC days, all those years of travel in the Corps— these had ingrained in him a restless temperament which now kept him always on the move. He explained, "Many years ago, when I was up in Oregon, I guess in about '39 or '40, I ran into an old gold prospector from Alaska, an old sourdough. He got me interested in gold. So, when I got out of the Marine Corps, I did a lot of gold prospecting, working in the west: Alaska, Washington, Oregon. I even went to Australia and New Zealand and places like that." Ever loyal and resilient, Leone went with him. She even said that she liked it. Some woman!

With this compulsion to travel, Dailey and Leone initially bought a motor home after he retired and covered the state of California. Then it began to feel too crowded there for them, so they moved to a tiny town on the Oregon coast, where they would walk the deserted beaches for miles.

In the summer of 1983 even that began to feel too civilized, so they took off again—this time for the remote areas of Alaska. There they came upon a small Eskimo village, Kotzebue, tucked away on the shores of the Bering Strait, above the Arctic Circle and directly across from Russian Siberia. No roads led to it. Settling here, they could be totally alone. To complete the isolation, he kept it secret that he had a telephone; he hardly ever picked up his mail; and he answered letters even more infrequently.

Of course, he retained enough sense of ordinary living to realize that the way-below-zero temperatures of Kotzebue in the long, brutal Arctic winters were not the best time and place for gold prospecting. So the two of them headed off as perpetual rolling stones, always trying new areas in warmer climates, always moving toward new horizons, always looking for gold. There were trips to the states of Washington, Arizona, and New Mexico, as well as to Hawaii,

Australia, and New Zealand. Not content with this vast range, they planned trips to Europe, South Africa, India, and China. As he characterized this restless energy, "Looking for gold, diamonds, and any kind of minerals that are worthwhile—that's been my life and I still do it." And at seventy-two years of age, the outdoorsman was still fit for this strenuous life, still just as active, trim, and steel muscled as he had been 40 years earlier.

Trying to analyze his psychological motivation, Dailey harked back to a conversation Chapman had had with him:

> When he called me in at Headquarters Marine Corps the day after I took over as the Sergeant Major of the Marine Corps, he sat me down and he said, "Dailey, you've been out in the field. You've been a small unit fighter. But in Washington, D.C. we think big. I want you to think big from here on out, not think little any more as you would down on the battalion or regiment or division level. You must think big, because you're over the whole Marine Corps; you're the 'top kick' of the whole Marine Corps."
>
> He taught me something that day. I'd been thinking little when I came out of the Arkansas Ozark mountains. I was such a little guy there. Then I got in the CCC and I started to think big. When General Chapman came in, he built on that. So in retirement I continued to think big—I was going to hit a big gold mine some day or a diamond mine. That was my work and I would be big. So that was my philosophy in civilian life.

These constant travels made Dailey almost an invisible man to his old comrades in arms—generals and NCOs alike. He truly was isolated. A later Sergeant Major of the Marine Corps wanted to invite him to be a guest speaker at a staff NCO seminar, but it "took two or three months to get ahold of him."

Another time, a sergeant major at the Marine Corps Supply Center in Barstow, California, wanted to have Dailey as the honored guest at the enlisted ball on the Marine Corps birthday. He called the Sergeant Major of the Marine Corps and was told that Headquarters didn't have the faintest idea of where to locate Dailey—"Try his daughter in California." A letter to him at her address brought a resounding silence. Three months later, Dailey walked into the man's office, dusty and in heavy boots, "He looked like a prospector but underneath the Sergeant Major of the Marine Corps was still there; there was no question about that." Dailey explained that he'd been moving around in the southwest desert the whole time, looking for gold, and only picked up his mail every few months. He then agreed to come to the ball, but only in civilian clothes, although as a concession, he would wear his miniature medals.

It was clear that Dailey set his own style and spent his days exactly in the way that he wanted. One of his successors, Sergeant Major John Massaro, later summed him up, "The only title I could put on him is 'free spirit.'"

The carefree outdoor life in the wilderness that he shared with his wife for fourteen years suffered a grievous shock in November, 1987. Leone died. With Leone gone, Dailey knew that his life had to go on; he was lonesome now and the fact that his marriage had been so good made him receptive, in time, to the idea of remarrying. Leone's best friend wanted him "to meet somebody who was good," so she introduced him to a fine lady she knew, June Thompson. A visit up north was arranged, and Dailey then "showed her all over Alaska" in·1988. Things quickly got very serious, but he took pains to clarify the central issue, "If you don't want to travel, you'd better not marry me." Her reply was succinct, "I want to travel." With that understanding, they made the trip to Utah, and were married December 9, 1988, in the Mormon Temple in Salt Lake City. From there it was "back to the outdoors," or, in Dailey's words, "We've been gone ever since. I liked to know what's on the other side of that river, so she got to travel a lot!"

One fundamental strength underpinned this itinerant life. As Dailey volunteered:

> The Church played the biggest part in my life, the LDS, the Mormon religion. I gave it credit for being the Sergeant Major of the Marine Corps. It really helped me in my career. Being a Mormon, I didn't spend a lot of time at the bar. I didn't drink; I didn't smoke; I tried to do hard work. And I think it played a big part in having Leone as a wife, and then having June as an LDS wife. We went to church every Sunday, and we had prayer every morning together as well as at night. We prayed all the time, and we taught our children to pray.

When they did surface in civilization, on returning from some remote place, a priority was to contact their married children: two of his and three of hers. Connie Dailey had been born in February, 1949, and graduated from the Mormon's Brigham Young University. Her sister, Jan, was born in September, 1950, spent three years at BYU and then graduated from Western Kentucky. Their memories of their father are strong—little things, perhaps, but still revealing because they provide a different perspective of Dailey. Connie put it this way, "We never lived on a military base. (Dad felt it wasn't the right place to raise a family.) Most of the time I only remember Dad coming home on weekends, feeling that work and family didn't mix."

When Dailey went aboard the USS *Bremerton*, she continued, "My Dad tended towards being overweight. I remembered him being round and jolly at that time. He was gone out to sea for six months. Without saying a word, he starved himself. When he got off the ship my mother, sister, and I were all waiting. We did not recognize him, he was so thin. It was a great shock to my mother! My Dad always prided himself on how he looked in his uniform. He never put many pounds back on after that."

Ever conscious of his own sketchy education, Dailey was intensely committed to his daughters' schooling. Connie observed:

> My Dad regarded education very highly and made sure both my sister and I had a good education. We have both done post-graduate work above our BA and BS degrees.
>
> When my Dad was the Sergeant Major of the Marine Corps, I was a college student active in anti-war demonstrations. This didn't seem to bother my Dad at all. He felt he was doing what was right when he went to

Vietnam, but he also believed in my right to disagree with the government. My boyfriend then (and husband now) had long hair—a far cry from a Marine hair cut. He liked to tease me, in a good-natured way, about getting him to a Marine barber.

Both daughters returned time and again in their memories to the over-riding theme of travel, travel, travel. In Connie's words, "Home was where my Father hung his hat. I believed he would never stop roaming the earth. My Mother always said they both had gypsy blood."

Jan for her part recollected:

> Most of my childhood memories of my Dad were on vacations. He loved to travel! He had some rather unorthodox theories about vacations: he didn't like motels or tents. He just pulled up to a camp ground, usually very late, and we threw our sleeping bags on the ground (or sometimes, if we were living in luxury, on camp cots) and slept under the stars. Actually we slept in the car most of the time. My Dad liked to drive all night. We often stayed in those campgrounds during the day while my Dad slept. Then we would travel all night again.

> I've awakened in some strange places—tall redwood trees, the sound of alligators in Florida swamps, mountain vistas, deserts, etc. I once asked him why he liked to drive at night, and he said that it was because of all the wars he had been in; he didn't like sitting still at night-time.

Dailey has been a man with two driving passions. First, the Corps: "I kept the same feeling afterwards for the Marine Corps that I had the first time I came in. Those years that I was out of the Marine Corps, I didn't lose my love for it."

And second, the future: "My future plans are travel until I'm to the end of my time. I hope it's a long time!" Life in his remote, isolated village in Alaska led Daily to an unusual conviction: "I am going to be doing a lot of research in the Arctic Ocean area, because I believe the earth is hollow, and there's an opening up in the North Country. I'm healthy. I'm a vegetarian; I eat some fish, but I don't eat meat. I'm in good health. I walk many miles every day. June likes to walk; we walk together and we stay outside. I don't stay inside a building too long." Where he has stayed is outside, traveling and prospecting, the ultimate outdoorsman.

Chapter 7

THE COWBOY WITH
THE THIRST FOR KNOWLEDGE
Sergeant Major Clinton A. Puckett

Joseph Dailey's successor was Clinton Puckett, and one of the most revealing ways to understand the new Sergeant Major of the Marine Corps was to look at his personal, family life. The characteristics of that domestic life—strong initiative, personal flexibility, unwavering focus, driving motivation, strong interpersonal relationships and a self-taught pattern of reading and learning—revealed the essential qualities of his professional life as well. Thus, one can usefully begin a look at Puckett's career, both active duty and retired, through the lens of home, wife, family, and his personal interests.

His retirement home was a modest one, in the shadow of the Navy Yard in Bremerton, Washington, close to where the Marine Barracks formerly stood. Two of his wall decorations bespoke his profession. There was an old-time campaign hat, reserved for Marine Corps drill instructors, which was now bronzed and mounted on a testimonial plaque, and a clock with the Marine Corps emblem. Books were evident everywhere.

He didn't look at all like the big, tall, dominating sergeant major a civilian would picture in his mind's eye. Short at five feet, nine inches, slender at 154 pounds, hair closely cropped but vanishing in front and white above his ears, he had a quiet, studious air about him. His hands, however, were callused from hard labor. The voice was serious, although an occasional smile crinkled his face. The eyes were brilliant blue, alert and observant. This was a careful, thoughtful man. His wife, Liz, was seven-eights American Indian from the Suquamish Tribe. Their relationship went back over forty years to a chance meeting.

Coming ashore in Bremerton from sea duty on a cruiser, Puckett met an attractive young lady named Elizabeth Napoleon at a dance in 1948. Kidding around, he introduced himself as "Tommy Puckett," and that was her nickname for him ever after. They met again when she went down to San Diego for a visit in 1951, and this time it was decisive. They decided to get married, and, to speed things up, went over to Yuma, Arizona. There they were wed on July 7. She resigned her job at the Bremerton Naval Hospital to join her new husband, but in a few short months he was sent overseas, so she had to go home to Bremerton again. On his return, he was welcomed by a five-month-old baby girl, Nancy.

A cyclical pattern had been established: "That's all the Marine Corps knew," Liz said. They would be together in San Diego or Camp Pendleton, then he would go overseas on an unaccompanied tour of duty, while she moved back to Bremerton until he returned again. In 1954 a second daughter, Kathy, joined their family. A happy time together in Hawaii from 1959 to 1962, and a second trip there in 1969-70 were their only respites from the cycle of repeated separations.

Life as a Marine Corps wife was obviously not easy, but Liz handled it with skill:

> We just took it for granted that we had to be there and do it without worrying him. I think that in all the years that he was away, only one time did I ever really tell him when the kids were sick. When I told Tommy, he was going to come right home, because he got very excited where the kids were concerned. But I said to him, "No, you don't come home for this. The Navy's got us all covered."
>
> Actually we were very lucky because, when he was overseas, we always came home here to Bremerton, and the colonel of the barracks would call or come by or the sergeant major would, and they would tell me that if I needed anything they were there to help. So we always tried never to bother him when he was gone.
>
> He was not the type to say bad things, you know. He never got excited or yelled. When I was having my second daughter, Kathy, we went into the hospital, and I told the corpsman there that I was going to have a baby. The corpsman didn't hear me, and my husband came up and

yelled at the corpsman. The whole hospital heard him! The nurses came running out with a gurney and put me on it. I was shocked! I just couldn't believe that he could open his mouth and yell that loud. I think that was one of the very few times ever that I could really say that he got upset.

As for the kids, I would tell him that everybody thought, because he was the Sergeant Major of the Marine Corps or because he was a DI, that the kids were scared of him or he yelled at them like they do in the movies. When I told him to talk to the kids, he talked to them real low and I thought, "Well, I could do that myself."

There came a time in 1970 when they moved to Washington. With Headquarters duty for her husband, Liz recalled:

It was no different actually, just different people. Wherever we've been we've always had fun. We've always made the best of it. The only thing different there was that I had to wear formal clothes, and I'd rather be in a sweatshirt and blue jeans. When he was Sergeant Major of the Corps, every week that he was home we were committed at least five evenings a week. When there was a party or something in Washington, we had our invitation, and he never turned down an invitation.

There were occasional "command performances" for Liz as the wife of the Sergeant Major of the Marine Corps. For example, at one point in the Washington tour of duty, a company was preparing advertisements for the military services. Puckett came home and said, "They requested you to go to New York, and listen to the Marine advertisements and add your input." Many other wives from the different services were also involved, but Liz answered, "I'm not going." He replied, "Yes, you are going," so then she agreed, "Okay, I can go." When the women arrived in New York, a man said, "Now would you please, before you have anything to say, hold up your hand because we're taping." Liz continued the story:

So I sat there, and I was there a long time and never said anything. It was making me nervous. There was this one wife whose husband was Navy and her daddy was an admiral, and she went on and on. She just wanted to sound like she had it so bad. It really made me mad.

Finally I had enough of her and I raised my hand. The man called my name, and I said, "I just want you to understand that I have two daughters, and they've gone through sixteen or eighteen different schools and six different high schools. I just don't see where it bothered them. I don't see where people think that military brats have it so rough. They come out—maybe not the best—but they're just average."

Liz, with her Indian heritage and appearance, had some interesting times in the social swirl of Washington:

My dad was full blood and my mother had just a smidgen of white blood. The kids were seven-sixteenths blood. We would go to the embassy parties, and it would be almost embarrassing because I had never lived on the reservation; I had only visited the reservation when I was a kid.

That would come up in conversation, because I was dark enough so people knew that I was a different nationality. As soon as they would find out that I was Indian, they would expect me to know everything about that. Well, let's face it, I didn't.

With the strong emotions Puckett felt for family life, these experiences of Liz's were truly important to him as well. This empathy is a key to understanding the man as a deeply caring human being.

Together they reached a family watershed in 1975. A radical change of pace in Puckett's professional life—retirement—had an immediate and profound impact on their domestic life. The first week of his doing nothing was a real shock to them both. Liz described her husband, "He never said anything. He never cussed or fussed or growled, but with the look on his face when he was unhappy, he might just as well have; God, he looked miserable!"

Things soon took a turn for the better, as the "Marine underground" of Washington connections went to work. Another retired sergeant major who had the right contacts went to see the personnel director of the Veterans Administration (VA). This man just happened to be a retired Marine captain who greatly admired sergeants major. As a result, Puckett quickly went to work for the VA in Washington. After a few years, the family moved to the VA Regional Office near Augusta, Maine. There they bought a big house, and began a habit of renovation they continued long after.

Transferred to Vancouver, Washington, they redid their house there and lived in it for nearly two years, followed by a VA assignment in Seattle. After thirteen years with the VA, Puckett came to feel that "he'd had enough." Liz's first reaction was one of nervousness, but then, always ready to cope with changes, she exclaimed, "Goodness, now we're really going to have a ball!"

And so they returned for the final time to Bremerton, with Puckett making his second retirement on March 30, 1988. Keeping busy, he took off alone for five weeks in Vancouver, finishing the refurbishing of the house there as a rental investment, while Liz carried on at home. Giving free rein to his fascination with home renovation, he picked up another house in Bremerton and approached Liz, "Well, let's go over there and paint it." She replied, "You've got to be kidding!" But he wasn't, so over they went, fixed it up, and moved in. The urge to move continued, so that house was also put up for rent, and they made one last trip to their final home.

They were an unusual married couple, a real team with an enormous capacity for accomplishing things. For most people the multiple real estate ventures would have been more than enough to keep them busy. While those outside ventures were going on, the inside of each of their houses in turn boiled with the activity of children. Besides their own Nancy, Kathy, and Chris, they had a pattern of taking in still more young people. Because of Puckett's life-long thirst for knowledge and his continuing devotion to the Spanish language, there was one from Spain and then one from Mexico, plus a flow of "kids who had problems in Bremerton." They took it all in stride. As Liz said, "These young people just came into your home and you didn't wonder about it."

Life as a family man was, of course, only one important aspect of Clint Puckett. The other dominant factor was a long career devoted to professional advancement in the Marine Corps. In a tiny town in the back country of Oklahoma, Waurika, he was born on March 6, 1926. Shortly thereafter his family moved to Roswell, New Mexico, where Puckett went to grammar school and started high school. He never finished, and that abbreviated education proved to be a spur to a learning process for the whole rest of his life.

Leaving school, Puckett worked for a year as a cowboy on various ranches in the surrounding area. Then something more compelling took over his life, as he explained:

> World War II was on, and, of course, patriotism was running very high. There must have been 15 or 20 boys my age, friends who considered going to join the Corps. Besides, I had three brothers who were excited about military careers; one later joined the Navy and the other two went into the Marine Corps. I always wanted to jump out of airplanes, however, so I was going to join the airborne forces. But when I went to the recruiting station in Santa Fe on February 18, 1944, the Army recruiter told me that I had to wait until I was drafted, number one, and then, number two, volunteer for airborne and perhaps I would be selected. So I said, "Okay, if that's the way it is, I'll join the Marine Corps."
>
> Incidentally, I was the only one of all my friends to join the Corps. The reason was that we were seventeen years old and consequently needed parental consent. So it wasn't only that my friends didn't want to join the Corps; some parents simply refused to sign.
>
> What was it like? Today everyone knows several people who've had military service. It was not so in 1944. So, if I set foot on the moon today, I would not feel nearly as out of place as I did when I walked aboard the recruit depot at San Diego in 1944.

It was an enormous change from cowboy to Marine private, but Puckett successfully negotiated boot camp and was then sent to the 5th Division at Camp Pendleton. Soon the whole division moved, in August, 1944, to Camp Tarawa on the island of Hawaii. Although designated a rifleman, Puckett, to his confusion, was assigned not to a rifle company, but as the only infantryman in the joint assault signal company. That took him into the bloody assault on Iwo Jima on February 19, 1945. Working ashore with a battalion of the 28th Marines, his job was to relay information to the ships offshore for supporting naval gunfire. Thus he was present for one of the most electrifying moments of World War II: "Even after all these years, I'll never forget the feeling after five days in combat, looking up and seeing Old Glory waving from the top of Mount Suribachi. It was just indescribable."

On the eighth day a vicious Japanese mortar barrage landed right next to Puckett, and he suffered a concussion which caused his evacuation. There was no Purple Heart for this, for, as he noted in a matter-of-fact tone, "there were many, many Marines in those days who, if they weren't badly wounded, just sloughed it off."

Returned to the United States, he soon recovered and was assigned as a military policeman at Camp Pendleton. In April, 1946, exactly twenty-six months after joining up, Puckett's enlistment expired and he was discharged from the Marine Corps. During that entire time he had met only one Marine, a "professional private," who had served prior to the war. Now everyone he knew was going home, and he was, too. There was simply no thought of re-enlisting at that time.

Back in Roswell, after a brief interval drilling water wells with his brother-in-law, he bought a riding stable to rent saddle horses to dude ranch visitors. There was a serious romance in his life at that time, but a crushing blow fell when the girl married someone else. That did it; his bruised reaction was, "It's the Marine Corps for me." Signing up again in July, 1947, he returned as a private first class (PFC) to the San Diego Recruit Depot. There he was, for a short time, a member of Post Troops. Although his Military Occupational Specialty (MOS) was as a military policeman, he was put to work in a communications store room. One day a request came in to the depot to fill a quota for Marines to serve aboard the heavy cruiser, U.S.S. *Columbus*. Since Puckett had been working outside his MOS, he was selected as one of those to go to sea duty in September, 1947.

It was a radically new life: going on board at San Pedro, California, a spell in dry dock, and then heading for the Atlantic Ocean through the Panama Canal. The Marine Detachment numbered forty-six, many of them on one-year enlistments and thus with little experience, "probably the biggest bunch of characters that I have ever known in my entire life." Puckett, still a PFC but a little bit older and with a combat record, was made a squad leader. Then, in May, 1948, he was promoted to corporal by a commanding officer who took a professional interest in the young man, and "probably more than any other senior Marine in all my service, he tried to show me what being an NCO was all about."

The ship made two trips to Europe. In the summer of 1948 it was a cruise for midshipmen from the Naval Academy. The next summer, the *Columbus* served as the admiral's flagship, based in Plymouth, England. As Puckett later sketched it, "We were constantly running around Europe. Our longest cruise was 10 weeks and the longest we ever stayed in port was three weeks. Our ship hit fifty-two foreign ports and fourteen different countries in a fifteen-month period. And I was the greatest 'liberty hound' on board!"

When the *Columbus* finally returned to the Charleston Navy Yard in Boston, Puckett's tour of sea duty ended. Marines with less than six months left to do in their enlistment were assigned to recruit depots. Because Puckett had originally joined west of the Mississippi, he was sent to San Diego. Arriving there in 1950, he was interviewed by the depot sergeant major and given a choice. Did he want to go to the guard company or the drill field? "The choice was obvious. I did not want to be an MP."

Since these were the days before there was such a thing as a Drill Instructors School, his training took place informally by osmosis in the drill instructors' lounge: "We learned from each other. It was as simple as that. We mimicked those men who were good, and discarded the voices and activities of those who were not."

A few months later the Korean War began, and the Marine Corps pulled out its most experienced NCOs from all over the world to form the 1st Provisional Brigade for immediate combat. This thrust new responsibilities on Puckett, "Corporal drill instructors who had experience became senior DIs. At one point I was the senior DI of two platoons, and upon their graduation I got a letter from the father of one of the recruits who addressed me, in the letter, as the 'Commandant of Platoon Such-and-Such.' It was a letter of thanks. He said that I had accomplished, in eight short weeks, what he had failed to do in 18 years: make a man of his son."

The heavy action in Korea made continuous demands on manpower, and so, in September, 1951, Puckett, now a sergeant, joined a rifle company in the 5th Marines in Korea. With the wartime acceleration in promotions, he made staff sergeant in October, 1951. As a result, his company commander wanted him to take charge of a machine gun section, but Puckett resisted, "I hated machine guns. I wanted nothing to do with them; I wanted a rifleman's job." He received it as a platoon guide, which led to a perilous situation in June, 1952.

He had taken a daylight reconnaissance patrol out in the saddle between two outposts that became famous later as Reno and Vegas. On that patrol, he found that the Chinese Communists were preparing new positions in an old trench line. That area had changed hands several times over the past months, so he returned to his own area to work up an ambush plan for that night: two fire teams, reinforced with an A-6 machine gun. Puckett recounted what happened next:

> We moved out late in the afternoon, going in the direction of an outpost manned by another company, and then moved up to the saddle at dusk and set up. Fifteen minutes later we made contact with a Chinese force, which was of such strength that it shattered my patrol. I stepped into a hole in the side of the trench to provide cover, and I heard my Marines yelling that they were wounded, and then I heard Chinese voices all around there. They traveled in three-man burp gun teams, and I could hear them moving up the trench. When they approached my position, like three, four feet away, I opened up with my weapon, which was a Thompson submachine gun, into the chest of the lead Chinese.
>
> After I dropped the lead man in their burp gun team, the other two members pulled back down the trench and sprayed it with fire, pelting me with rocks and pebbles. Their grenades and small arms fire then abated a bit. Chinese soldiers continued to yell directions, but I could no longer hear Marine voices. A few moments later I heard another burp gun team coming down the trench from the other direction. That meant that my men had either been killed or they were no longer in the trench. When the team sounded as if they were about ten feet from my hole, I sprang up, wheeled around, and shot the three of them (thus accounting for four dead). Then I quickly vacated the premises.

When he got up to the outpost of the other company, he discovered that he was the only one of his team there. But a platoon leader consented to give him two of his own Marines to go back down to the trench area. There they made enemy contact again, and Puckett continued:

> My Thompson sub jammed. First of all it misfired. I jerked the operating rod to the rear, since a Thompson fires on the forward movement of the bolt. In such a situation, that bolt going forward to pick up that .45 caliber round sounds like a freight train coming round the bend. I felt that I could have sung "Old Lang Syne" three times before it ever hit home. And when it did, it went clunk! I jerked it to the rear, fired two or three more rounds, and it jammed again. So I got all my grenades off in the air at once and left again.
>
> On my way back to the outpost I discovered most of the members of my patrol, and we helped carry the more severely wounded up to the outpost. When we got back to the outpost, I told the platoon leader that he had lost his two Marines who had gone with me. He assured me that that was the same thing they had told him about me. So we all survived!
>
> As it turned out, out of the sixteen men on that patrol (fifteen Marines and one corpsman), all were wounded except one man. I got grenade fragments in my left hand, which resulted in a Purple Heart Medal.

That kind of leadership and courage did not go unnoticed. Following the guidelines that required truly exceptional performance in maximum danger, a recommendation for a Navy Cross made its way through all the upper echelons of command to the Secretary of the Navy. He concurred and made the award, citing Puckett for "extraordinary heroism...valiant leadership, and inspiring fighting spirit...."

Not long after, Puckett's tour of duty in Korea ended, and he was sent briefly to Camp Pendleton and then back to San Diego in 1953. There he was assigned to the newly created Drill Instructors School. With his previous experience as a DI, Puckett sailed through the course, graduating first in his class, which led to his assignment as an instructor at the school. He was by now a Technical Sergeant.

There was a temporary interlude in the summer of 1954, when Reserve Marines trained there in San Diego. Puckett worked closely with them, and ended up their chief enlisted Marine, called a field sergeant major.

On his return to his previous billet at the school, he recalled:

> We had just some unbelievably good Marines: some of the most outstanding Marines that I served with in my entire career. It was a tough, demanding job: very prestigious. From the entire depot, we could select any Marine whom we wanted to work at the school. Many of the staff NCOs, though, did not want to join us because of the rigorous schedule and hard work involved. But there was one very young, sharp special subjects instructor in the recruit training regiment who was eager to come to the school. This was John Massaro, who had been in my battalion in Korea, and he would later follow in my footsteps.

Massaro remembered well those times with Puckett, "On many occasions, he came down and monitored the instruction that I was giving. Prior to my finishing that tour, I also went to Drill Instructors School as a student and later on as an instructor. About a year of that period of time I spent instructing right along with Clint Puckett, who was the drill master."

By July, 1955, it was Puckett's turn to go overseas again. Although most of his contemporaries were going to Okinawa, in the mysterious workings of the military, he was unexpectedly sent to serve with the Korean Marine Corps as an advisor. Landing in Seoul, he boarded a truck, headed north, and found himself in exactly the same area where he had been three years earlier. The next day, however, his orders were changed and he went south to Chinhae near the port of Pusan, where the 1st Provisional Marine Brigade had first landed five years earlier. As he described it:

> It was an old Japanese seaplane base: a combination of recruit depot, infantry training regiment, supply depot, naval academy, all of these things together. I was the only infantry advisor there for many months, although there were thirteen enlisted U.S. Marines and three U.S. Marine officers.
>
> At that point in time, the Korean Marines had tremendous spirit but no depth. That's all there was to it; they were not professional. As I would approach a training area, they would have a Korean Marine posted to watch for my jeep. His job was to wake up the officers and staff NCOs as I approached.
>
> I was an advisor to the recruit training depot, the equivalent of an infantry training regiment, as well as to their demonstration battalion. I also visited their naval academy—anything that had to do with infantry, I visited and made reports, including suggestions on how to improve their training. While I was there I made master sergeant in October, 1955.

One particular training experience stuck in Puckett's mind:

> It was difficult to measure progress. As one particular example, they had a field firing exercise where they fired at a huge rock. The vegetation was beaten down around the rock. I thought it was tremendous, because any time the bullets ricocheted off the rock you could tell it was a hit. But they were not satisfied. They wanted to build a rifle range, and they did. The butts were so beautifully landscaped with rocks and grass and water channelled around it: a beautiful job....
>
> There was one critical problem: the targets they built were so close to the earth berm that, when you ran the target up, it scraped the paper off the target! That is one memorable case of advising them on how to operate which I'll never forget.

One of his interpreters—amazingly—had been his company interpreter when he was there during the war: a PFC Lee. They were friends when he was there earlier on his combat tour, and they became fast friends on that later tour.

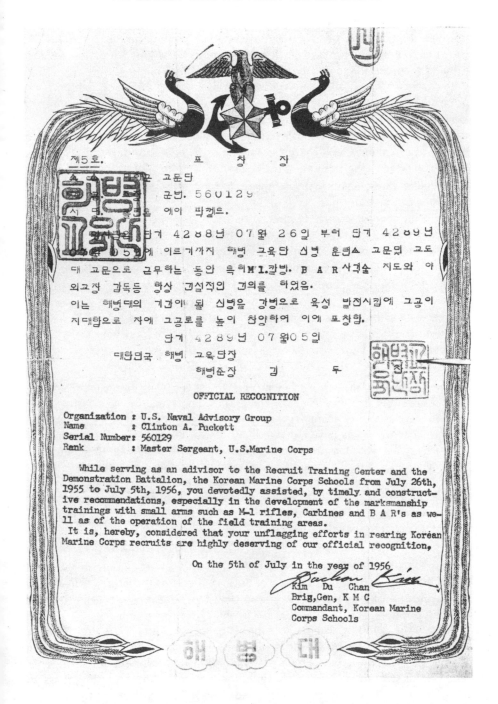

In rather ragged English, the Korean Marine Corps officially expresses its appreciation to a U.S. Marine master sergeant in 1956.

Fourteen months of that unusual duty came to an end in September, 1956, and Puckett returned to Camp Pendleton. The Commandant had reinstated the titles of first sergeant and sergeant major, so he asked for a first sergeant's job and received it in a company of the 2d Infantry Training Regiment. Along with administrative duties, he ran field exercises with the men of the company. (Upon finishing recruit training, all Marines then, regardless of their ultimate assigned technical specialty, went through basic infantry training first.)

Puckett made a lateral transfer in the spring of 1957, becoming the regimental operations chief (S-3). There he had 150 staff NCOs under him, as he was responsible for all the training of the regiment. That brought his formal promotion, making him officially a first sergeant. In May, 1957, the word came through that the Commandant had created a new billet, Sergeant Major of the Marine Corps. That news lit a fire in Puckett, "As soon as the position was established, that became my goal in life."

This same month, a year later, was marked by a very emotional experience. He received special orders to fly to Washington to represent the Marine Corps in the Memorial Day ceremonies at the Tomb of the Unknown Soldier in Arlington Cemetery. He was chosen from eight active duty enlisted Marines who had been awarded the Navy Cross, along with two staff sergeants. They would follow in the footsteps of the one Marine who had helped bear the body of America's World War I Unknown Soldier to the Tomb thirty-seven years earlier.

Puckett recalled that day with a tremor still in his voice:

> I have had many honors in my time. (I was very, very fortunate in that regard.) But that was singularly the greatest honor that I have ever had: to serve as a body bearer for the interment, at Arlington Cemetery, of the Unknown Soldiers of World War II and Korea. We trained at Fort Myer, in Virginia, with the Army's Old Guard, and were even made honorary members of the Old Guard. We were originally stationed at the Marine Barracks in Washington, D.C., but you had to practice with caskets, and you can't very well carry caskets around the Capitol Building in daylight hours. Consequently we trained in the wee hours of the morning. It was a tremendous experience.

Then another transfer brought him, in April, 1959, to the Marine Barracks at Pearl Harbor. As first sergeant of the guard and security company, Puckett found that "it was a wonderful tour of duty: quarters on the post, a four-minute walk from the office, an historic site, a beautiful setting. I was able to install evening parades as a regular feature in the barracks routine."

February, 1960, marked one more big step in Puckett's career. He was selected to be a sergeant major, a distinction hard to achieve in a peacetime Marine Corps with fewer sergeants major than full colonels. As soon as he received his warrant, he wrote a letter to the Commandant requesting reassignment to the next available sergeant major billet. Passing through the chain of command on its way, the letter caught the eye of "some staff officer who saw it as an effort to leave Pearl Harbor, so new orders were not forthcoming."

Clad in a shooter's uniform, Puckett wins the overall aggregate trophy at Pearl Harbor in 1961.

Staying on, Puckett found an opportunity to develop a new skill: competitive shooting. There were intramural matches island-wide for Marines, as well as Pacific Division Matches. While he modestly classed himself as "a rank amateur" in the latter, he cut quite a swath in the former. There the major trophy was for the top aggregate score in both rifle and pistol, and he became the first Marine to win it for two consecutive quarters. His talent would bear fruit later in combat.

Finally, in May, 1962, he received the sergeant major billet he had sought earlier. He returned again to Camp Pendleton, to the 1st Reconnaissance Battalion of the 1st Division. The training there concentrated on "means of entry." This meant intensive practice with rubber boats, landing from submarines and small craft, mountain climbing, and the like. "I was still young enough to thoroughly enjoy playing PFC!"

The battalion was located in a barracks on the beach, and the force reconnaissance company had its office on the second deck there. This enabled Puckett to observe with approbation the gunnery sergeant of that company, a friend from their days together as DIs, John Massaro. Two years of "recon" training ended when Puckett was moved over to another area of Camp Pendleton, to take over as a battalion sergeant major in the 5th Marines in April, 1964.

It was a pregnant juncture in Marine Corps history. Although the conflict in Vietnam was in its early stages, it was already steadily expanding. Some time earlier the Corps had instituted a "transplacement" cycle system. This called for units such as battalions or squadrons to move as an organic whole to the Western Pacific and replace similar units there, which would then rotate back to stateside duty. With the 5th Marines about to go overseas, Puckett found some good elements in his new assignment, "For the first time in my career, if you rated a staff sergeant and two lance corporals, you actually had two lance corporals and a staff sergeant. You had second lieutenants commanding platoons. You had captains as company commanders. The battalion was at total strength. We were together for the entire stateside cycle, and that battalion hadn't changed at the end of the cycle when we transplaced, the last battalion to do so as a unit."

After a brief stop in Okinawa for final combat training, the battalion arrived in Vietnam in September, 1965, and was redesignated as part of the 3d Marines: same people, new label. Taking up a Tactical Area of Operational Responsibility (TAOR) in the northwest segment of the Da Nang enclave, the battalion had a complex and difficult mission. Puckett explained it:

> When we first got there, we had companies deployed around our TAOR. And as we drove down the road in our Mighty Mites, the helicopter-transportable jeep made of aluminum (a worthless piece of trash), we would see a Vietnamese wearing black pajamas and a coolie hat; perhaps if it was raining he might be wearing a palm leaf rain cape, barefooted or sandals, with some kind of weapon slung over his shoulder. It might be a Thompson sub or an M1 carbine. So the question was always, "Is he a Viet Cong or isn't he?" The only way you could really tell was, if he smiled at you, you could almost safely presume that he was friendly.
>
> Those were Popular Force [PF] troops under the command of the village chief, and, when Marines would go out on patrol, they would come very, very close to having fire fights at night with these Popular Force troops also on patrol. Fortunately, within my battalion, we never did, but we came very, very close many times.
>
> It was frustrating to our Marines, because they would see someone out in the brush in a makeshift uniform such as I've described. They would capture him, take him to the village chief, and the village chief would say, "This is one of my PFs. Moreover this is the third time you've arrested this cat this week." So it made us seem stupid to the village chief, and of course we became suspicious of him, because we would say, "No matter how many VC we capture, you always say that they're your PFs."

To deal with the problem, the battalion commander initiated a program of putting a squad of Marines down in the village with a platoon of Popular Force. It worked so well that he rapidly expanded that into a company. Since this was an innovative step, beyond normal operations, the first thought was that the Marine company commander would be one of the battalion staff officers. They, however, already had full-time jobs and were not interested in that assignment. Thus the battalion commander asked Puckett if he would be willing to take that job, and he jumped at it. This put him in a unique position,

"I was one of the few enlisted Marines who commanded a 286-man company in combat in Vietnam. I had a platoon in three different villages, and I moved from one to the other. So, while I had a company headquarters in one village, I frequently was in the other two. And we sure had our share of fire fights with the Viet Cong."

That extemporaneous role for a sergeant major provoked a bit of discussion among some officers. As Puckett recounted it:

> Some officers resented it, because the sergeant major was the only man in the battalion to whom you couldn't say, "Your job is such and such from this hour to that hour." I figured that my job was to be "in charge of everything within sight or hearing and ultimately responsible for nothing. Get involved with everything having to do with the enlisted Marines, but remember that there's always an officer who is ultimately responsible." Therefore, it requires a great deal of tact and diplomacy to be able to get something done with the concurrence and support of a company commander, and the S-3 [operations] officer, and the battalion commanding officer. It's difficult!
>
> The job of sergeant major was obviously, to me, a major topic of conversation in the Officers Club. In fact, year after year (and I was a sergeant major for a long time) each battalion commander whom I got would say, "Okay, Sergeant Major, let's sit down and discuss what your job is." They didn't know. The job of the sergeant major depended largely on the strength and background of the individual concerned.

Puckett went on to give another example of the fluid role of a sergeant major, citing the "Mixmaster" procedure in Vietnam where three and a half of his companies would be called a "battalion," and then sent off on an operation. The men remaining behind, augmented by rifle companies from other battalions, still had to fulfill all the original responsibilities within the battalion's TAOR. Yet nearly 75 percent of the original battalion had gone off on that operation.

Puckett outlined the duties that befell him:

> Normally, the executive officer is left in charge of the part of the battalion that stays behind. My battalion commander left me behind on an operation, and I'll hate him until the day he dies (or I die) for leaving me back there and not letting me go out with my Marines. With the shortage of officers, I was acting as the S-2 [intelligence officer]. There were only two other officers, other than the executive officer, left there with the battalion. So we were operating the battalion in twelve-hour shifts, with this captain and me running the Combat Operations Center. During my twelve-hour tour, I was in fact operating in the name of the battalion commander.
>
> I was giving directions, hopefully right directions, and done tactfully and respectfully, to company commanders. During the daylight, on more than one occasion, the executive officer (who commanded the battalion) had to go to Da Nang. The S-3 had to go to the regimental headquarters. That left me in command of the battalion! I commanded the battalion under those conditions for up to six hours: very unusual.

By September, 1966, Puckett's Vietnam duty had drawn to a close. The quality of his leadership there had been such that he was awarded (two years later) a Navy Commendation Medal with Combat "V." As one of his peers commented, "Clint was one of those guys who took care of the troops. He was deeply interested in them and really did one great job on their behalf."

In a major shift in duties, he now went on the staff of the inspector-instructor of a battalion of the 4th Division (Reserve) in San Bruno, California. This was not by choice, he confessed:

> First of all, I fought it. I did not want to go on independent duty; I wanted to stay in the infantry. As it turned out, it was one of the most interesting, challenging, and, I think, rewarding tours of duty I ever had. The Reserves wanted to do a good job. They were faced with mobilization, and they never knew, from week to week, whether or not the unit would be activated.

> The sergeant major of my unit had assumed all the responsibility for getting our Reserves to their summer training. If he had dropped dead of a heart attack, the battalion couldn't have gone at all, because only he knew what to do and how to do it. He did almost everything alone. He just didn't have any idea of how to operate properly as a sergeant major—simply because he had no training for that rank and no one had ever shown him.

> With a little coaching from me, that battalion made (through him and his staff NCOs) what I thought was significant progress in readiness during my two-year tour of duty with it.

> With our battalion, though, there was a constant problem of getting sufficient training. This was also during the Haight-Ashbury heyday. There was a lot of anti-war, anti-military sentiment reflected by some of the Reservists. Let's face it: many of them joined the Reserves to avoid active military service. It presented a constant leadership problem.

It was back to Vietnam again for Puckett in September, 1968, this time as regimental sergeant major of the 7th Marines. This was a good job, he remembered, "I had a regimental commander [Colonel Herbert Beckington] who felt that anything good that any of his Marines did made him look good. Unfortunately some officers feel that, if they recognize one of their Marines, it somehow detracts from their status. That regimental commander was not of that type. He let me go to the field to be with my Marines."

The opportunity to do that was not long in coming. On his previous tour in Vietnam, Puckett, as an old match shooter, had been greatly distressed to see the ineffective and improper use of two-man sniper teams. Now he was in a position to take some corrective action. He described the situation:

> In the very first week, on Hill 10 we saw North Vietnamese Army soldiers on a ridge line 1100 meters away, and the snipers were shooting at them and couldn't even scare them. Being in the regimental headquarters, I soon found that the snipers were not sufficiently trained. Their equipment was in a bad state of repair, and I started working with them. Their platoon

leader was one of the junior officers in regimental headquarters; this was an additional duty for him, and he didn't have the knowledge, the time, or the energy to devote to them.

I finally got frustrated and asked the regimental commander if I could take over those snipers as their platoon leader, on an additional duty basis. He agreed and, during July the following year my twenty-three or twenty-four men registered seventy-three confirmed kills and captured three of the enemy.

Back at regimental headquarters, Puckett quickly noticed the leadership qualities of two men. In one of his battalions there was a very able sergeant major named Henry Black, and in the headquarters company a fine young gunnery sergeant named David Sommers. Their careers would subsequently follow Puckett's to the top-most rung of the enlisted ladder.

Puckett himself got into heavy combat missions at that time. He recalled one such:

> We had a battalion in what was called the Arizona Territory where there was strong activity. As a matter of fact, there were a couple of North Vietnamese Army battalions which had been sent there to wipe out one of our parent battalions (which was providing a screening force on our side of a river for Operation Oklahoma Hills). We had several battalions under our operational control, including South Vietnamese battalions. One of these was from an adjacent regiment, across the river. It was going down late in the afternoon to link up with our parent battalion and I hitch-hiked along.
>
> Shortly after crossing the river, almost at sunset, we had contact and were forced to call a halt for that day. The next morning, as the battalion was preparing to move out, I looked in my hiding hole and discovered an enemy soldier, who led me to another hiding hole that was completely camouflaged, and I dug out two more NVA soldiers.

A close interrogation of the three captured men disclosed valuable intelligence information, and the regimental commander recommended Puckett for a medal. At the end of his tour of duty he received a Bronze Star with Combat "V" to add to his earlier awards.

Leaving Vietnam in September, 1969, he moved to the billet of sergeant major for Camp Smith in Hawaii. This was the headquarters for the Fleet Marine Force, Pacific (FMFPac). His stay there was brief, however, as he reflected:

> I went to Camp Smith for a three-year tour of duty. At that point in time, the sergeant major of FMFPac was planning to retire within the next two or three months. I was sent there, as the sergeant major of Camp Smith, with the knowledge that I would get a shot at being selected as the sergeant major of FMFPac when that other sergeant major retired.
>
> It didn't work out that way, because one of my regimental commanders from my second tour in Vietnam [then Colonel Beckington, later a lieutenant general] called me on the phone, and he told me that he was considering ordering me back to Headquarters Marine Corps for one of two

positions. One was the sergeant major of the Personnel Department, and the other was first sergeants/sergeants major monitor, who cuts orders on all first sergeants and sergeants major within the entire Marine Corps.

He told me that he realized I'd just gone there on a three-year tour of duty, and this was only eight months later. So he gave me an opportunity to contest the assignment before he cut my orders. He advised me to go home and talk with my wife, Liz, and the kids (who were in Hawaii with me), and then to call him back on Monday. My first reaction was, "General, I've never had a staff assignment. I'm an infantryman."

When Puckett, after a family conference, did not contest the assignment, off to Washington he went. Arriving there in July, 1970, he took over the duties of personnel sergeant major, "I discovered that the job was nothing less than taking care of all enlisted Marines." (Years later, in retirement, he expanded his scope further, serving on the Secretary of the Navy's Advisory Committee on Retired Personnel.)

Analyzing the way he now had to work, vis-a-vis the other top enlisted NCOs at Headquarters, Puckett put it this way:

There is a close working relationship between all three. The Sergeant Major of the Corps is on the road—travels—50 percent of the time. The personnel sergeant major rarely travels and is the point of contact for all enlisted Marines who come to Headquarters Marine Corps seeking reassignment, or a solution to their problems, unless they have someone else specifically to come to.

The first sergeants/sergeants major monitor's job has such a wide impact because of the people he cuts orders on. Thus he needs to coordinate with, and to get the opinions of, the sergeant major of the Personnel Department and the Sergeant Major of the Corps, particularly when you start talking about the most senior positions, those that have a boss who is a commanding general.

These three individuals know personally, or certainly by reputation, almost all sergeants major in the Corps. They know their background, their strengths, any weaknesses, and they are trying to fit round pegs in round holes. If you're talking about very senior positions, for example a division sergeant major or a wing sergeant major, then the three of us would try to identify someone who was available to go, and who would work well with that particular commanding general.

As sergeant major of the Personnel Department (and later as Sergeant Major of the Corps), I had commanding generals call me for lengthy discussions requesting the assignment of a senior sergeant major. They would simply refuse to believe that that's the job of the first sergeants/sergeants major monitor. I could influence him, but I couldn't tell him what to do.

Nevertheless, Puckett was able to influence the assignment of an old acquaintance, John Massaro, who was sent to Okinawa as the sergeant major of the air group there. Later on, Massaro commented, "That particular assignment was pretty much hand picked for me by Clint Puckett, who was the personnel sergeant major of the Marine Corps. By that time I'd also learned that other people knew more about what I needed than what I thought I needed to round out my career."

One of the men who came to Puckett for help was the first sergeant of the ceremonial guard company at the Washington Barracks. He needed a certain type of staff NCO for that particular high profile duty, and he knew where to go to find it. The inquirer was Leland Crawford—and he, too, would later climb to the peak.

After two and a half years in his sensitive personnel post, Puckett received a phone call one day in December, 1972, from the Commandant's office, "General Cushman would like to talk with you later on." In the quiet of that evening, long after everyone else had left for the day, the two men met. It was then that the Commandant revealed that he had selected Puckett to become Sergeant Major of the Marine Corps, adding, "Go home and tell your wife but no one else, until I make an official public announcement."

So it was that Puckett realized his goal, sixteen years after he had first secretly set his mind to it, and nearly twenty-eight years after he first enlisted as a private. Looking back, he admitted, "I used to be arrogant enough to think, 'I am going to become the Sergeant Major of the Corps.' But the closer I came, the more I realized it was like lightning striking twice. I knew that I was a contender. I knew of my competitors, but one never really knows. To say that I was elated won't scratch it." (His wife's reaction was much blunter, "He expected it.")

The selection process had followed the usual arduous course. Starting four months earlier, a board of nine colonels and lieutenant colonels had screened the records of some 300 of the most senior sergeants major in the Corps. They had selected twenty-five whom they considered "fully qualified." These were then whittled down to three finalists by a panel of three general officers, and then the Commandant, General Robert Cushman, made his personal choice.

There was one rough spot, however, before Puckett formally took office. Seeking to learn what lay ahead, he approached his predecessor, Joe Dailey. The response was brusque. Whether it was reluctance to turn over the reins, or because of personal friction between the two men (or even, conceivably, because of Dailey's dissatisfaction over the current functioning of the billet under Cushman?), Dailey never even congratulated Puckett on his selection for the billet.

The big day finally came on February 1, 1973, and the sixth Sergeant Major of the Marine Corps moved into his new office and took charge. A newspaper, in reporting the occasion, aptly termed him "The Enlisted Man's General."

What would be the ground rules in his working relationship with the Commandant? As Puckett remembered:

> One of the first things that happened was that General Cushman arranged for me to come in, and we discussed how I would operate. He decided that, because of the lack of facilities on his plane, my wife, Liz, could

Puckett (center) receives the Sword of the Sergeant Major of the Marine Corps from the Commandant, General Cushman (right), on January 31, 1973. Dailey, his predecessor (left), keeps his eyes straight ahead at rigid attention.

Official picture of Puckett as the new Sergeant Major of the Marine Corps in February, 1973, with his 19 ribbons topped by the Navy Cross.

make trips with us as long as they were not overnight trips. I had posed the question of what he wanted on this because some of the wives of the senior enlisted men from the other services traveled with them quite frequently. I just wanted it clarified.

He also told me that he did not want written trip reports. He would like me to brief him, verbally, after the trips, and he stressed that he wanted me along when he visited major Marine commands world-wide. Those were the only directions he gave me.

So Puckett was, in many ways, on his own, but the twenty-eight years of widely varied service stood him in good stead. He had little trouble in taking hold of the job. Frank Rauber had once described him as "more of a detail man than some others," and this ability enabled Puckett to keep close tabs on the voluminous flow of business. Beside the manifold duties at Headquarters, he was on the road 50 percent of the time, with half of that involving travel with the Commandant. They started off each year, as the Commandant's rule, with visits to each of the recruit depots, followed by trips to most major commands once during the year. Overseas, they made at least one trip to the Pacific and one to Europe each year. The situations they encountered are best described in Puckett's own words:

> When we went overseas, one must understand that the Commandant was invited to a foreign country as a guest of that country. While there, he would visit the foreign Marines, if they existed. Whether Taiwan, Thailand, Indonesia, Philippine Marines, Dutch Marines, or the Royal Marines, he was there to visit the Marine Corps of those countries. Of course, we always have a Marine Security Guard with our Department of State there, and when we would go to one of those countries we always visited them also. I, of course, got into it in a little more depth. I frequently stayed there attending a dinner with them, inspecting, listening, and so forth. And this ranged all the way from Paris to Hong Kong.
>
> The foreign Marine units would present a sharp contrast from one country to the other. (Although all Marines, U.S. or Chinese, have one thing in common and that's esprit de corps, and the uniforms were similar also.) Some of the corps that we visited were not stationed at a base, but were deployed in the field, Korean Marines as an example. And the same thing on Taiwan. The Philippine Marines were committed to combat with the Communists when we were there, and they were suffering casualties. That's a very, very small corps, but the uniforms are very similar; the attitude or esprit de corps are close copies of U.S. Marines.
>
> The Dutch Marines had both draftees and volunteer forces. The volunteer forces were very much like our Marines I remember from World War II. And they spoke excellent English. Except for the emblem that they wore, it was hard to tell them from the U.S. Marines. But the draftees: long hair, and they were rather different!
>
> At most places the reception, the treatment of me, was just unbelievable in the red carpet that was rolled out and the events that were scheduled.

Some foreign corps staff NCOs don't have any real status, and I had plaques that I presented particularly to them. We visited Taiwan and we were put up at the Grand Hotel where our Marines were deployed. We only had two American Marines there, a bird [full] colonel and a gunnery sergeant. The gunnery sergeant came up to my room, and I told him about the plaque which I wanted to present. He told me, "Well, Sergeant Major, the only difference between their master sergeant and a private is in pay! They work side by side doing the same job; they have no prestige whatsoever, no position, no station. Everything is for the officers."

The next morning Puckett was on a tour, and a bright, alert young Chinese Marine approached him. He spoke excellent English and had trained at the U.S. Marine Camp Hansen on Okinawa. He informed Puckett that he was the Sergeant Major of the Chinese Marines. The American gunnery sergeant later maintained that, the day before the Commandant's group arrived, that man had been a lieutenant colonel and the Chinese had simply named him "Sergeant Major" just because Puckett was visiting there with that rank.

The story of the trips continued:

When I visited Korea with the Commandant, I met the Sergeant Major of the Republic of Korea Army who had only eight years in that grade. Then there was the Sergeant Major of the Philippine Marines and also the Sergeant Major of the Chinese Marines. What I'm saying is that there are senior enlisted now in any number of countries around the world, but it all stems from three gentlemen who set the pattern: Bill Bestwick, Frank Rauber, and Tom McHugh.

As to our Legation Guards, I was amazed to find the status of the Marines. Every place we have an embassy or legation we have what we call a Marine House. They may very well be in a hotel or on a certain floor, perhaps in a villa, maybe (as in the case of Thailand) they have twin quarters with a beautiful swimming pool in between.

I particularly recall Luxembourg. We had five men there with a staff sergeant in charge; that staff sergeant had been the armorer with my regimental sniper platoon in Vietnam, so I knew him very well. I found that on Friday evening they opened the Marine House and, of course, its bar. (I think that's where the phrase "TGIF" came from.) They always have a party then at the Marine House. And the drinks are something like 15 cents, 25 cents.

But over the year, they accumulate quite a sizable fund and they stockpile that. Those five Marines, for the Marine Corps birthday, put on a celebration that cost them $20,000! And in such places as Luxembourg, if you are not invited to the social event of the year, the Marine Corps Birthday Ball, you have not yet arrived.

When Puckett would come back from any trip, he would report to the Commandant what he had found: strengths, weaknesses, needs, or leadership of the commanders. When he visited the Marine Corps Recruit Depot in San Diego, for instance, he reported to Cushman the superior leadership of the commanding general there, and that was obviously pleasant for the Commandant to hear. When appropriate, Puckett also pinpointed a problem:

> Only one time in my two years and four months' tour was I required to give a bad report. That time, I was very disturbed about an I&I staff. The sergeant major had not moved his family there and was very disgruntled. The I&I staff looked terrible; their attitude was very bad. The Reserve Training Center was in horrible shape. The I&I himself, a lieutenant colonel, had a big pot gut. It was awful.

> I always had tried the best that I could to stay away from officers' business; that was not my area. But in this case, there were two people who were responsible for that fiasco: the lieutenant colonel and the sergeant major. When I reported this to the Commandant, he picked up the phone and called the inspector general and said, "Within two days I want someone to go take a look."

> Things were so busy that I might get behind in my reports—even with my eleven- to fourteen-hour work days. Once I had to summarize five trips in a single meeting with General Cushman.

Although the two men would get together in the Commandant's office whenever either of them felt that it was necessary, these meetings were infrequent—"He had his job; I had my job."

Puckett felt strongly about wide-scale communication with enlisted Marines in the field. To this end, he began in 1974 a regular monthly column in *Leatherneck*, a magazine which goes to Marine units around the world. A typical column was a blend of comment on the function of NCOs and on barracks life in the 1970s:

> The NCO's role is too important to be taken lightly. Learn to give orders in a manner which will evoke instant and cheerful obedience. An order issued as an ultimatum challenges the self-respect of the Marine, thereby inviting disobedience.

> Accept the challenge of wrestling with problems, but never let it be said of you, "The only way anyone would follow him is out of idle curiosity." Put your head down, your canteens up, and push!...

> Throughout our history, barracks population was a mix of young Marines and seasoned NCOs. It was not uncommon for staff NCOs to occupy rooms within troop barracks. Higher pay for lower ranking military personnel has induced a large number of NCOs to get married and move ashore. Few bachelor staff NCOs now live aboard stateside posts because of Department of Defense policy....

> Seven months ago, the Commandant directed that, to the extent practicable, staff NCOs be present in the barracks at all hours of the day. His purpose was to restore habitual supervision in the traditional sense, in order to solve our leadership problems.

> With this supervision, and with your help, order will be restored. The barracks thief and the troublemaker need your [disinterest] to survive. When those who will not learn to respect the personal and property rights of others are identified and discharged, a wholesome atmosphere will return to the barracks.

Out in the field: a visit to Camp Lejeune in 1973. The press, as always, throw questions at Cushman (left) and Puckett (right).

A trip to San Bernadino, California, in 1974 caused Puckett to break out his dress blues, full medals, and a rare smile.
Puckett photo

This talent for writing caught the eye of the Commandant, and one day his military secretary called Puckett to come into Cushman's office. A lieutenant colonel who was a gifted writer was there also, but the general turned to Puckett, "Sergeant Major, you're always writing. Here's something that I want you to address for me," and he then outlined the problem of the moment.

There were always discussions about personnel assignments, and in November, 1974, the sergeants major monitor came to Puckett to get his opinion on one. As a result, Henry Black, his old acquaintance from the 7th Marines in Vietnam (and soon to be his successor), came to be transferred from duty in the western Pacific to the Marine Corps Development and Education Command in Quantico, Virginia.

Puckett had always had a fascination with the "uncommon" men who had played a special role in the Corps. His thoughts kept reverting to Bill Bestwick, Frank Rauber, and Tom McHugh, and an injustice troubled him, "They did not get the special pay that the most senior enlisted men have enjoyed since that time. I talked with the Non-Commissioned Officers Association [NCOA] about this, and they sponsored a bill to give them proper recompense in retired pay." (Later on, in retirement, Puckett noted with satisfaction, "It's now the law, and those three were included, retroactively, in that special pay.")

If he had chosen to, he could have said more about that pay issue. The inequity for the first three Sergeants Major of the Marine Corps was well known at Headquarters, and there had been a lot of long, drawn out discussion—but no action. So Puckett, on his own initiative, tapped the "Marine underground" of connections in Washington. A retired sergeant major, C. A. "Mack" McKinney, was the legislative director for the NCOA, and Puckett challenged him to tackle the problem.

Getting a special purpose bill passed in Congress is a very laborious and difficult undertaking, and one Reserve organization had already declined to attempt it. The sergeant major, however, answered Puckett's plea with, "Give it to me; I'll do it." There followed long months of drafting wording and lining up support. Fulsome biographies appeared in the Congressional Record. Countless phone calls, letters, and memoranda were required. As McKinney recounted the complex maneuverings:

> We got the thing through the House without any problem at all, but when we got over on the Senate side, we were facing a problem with Senator Stennis' office. Senator Stennis, at that time, had a staff director who felt there were more important pieces of legislation, and decided, more or less, to put a hold on this thing.
>
> The man who introduced this bill for me was Senator Morgan from North Carolina. When it got down to the last day of that session of Congress, right before they adjourned, Senator Morgan was advised that Stennis' staff director had put a hold on this particular piece of legislation, and Senator Morgan went flying over to Senator Stennis. He asked him, "Who in the hell is in charge of the committee: the staff people or the Senators?" Of course Senator Stennis replied that certainly they were, so Morgan said, "Then I want this piece of legislation passed today." Thus it went on the floor and was passed by a voice vote.

The extent of this achievement becomes obvious when the time it took is considered. Puckett's original request was made in 1974, and even his successor had retired before the successful conclusion in the fall of 1978—four years later!

The effects of the bill were curiously diverse. Bill Bestwick was dead, and there were no residual family benefits in the bill. Frank Rauber enjoyed the full benefit, something on the order of $250 a month additional. Tom McHugh, because he had stayed on active duty after his tenure as the Sergeant Major of the Marine Corps, had then received cost of living adjustments which brought him up to a higher pay level than the bill would have provided.

Besides these special Marines, Puckett was alert to wider contacts. Sergeant Major McKinney, who had worked on the retirement pay bill, kept after him:

> My idea was to get more and more enlisted people involved in the area of knowing Congressmen, and being able to walk up to a Congressman and feel that they could speak to him openly. So when we had luncheons to honor certain members of Congress, I could always count on Clint to bring a group of sergeants major over.
>
> Beyond that, Clint was the first Sergeant Major of the Corps who ever came to the Non-Commissioned Officers Association convention. He was a member of another organization, didn't feel like he needed to be with NCOA. Nevertheless, I brought him down to San Antonio, and he sat through the convention and then joined the NCOA. Subsequently he served as a representative and advisor to the board.

Back at Headquarters Puckett had to deal with a variety of generals. He never forgot one episode which could have been a most unpleasant confrontation, but turned out happily in the end, "I worked very, very extensively with the Personnel Department. That's where all the Marines are, and all the services to the Marines in the field. I sat on the Commandant's Enlisted Performance Board; I sat as a member of the Uniform Board, and so on. So I had contact with many, many of the branch heads that dealt with people, with Marines. With one exception, they were very supportive and helpful."

At this time in the mid-seventies, the Marine Corps was having more difficulty in finding quality recruits, so it decided to call to active duty selected staff NCOs from the Reserves. The plan was that they would recruit for Marine reservists, and leave the regular recruiters free then to recruit regular Marines. Some of those called back were young staff sergeants, Vietnam veterans, who had only been out of active duty for six months. Now they suited up in dress blues and did a magnificent job. Complications soon developed, as Puckett noted:

> The rules of the game at the start were, if they had been out more than something like twenty-four hours, then they could reenlist with only the rank of sergeant, with a new date of rank from the date of reenlistment. That was obviously a faulty system. It was penalizing these fine young Marines who had hardly missed a step in reenlisting. Then someone sold Major General Michael Ryan, who was the Director of Reserves, on recom-

mending the integration of Reserves serving in such positions into the regular forces, retaining their original rank and their date of rank.

Now, for those staff sergeants who had been out only six months, what's the big deal? None! However, in one case there was a first sergeant in New Mexico who had less than two and a half years' service as a first sergeant. His date of rank was such that, had he been integrated, the next year he would have been eligible for sergeant major: less than a four-year cruise of active duty, and now a possible sergeant major!

The paperwork for that man's integration moved apparently inexorably through channels. Signing off were Brigadier General Edward Wilcox in personnel management, Lieutenant General Samuel Jaskilka, the director of manpower, and the chief of staff, Lieutenant General John McLaughlin. However, when it got to the assistant commandant, General Earl Anderson, he said (in Puckett's own whimsical words), "Send that paper over to dummy Clint Puckett and see what he has to say." The sergeant major's reaction was, "Baloney!", and the Commandant supported his objection. There was a sequel:

> The Director of Reserve and I met in the passageway three or four days later. We were going to a briefing with the Commandant at that point. General Ryan said, "Sergeant Major, I've got an idea kicking around [about how to solve this Reservist problem]. I'd like to discuss it with you." I replied, "Aye, aye, sir. I'll make an appointment with the general's secretary and come down and talk." It turned out to be an excellent idea, and I supported it wholeheartedly. So this was the quality of leadership of officers such as General Ryan, who didn't get pushed out of shape because I had sabotaged something that he had previously signed.

In Puckett's time about 900 to 1,000 letters a year were written to the Sergeant Major of the Marine Corps. Most of them dealt with promotion questions, but the letters covered every conceivable problem. Puckett gave an example:

> Once I got a letter from a gunnery sergeant out in Kaneohe Bay. It was a bitch letter, "I have asked for a fitness report readout. I haven't gotten it. I went to the Degree Completion Program; I've got my degree. I've asked for a change of MOS, and I've heard nothing. Sergeant Major, the Marine Corps is treating me shabbily. What the heck is going on?"
>
> I wrote him back, "Dear Gunny, what the heck are you bitching about? You're not in Okinawa!" (By this time the Marine Corps was way out of Vietnam.) "The Marine Corps just sent you to college, paid you full pay and allowances to get your degree. What are you complaining about? Incidentally, your fitness report readout is in the mail, and the Personnel Department informs me that your change of MOS has been approved."
>
> A week later, I got a letter from that gunnery sergeant out in K Bay. He said, "Sergeant Major, I want to thank you. It's been a long time since anyone has chewed me out like that. You're absolutely right. I deserve every bit of

it, and you'll never hear another peep out of me." I then wrote him a follow-up that said, "Attaboy," and I clipped that correspondence together and sent it to the Commandant.

Throughout his entire career, one problem had never left Puckett's mind: he had started out as a young man with practically no education, and he quickly came to see this as a major impediment to a full and meaningful life, far beyond the professional requirements for career advancement. Looking back in retrospect, he spoke vehemently, "As a high school dropout, it occurred to me very early on that I didn't have sufficient education to be able to function properly, that I needed more education."

To remedy this, he started studying through correspondence courses, and, in 1951, passed his high school equivalency test. Continuing on after that, even in Vietnam, he completed not only twenty-four college-level academic correspondence courses through the Marine Corps Institute and the Army's correspondence school, but also correspondence courses through the University of New Mexico. His night school subjects ranged from English to Spanish to political science. Those mail courses taught him to read, write, and speak Spanish, but to improve his fluency, he continued to work diligently on his own to master the language more fully (reading, for example, Cortez' letters on the conquest of Mexico). He was, in truth, "the cowboy with the thirst for knowledge!"

This zeal of Puckett's was well known by his peers. As Sergeant Major John Massaro summarized it, "The unique thing, I think, about Sergeant Major Puckett, that set him aside from a lot of other sergeants major, was his drive to educate himself in areas that were not necessarily pertinent to the Marine Corps. He had a great desire to learn foreign languages and develop skills and talents that weren't necessarily associated with the Marine Corps, but did not, at the same time, detract from his Marine Corps duties and being a good Marine."

The haunting drive for learning carried over from his personal life into a passionate commitment to professional education for all Marines, and staff NCOs in particular. His columns in *Leatherneck* carried his messages on leadership and education far and wide. On every trip he would speak about it. He constantly gave his support to seminars and symposiums. It was his burning cause, "my greatest contribution," he felt.

Throughout his tour as Sergeant Major of the Marine Corps, Puckett's life kept intersecting with the other rising stars who would follow him in the top spot. Leland Crawford, then a sergeant major at the recruit depot in San Diego, never forgot a visit there by Puckett, "He was the educated one, a very smart individual, did a lot of writing. We all thought he was going to get all the staff NCOs into the theater and talk to us, and instead he put us all at the bar, drinking beer, and took all the wives back there and talked to them!"

Another sergeant major, Robert Cleary, when he was with the Marine Security Guard across the street from Headquarters, also had vivid memories of Puckett, "He was very articulate, very concerned at that time with the education of our staff noncommissioned officers and naturally our Marine enlisted. He was pushing everything that he could along in that direction." Henry Black remembered:

> Clint was sharp. Some people liked him; some didn't. That goes for all of us, naturally. I had no idea, when we were both in the 7th Marines in Vietnam, that I would be relieving him later on as the Sergeant Major of the Corps, but when that time came, he was very thorough. He took pains to ensure that I understood everything I was to do at Headquarters.
>
> For instance, he cautioned me on responding to young Marines' correspondence, which the sergeant major does an awful lot, and not delegating it to somebody else to take care of. You had to get personally involved, he said, with the problem that was presented to you through the mail or over the telephone and resolve it, and then tell it like it was. Clint gave me good advice.

Then there was John Massaro again. Headquarters was assigning him to recruiting duty in Salt Lake City. It probably would have been his last career tour, and as a devout Mormon, Massaro was ready to go. Puckett heard about this, called Massaro into his office, and said, "You don't want to do that. Change your mind. You'll get another chance [at selection as Sergeant Major of the Marine Corps]...."—a prophetic piece of advice!

It was part of an inevitable cycle that those diverse experiences had to end. With the retirement of General Cushman slated for June, 1975, Puckett put his own affairs in order. There was one final column of farewell in *Leatherneck*:

> As I reluctantly break ranks after thirty years of active service, I leave this message: Some of the most joyous and care-free years of my life were spent in the barracks or in a tent. There I learned the true meaning of the word integrity, and my character was molded by association with my fellow barracks dwellers. There I learned to judge a man by what he was inside....
>
> Have fun! Enjoy to the fullest these years of service to your Country and Corps. But be honest and trustworthy, work hard and serve honorably. Do your part to ensure that another Sergeant Major of the Marine Corps now serving in your ranks, receives the proper influence—the Sergeant Major of the Marine Corps, year 2002.

Nevertheless, it was a difficult and emotional experience for Puckett, although he was reconciled to the inevitability:

> On June 1, 1975, I transferred (reluctantly) to the Retired List. Let me explain my feelings. In the five years I was there at Headquarters, both as sergeant major of the personnel department and Sergeant Major of the Corps, I had many contacts from Marines who were—to call them "outstanding" is truly an understatement—forty-seven, forty-eight years old, at the apex of their careers, could and did run ten miles a day. They told me, "I've spent my entire adult life in this green suit. To throw me out now is a crime!"

I understood their feelings, but, if you allow service beyond thirty years, would it be any easier when they had thirty-three, thirty-six years' service? And, if you allow that, then PFCs can't make lance corporal and first sergeants can't make sergeant major. You end up with a Corps of old men. Understand that, when I had six years in grade as a sergeant major, I was still the junior sergeant major in my regiment. As a consequence, although I hated to go, I didn't have the guts to ask to stay beyond thirty.

On May 29, the traditional retirement ceremony was held at the Washington Barracks. General Cushman made some complimentary comments, "Truly a Marine's Marine"; "accumulated wisdom of a long and distinguished career"; "I le did more than continue the march—he accelerated the pace." Then followed the award of a Legion of Merit signed by the Secretary of the Navy with more plaudits, "...extraordinary judgement and ingenuity...exceptional professional competence and keen foresight...superb performance, perseverance, and selfless devotion to duty...."

The Sword of Office was passed to his successor, Henry Black, and on May 31, 1975, Clint Puckett finished his last day as Sergeant Major of the Marine Corps, and his last day in three decades of active duty. Then he headed home to the family life that was so important to him, undoubtedly to pick up a book and start studying again!

Chapter 8

TELL IT LIKE IT IS

Sergeant Major Henry H. Black

I never asked for anything unless it was a challenge." "I upset some generals [and other officers and staff NCOs] in the Marine Corps. I really did, because I told it like it was." So spoke a rough, tough man who became the seventh Sergeant Major of the Marine Corps, following Clint Puckett's retirement in 1975. All of the other men who attained that billet obviously had a somewhat similar characteristic of holding firm convictions and acting on those beliefs. They had, however, a compensating balance of using a self-restrained diplomatic approach to contentious situations. This man was different, for he had an unbending, let-the-chips-fall-where-they-may style that was distinctively his own. Loyal, starched, direct, unswerving to a unique degree, Henry Black never shied away from confrontation when principles (or the policies of his commanding officer) were involved.'

His peers had pungent memories. One of those who knew him, Sergeant Major Robert Cleary, observed, "He was a wringer. If you were overweight, the reputation in the field was, 'Stay out of Sergeant Major Black's way or he'll get you.' Not really 'get you,' but you'd best be able to pass the Physical Fitness Test and look good. He was one hell of a fine Marine, but stubborn.''

Another, Sergeant Major Leland Crawford, put it this way, "He had nerve. He wasn't afraid to go up to someone, if they had a deficiency, and tell them that they were screwed up. I liked that about him. I took old Henry one Saturday evening to our staff NCO club. He sat there at the bar stool, and I'll bet you that he reprimanded fifteen staff NCOs for appearance and weight control. That's what I mean: he had guts. He didn't give a damn, and I liked that!''

This single-minded attitude was not just some personal fixation of Black's but was, rather, his way of faithfully implementing a fiat of his Commandant that "there will be *no* fat Marines. Military appearance is an absolute requirement to be a Marine, and there will be *no* deviation from it." Naturally, this kind of a head-on, hard-nosed approach ruffled more than a few feathers. Still another fellow sergeant major commented on the negative side of Black's steely style:

> Unfortunately, he had a way about him that was...I guess it could best be described as abrasive, and perhaps he didn't make the impression that he could have. In dealing with the junior Marines, I think he did quite well. It was more with the senior staff NCOs that he would tend to confront— perhaps that was just his way.
>
> I think the problem that he might have had was the way he did it. You can chew somebody out and leave them still feeling good, or you can chew somebody out and leave them feeling kind of bitter. Unfortunately, I think he had a tendency to do the latter. I'll never forget when he called me up one day and got all over me because he had seen a copy of our local newspaper and we had a master sergeant re-enlisting who looked like he might be over-weight. Actually he was within the limits, but the way he was standing in the picture made him look that way.

(What that sergeant major didn't know was that the Commandant himself had seen the photograph and directed Black to check it out.)

Then there were the officers—the recruiting officer, the mess officer, the PX officer, and several high-ranking generals—who flared up when Black would stubbornly insist on the correction of a problem or fight for a principle he felt was right. Of course, when he admired the way an officer did his job, a real empathy would develop and the men would work smoothly together. That was the nature of a very distinctive individual, and, while there were those he upset, the record clearly shows the high regard in which he was held by most and the outstanding level of his accomplishments.

His life began in Imperial, a tiny town a few miles west of Pittsburgh, Pennsylvania. James and Hazel Black lived there with their fourteen children. The father had had many varied experiences: Navy before World War I, then Army combat in France, then coal mining and railroading. The last paid well and life proceeded smoothly as the family grew one by one during the twenties. On February 9, 1929, the seventh son was born and named Henry.

That fall came the total crash of the stock market and the Great Depression. Life in the Black family took a terrible turn for the worse. The family was forced to move frequently, "keeping ahead of the rental agents." A "bathroom" meant a privy out back and any old wash tub in the house. They started to build a home, but never finished it. In later years, Henry Black recalled the family's grim struggle for existence:

> With the size of our family, it was live off the land, truck farming, hauling coal, etc. As the oldest boy at home, I used to pick coal on the slate dumps; get up at 4:00 in the morning, walk five or six miles, and work all day and into the night, including weekends, picking coal. Then my dad would come up with a truck, and we'd load it lump by lump and take it and try to sell it. In fact, I had to spend so much time doing this that I missed a lot of school and lost my position on the basketball team.
>
> We did other things as well. We raised vegetables; we would sell them house to house. We'd have to go to Pittsburgh to do that.

The years of this bare-bones existence went painfully by, indelibly affecting the future personality of the young man. When World War II broke upon the country, the older brothers enlisted, but Henry was too young, a student at Findley High School. Nevertheless, he too tried to enlist, but, at age sixteen, he could not get his parents' permission. After he graduated from high school, it didn't take him long to make up for lost time, "They started the military draft, and I didn't want to be part of that. Then my brother, Al, joined the Marines and, when he came home on recruit leave, he looked sharp, and a few months later I followed him, enlisting on April 12, 1948."

Boot camp at Parris Island was not the usual shock to a nineteen-year-old, for growing up with eleven brothers proved to be a good preparation. There was also the stern, rough way he had been raised which stood him in good stead:

> My dad had very strong discipline in our family, if you didn't carry out what you were responsible to do in our home life. When you lacked something or you didn't do it, then you were in trouble with Dad, and you got punished.
>
> I went to boot camp, and it was no different. My first night there, one recruit said something to the drill instructor, and the DI, a small man, just picked him up and threw him through the air. I mean, I'd never seen a man with such power. Then I asked a dumb question and the DI picked me up and threw me against the bulkhead. So from there on, I believed in what he was trying to do for us, and I think I'll never forget him! In spite of his shortcomings, I totally respected the man, so we never reported any of his maltreatment.

Through all of this, Black gained a solid foundation for the years to come, "There were a lot of intangible things the drill instructor instilled in you. He taught you love of Corps and he taught you dedication, which you have to have also from your home."

Finishing his recruit training, Black was ordered to the 8th Marines, 2d

Division, at Camp Lejeune. Memories of that duty remained with him forty years later. For example, he described his first sergeant then, "When he got a little upset with the troops, you could hear him from one end of the area to the other!" And then there was his regiment's May, 1949, deployment to the U.S. Sixth Fleet in the Mediterranean. It was an eye-opener for a young kid from a small town:

> I'd never been around the Navy; that was the first thing that hit me. The boatswain's mates kept pushing us around, "You can't sit here," "You can't do this," "You can't do that." But anyway, we soon made friends and got on with life together. For a young single Marine (and I liked to go on liberty), it was the most enjoyable tour of duty that I ever had in the Marine Corps.
>
> I went to Naples and Marseilles; in fact I danced with the famous movie star, Rita Hayworth, when she came aboard the carrier *Coral Sea*. I also went to Athens; I went to Tangiers: that was unbelievable. You know, it's a different world. I went around the whole Mediterranean, in fact we even went—right after Israel was formed as a country—into a sea port there. We were pulling the Marine detachment of the UN forces out.

After returning to Lejeune in September, Black was transferred from his rifle company to the headquarters and service company of the 6th Marines. A few months later, there was a call for volunteers (on Christmas Eve, of all times) to go back to "the Med." Black agreed and so had a second, enjoyable trip there. On his return, the invasion of South Korea in June, 1950, left little doubt what the future held. His battalion soon received orders to go by train to Camp Pendleton in California. Black's mother and father journeyed to Jacksonville, North Carolina, to see him off.

Early July was a time of enormous, frenetic activity at Camp Pendleton, as extreme measures were taken to flesh out a brigade and ship it out immediately for combat. This chaotic period brought a change in the designation of Black's unit in August. Now it became the basis for the newly reactivated 1st Marines, whose colonel was the redoubtable Lewis "Chesty" Puller, a renowned combat leader who had already been awarded in his long career an incredible total of four Navy Crosses for heroism—and would later receive a fifth for his performance in Korea.

Puller melded the regiment together in ten days, and it sailed in late August for Kobe, Japan, and then almost immediately for Korea. Black nearly missed the famous landing on September 15 at Inchon, far behind the enemy's lines. The old Landing Ship, Tank (LST) vessel on which he was embarked was hit by a typhoon, lost the use of an engine, and had to drop out of the convoy. Emergency repairs were made, and they arrived just barely in time for the assault.

The dramatic, surprise landing, against all odds, came off as planned, and led to an immediate push inland. Black was originally assigned as a driver for the battalion supply officer. This was not quite what he had in mind, "I didn't want any part of that, and I got it switched so that I went and drove for the commanding officer of a rifle company." That put Black in the midst of the successful drive to capture the capital of Seoul, which was stormed in hand-to-hand fighting: house to house, street by street, working with tanks at point-blank range.

His unit was then ordered back on board an LST for the next operation. The ship took them around the Korean Peninsula, from the west coast to Won-san on the east coast, encountering another typhoon en route. This landing was a little different. Instead of a hail of enemy fire, there was a sign (put up by the Navy) awaiting them on the beach, "Bob Hope was here."

His battalion moved quickly inland to a key highway junction, Majon-ni. The area was swarming with North Korean soldiers, and as Black succinctly commented, "We got into some shit real quick. But one new friend we introduced the enemy to was our 'Bouncing Betty'—a personnel mine that would bounce up off the ground and then explode." There was one wild day in particular:

> We were on a patrol out of Majon-ni. We had been going on patrol, platoon-size, out this road for two or three weeks. I went every day. We were the point; my company jeep was up front always. They had blown the road up in front of us, and then they had us in a horse shoe and pounded us all day. We had about 80 percent casualties that day. I watched our machine guns be put in place trying to return fire, and as fast as men got behind the gun, they got killed. They just kept putting the gun on top of the dead Marines. This was to my left, and you could hear the wounded shouting, so I just got back to a vehicle and started loading them up and hauling them out under fire.
>
> As I was loading them they were screaming. There was no way I could return fire. We were in a ditch with a cliff and they were right above us, rolling grenades and boulders down on top of us. They had us! After about six hours, I'd made two or three trips in and out, and the vehicle got hit. It was another hairy moment! The battalion surgeon—a fine man—was back in the rear, and he said to me, "Don't go back." But I just kept going back...you get to a point where you don't give a damn.

Black's courageous conduct brought him a Bronze Star. The citation from the division's commanding general called it a "heroic achievement" and praised his "unerring devotion to duty and aggressive actions."

That was a pretty good start for a twenty-one-year-old corporal, but there was more to come a little over three weeks later. Black's battalion was pulled out of Majon-ni, and rejoined other Marine units in a long convoy. It was headed on a fateful trip north. The operation began as a plan to have the whole 1st Division drive to the Chosin Reservoir near the Chinese border, a proposed zone of action 200 miles long and 60 miles wide. As the division worked its way towards its objective, more and more contacts were made with Chinese "volunteers," the thermometer continued to plummet, and the snow deepened. Despite pressure from higher (Army) headquarters to plunge north towards the Chinese border, once the division reached the Chosin, it concentrated its regiments as a precaution. It was a crucial command decision, for enormous masses of Chinese troops then struck the Marines with unbridled ferocity. Further advance was obviously impossible, and total annihilation of the isolated division seemed possible. "Attacking in another direction," the division fought its way south out of the trap.

Black's experiences paralleled those of Tom McHugh in a neighboring regiment: horrendous cold (without the shoe-pacs meant for sub-zero wear) and continuous combat with the Chinese surrounding them on both sides of the long divisional column stretched out along the only existing road. The Chinese poured in the human-wave attacks day and night. Black vividly recalled one particular day:

> In Hagaru-ri we really got hit. I don't know how many there were of them, but the next morning we had 700 dead Chinamen within our lines and behind our lines. I don't know how many of their regiments hit us. Our CP had been over-run, and our ammunition dump was there. Another Marine and I—we kept loading the jeep trailer with ammo and bringing it back to our 60mm mortar people and the others. We got hit by white phosphorus shells one time: burned our coats and so forth. I made two or three trips. It was a nasty situation: heavy fire, a long night, and a lot of enemy pressure—combat at its most intense.
>
> I'd been in fire fights before in Seoul and when I won my Bronze Star, but this was really unique. We had a perimeter defense that was unbelievable: only one battalion and supporting troops for the entire Hagaru area, including our gouged-out airstrip. But I made trip after trip until we got all the ammo. This was going out to where the enemy was. As in any fire fight, everything was very confusing.

He was awarded a Silver Star (one level below the Navy Cross) for his bravery in that battle. The citation from his commanding general noted his "conspicuous gallantry and intrepidity" and his "absolute disregard for his own personal safety...."

In a long, slow, painful breakout, the Marines cut their way through the encirclement. "It seemed like an eternity" to Black, but they finally fought their way back to the coast. The division had overcome thirteen Chinese divisions in a remarkable feat of arms.

Surviving these dramatic encounters, Black got the good news in May, 1951: orders to return to the States. There he was sent to the quiet post of the Marine Security Guard at the Naval Proving Ground in Dahlgren, Virginia. It proved to be dull work, after what he had been through, but his promotion to sergeant came through, and something even more important occurred. He met a young lady, Fannie Samuel, from King George, Virginia, at an American Legion dance in nearby Colonial Beach that summer. He later confessed, "I only danced with her once." That was all it took. Their relationship flourished and led to an engagement in August. The following month they were married in the country church in King George.

Promotion to staff sergeant came through in 1952, and in the following year, he received orders to report to the 2d Division at Camp Lejeune. He didn't like what he found, "We had only a skeleton force there, waiting for the main body of the battalion to return from maneuvers. It was just a few people compared to a combat battalion I was used to. I thought, 'Hell, I don't know anybody here.' So on the spur of the moment I said, 'Well, I'll apply,' when they came around and asked for people to apply for recruiting duty."

He was sent to Recruiters' School in Parris Island. What memories must have gone through his mind, when he returned to the site of his recruit training five years later as a twice-decorated veteran NCO.

Completing the school in July, 1953, Black was sent to the Recruiting Substation in Allentown, Pennsylvania. This tour of duty proved to be a mixture of professional success and personal hardship for a man who now had to support both a wife and a son. Black remembered in a tone of bitterness:

> We had no medical assistance for dependents. We lived on very little...it was humble living! We really had hardships financially: trying to live in that type of community on the income we had. But we managed. My wife, after she had the first baby, quit her job. We learned to live, I think, on about $170.00 a month.
>
> As for recruiting, this was Pennsylvania Dutch country, and they're very hard to get to know, but, once they get to know you they're very nice people. We did very well up there in Allentown, even though it's always tougher for the Marine Corps to recruit right after a war than for the Air Force or the Navy.

After serving his required time as a recruiter, Black was asked if he would extend his tour of duty in Allentown. His gruff reply, "No way!" He wanted to return to the infantry duty he preferred. In August, 1956, he got his wish when he was sent to the 9th Marines who were part of the 3d Division on Okinawa. Now a gunnery (or tech) sergeant, his job there was to take charge of a heavy machine gun platoon. Because it had no officer, he served as platoon commander and platoon sergeant combined. His platoon turned out to be the last one in the division to have "the old, water-cooled, .30 caliber heavies," and he loved them!

The 3d Division was the Marine "ready force" for the Western Pacific, so Black and his platoon moved around widely. "We went up to Japan and climbed Mt. Fuji a few times." But there was another visit to Japan that was far less strenuous and more important to his future career. He was able to attend an administrative school there for six weeks which prepared him for First Sergeants School later on. After that, there was still another trip:

> We went down to the Philippines, and we were everywhere—mainly in the field. The 9th Marines lived in the field. We humped our ass off in that heat. Okinawa's hot—it was hot while we were there—but the Philippines were even hotter. We were on an eight-day-straight training schedule, regardless of what day. If it was Christmas, you were in the field, and then

Platoon leader Black sits proudly behind his favorite weapon, the old water-cooled .30 caliber heavy machine gun, while in the 9th Marines on Okinawa in 1957.
Black photo

A 1969 reunion in Vietnam: Black (right), while serving as a battalion sergeant major in the 7th Marines, has a visit with his brother Al, now a master gunnery sergeant in Da Nang.
Black photo

a day for inspection, and then a day off, and then back for eight days. I guess somebody must have gotten upset about that, and they later changed it. But I loved that tour with the 9th Marines!

It couldn't last, and his turn for stateside duty rolled around in November, 1957. He volunteered for Parris Island to attend the Drill Instructors School. That turned out to be a natural for him. He later recalled, "I came out number one in the school, and people thought I was crazy for volunteering to go to the drill field. My philosophy in the Marine Corps was that I never asked for anything unless it was a challenge. (I think it paid off in my record, because I later volunteered, when I was married with kids, to go back to Vietnam.) I liked the adventure of the Marine Corps. At a Marine barracks or recruiting station there was no adventure, not to me anyway."

That kind of "gung-ho" attitude brought results. He climbed successively from junior to senior to chief drill instructor in the recruit training regiment. At the same time he received his warrant as a master sergeant, which helped his family's finances since twin girls, Catherine and Debora, had arrived in August, 1958, to join five-year-old Michael. Reflecting on his experiences at Parris Island, Black noted:

> The outstanding thing was the competition between platoons. Their drill instructors were, all of them, tremendous. Naturally, we had a couple of characters. There were also, of course, a few who used maltreatment, but they got caught and paid the price. The hot item was how you handled troops.
>
> We did have one platoon of all college graduates. I think they had a General Classification Test average of 124. Another drill instructor had that platoon, and I guess they were the sorriest group that graduated out of the whole four-platoon series. It was hard work at Parris Island, routine, you know, but it was an adventure, I felt.

The Marine Corps doesn't often ask you what you'd like—even if you are a master sergeant. So it was that Black reluctantly was sent back, in August, 1960, to recruiting duty in Wheeling, West Virginia. As was his nature, he gritted his teeth and gave it his best effort for the next four years. He did well, bringing a steady flow of new young recruits into the Corps. In fact, he added a new young man of his own, for David, his second son, was born in March, 1964. During that same period, the Corps changed its NCO structure, and so Black (while remaining in the same E-7 pay grade) was redesignated a "gunnery sergeant."

Finally, in August, 1964, he returned to what he wanted—a rifle company when he came back to his old regiment, the 8th Marines, at Camp Lejeune. Here he was promoted to E-8 and served as a company first sergeant, part of the Marine "ready force" on the east coast. The 2d Division was in constant training. Black went, in October, with his regiment for Operation Steel Pike, a practice amphibious landing in Spain. This was a huge, complex exercise, involving over 20,000 U.S. Marines, 2,000 Spanish Marines, 500 American merchant seamen, 60 ships, and thousands of U.S. Navy sailors, "the largest single amphibious maneuver over long distance in peacetime." Black's regiment landed all its personnel, equipment, and supplies entirely by helicopter, a first in the Corps' history.

Soon after he returned to Lejeune, there was a trip to Camp Drum in upper New York State for specialized training for a different exigency. He was part of a detachment sent in February, 1965, to the frigid area of Watertown for cold weather exercises including the first testing of troop-carrying helicopters in sub-zero weather.

That proved ironic when a "Red Alert" was flashed to Lejeune shortly afterwards, "Be ready to move out on an emergency deployment to protect American lives in the street fighting now going on in the Dominican Republic!" In May, Black's battalion moved quickly by truck to the Marine air station at nearby Cherry Point, North Carolina, and boarded its transport aircraft. Less than twenty hours later, the battalion was in Santo Domingo, almost 1,200 strong and ready to protect the American Embassy. Whether frozen in New York or boiling in the tropical heat of the Caribbean, the "ready force" had shown it really was ready to move on a moment's notice and then speedily reach its target. Black later recounted his experiences:

> Down there it was weird. We were setting up machine gun emplacements on people's front porches on the street. There were no real fire fights that we got into. It was sniping and that type of thing. We really had no casualties.
>
> There was one day when we were standing out by a road block, and we had tanks down there. We had this young lieutenant who was walking around, and all at once our water cans near him started dancing down the street. I knew he was under sniper fire. It was comic in that it was so peaceful and so beautiful in the area right along the water there. That was his introduction to combat, when the water cans started flying around. The rounds of ammo started hitting them (they were empty) and started moving them down the street at the road block.
>
> Like any young Marine in those situations, we had to watch our men so they didn't get too familiar with the ladies and all that stuff. It was a good experience for the young Marine who had never carried live ammo on him. There were all kinds of regulations about when you could load, when you couldn't, and so forth.
>
> One time down there, the gunnery sergeant and I and our captain were laying down in some kind of a breeze-way. We were all stretched out at about 3:00 in the morning. They had terrible rats down there, as big as cats, and we were laying down side by side, and these rats ran right over us, about a dozen of them. That was the worst part of the whole operation... you'd look up a telephone pole, you'd look at a rat coming down a pole. It was unbelievable how big!

After this comic-opera scenario, which ended in June, came the real thing. In January, 1966, Black was sent to rejoin another of his old regiments, the 1st Marines, who were heavily engaged in the growing struggle in Vietnam. His battalion commanding officer this time was a "character," but a combat-proven character, already a holder of the Navy Cross, soon to be awarded another. (Formally named Lieutenant Colonel Van Bell, he was called admiringly by his men "Ding Dong" Bell.) As first sergeant of a rifle company, Black later explained:

> We were outside of Da Nang at first. Of course, we didn't move around much. We had small unit operations, company size, strictly maintaining the area of responsibility that the battalion had. The division headquarters was right behind, a couple of big mountains over. You know, the normal thing that went on in Vietnam was small-unit (squad) type of operation. I used to go out on some of the ambushes.
>
> One time later we were on a patrol. We were on tanks, up south of Hue, in a cemetery area; we were moving out the road, and we didn't get a mile. I was riding on the fender of a tank, and we just blew up. It hit right under me and I went flying! A land mine blew the tank track and blew me. Then a couple of tanks behind, they hit a mine which we had missed. Of course, we had some guys walking along and they got hit with shrapnel.

This little episode added a Purple Heart to Black's other decorations. He was lucky nothing more serious happened when his battalion took part in Operation Hastings in July, 1966, "the most ferocious fighting of the war up to that time."

February, 1967, brought orders to return to the U.S. He was to go to the staff of the inspector and instructor of a Reserve unit in Newcastle, Pennsylvania. Black's reaction was typically direct, "The hell with this! Enough is enough. No more independent duty!" So, for the first time in his life, he went to Headquarters to press personally for a change in orders so he could go to a regular unit base. Someone (the Sergeant Major of the Marine Corps?) took a look at his superb track record and changed his orders to Quantico.

Arriving there, he was assigned as first sergeant of a casual company. As he later recollected:

> That was an exciting tour. We had the guys waiting for action on Bad Conduct Discharges who were just out of the brig. We had from the worst Marine to the greatest: some good men waiting for discharge, and some waiting to go to prison. When I reported in there I had never seen a place like that.
>
> There was, for example, the company's chief clerk, who was a sergeant, and I started getting calls on his indebtedness. One day it really came to a point, after I had counseled him and talked to him about it. I got one more call, so I called him in and I said, "Take care of this; I don't want any more of this." So he did. He went out and robbed a bank in Quantico, at noon! He put an overcoat on (it was 100 degrees outside and he walked in with an overcoat on), and said, "Hold up!" Of course, they caught him. The poor guy got $900.00, and he was $10,000 or $15,000 in debt. That's how he was going to settle his financial problems. My wife still laughs about that one; my counseling must have really gotten to him!

After his peculiar experiences in the casual company for a year, Black's life returned to normal with a transfer to a different side of Quantico. He had been selected for sergeant major while in Vietnam, and now the promotion came through. He moved into the billet of sergeant major of the headquarters battalion, Marine Corps Development and Education Command. This was the Corps' "think tank" with bright, young staff officers working on such concerns as new weapons, tactics analysis, and advanced professional education. (There was no Staff NCO Academy then.)

Given Black's nature and his affinity for a rifle unit out in the field, this kind of rarified atmosphere was really not for him. Some sensitive discussions ensued with his wife, Fannie, a true Marine wife. "She never in my life objected to any move I volunteered for," he said proudly. He made up his mind. Family or not, he volunteered to go back for a second tour in Vietnam, which was so in keeping with his basic fighting nature.

The Corps naturally was happy to have such a combat-seasoned veteran back on the firing line, so, in June of 1969, he was transferred to Vietnam to serve as sergeant major of the 2d Battalion, 7th Marines. It was to be "a tough tour of duty," as he admitted later. (In this new billet he naturally encountered the regimental sergeant major, Clint Puckett, who would go on to be Sergeant Major of the Marine Corps and later have an effect on Black's career.)

The battalion saw plenty of action, and Black was in his element: "We had good operations." There were two that were special. He later gave the details:

> We were down in the Hiep Duc, they called it. We were operating out of Fire Base Ross, having started out with two rifle companies on this operation. Regiment was up on a mountain looking at us through telescopic lenses. But we were fragmented so when we got down there, we got into some very heavy shit.
>
> Then we get this other company in, and our commanding officer puts them right in one little area, and they got hit by really heavy mortar fire; it was unbelievable. They hit them right dead center. We were right there, too. It was unbelievable the next morning: the casualties. They didn't have any holes, they didn't have nothing! Just blew them away—sad.
>
> At the same time our CP [Command Post] also got hit heavily. We were really into it down there! We had objectives to move toward, but—because of enemy fire—we were sort of stale-mated. The North Vietnamese (the first time I had ever seen them in uniform) were counter-attacking our command CP group, at noon, trying to over-run the CP.
>
> I noticed a lot of people hiding in their hole instead of returning fire, and that just upset me. So I was kicking ass and I mean really kicking ass! When I saw officers hiding in holes, it just made me sick. Nobody was doing anything with the command group or the troops to get them to protect themselves and engage the enemy. I took this upon myself. The whole damn operation was unbelievable.

Black's commanding officer (CO) was relieved of his duties, and a new CO was sent in, Lieutenant Colonel Joseph Hopkins. "He was a real field officer (who later made general)," and he was quick to appreciate the outstanding leadership that Black had shown under maximum pressure. He recommended an award of the Legion of Merit, but this was altered at the division headquarters, and Black received his second Bronze Star with Combat "V." His citation from the Commanding General, FMFPac, Lieutenant General Henry Buse, said in part:

> ...the lead elements came under a heavy volume of fire from a large hostile force concealed in the rugged terrain. Reacting instantly, Sergeant Major Black organized a reaction unit of command group personnel, and skillfully deployed the Marines into advantageous fighting positions from which they delivered suppressive fire against the enemy, which enabled the lead platoon to resume its advance. Ignoring the hostile fire impacting around him, he then boldly moved across the hazardous terrain to assist in treating the casualties and carrying them to medical evacuation helicopters.

The citation went on to commend Black's bravery in a bloody engagement three days later:

> ...as the command group was moving to a new location, the Marines were subjected to a fusillade of mortar, rocket-propelled grenade, and small arms fire from all directions. Realizing the need for immediate action, Sergeant Major Black established a defensive perimeter and, repeatedly exposing himself to the intense enemy fire, moved from one fighting position to another, encouraging his men and directing their suppressive fire at the numerically superior force. His heroic and aggressive leadership so inspired his men that they turned a potential disaster into a decisive victory....

The other operation that was etched in his memory came shortly thereafter. Black described it:

> While we were at Fire Base Ross, I'd go out on operations all the time with the rifle companies. We went out on one operation and the start was comic. Lieutenant Colonel Arthur Folsom...I was going to go with him in the command Huey helicopter. But he said, "Sergeant Major, it's all filled up with radiomen and forward observers. So if you don't mind, you can jump in that bird."
>
> So I replied, "I'll go with this company." I got on their bird, and the company CO was on it. We were about the fourth chopper in. We landed in a hot zone and they were ripping us! The old chopper dropped on top of a little mountain pinnacle, and that bird could hardly sit down. We were the last. After they put, I think, two squads in, then we came in. That chopper pilot dumped us out, and we came rolling down. It's hard to describe, but it was not like a normal landing that you make, because he wanted out of there! So he got out, and we were up there (with three days' food) for about six days, I guess, or seven.

A lot of the young troops didn't even have their full rations with them. Eventually, it was foggy and cold and miserable before we got off there. Of course we hadn't eaten in three or four days. I shared my chow with the troops, but I'll tell you we were hungry when we got down off of there!

Besides these particular operations, I had a lot to do on a day-to-day basis. Down at Fire Base Ross, we got regularly mortared really heavily. I would go out and check to see how things were...what was going on. I didn't jump in a hole and stay there. I just kept moving around and checking things. We really got hit! They knew how to use their Chinese mortars, 120s and all sizes.

A sergeant major who took care of his men with such courage and diligence did not go unnoticed. A third Bronze Star with Combat "V" was awarded to Black as he neared the end of this violent tour of duty. His citation covered a broad period, June, 1969, to March, 1970, and said in part:

Particularly noteworthy were his actions on the night of 16 September, 1969, when his battalion was occupying defensive positions at Fire Support Base Ross and came under an intense rocket, mortar, and rocket-propelled grenade attack. With complete disregard for his own safety, Sergeant Major Black fearlessly moved throughout the defensive perimeter, personally carrying several wounded Marines to safety and shouting encouragement to his men....

Orders returning him to the United States arrived in April, 1970. Headquarters had decided that a man with that many combat ribbons would be a splendid representative to the public, and that he should go once more on recruiting duty. Black was appalled and naturally went at the problem head on, "When the orders came, I called the sergeants major monitor at Headquarters and just about went crazy. He said that they would only put successful Marines back at recruiting, and that I knew the recruiting game inside and out. Well, I was a sergeant major and he was my monitor, but I'll tell you, I raised some hell about that. I repeated, 'Enough's enough,' because I wanted to be with the real Marine Corps. But in the end, I had to go down there." Accordingly, his next two years were spent in Richmond, Virginia, as the sergeant major of the recruiting station there.

For most men, this would be a quiet, peaceful tour of duty. Not with Black! Once he got the picture of what was going on there, his basic intolerance of shoddy performance erupted, and all hell broke loose. As he later explained with brutal frankness:

I'll tell you, I just tore that whole organization up. I had my CO relieved. The Fourth District colonel later called the new CO who came in, and he said, "Watch that sergeant major. He's a trouble-maker." But I had to have that previous asshole relieved within three months for enlisting recruits that were not fit to even do anything except make a quota.

I had just come back from my second tour in Vietnam, and I knew what I had been through there with some of these malcontents and misfits.

I just said, "Put it all on the line." But, I got a citation when I left, because under the new CO we brought our work up to par. We did it with honesty, but I also did it with force.

In fact, I pretty near beat the hell out of a gunnery sergeant there one time. He wasn't doing his job at all, and then he was lying. He was trying to bullshit me. Hey! I knew recruiting; I could tell when somebody was not being honest with me. I knew the guys who were having trouble and those who were honest, giving it their best effort. I knew this guy wasn't, so I told him, "Come on outside. We'll get with it, right now." Well, we didn't have to. I gave him the offer, but he backed off, and he then became one of my better recruiters.

This tour revealed clearly several basic facets of Black's strong temperament: he wanted to be with the infantry; he fought the recruiting assignment, but once he had to do it, in typical fashion, he gave it his best shot; he was quick to confront anyone who was cutting corners, regardless of the furor that created; he would back up the standards he set for enlisted personnel with his fists, if need be; and he asked the monitor, "As soon as you can, get me off this duty."

The results were clearly documented by the Navy Achievement Medal subsequently awarded to him by the Secretary of the Navy, with a citation, signed by the Commandant, which noted "the superior performance of his duties...displaying the highest degree of leadership and dedication. Establishing sound policies and demanding continued professionalism from his men, he inspired the recruiters of Recruiting Station, Richmond to establish the largest pool of recruits throughout the Recruiting Service."

When it came time to move on to his next post, his first choice was to go to the 1st Division at Camp Pendleton, but there were no openings at that time for his rank. In an accommodating mood this time, the monitor asked him, "Would you like to go to the Marine Barracks, Bremerton, Washington?" A family conference ensued, "My wife had never gone anywhere west in the Marine Corps. It had been between Camp Lejeune, Quantico, and Parris Island. After all my adventures I thought, 'It would be nice if she had a tour somewhere else.' So I asked Fannie and she said that she had never been to the west coast, and there's where we headed in August, 1972."

Again, in what normally would be a routine tour, there turned out to be a problem with an inferior officer. As was already clearly the pattern of his career, this was not something with which Black put up calmly, "It was unbelievable! It was some experience! We had a CO there who was a spoiled little brat, a lieutenant colonel who would throw little tantrums and that kind of shit. And he had problems in his personal relations with his officers. His executive officer was a major whom he hated. It was something down there! So I left pretty readily."

By this time, Black had put in over three and a half years of stateside duty, and the itch was strong to get overseas and back with a Fleet Marine Force unit. Accordingly, in November, 1973, he welcomed orders to move to Japan as sergeant major of the 1st Aircraft Wing at Iwakuni. This was a broad responsibility. "It was the first really big organization that I was ever in. Before that, it had been service at a battalion level." Black later summarized these experiences:

> That was my first tour with a wing, and I really learned to respect where they come from and the good Marines they are. You know, in the infantry they always put down the air, but that was a hard-working time, just an excellent tour. I worked for an outstanding commanding general [Major General Frank Lang], and he could fly anything in the wing. We'd go off— we might go down to Taipei; we'd go to Okinawa, to the Philippines. It was interesting. Then we got a new commanding general [Major General Victor Armstrong], and he was just as outstanding. He and I pulled a couple of great liberties together down in the Philippines.
>
> One day we had these guys on strike. I'm in the general's office talking about something. I look out the window and there's two or three Marines and they had these placards. The general also looks out and he says, "Sergeant Major, I don't believe what I'm seeing!" They were on strike, protesting some damn thing. We'd had a few racial problems in the barracks, but I don't know what this was about. It was crazy! I just got on the phone right in the general's office and called the Military Police. They came in and I said, "Arrest them." They locked them up, and then got ahold of their CO. It was incredible!

The quality of Black's work at Iwakuni was evaluated by an "old pro." Sergeant Major John Massaro, who had already made a name for himself and would later go on to still more prominence, was at that time working with the inspector general (I.G.) at Headquarters. When the I.G. and his sergeant major would return to Headquarters from a field trip, there were unsparingly honest reports on what they had seen, distributed to the most senior generals and the Sergeant Major of the Marine Corps. Careers could rise and fall on the basis of these. Massaro made clear Black's relentless devotion to physical fitness, with its crucial effect on a Marine's combat performance, and prefigured his later focus on eliminating fat, out-of-condition men:

> When I really got acquainted with him, he was the wing sergeant major of the 1st Marine Aircraft Wing in Iwakuni, Japan, when I made an inspection trip over there with the Inspection Division. Probably, when I got back, I wrote up one of the most complimentary reports, as far as the sergeant major and the staff noncommissioned officers were concerned, of any inspection trip that I participated in, because of their drive and their desire to comply with the policies of the Commandant of the Marine Corps in particular with regard to the physical fitness program.
>
> It was during those trying years when the Marine Corps was kind of struggling to get everything back on an even keel. The effort that they displayed there, in their desire to comply with these directives, was nothing short of exemplary, and this was how I stated it in my report to the inspector general.

At the end of a year in Japan Black was due to move again. A conversation took place at Headquarters, with the sergeants major monitor asking the Sergeant Major of the Marine Corps what he thought. Clint Puckett recalled the good opinion he had formed of Black when they had served together in the 7th Marines. Thus, in November, 1974, Black returned to Quantico as sergeant major of the Marine Corps Development and Education Command. Once more he found a situation not to his liking and made his usual blunt assessment:

> It was a shambles. The sergeant major who had been there, he shouldn't have been wearing sergeant major chevrons. He had an office at the other end of the building from the commanding general, and I can understand why the general wouldn't have him close by! Right off the bat, I requested a move to put my office where it should have been, near my general. However, the chief of staff initially blocked my attempt to move.
>
> But then a new general [Lieutenant General Edward Fris] came in— crew-cut, grey hair—one of the greatest men I ever worked for. He was an aviator, and he immediately had me moved close by from where I had been down at the other end of the damn Lejeune Hall. He was tremendous! He and I would go around at 4:00 in the morning in Quantico to check the mess hall. He would say, "I want to know, Sergeant Major, what they're feeding the early watch."
>
> So we'd go into the mess hall, and he'd ask, "I want to see your menu." He wouldn't say, "Sergeant Major, you go get it." He'd go get it. I'd be walking around checking things, checking what was on the chow line. He would ask, "Is that on the line, Sergeant Major?" I'd answer, "No." Then he'd say, "It should be, it's on the menu." Well, needless to add, the mess officer of the base and I weren't on too friendly terms!

Black found out that the enlisted men who did the training at Officers Candidate School had a problem when they got back from the field. Everything was closed out at the Basic School, and they were twenty miles or so from the main part of the base. There was no bus service and they didn't even have a club there. Black told his general about that and recalled Fris' quick reaction:

> "Well, Sergeant Major, let's you and I go out there." So he and I went out. At 3:30 they were closing the "gedunk stand" where you could get a hamburger and french fries and a milk shake. It was run by our PX system. When the general went up there, this lady, a civilian, said, "I'm sorry, I can't..." He ordered a hamburger, testing. She replied, "No, we're closed." All he said was, "Allright." The next day it was open!
>
> And we got into other things. Drinking was a big thing then for young Marines. I told him, "You know, General, you can't buy a milk shake on this base?" He said, "I can't believe that." I challenged him to see if we could go out and find one. This is the kind of man he was; he would take the time for these things as a three-star general. We had milk shakes on the base within two weeks. Needless to say, the PX officer and I weren't on good terms either!

By January, 1975, Black was well into his new job. He now had over twenty-six years of active service to go with all his combat medals, and it seemed clear that he was entering the home stretch of his career. At this precise time, however, the wheels of fate began turning at Headquarters. In mid-January the Enlisted Performance Board there met to begin the careful process of making nominations for the next Sergeant Major of the Marine Corps. The Commandant, General Robert Cushman, had decreed new ground rules:

> 1. *All* sergeants major are to be considered, even if they do not have a combat record (allowing women sergeants major an equal opportunity for the first time).
>
> 2. The previous exclusion of those with more than 28 years in service (because they could not fill the minimum of two years in the billet without exceeding the 30-year deadline) was waived.
>
> 3. The maximum age limit of 55 would remain.

Following these guidelines, the board reviewed the records of all 475 sergeants major on active duty—from the most senior to the most junior. It was a huge task, but logic (and tradition) indicated the resulting nominations would contain a high percentage of senior combat men.

The fifty best-qualified names were then passed along to a five-member general officer board convened in mid-February. Clint Puckett, as the retiring Sergeant Major of the Marine Corps, was an ex-officio member of this board, and had his opportunity to give an evaluation of Black's career. They chose the three finalists, one of whom was Black, for Cushman's ultimate selection.

In March, Cushman made his decision. The new Sergeant Major of the Marine Corps would be Black. He was the first Marine to serve in the billet who did not have World War II experience. The scene now shifted to Quantico, as Black later explained:

> I used to go down to the gym every day and play basketball, pick-up teams with the young troops. Rank had no privilege on that basketball court, I swear. Those young kids would try to tear you up, but I could hold my own. It kept me in good shape. One day they sent the general's sedan after me. They wanted me back at Quantico headquarters.
>
> So I got dressed and got in the car. I went up there and General Fris was smiling. He said, "You've got it!" It was so nice; it couldn't have come from a nicer gentleman. That's how I learned about it. I'd heard stories about how they selected them. You always hear this thing about political pull and all that. I had no political pull.

And that's an understatement! With Black's direct, highly confrontational style, it was obvious that his selection was based on a superb record of professional achievement, rather than on any diplomatic maneuvering.

Clint Puckett, as the outgoing Sergeant Major of the Marine Corps, handled the change-over in typically meticulous style. Black, when later asked about his transition into such a complex job, gave full credit to Puckett:

Clint was sharp, and he was very thorough. He was a very detailed man, having been quite a shooter, and, you know, those guys always make notes. He insisted I get up there early. I wouldn't be taking over until June, but he got me up there in April. Well, I would be new on the block, so I said, "If that's what you want, I'm not going to argue...."

At times it got boring during this break-in, as you might call it, on the administrative procedures. He took pains to ensure that I understood everything I was to do, things that had to be done at Headquarters.

He was very insistent about responding to young Marines' correspondence (which the sergeant major does an awful lot), and not delegating it to somebody else to take care of. You had to personally get involved with the problem that was presented to you through the mail or over the telephone, and then resolve it and tell it like it was. Clint gave me good advice.

The ceremony took place on May 29, 1975. Puckett passed the Sword of Office to Black at the usual impressive ceremony at the Washington Barracks, and Black, in his forthright remarks, sounded a keynote to the enlisted personnel of the Corps which would typify his forthcoming tour of duty, "Get in step with the Corps or fall out of ranks." As the new sergeant major took over and moved into his office on June 1, he came into contact immediately with a wide range of the Headquarters staff. What they saw was a man only five feet, eight inches tall, with 160 lean pounds, black hair, and bluish eyes, but clearly a hardened veteran NCO with impressive ribbons and a wide range of experience.

There was a curious footnote to the timing of Black's arrival. Given the intimate way in which the man in that billet must mesh with his Commandant, it was odd that Cushman selected Black when he was retiring in one month—thus leaving the new incoming Commandant, General Louis Wilson, with a key aide whom he inherited rather than picked himself.

Wilson, after being selected as Commandant and before taking office, naturally gave this incongruity much thought. He had not known Black previously, and there was another senior sergeant major with whom he had worked closely and for whom he had a very high regard. Commandants are expected to be skillful managers of a large, complex organization that has more than its share of strong personalities, unique traditions, and interlocking relationships. So Wilson did the wise thing. Instead of acting on his own impulse, he talked the problem over with his chief of staff, Lieutenant General Leslie Brown, admitting that he "leaned in the direction" of making a direct, personal selection of a man he already knew. Brown, however, pointed out the importance of the careful process which had led up to the board's previous recommendation of Black.

This opinion fitted in well with Wilson's basic philosophy that "the Commandant shouldn't be an over-all monarch, as it were, but should usually reflect the views of the Marine Corps in general." Even though Wilson had originally "forgotten that Black had been selected by General Cushman," he was quickly reminded of it when Black, on his own initiative, went in to see him in his "transition office." The sergeant major offered to stand aside if the new Commandant wished to repeat the nominating process. Wilson made a decision to retain Black, "Therefore, he became the Sergeant Major of the Marine Corps, which I certainly did not regret."

Black served one brief month under Cushman, and then set about developing a smooth working relationship with Wilson, his new boss. The many years of active duty, under a heterogeneous range of former COs, now stood him in good stead. Here was a man who drove himself to produce his best and expected the same from others. He had lost none of his uncompromising, head-on commitment to carry through what he felt was right—often regardless of the attitudes or feelings of others—but he was able at the same time to attune this dedication to excellence to the implementation of the plans and goals of a CO he respected. This was the paradox of the man, and perhaps the secret of his success.

One of the things about Wilson that Black immediately identified with was his combat record. The new Commandant had been awarded the Medal of Honor. It had come from a night of frantic, hand-to-hand fighting on Guam in July, 1944, when then-Captain Wilson had been wounded three times, and, among the other heroic deeds, killed with his pistol at close range a sword-swinging Japanese officer.

The two men who had not known each other began their new work together. Access, communication, and support were vital requirements for Black to do his job according to his own high standards. He found Wilson receptive. As he later evaluated the Commandant's style:

> One thing, with General Wilson, I could go in there to his office any time. Of course I had the common courtesy to know when he was tied up. His secretary was Colonel Ross Mulford, and I had good relations with him. He knew when I could get in, and he would always let me know, right on the ball. So I had good access to the general; he backed me in everything I did.
>
> Wilson was not the type of general officer you got close to, you know, personally. Professionally, right on. He had a sense of humor. We used to play volleyball at picnics and so forth. But you didn't fool around on business. Wilson was a man who didn't waste time, yours or his. He could get right to the point.

This "all-business" style was a striking characteristic of Wilson's. Speaking of his relationship with Black he later confessed, "Rarely did we have any comraderie, which wouldn't bother me a bit because I just didn't do that (whether we were on the airplane or at Headquarters): to go have a beer and so forth. I wouldn't have minded a bit, but that was not my style. We did, however, have some volleyball games together; I enjoyed that exercise."

Wilson, after years of service in major commands naturally brought with him to the post of Commandant certain personal perceptions and concepts of the proper role of the Sergeant Major of the Marine Corps. He later defined his views:

May 29, 1975: Black (right) has just received the Sword of Office of the Sergeant Major of the Marine Corps from the Commandant at the retirement ceremony for his predecessor, Clinton A. Puckett (left).

Official portrait of Black as Sergeant Major of the Marine Corps in May, 1975. He would later add a Legion of Merit Medal to the ribbons here.

First of all, this was a personal thing; I believed that the relationship between the sergeant major and the Commandant had to be personal.

I recall that, in earlier years as a commanding general, in dealing with the Sergeant Major of the Marine Corps, there was an atmosphere about him that permeated the Corps: that somehow he was a spy from Headquarters, a spy from the Commandant, who was going around talking to NCOs and then reflecting their views to the Commandant outside the chain of command. Now, I'm being very frank about this, and other people may or may not have admitted it.

I felt that I did not want this to happen, nor did I want the commanding generals and commanding officers of units that he visited to feel that somehow he was going to report to me what he considered to be shortcomings, or, in fact, "the views of the majority of NCOs" or "what the enlisted men are thinking," as opposed to coming through the chain of command. Now I needed to know that, but I didn't need to know it from a semi-official source, which the sergeant major really was.

On the other hand, the sergeant major provides a very valuable service in that enlisted personnel can feel that they can come to him and tell him their views, their problems, or the general morale of commands—which can be reported to the Commandant and which he would have no other way of knowing. Therein lies a dilemma.

So my relationship with the sergeant major, which I discussed with him, was basically this: "You have an office down the hall. I trust that you are available to every enlisted person in the Marine Corps. If that gets too onerous, let me know." That never occurred.

There was, in this point of view of Wilson's, a curious dichotomy. He himself admitted it was "a dilemma." How can one reconcile the natural desire to eliminate the past perception by some of the Sergeant Major of the Marine Corps as a "spy," or eliminate the pattern of relaying directly to the Commandant "what the enlisted men are thinking," and still have what Wilson *did* want for his sergeant major: enlisted personnel can "tell him their views...which can be reported to the Commandant?"

It is a fine line between the two, calling for judgment. Fortunately, after decades of active duty, the two men had the skill and experience to work it out satisfactorily. They realized it was a matter of style, of perception in the field, and of communications procedures. In the final analysis, Black managed a neat juggling act. While remaining sensitive to the Commandant's initial concerns, he still managed to move full speed ahead with his own hard-charging, plain-spoken way of carrying out to the fullest the responsibilities of his job as he saw them.

Besides the Commandant, Black had to develop a close working relationship with another key person at Headquarters: the sergeants major/first sergeants monitor. As he later explained, "I talked to him when I came in. We agreed that we would touch base, if it was a major command, about whom he was going to put in there. I told him, 'I can give you my input, but you are the man. This is between you and your boss, but I will give you my feelings on it.' We worked well there."

As had been the custom for years, Black accompanied the Commandant on his travels. Wilson later reflected:

> Whenever I made a trip to go to a command in the form of an official visit, he went with me. I told him, "I don't want you to stay around with me," (You know the old days when the sergeant major used to write down, when the commanding officer would inspect, "Joe Schmo had a dirty rifle," and then threw it away promptly.) but I said, "Stay away from me. You're not my aide, and I want you to look at the command here, and be available to the enlisted men to come and see you."
>
> Then, on the way back, we would have a visit (as we did on every trip that we made in an aircraft). We sat aside, and he would have notes, and I would either make mental notes on it or he would write it up when we came back...nothing official and you would find nothing in the files, I'm sure, which indicated that the sergeant major had found the following discrepancies or whatever on such and such a day. That was basically the relationship that I told him that I wanted him to have with me. And it worked out quite satisfactorily.

Black would notify in advance the sergeant major of the unit they would be visiting, and he, in turn, would pass the word that the Sergeant Major of the Marine Corps would be there and available if anyone had anything they wished to discuss with him. Wilson related the outcome:

> Later he would come in to my office and say, "Well, General, there were fifteen people that came in to see me, and their questions were basically along this line." Well that, then, would prompt, or perhaps not prompt, questions from me as to specifics. It often had to do with pay—mostly personal issues, let's face it.
>
> I don't suppose, except for the sergeant major's personal evaluation as to the morale of the command or his general comments on the overall appearance of the command, that there was any time that a senior NCO had come to him to say, "Let me tell that there is in this command...." or "There is in this area a general dissatisfaction..." You never hear of satisfaction; you always hear of dissatisfactions, of course.

The Commandant had a reputation of saying that there would be *no* fat Marines. Accordingly, the Corps discharged hundreds of people who simply would not lose weight. The word quickly went out to air and ground units that a military appearance was absolutely a requirement to be a Marine, and there would be *no* deviation from it. Wilson explained:

> When we would be reviewing what Black had observed or heard on our return trip from a base, without being specific, I would ask, "How about the weight loss?" "Well," he'd reply, "I noticed that there was some weight loss here, but I did find two or three fat people." Then I'd ask, "What unit were they in?" and he would indicate or not. But I did not really want him to go out to the NCO Club at night, and directly say, "Okay, John C. Portly, how much do you weigh?" or things like that. He wasn't a spy, as it were, but I wanted an overall evaluation, and then I would take it from there.

When it came to the question of overseas trips, Wilson followed a different procedure than many of the other Commandants. If it was a U.S. Marine unit, Black would be there, but not so if Wilson was going to a foreign Marine Corps. He looked at it this way:

> If in fact I went to pay an official visit, for instance to the Spanish Marine Corps or to KKO (which was the Indonesian Marine Corps), or the Royal Marine Corps, I did not take the sergeant major. As a matter of fact, he wasn't invited in the sense that, when a message came in from the Commandant of the Royal Marines, for example, there was no indication that "the Sergeant Major of the U.S. Marine Corps is hereby invited."
>
> On the other hand, if I had gone back in a communication and said, "I would like to bring the sergeant major," I'm sure they would have said, "Okay." But this was more of a visit of equals, as it were, than to look at things from an enlisted point of view. I really don't know what the Royal Marines' enlisted personnel could have contributed through my sergeant major for the U.S. Marine Corps.

On the vast majority of the trips that Black did make with the Commandant, his strongly-motivated personality and aggressive initiative sometimes led him to do more than Wilson was probably aware of. There were humorous results sometimes. He later told a story with a smile, "We went on a trip in Guam. The first time I went up to the gate, and they had nuclear storage there, and here's this kid in dress blues; sharp looking. I always got out of my vehicle, so I went in his booth. There he was in dress blues and tennis shoes. I told the general, as a joke, 'You know the old saying we used to hear, "Dress blues and tennis shoes." Well, General, I found one today!' He didn't get excited about it; he just laughed."

A more serious note soon appeared, however. Black went on:

> With their reaction force for nuclear security there you couldn't even get ahold of any of the higher-ups quickly. I tested the system. I asked the guard at the gate, "Whom do you call? Where do you call? Where does he live? What is his phone number?" All he could answer was, "He lives in quarters on the base. He's married and that's an accompanied tour." He really wasn't able to call direct if there had been an emergency. It was a very fragmented, very loose situation.

In a more personal vein, there were gracious, thoughtful things that Black did on his trips. Arriving alone at one base, he was taken to dinner by the local sergeant major, George Rogers, and his wife. In appreciation for their hospitality, he presented the wife with a handsome little pocket knife, engraved with "Henry H. Black, Sergeant Major of the Marine Corps." She still treasures that knife.

Much more frequently, however, trips revealed problems, and Black was not a man to back away from strongly confronting these. As he later recounted:

> I got a reputation going around the Marine Corps on these trips. Wilson would go his way on a visit. I didn't follow in his tracks. We agreed, that's

no good; so when he'd go one way, I'd go another way. Mine was strictly with the troops. What I saw, I would report back, I would investigate.

I upset some generals in the Marine Corps; I really did; because I told it like it was. They thought I owed them some allegiance not to tell the Commandant. Well, if I didn't tell the Commandant, what the hell was the use of me being there? It wasn't trivial stuff; living conditions are important, for example. I'd had a casual company, and I'd seen one out at El Toro that wasn't fit for hogs and also at Camp Pendleton. Things were done: Wilson went at them and there were improvements.

I'd go to early chow at another place and ask the cook, "What's on the menu for breakfast?" Well, at early chow he wasn't feeding the normal breakfast. He didn't get up early enough. I'd take that to the sergeant major there, and tell him to take care of it.

When I saw trends and major problems, that's when I unloaded on the Commandant...even if it was a sergeant major. Once Wilson and I were going to get on the aircraft to fly to the next stop. The wing brigadier general came up to me and asked to talk to me privately. I answered, "Yes, sir." Then he said, "We've got to do something with my sergeant major." I replied, "I know. He's sorry. He spends too much time out in the town. He just isn't professional." So, I mentioned this to the Commandant on our flight down to the Philippines.

I guess Wilson got on the radio or something, and when I later flew into FMFPac, the Deputy FMFPac Commander called me into his office. He exclaimed, "What are you telling the Commandant this story for?" I said, "I don't know what you are talking about. That's my responsibility!" He barked, "It's not true!" So he got the general who told me this on the phone and he denied everything. That really upset me. But I didn't back off. I let the Commandant know about all that. It didn't make me too popular around FMFPac with the deputy!

Curiously, when asked about this incident years later, Wilson stated that he did not remember it. (Of course, as Commandant, there were many big issues on his mind.) He went on, however, to detail his views of how such a problem should properly be handled by a general officer:

In effect, I'm sure that if a general wanted to get somebody out, it had been my policy that he should step up and be counted. And if, in fact, they wanted a sergeant major to leave, they ought to write a letter and talk to the commanding general about it. My sergeant major was not there to be a sounding board for generals. The sergeant major was there to be a champion for, and one who understood, enlisted men.

It was known as "bulkheading" in the old days in the Navy, when the enlisted men would be outside the officers' wardroom and talk loudly so that the people in the wardroom could hear it. So generals, if they wanted to say anything to the Commandant or to the commanding general, they ought to say it and not "bulkhead" about it.

Anytime the Sergeant Major of the Marine Corps visits a base, he always checks out the food. Here Black discusses it with another sergeant major during a visit to FMF, Atlantic, Headquarters in Norfolk, Virginia in 1975.

Black photo

April, 1976, visit with the Commandant to the Marine base at Kaneohe Bay, Hawaii: Black checks out the equipment of a "recon" Marine (top). Note rope for rapelling cliffs and underwater scuba gear. Then he moves on to inspect a 105mm artillery piece (bottom).

An airplane hangar (top) provides a good location to pass the latest word to the troops during a September, 1976, visit to the El Toro Air Station in Santa Ana, California. In a more relaxed moment on the same trip, Black breaks out in a smile as he talks with two young Marines (bottom).

Black photo

The old style campaign hat is a treasured symbol of the Marine drill instructor. This one has been bronzed and mounted to a plaque to present to a DI on the completion of his tour of duty. Black (left) served as master of ceremonies during a 1976 visit to the recruit depot at Parris Island.

Black photo

Black also remembered:

> There was another aggravating time with a different general. He was at Parris Island; he called up and really chewed my ass out. It was his own sergeant major's fault. That man had called me with a request for an assignment to a major field command before he retired, and I had referred him to the monitor, who then cut his orders for the 3d Division. The general didn't want to lose him and he raised hell with me. He cussed me out and everything. I said, "I'm not taking this shit."
>
> So I went right in and saw Wilson. I walked right in and didn't even knock. Wilson got on his phone before I left the office, and he said, "Get me that general!" This was what I liked about Wilson; he backed me 100 percent. He had him on the phone before I left. By the time I got to my desk that phone was ringing within two minutes, and that general was apologizing. I'm serious! That's how Wilson backed me.

Another time Black came back to Headquarters from a trip with the Commandant, and a general there "thought that I should report to him before I told the Commandant, but I said, 'No,' to him. He was a three-star, but I worked for the Commandant. Then he repeated, 'Well you should have done this...' I replied, 'I report to the Commandant.' So I made my trip report directly to the Commandant on everything I did out there." It was crystal clear that, regardless of rank, Black always stood his ground uncompromisingly.

With so many trips required of him, it would have been nice if his wife could have accompanied him. Wilson's wife generally went with her husband, and Black commented, "When we would go to a base, do you know who talked with the wives? The Commandant's wife would, but I talked to them, too. It would have been nice if my wife could have been there. But we made only one trip together—to a scholarship charity event in New York City. I never asked anyone for anything, and I would never think of asking the Commandant, or anyone else, if my wife could go. If he had wanted her to go, he would have said so."

One of the useful Headquarters meetings for Black was an innovation of Wilson's: a weekly assembly of all his senior staff. There Black was able to give any comment he wished to make on enlisted matters. Apparently, he could practice diplomacy on occasion, for his daily contacts with the generals there went smoothly. Wilson noted, "The fact is that I never heard a word of complaint from any of these senior officers. He performed like I wanted a sergeant major to perform."

With Black's deeply felt convictions about professional improvement, he—not surprisingly—acted. Before he became Sergeant Major of the Marine Corps, his predecessor, Clint Puckett, had assembled an informal gathering of sergeants major to make recommendations on issues important to the enlisted personnel of the Corps. Black took his usual initiative and organized the first formal, full-scale Sergeants Major Symposium. It was typical of him that he felt that the voice of the enlisted personnel should be heard in a systematic way, at the highest policy levels of the Corps.

Thus it was that, in July, 1976, he assembled fifty sergeants major from all over the Corps. Black served as chairman. The assemblage included Robert Cleary, the personnel sergeant major at Headquarters, and John Massaro, sergeant major of the 1st Division at Camp Pendleton—both of whom would later rise to take over the top spot. In addition, Wilson came to express his views and put the Commandant's stamp on the importance of the meeting. He was joined by the heads of the various Headquarters staff divisions.

In typical Black style, the tone was, "Buckle down and get with it!" They met for three full days, beginning at 7:30 a.m., to evaluate 119 separate suggestions from major field commands all over the world. The recommendations ranged over a vast area of concerns: fundamentals like staff NCO living quarters, promotions, drill instructors, recruiting duty, fitness reports, the Staff NCO Academy, marksmanship, and dress blue uniform regulations, as well as more esoteric subjects, such as the color of socks to be worn with the utility uniforms of Women Marines, bumper stickers, and haircut regulations for Reservists (in a hippy age).

The recommendations were individually accepted, rejected, or modified, and then were passed on to the appropriate staff divisions at Headquarters. It was a well-organized start of a useful procedure that continued every second year thereafter.

Cleary, with his power base in personnel, was a man with determination and convictions as strong as Black's. As is natural with two men who had more than earned their stripes, they could not always agree on every individual decision. Cleary later recollected, "Black was stubborn, and I used to argue with him once in a while about an overweight person, saying, 'Give him another chance...that sort of thing, because this guy didn't get overweight over night.' I would point out, 'The Marine Corps has a responsibility too. Who's watching him? What type of supervision is he getting in the field?' Black would sometimes give a little."

As might be expected, the sergeant major was often called upon to represent the Marine Corps on public occasions. One of these was the annual Marine Corps Service held at the Washington National Cathedral on the Sunday nearest the Corps' birthday, November 10. In 1976, Black was cast in a role somewhat different from his previous experiences. Clad in dress blues, his chest blazing with an impressive array of medals, he mounted the steps of the Cathedral's ornate Gothic lectern, and read the First Lesson from the Book of Psalms.

A different requirement came at him from a wholly new direction. Puckett had previously started the practice of writing articles to reach a broad cross-section of enlisted Marines through their own special magazine, *Leatherneck*. When asked to continue this practice, Black was taken aback (for one of the rare times in his life). He later admitted, "I was shocked that I had to write articles because I'm not a writer. I tried to write on things that I'd seen in the Corps and on issues that needed attention...making it as readable as possible without being dull."

Although this type of obligation was certainly not Black's favorite, he dove in anyway. A typical column, on the hypersensitive subject of promotions, laid out the full details of how the Sergeant Major of the Marine Corps would handle an inquiry:

> The majority of the mail I receive consists of inquiries from Marines attempting to find a specific reason as to why they have failed to be selected. Upon receiving correspondence of this nature, I draw the individual's case file and review his or her entire history as a Marine. Initially, I insure the member did in fact compete before the current board in the correct zone, as well as all boards for which the member has been eligible to compete....
>
> Some Marines fail to realize the importance of their photographs. I review them for personal appearance and proper weight. In checking their photos for personal appearance, I review them as if the individual were standing a formal inspection; i.e. proper grooming, footwear, sharpness and fit of the uniform and decorations/awards worn and entitlement.
>
> Next, I review each fitness report since promotion to their current rank, or in the case of those individuals with a relatively short amount of time in grade, I review all fitness reports for the preceding five years. Initially I check for missing fitness reports and physical fitness test results. If I discover any fitness reports are missing, I notify the Marine and the Fitness Report Branch.
>
> I also screen the entire service record for any information which may be derogatory in nature.... I also check it for awards, meritorious masts,

On a 1976 visit to the Marine air station at Kaneohe, Hawaii, Black (right) makes a careful inspection of the correctional facility's squad bay.

letters of appreciation, special recognition received and off-duty education or correspondence courses.

After my initial review of the fitness reports, I then go back and conduct an in-depth review of each report, both the markings and the written comments. By so doing, a mental picture can be drawn of the Marine.

There's more to the column—and it's not poetical writing—but it does make clear the careful, time-consuming effort that the senior enlisted man of the Corps would make on behalf of the most obscure corporal.

Thus the busy months went by for Black. Meanwhile, his health was deteriorating. Like any Marine who had devoted his whole adult life to a career in the Corps, he had expected to "go out on thirty." It was not to be. The years of pressure and conflict, in war and peace, had taken their toll. Sadly, he faced reality:

> I was really having physical problems: very severe stomach pains, and a hernia. I used to go out on trips, and I'd be seriously sick, but I never let it be known. It got so bad that I finally went to see the medical people. The Veterans' Administration [V.A.] found an ulcer (which the Navy couldn't find, sorry to say). Then there were other things. With my acidy stomach, anything I ate didn't agree with me.
>
> The tenseness of the job—and it is tense if you take it seriously—didn't help me either. And I thought, "There's another guy who can come along and replace me very easily. Don't put up with the aggravation." So I told the Commandant, "Physically, I'm hurting and I've got to do something." So I went out.... I should have retired in '78. That would have been thirty years. I went out at twenty-nine and a half.

It was hard to take, retiring early, but he went out in style. There was the full formal ceremony at the Washington Barracks on March 31, 1977, as his successor took over. Wilson made a glowing summation of Black's contributions to the Corps, and then stepped forward to pin on him the Legion of Merit. This was normally awarded only to officers, but Black was an uncommon man who had always stood for—and fought cantankerously for— what he felt was right for his Corps. Of course, the Commandant had had a hand in the process of the award. A citation had been drafted at Headquarters and sent to the Secretary of the Navy for his approval and signature. The formal citation summarized Black's accomplishments:

> Throughout his tenure, Sergeant Major Black consistently demonstrated mature judgment and resourcefulness in discharging his duties as the Commandant of the Marine Corps' principal enlisted assistant. Upon assuming the billet as Sergeant Major of the Marine Corps, he brought to his position the accumulated wisdom of a long and distinguished career, which he applied indefatigably to the improvement of the morale and welfare of the individual Marine....
>
> In addition, in his extensive travels and numerous appearances in the civilian as well as military community, and his sage messages to the Corps,

Sergeant Major Black set a philosophical and moral tone for all Marines to emulate. Equally noteworthy were his perceptive and knowledgeable suggestions and recommendations to the Commandant of the Marine Corps and to the Headquarters Staff, which resulted in the implementation and adoption of a number of innovative and far-reaching policies and procedures....

Now Black was out in the cold, just another forty-eight-year-old, unemployed man who had spent his best years in a world remote from the comprehension of civilian employers. How could they possibly comprehend the guts, the leadership, the power that had characterized his life? On his first day as a civilian, Black faced the reality, "I came into the Corps for travel and adventure, and I got both. Sometimes I got a little more adventure than I wanted. Now I'm looking for employment."

A man with his kind of backbone, however, would always be fortified by the credo on a plaque he kept with him. It said, "For those who have fought for it, life has a flavor the protected will never know." He plunged in to tackle his new world. After all, he had Debora and Catherine who were then freshmen at Mary Washington College, David who was a student at Wright Intermediate School, and Michael, a sergeant in the Corps. In addition, there was, of course, Fannie and their home in Fredericksburg, Virginia. (They had bought this in 1975, when he was Sergeant Major of the Marine Corps, and he had spent countless hours commuting from there to Washington.)

As he later described his situation then:

I had to find a job. I was off two weeks, and I couldn't stand it. We had a yard sale, made $500.00 selling our junk. We didn't have much because we'd moved twenty-nine times in twenty-four years, my wife and I. That's not only from station to station, that's also moving within one tour of duty. I owned this home, and had a good mortgage. It didn't cost much, only $44,000 originally.

But I had never previously given much thought to a civilian job. Then Puckett brought me over to the V.A. and I was introduced around. I didn't hear from them, so I went over to this golf course after two weeks. I wanted to work. I was bored! So I put in an application to work around the golf course, greens keeper, whatever, just to work. I also needed the money.

The day I was going to work there, a car salesman called and wanted me to come over. "You want to sell cars?" I said, "Hell, I'll sell cars. I'll do anything once." I worked there four months selling cars, and I sold a few with no experience. Military retirement pay doesn't cover your expenses. Then I heard from the V.A. and I went with them. I've been there ever since.

When I was on active duty, sergeants major always called each other "Sergeant Major"; we didn't use nicknames. Once I got into the V.A., I decided "Henry" was too square sounding, so I switched to "Hank."

A quieter, more relaxed tone slipped into his voice as he looked at his life then. The privations and confrontations and ulcers of the past receded into memory, and the happiness of a man living a satisfying family life came out, "I could never stop working now. The money's good, and my wife and I don't have to worry about end-of-the-month bills; our children are all raised. We've done a lot of work on our house. I bought her a new Cougar car. (Of course, I'm paying for it!) I'm thinking when I'm sixty-two to sixty-five I'll pull the pin on this V.A. job. We love our home in Fredericksburg. Fannie will not leave it. After all, she had to move all those times in past years!"

There were two main relaxations he enjoyed:

> Always in the Marine Corps, whether we lived on base or off, I always kept the nicest yard. I worked hard, and it was relaxing being a gardener. I loved this; I kept up my grass and hedge and everything. So, when I retired, for about five years I'd paint and strip paint and cut the grass and work around the house. It's all I did in my spare time.
>
> One day a general (whom I'd known as a lieutenant in Korea in 1950) called me, and I went up to Washington for golf and a retirement briefing. So we went golfing. I found that I sort of liked it. I'd golfed now and then throughout the time in the Marine Corps, but not regularly. My wife said, "Why don't you take up golf?" so I bought a damn set of golf clubs. A buddy of mine said, "Join the country club." So I joined the country club; it didn't cost too much. I haven't missed a weekend since. Then I bought my wife a lawn mower, and she had to cut the grass!

Apparently Fannie handled this responsibility with aplomb, for she was always a "doer." The entire time her husband was in the Corps, she taught Sunday School—and continued to do so at a nearby Methodist church after he retired. (Forced into a corner, he had to confess that he did not regularly join her at Sunday services.) Black went on to recount with pride, "She was the president of the Wives' Club at Quantico. She did a lovely job; not just I but the generals there then would tell you that. She participated in raising funds for scholarships for children. You know, she's not one to just sit back and say, 'Take care of me.' She got out on her own and did a lot of things for the base and the community, and she still does."

How to summarize a man of such diverse characteristics? Surely one of the best insights must be the evaluation of his Commandant, General Wilson:

> Of course, I would not have ever had a sergeant major who was not what I consider to be the epitome of military bearing and those things which I insisted all of Marines try to adhere to, because he served as an example. His combat record was something which was enviable for Marines. These are things which I looked for and found in him. I found that he was quiet; he was thoughtful; was not prone to giving exaggerated statements; but nevertheless one who would give his answer to my questions without being overly verbose. We weren't in the business of telling "sea stories!" He performed like I wanted my sergeant major to perform.

Black's own summary was straight from his heart, "I loved the time I put in the Marine Corps. I didn't consider it a career; I considered it an adventure every day. I really did. 99 to 100 percent of it was great, and of course, where there were problems, those were minor things. Of course, it's unusual, but I never went back to Headquarters after I retired. When I took the uniform off, I took it off! The Corps was in their hands now, and I kept my nose out of it. I thought that's the way it should be."

That's the way it was for the man who would always "tell it like it is."

Chapter 9

THE RECON MAN
Sergeant Major John R. Massaro

A "recon man"—what does it mean? As a contraction of "reconnaissance," the easy answer is in the dictionary: "an exploratory military survey...by the probes of small land units of enemy territory and of enemy installations, movements, activities, and strength."

But the answer in the Marine Corps is more complex in subtle ways. There are the intangibles, invisible but crucial, that lie at the heart of this answer. The driving inner sense of motivation, dedication, and cooperation is palpable. Then there are the carefully selected men, the demanding specialized training, the unusual technical equipment, the isolated danger of their mission, and the high-stress physical conditioning, with all of these elements bound together in a fierce unit esprit de corps.

Thus it is no surprise that those Marines who proudly carry the designation of a "recon man" are convinced that they are a special breed. Their skills must include, above and beyond ordinary combat training, familiarity with submarines, rubber boats, scuba diving, parachutes, mountain training, and long distance runs. Pride has unfailingly been a basic characteristic of the whole Corps since its founding on November 10, 1775, but the "recon" units have always felt they had a particular and distinctive role: an elite few with a priority mission which required the most physically demanding, highly refined skills of anyone, anywhere, anytime.

These were the key elements that dominated the most characteristic Marine assignments of John Massaro. In 1979, at the end of his career as Sergeant Major of the Marine Corps, above the multiple rows of ribbons on his uniform, he wore his two proudest insignia: Parachutist and Scuba Diver, symbols of a "recon man." These badges of honor came from earlier years of hard work and outstanding performance in a series of "recon" units.

His first exposure was when he was in a rifle outfit thirty years earlier. As a private first class, fresh out of boot camp in 1949, Massaro was serving as an infantryman in the 6th Marines at Camp Pendleton. There he got his first training in submarine and rubber boat work. After this initial experience, Massaro's next contact with this type of training came after several intervening assignments, including a tour of duty in the Korean war. His involvement in full-time "recon" work came about in an accidental way. In August, 1955, when he reported in at Camp Pendleton, the assignment NCO asked him, "Where do you want to go?" and, having been in the 5th Marines in Korea, he replied, "5th Marines." Massaro later recounted what happened next:

> He ranted and raved a little bit and said, "No way, no way! I'll tell you what: I'll make you a deal. Every day they're hounding me to send somebody down to the division reconnaissance company and nobody wants to go down there."
>
> In my recollections from Korea, I really didn't have that great a respect for reconnaissance work, so I didn't want to go down there either. But, in the meantime, he had told me that if I'd go down there for an interview, whether I stayed or not, he'd send me to the 5th Marines. It was kind of a no-lose situation.

Thus Massaro spent about half a day there with the company first sergeant and some of the staff NCOs and talked to some of the troops. Then the company commander had the first sergeant bring him into his office, and they had a talk. Massaro remembered:

> All this time I'm thinking back to Korea: on the patrol routes that I ran every two or three nights, Recon would come up and run them about once a month. Every time you picked up the division newspaper there were big articles of how great these guys were. They were doing once a month what I did nearly every night.
>
> So now I thought, "Hey, I don't need this." But I patiently listened to the captain and when he was all finished he said, "Well, what do you think?" I answered, "Well, Captain, I think you've got a good outfit here, but I think I'd be better off down in the 5th Marines." He never lost his

cool; he just very calmly sat there, and then he said, "That's your decision to make. But you probably couldn't hack it here anyhow." Needless to say, that was the turning point, and that's how I got started in reconnaissance type work. It turned out to be one of the best things that ever happened to me.

Massaro began that tour as a staff sergeant, but in November of 1955 was promoted to be a technical sergeant, serving as a company gunnery sergeant in the 1st Division's Reconnaissance Company. As he threw himself into his new duties, his opinion of recon men and the job they were trained for began to change completely. He was hooked. To develop his expertise further, he requested assignment to the Army Airborne School at Fort Benning, Georgia. In February, 1957, it was approved. For three weeks he attended jump school with five other enlisted Marines and two young captains. (One of the latter was named Paul X. Kelley, and he would go on to become Commandant almost thirty years later.) Besides earning his parachute wings insignia, Massaro left the airborne school with one other distinguishing characteristic, "whitewalls." These were jump school haircuts that left a man nearly nude above his ears, and Massaro adopted that ultra-close cut as a permanent style.

On his return to Pendleton, he was immediately plunged into typical reconnaissance work. As he later recounted:

> Our company began to train one of the battalions of the 7th Marines to become eventually a reconnaissance battalion. We spent the next several weeks in various types of training: rubber boat work, motorized, overland, and beach reconnaissance—all those things associated with the gathering of information. Then, in May of 1957, that particular battalion was designated the division "recon" battalion, and we were designated C Company in that battalion.
>
> After that we began to receive more of the normal other assignments that you get in any battalion, where you have to provide additional people for the guard and for mess duty or fire watch. Those were assignments that we hadn't previously had, and this detracted somewhat from our previous level of efficiency and proficiency, which we had been able to enjoy as an independent company conducting our own training as decided by our company commander. I stayed there in the "recon" battalion until June, 1957.

Massaro went on to extol the superior quality of the men in his reconnaissance unit, pointing out proudly that, during his entire tour of that duty, "we only had two office hours [disciplinary actions]." There was, however, some friction with others: "As a matter of fact, we got into a little bit of trouble with the division assignment people, because we would go over to the casual company and interview everybody coming through it for possible assignment to the division 'recon' company. That's how we got the cream of the crop; we got these Marines that stood a click above everybody else. Marines' Marines were what they were!"

The little squabbles over assignments never diminished Massaro's satisfaction in the achievements of his "recon" company. However, significant changes occurred which forced him to reconsider his situation:

> It was very difficult for me to consider leaving that particular company. But at this time the decision to establish a force reconnaissance company had already been made. Things had finally gotten to the point in my battalion where I was very disappointed. We just weren't able to do the things we'd previously been able to do, as far as accomplishing our missions in the field.
>
> Force "recon" had been periodically sending staff NCOs out to where we were, and they would ask me and the other parachute-qualified and scuba-qualified Marines if we wanted to go into their company. Well, because I wouldn't go, none of the others would go. Finally, when I could see that things were going to go continually downhill from what I believed our reconnaissance unit should be, I went to my company commander and I told him, "Captain, I don't want to leave, but...."

With his move to the force reconnaissance company, Massaro became platoon sergeant of a platoon that was both "parachute and scuba qualified." Thus he was able to go to scuba school, "We had a preliminary three-week course at Pendleton that was administered by people from our own company who were already scuba-qualified. Then from there we went to the sub base at Pearl Harbor for our actual qualification. There they put us through the 125-foot diving tower, and we made all of our qualification dives at Pearl Harbor."

In June, 1959, Massaro received his official gunnery sergeant warrant, even though he had been performing those duties previously. On a few occasions after that, for a short period of time, he also acted as company first sergeant.

November that year brought orders for a change of station. He'd had over four years of devotion to every phase of the intensive training that put a stamp on him as a "recon man" for all the rest of his career. His new duty assignment to aviation was a total change of pace. Massaro was not pleased, "I had absolutely no desire to go to an air wing. Being an infantry Marine, my only wish, when I knew that I had to leave Pendleton, was to go to the 3d Division." As always, the Corps had the last word. He was sent to the 1st Marine Aircraft Wing (1st MAW) in Iwakuni, Japan. Evaluating this move later, Massaro mused, "All these things that I didn't particularly want, somebody somewhere was taking care of me, and they turned out to be real blessings."

There was one parting incident at Pendleton. The gung-ho, hard-charging "recon man" got a call from the wise old master sergeant who was operations chief in force recon and had had previous tours of duty with an air wing. Massaro long remembered his advice:

> "Gunny, we're going to have to sit down and have a little chat here," he told me. So he assigned me a time that I could come in and just sit down and have a leisurely talk with him. Then he said to me, "Gunny, I'm going to tell you something right now. You can take it for what it's worth, or do what you please, but you'll never last in the air wing doing what you do here."

For most of the Marines that we had in our "recon" company, as company gunnery sergeant I had pretty much ruled them with an iron hand. If I found a Coke bottle setting on the window sill, I simply dropped it on the deck and it broke right there. If I found a wall locker that was open, when that Marine came back he found all of his clothing on the deck, scattered about. They appreciated it in the long run, I think: most of them did anyhow. So everybody pretty much knew what to expect from me.

If I had something that would go wrong in the barracks, where there might be a little disturbance the night before, I didn't hesitate at the next morning's formation to invite those responsible to step out of ranks if they felt so inclined, and I'd bust their nose for them right there, and we wouldn't have any more of these problems!

It began to dawn on Massaro that in going from an environment like that, where people understood rigid discipline, to an air wing where discipline would be somewhat lax, he probably would not last very long unless he took the advice of the master sergeant:

They're only interested in one thing in the air wing, and that's how many aircraft they're flying on a day-to-day basis. They really don't care too much about haircuts, or shined brass, or shined boots. So you're going to have to go over there and really change what you now believe to be right, and find another way to implement some of your ideas. I think that by example some of the things you do will rub off, and then I think that you'll get good results. But if you try to use the same tactics you used here....

So Massaro left force "recon" to face a drastically different world, and he later admitted, "That master sergeant's counseling probably did more to help me get into that tour and get through it than anything else." Throughout the time he was serving with the air wing, the dyed-in-the-wool "recon man" strove to maintain his special qualifications. During the summer of 1960, Massaro was able to wangle orders to Okinawa to re-qualify as a scuba diver. (The rules required periodic requalification.) To maintain his parachute qualification, Massaro helped spark the formation of a sport parachute club at the air wing base. This enabled him and a half dozen other qualified Marines to participate for six days in a competition-demonstration put on by the Army, the First Far East Sport Parachute Meet.

After slightly more than a year with the air wing, Massaro requested duty with the 1st Division, and in January, 1961, the orders came through. Being a savvy gunnery sergeant with over twelve years of experience in the ways of the Corps, when he got back to Camp Pendleton he made a little detour before reporting in to division headquarters. Who could tell in advance where the sergeant major there might assign him? So he went first to the force "recon" company and met with the company commander (who knew an old pro "recon man" when he saw one). That officer called division headquarters and made a few arrangements, so when Massaro reported in officially, the die had already been cast, and he came straight back home again to his old outfit, the 1st Force Reconnaissance Company.

There was another happy reunion during this period. In May, 1962, the new sergeant major, Clinton Puckett, reported in for the 1st Reconnaissance Battalion. He was an old friend from Korea and a previous tour of duty as D.I.s together at San Diego. Massaro's company had its headquarters in the same building as Puckett's battalion CP. Now they were "recon men" together. And Puckett's favorable opinion of Massaro was further strengthened: "Now he was a gunny, there was no change from the time he was a young staff sergeant; he was still very sober, very stern, still stood out even among outstanding Marines."

There was another relationship then that Massaro later looked back on "somewhat in shame; it was something that started out badly but turned out in the end to be good—and the good far outweighed the bad." He recalled:

> We had a supply officer and, of course, he ran his supply building about the same way that I ran my company gunnery sergeant job. Sometimes these things came in conflict with each other. We had no—I guess you might say—real admiration for each other, although initially there were no real hostilities between us either. I had taken him through what we called "junior jump school," and I'm sure that some of the pain that I inflicted upon him, while he was going through the school, stuck in his mind.
>
> But one day, while things were (I thought) going rather smoothly, one of my platoon sergeants came to me and said, "Gunny, this supply warehouse situation has got to be changed. The captain just threw me out of there because I was wearing tennis shoes with my utility uniform. We were just getting ready to go out on a dive, and it would be ridiculous to wear boots and then change to my tennis shoes at the boat and everything."
>
> So I became somewhat infuriated and went to see my company commander. As a result, I assume that my company commander had that captain in and had a few harsh words for him. For a short period of time, why, there were—I'm afraid—some strained feelings between that captain and myself.

Some months later, most of Massaro's company left to go to WestPac, but he stayed behind. Then that same captain was assigned as his company commander. As company first sergeant, Massaro said to himself, "Oh, boy, I've had it now. I had my day; now he's going to have his." They went through an extended period of feeling each other out suspiciously. Gradually, however, the captain fell into a pattern of asking his first sergeant for a recommendation after the weekly barracks inspection. Each time, Massaro would suggest an earlier and earlier afternoon hour to release the men on liberty, and the captain would agree. Finally, inspection was finished very early one week, and Massaro later remembered with a smile:

> The captain asked, "Well, what do you recommend, First Sergeant?" I replied, "Sound liberty call right now." He said, "Post the duty NCO and sound it." Some time after that day he commented to me, "First Sergeant, you're trying to get into my knickers," or something like that!

But, from that day forward, I guess you'd have to say that our relationship was nothing but the finest. The captain was quite instrumental in at least one, and possibly two, Meritorious Masts [commanding officers commendation] that I got before I left that particular company. I'm sure that helped when promotion time rolled around.

That tour of reconnaissance duty ended in April of 1963, but, after another interlude on the drill field, Massaro was soon returned to his specialty. While independent duty (away from the regular field units) was not something he liked, his orders in January, 1966, combined independent duty with his true love, "recon" work. He went to the 4th Reconnaissance Company, a Reserve unit, in San Bernadino, California, as a member of the I&I staff. As he later recollected:

The primary mission of the I&I staff was to train Reserves adequately so that, in the event that they were mobilized, they could satisfactorily carry out their mission. Thus the work I did there was basically the same type of instruction that you'd be giving to Marines of the regular establishment. We had one weekend a month that they drilled, and we had them for the whole weekend. In our particular unit, we did a lot of field work, and oftentimes we kept them over night. So they didn't just come to the training center and spend eight hours and leave.

The I&I that I had during most of my tour there was a major who had been to Vietnam and come back. Together we made some rather significant changes to our Reserve training program. Parachute jumps, for example: prior to his coming they were pretty much an all-day affair, and you didn't accomplish anything other than the jump itself. Once he got there we discussed that problem, and we said, "There will be no more administrative jumps. Henceforth jumps will be tactical, and all administrative jumps will be conducted on a non-drill weekend. If you've come here to train and you want to jump out of an airplane, then you're going to do something in conjunction with it. You're going to have some type of a reconnaissance mission to perform in conjunction with that."

There were other responsibilities which were thrust upon Massaro in addition to the reconnaissance training. One of these was the Casualty Assistance Program. He described it this way:

Unfortunately, during that period of time, we were still engaged in Vietnam. For any Marine from the San Bernadino area, either killed in action [KIA] or wounded in action [WIA], we had to make a report to the next of kin. During the period of time that I was there, we had thirty-five KIAs and 120 WIAs.

So a large portion of our time was utilized making casualty calls. Ordinarily, even with a WIA casualty call, it would usually necessitate anywhere from one to three, four, or five visits to the family—until the Marine was either back to duty or back in the hospital. Then on a KIA, you had to make all the arrangements for the funeral. After the burial you had to make all the arrangements to get the next of kin everything that they were entitled to.

In addition, San Bernadino was quite a Marine area, and we were frequently called upon to participate in various activities throughout the community. These responsibilities, later on, really were a benefit to me, because I'd never done anything like them before. They had an organization called "Santa Claus Incorporated," that helped us collect toys for the needy children, and there were other activities, such as Little League baseball, where they frequently asked for our color guards.

A transfer in November, 1967, marked the end of Massaro's last specific assignment as a "recon man," but the habits and style of that special life remained a central feature of all the rest of his career. The intangible resources that he had acquired proved to be invaluable assets in the wide variety of his other assignments.

Where had it all begun? Born in Cleveland, Ohio, on May 22, 1930, John Massaro went to first grade in a school in Wooster. But then his family moved to Orrville, twenty miles south of Akron, where his father worked in a wood preserving plant. The young man attended Orrville High School, where he played on the undefeated football team and was active in the Future Farmers of America. When he graduated in 1948, his dream was to study agriculture at Ohio State University. It was not to be because his father could not afford the tuition.

The eighteen-year-old Massaro had only been out of the state of Ohio twice. Now he wanted to see some of the world. His football coach was an old navy man and suggested that career as a way for Massaro to satisfy his urge to travel. With that in mind, Massaro and a close friend decided to pay a visit to the Navy recruiter in Wooster, only ten miles away. As he later recalled:

> I never intended to enlist in the Marine Corps. We went into the Navy Recruiting Office and were interviewed and administered a very brief and, I'd say, somewhat simple test. They determined that, at least at that point, we were qualified for enlistment. However, they had an eight- to nine-week waiting list, and we wanted to go the next day, which they told us would be impossible.
>
> So we went back outside and we were standing on the sidewalk and got to talking, and this buddy of mine said, "Well, let's go over and talk to the Marine recruiter." Initially I was opposed to that idea, because of our football coach's stories, so I told him, "No, I don't think we want to do that." But he answered, "Hey, fair is fair. We came over here to the Navy recruiter. Let's at least go down and talk to the Marine guy."
>
> We located his office and went in and had a brief interview with him. He gave us basically the same test that the Navy did. We passed that. He asked, "When do you want to go?" We said, "Tomorrow." He replied, "Impossible, no way! Maybe in two or three weeks I could get you in,

but that would be the earliest." So we said, "Well, if that's the case, we appreciate your time, but no thanks." His response was, "What do you mean?" We answered, "We've already been over to the Navy recruiter, and that's really where we intended to go in the first place. If we've got to wait three weeks to go in the Marine Corps, we might as well wait another few weeks and go in the Navy."

So he came back, "Just a minute. Let me make a phone call." (To this day, and having later had recruiting duty myself, I doubt very seriously that he called any further than the local bar or some beer joint.) But when he made this phone call everything was "Yes, sir," and "No, sir," and "Thank you very much, sir." When he hung up he said, "You know, you've got to be two of the luckiest guys that ever walked the face of the earth." We asked, "Why is that?" and he replied, "You know, they just happened to have two openings. I can get you in tomorrow. But you'll have to be over here at 6:00 in the morning to catch the bus to go up to Cleveland for your physical and your processing."

We said, "Oh, that'll be no problem. We can do that." Then he added, "There's one more thing that we have to do. I've got to run a local police check on you. Have you ever been in any trouble?" Although we'd had some minor difficulties, as kids did back in those days, there was nothing really serious, we told him.

The recruiter quickly took the two young men over to Orrville for an interview with the burly town marshall there. Massaro recalled the scene:

When the old marshall opened the door he just dwarfed all of us. Standing there he asked, "Yes, what can I do for you?" The recruiter said, "Well, I was wondering about these two young men that I have here. They've applied for enlistment in the Marine Corps, and I've got to know what kind of boys they are—what kind of a record they have." You could just see the wheels turning in the marshall's head, "Boy, here's two more of these guys that I'll get out of town in a hurry." He answered, "These are two good boys. You couldn't do better than getting these two. These are two real fine boys." As far as I know, that was the end of the police check.

The next morning the two young men went on the bus to Cleveland. They were processed that day, August 6, 1948, and were on the train towards Parris Island that night.

Looking back at boot camp, Massaro later confessed:

I had some shocks, just like everybody else, from a disciplinary standpoint. Although I think that most young men back in those days were raised in a somewhat more disciplined environment. Also, having played sports in high school and worked with the Future Farmers of America and things like that, I knew a little bit about what discipline was—but certainly not what Marine Corps discipline was.

The most humorous thing that happened to me down there (although I didn't think so at the time) was when one of our drill instructors called me out of ranks. He said, "I want you to do an about face for the entire platoon." When I got out there my mind just went blank. I couldn't think any more of how to do an about face than the man in the moon. This infuriated him considerably! So he had me do a lap with my rifle around the barracks. I came back around, and he said, "All right, do an about face." I still couldn't think how to do it, so around the buildings I went again.

By the time I got around the back of the buildings the second time I told myself, "Hey, this could go on all day and you ain't going to last that long." So I stopped behind the building and thought for a few seconds and figured out what I needed to do to perform an about face. When I came around that second time, he repeated, "All right, do an about face." And so I finally did an about face and was able to end up right back in my spot in the ranks.

As the end of boot camp drew near, Massaro gave thought to what duty he would request. His choice was Sea School for duty aboard ship. He was not selected, and thus began, in his words, "a pattern of events that continued throughout my entire Marine Corps career: I got very few of the things that I ever asked for, but it always turned out to be a blessing in disguise. For instance, I later came to understand that being aboard ship was the last place I wanted to be."

Many of his fellow recruits stayed in Parris Island with him in a casual company there. In November, 1948, orders arrived transferring him (via a five-day troop train trip) to the 6th Marines in the 1st Division at Camp Pendleton.

That infantry duty ended when he was shifted for four dull months to a warehouse job in Base Troops. In March, 1950, Massaro was sent to a post that appeared to be equally routine: the U.S. Navy Supply Depot in Clearfield, Utah. There he served as a gate guard and as a turnkey in the brig. His life took a decided turn away from the routine when a friend arranged for a blind date for him late that year. A young blonde lady named NeDean Ford from the nearby town of Roy made a deep impression on the twenty-year old Marine, and they started seeing each other frequently.

Just at this time, the Corps intruded on their romance. The Korean War had broken out, and many of Massaro's friends at Clearfield were leaving for combat. Now a corporal, he wanted to join them, but instead, because he had a General Classification Test (GCT) score of over 100, he was ordered to the recruit depot in San Diego in January, 1951.

Arriving reluctantly in San Diego, Massaro faced a whole new set of circumstances. As he later commented:

My first assignment was to a recruit training battalion. There was no D.I. School at that time, so you simply went down and began to work after a very brief indoctrination, which mainly dealt with some of the do's and don'ts. There weren't too many don'ts back in those days! They assigned me to work with a staff sergeant, and that was one of those blessings in disguise because of the things that he directed me to do.

One of the first things was that he made me responsible to teach all the drill. Although I had drilled troops before in the infantry and at

Clearfield, I certainly was not qualified as a D.I. who was supposed to be an expert in teaching people how to drill. So just about every night I had to look at the training schedule and see what I had to teach the next day. Then, after I put the platoon to bed, I'd spend an hour or two every night with the syllabus, trying to determine how I was going to teach those things the next day. And that's how I got to be a drill instructor!

Massaro's mind was focused on more than the drill manual, however. There were frequent communications back and forth with Roy, Utah, with the result that NeDean accepted his marriage proposal. In those days this required careful observance of the Corps' strict regulations. "You needed to have your commanding officer's approval to get married. Back then you also needed an out-of-bounds pass if you were going to go a certain distance from the base. Finally, if you were going to be gone more than a certain period of time, you needed a special liberty chit."

Having surmounted all these hurdles, he headed for Las Vegas to meet NeDean coming from Roy. An unexpected obstacle arose. Massaro "thought that in Nevada it didn't matter how old you were; as long as you could walk in and lay your money up on the counter, they'd marry you. But when we got into the courthouse to get our marriage license, I was only twenty. They wouldn't give us a marriage license, so I had to call home and talk to my mom and dad. They then had to go to a notary public, and have a certified telegram sent out to Las Vegas so we could get married. It happened on February 10, 1951."

Back at the recruit depot in San Diego, Massaro moved on from the drill field to the Special Subjects Branch, teaching map, compass, aerophotography, interior guard, as well as the history, mission, and traditions of the Corps. Wartime promotions were now coming through a lot faster, and he climbed quickly to sergeant and then to staff sergeant.

April, 1952, brought a big change when he was sent up the coast to Camp Pendleton for combat field training, immediately followed by duty with the 1st Division in Korea. His arrival there had a curious twist to it:

While we were still at battalion headquarters, the sergeant major asked if any of us had any problems. I said, "Well, Sergeant Major, I don't know if you'd call it a problem or not, but my time ran out when I was aboard the ship coming over here." Originally that sergeant major wanted to send me back to the States to be discharged, but I didn't come 7000 miles to turn around and go back. I wanted to find out a little bit about this thing called war. So I re-enlisted for three more years.

Assigned then to the 5th Marines, Massaro became acquainted with Clint Puckett, who was in his same battalion. The veterans there saw the new man quickly adapt to infantry combat, part of the time as a squad leader and part of it as a platoon guide and later as a platoon sergeant. He later summarized the situation:

We were on the 38th parallel. The division's area of responsibility at that time, on the left flank, tied in with the Korean Marines, and then on the right flank tied in with the Turks and the British. So we had the majority of the left portion of the main line of resistance as it was then established, just forward of the Imjin River.

In one position we were in, our platoon straddled the Panmunjom Road, and the peace talks there were already in progress at that time. So from the outpost that we had forward of our main line, you could take binoculars and you could look right down on Panmunjom. You never stayed in these positions very long; you moved every two, three weeks to a different position.

It didn't take the newly-arrived Massaro long to distinguish himself. A few weeks later he had a memorable night. As he later gave the details:

I was still a squad leader then. We were out on patrol one night, probably 1000 to 1500 meters forward of the main line of resistance. We got ambushed by the Chinese and the patrol leader, who was our platoon commander, got hit, as did several members of the squad. It was my job, so I just instinctively took over and set up a line of defense. We cleared the ambush and, when it was safe, I had everybody start pulling back. As they started to pull back, I just kept a couple of the troops back in the rear with myself, and we set up a rear guard, so we could all pull back to the main line without taking any further casualties.

This casual sounding summary of Massaro's was underscored when the commanding general of the 1st Division, Major General Edwin Pollock, awarded him a Navy Commendation Medal with Combat "V." The citation noted in part:

...Throughout the assault, he skillfully aided the patrol leader, helping direct elements of the patrol until contact with the enemy was broken.

During the evacuation of four wounded men, he courageously directed a rear guard action, and assumed charge of the unit when the patrol leader was seriously wounded. His initiative, professional skill, and encouragement contributed materially to the success of the operation and helped prevent further casualties, and served as an inspiration to all who observed him....

A year later the time came for rotation back to the States. But, when he received his new duty assignment in August, 1953, he reacted strongly:

When I got orders in Korea to come back to the United States again, I found out that I was going back to the recruit depot in San Diego. I'd had that one tour of duty on the drill field, and I wasn't really that desirous of going back to it again. I was a little disappointed; I felt that I deserved something different from that, because we didn't look on drill instructor duty as being all that great, especially the second time around. But, once again, it turned out to be a blessing in disguise.

When Massaro arrived at the recruit depot, he was originally assigned as a special subjects instructor in the recruit battalion, the same job he had had on his previous tour there. His battalion finished its training about January, 1954,

The unwrinkled face, the smile of youth, the 1951 pith helmet, and the new corporal's chevrons—Massaro as a brand new D.I. at the recruit depot in San Diego.
Massaro photo

Ten months of combat in Korea bring a sobering look (and a mustache) to Massaro, now a staff sergeant in the 5th Marines in January, 1953.

Massaro photo

and he thought that he had laid the groundwork to go to the bayonet course, as a bayonet instructor and a hand-to-hand combat instructor. However, he was told that he was going instead to the guard company. His reaction was natural:

> This really made me quite unhappy, but I went over to guard company. (You didn't question things back in those days; you did what you were told, and took whatever action you could later.) There I was informed that my assignment would be in the post brig; I would be an assistant turnkey. The hours really weren't bad compared to the hours you put in as a drill instructor, but I just didn't feel that I was suited for that type of duty. I decided right then and there that, if there was any way possible, I'd rather be back on the drill field as a working drill instructor than in the guard company.

Massaro took immediate action. He went to see the officer in charge of the Drill Instructors School. They struck a deal: the officer would arrange a transfer, but Massaro would have to become a student at the school. He continued the story:

> The next morning when I reported back in to the guard company, they told me, "There's been some mistake; you don't belong here at all. You're supposed to be up in the schools company."
> So I went up to that company, and I started through the course. I got about halfway through, and [since the Korean War was making heavy manpower demands] they had a shortage of drill instructors down in the recruit battalion again. So I went down and took through a platoon. It turned out to be one of the best platoons that I ever had. They set a depot record that lasted for a year or so, as far as the statistical things that they measure recruit training by.

When Massaro finished the school, in May, 1954, he came out number one in his class, but his next assignment was work with Reserves that summer, giving various types of instruction. About the time that the Reserve training program was ready to wind down, he got a message one day to go over to the officer in charge of D.I. School who asked him, "What are you doing over there?" Massaro replied, "Well, sir, that's where I was assigned when I finished the school." Then the officer said, "You don't belong over there. You belong over here. When you finish up over there in another week or ten days, you'll be coming back over here as an instructor." So he joined the other instructors, among whom was Clint Puckett. Puckett had earlier monitored several of the classes that Massaro had given in the recruit battalions. Now he was the drill master, and they were instructing right along together.

Massaro's time as a D.I. ran out in August, 1955, and he then moved on to the duty which would be the theme of his career, a "recon man." That tour at Pendleton was interrupted by an emergency, however. The drowning of six recruits at Parris Island in April, 1956, due to the negligence of a D.I. there, had sent reverberations all the way to San Diego, and drastic changes in training regulations and procedures were mandated for both boot camps. Brigadier General Alan Shapley was assigned to supervise the west coast process. Being a highly experienced D.I., Massaro was detached from his reconnaissance company for three months of temporary duty to take part in the shake-up at the recruit depot in San Diego. As he later described this assignment:

> One of the first things that they did there was to institute "series officers"; we'd never had them before. A "series" is four platoons that all go through recruit training at one time, a total of about 300 privates.

> My particular "series officer" was a lieutenant who was an infantry officer and understood the functioning of an infantry company. He called me in (I was a tech sergeant by this time), and he said, "Gunny, I've got an idea I've been mulling over in my mind. I'd like to know if you'd be agreeable, during the remainder of your tour down here, to participate in this particular idea." I answered, "What's that, sir?" He went on, "I've got an idea that we need a 'series gunnery sergeant' to assist the "series officer'." I agreed, and he got everything approved at the battalion level. As far as I know, I probably was the first "series gunnery sergeant" in recruit training.

Returning to his reconnaissance company, Massaro broadened his skills in 1957 by earning his parachute wings at jump school. After a little over four years at Camp Pendleton with the division and force reconnaissance companies, he went overseas in November, 1959, for an interim tour with the 1st Marine Aircraft Wing. While there, besides retaining his parachute and scuba qualifications, he expanded his professional skills in an area which he would later need in order to be considered a well rounded senior NCO. He remembered:

> I'd been there about two or three weeks when the squadron administrative chief (a master sergeant "01") called me in. He said, "Gunny, I've been looking through your record, and I need somebody to relieve me as the squadron administrative chief." I looked at him and I kind of laughed a little bit, and I objected, "I have no admin background." He replied, "No, but you've got the capability." Next I told him, "All I've ever been is a company first sergeant on a couple of occasions...."

> Before I was even finished he took me in to see the squadron commander, a major. He said, "Gunny, I'd like you to take this assignment. The master sergeant is already beyond his departure date to go back to the States. There's no relief in sight for him." The major knew that what I really wanted to go to was the wing NCO School as an instructor. So he continued, "If you'll take this job, I'll do everything I can to move you over to that assignment." By the time he was finished I had no choice. I said, "Major, I'll try it. I'll do the best I can for you."

Massaro initially expected it to be a temporary assignment, lasting until a replacement "01" got there: just keep the paperwork flowing smoothly through the office, and make sure people showed up on time and did their job. He was lucky because the master sergeant took about a week or so, beyond the time when he should have already been gone, to train him, "He taught me more in that short period of time than either of the two formal schools that I went to: one previous to that and one subsequent to that." The scope of this assignment was a revelation to Massaro:

> Our headquarters squadron for the wing had the entire wing head-quarters on our muster roles. We had 1000 people on those rolls at one time, from the commanding general right on down to the wing communications people, the wing band, and the group headquarters personnel.
>
> So here's a guy, with virtually no administrative experience at all, who's now responsible for the administration of records on individual Marines, their comings and goings (all of the drafts going in and out), and everything like that for the entire wing, filling an "01" billet. Nevertheless, I was slowly able to grasp all facets of administration for a headquarters squadron.

Toward the latter part of his tour at Iwakuni, a gunnery sergeant "01" did report in, and Massaro could have been relieved and gone on to another job. Back then the tour of duty was fifteen months, and he had already been there a year when that gunnery sergeant came in. However, Massaro's feeling was, "I'll just finish up my tour right here, because I know what I'm doing and I enjoy what I'm doing. I realized that, at some point in my career, this was probably going to be an invaluable experience. It gave me insight into just about every facet of administration that the Marine Corps has at various levels."

By January, 1961, Massaro was back at Camp Pendleton, where another tour with the force reconnaissance company lasted until April of 1963. When it came time for a different assignment, he was crystal clear about his preferences:

> Some of my peers were beginning to get orders from force recon, and from some of the other division units, to recruiting duty or I&I duty or various other types of independent duty. I had no desire to perform any of those duties! I felt that there were only two good duty stations in the Marine Corps, stateside, and one of them was Camp Pendleton and the other one was the recruit depot in San Diego. So I put in a request to go back to drill instructor duty. I was selected and did receive orders to go back to DI School.

When he came out of the school, he was assigned to a platoon and a series as a "bird dog," following along and observing what was going on. He then went to a series as a series gunnery sergeant. When the regular chief drill instructor got transferred a couple of months later, he was the senior gunnery sergeant in the company, and so he was assigned to the chief drill instructor job, "It was just like the company first sergeant in an infantry company. I made first sergeant officially in June, 1964, while I was still at the depot in San Diego. For a period of time, I was even filling a sergeant major's billet in the recruit training battalions. I was better prepared to do these jobs because, in late 1964, I attended the First Sergeants School at Parris Island."

Leaving San Diego in January, 1966, Massaro had his chance to impart the "recon" skills he had acquired through the years to the 4th Reconnaissance Company (Reserves) in San Bernadino.

From that assignment he shipped out in December of 1967 with orders to the 3d Engineer Battalion of the 3d Division in Vietnam as first sergeant of the support company. An interesting sequence of events took place on his arrival there—wonderfully illustrative of an old Marine truism, "Don't mess with a sergeant major, regardless of your rank!" Massaro later told the story:

> If I had to do it over, I might not even be here today because I would have done things differently then. When I reported in to the 3d Division, the division sergeant major was responsible for assignments of all first sergeants and all sergeants major coming in. (I'd been selected for sergeant major but not actually promoted.)
>
> He had four openings when four of us first sergeants reported in. Two of them were for the 11th Marines, and immediately two of those first sergeants said, "I'll take that." Then he had one for the 4th Marines that another first sergeant took real quick-like; and finally he had this engineer battalion billet. I told him, "I don't know anything about engineers, Sergeant Major." He said, "Well, you'll like it out there. You're right next to the tank battalion and they've got one of the best clubs in the whole area." (And here I didn't even drink!) So I thought, "Oh my gosh, what am I getting into?"

Facing this unwanted assignment, Massaro then bumped into a staff sergeant who had been his administrative chief in force reconnaissance, and he said, "Hey, don't worry about it, First Sergeant. The major who was our communications officer when we were in force 'recon' is now the XO [Executive Officer] of the 3d Recon Battalion here. We'll go over and see the major. He'll take care of this." Accordingly, they went over to the reconnaissance battalion, and the major took Massaro in to see the battalion commander, Lieutenant Colonel Jack Perrin. He exclaimed, "Hey, I need you right now! I'm short two first sergeants. I need one out at Khe Sanh. They don't have a first sergeant with our company out there. Don't do anything until I get a chance to talk to the sergeant major." Massaro later described what came next:

> So the lieutenant colonel met me at the division CP, and we went in to see the sergeant major. I never said a word; the lieutenant colonel did most of the talking. He said, "Sergeant Major, you promised me the next time that you had some first sergeants report in that I'd get one of them. Here you've got a guy with ten years' recon experience, and you're sending him out to the engineer battalion. I could use him, and you know that. Why can't you give him to me?" The old sergeant major told that lieutenant colonel, "Because he's going to the engineer battalion." Then they talked a little bit more and finally the sergeant major said, "Not no, but hell no! I said he's going to the engineer battalion, and that's where he's going!" And that's how I ended up in the engineer battalion out at a little place between Phu Bai and Hue City.

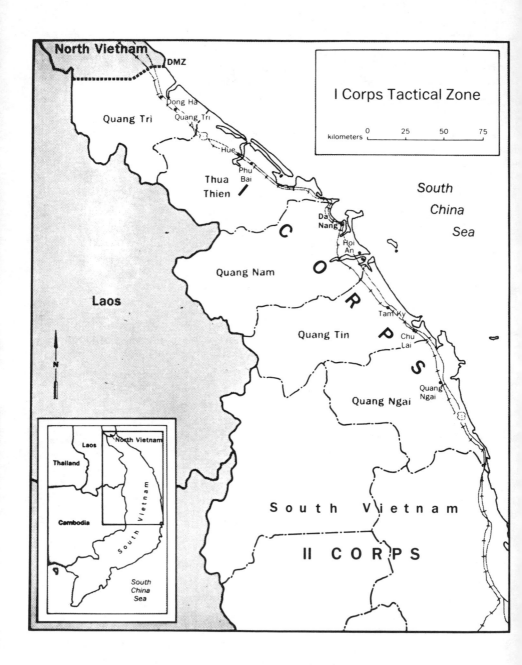

Even though he was disappointed not to have gotten his favorite billet as a "recon man," Massaro, in his typical way, dug in to do a conscientious job for the engineers. He started out as a company first sergeant, but then the battalion sergeant major rotated back to the States. With Massaro's warrant for sergeant major due soon, he was picked as the successor in this key position. (The warrant did come through in June, 1968.) His performance was so superior that he was awarded a second Navy Commendation Medal with Combat "V." (In the Marine Corps, the "V" is officially "a combat distinguishing device.") The citation of the commanding general of FMFPac, Lieutenant General Henry Buse, read in part:

> ...worked tirelessly and with meticulous attention to detail, as he conducted a comprehensive training program to increase the proficiency of his administrative personnel, thereby greatly enhancing the accuracy of his unit's reporting and administrative procedures.
>
> Reassigned as battalion sergeant major on 13 May, 1968, he traveled extensively throughout the northern I Corps Tactical Zone to the widely dispersed elements of his command to familiarize himself with the requirements of all enlisted personnel, and, demonstrating a sincere concern for the welfare of his men, provided advice and assistance to any Marine requesting his counsel....

In November, 1968, Joe Dailey took over as division sergeant major, and Massaro got acquainted with him then. Their paths would cross again....

This tour of Vietnam duty came to an end in January, 1969, when Massaro was ordered back to the States. Probably hoping to get back to a "recon" assignment, he found, to his dismay, that his new orders were for recruiting duty in San Francisco: "Being a newly-selected sergeant major, I had no burning desire to be out recruiting when I could be in the field somewhere. After all, they had all those battalions down at Camp Pendleton that could use a sergeant major."

It was a very difficult time to be given recruiting duty. The United States was torn by divisiveness over the war in Vietnam. It was a time of LSD, dropping out, hippie communes, and crowds of young people chanting, "Hell no! We won't go!" There was only one way Massaro knew how to do things: whether you like your assignment or not, get in there and do it right! "We had some difficult times during that period," he later admitted. "When I got there, things really weren't going all that great. But my recruiting officer had a fine feel for the job, and we worked hard; we tried to rebuild things and get them going, and we finally did. By the time I left we had made our quota for 26 consecutive months."

With a return to overseas duty looming at the end of his San Francisco tour, Massaro and NeDean had a discussion about the future. He had twenty-four years of active duty in a variety of places in the United States and the Far East, and it now seemed wise to put down some roots for his eventual retirement. Accordingly, when his new orders arrived, they went back on his leave to familiar territory, the Salt Lake City area, and looked around for a home to buy. Acting on a tip from a relative, they came down to the small town of Orem, some thirty miles south of Salt Lake City. The town streets there were laid out in geometrically spaced rectangles with numerical and directional sequences for their names. When they saw the attractive house at 309 South, 400 East, NeDean exclaimed, "We'll take it." Bringing the children from San Francisco, she moved in, a permanent family home at last!

Massaro meanwhile headed for Marine Aircraft Group (MAG) 36 at Futema, Okinawa, to take over as group sergeant major in August, 1972. Here again, the path of his career had intersected with an old friend. He later sketched the background:

> That particular assignment was pretty much hand picked for me by Sergeant Major Puckett, who by that time was the personnel sergeant major of the Marine Corps. By that time I'd also learned that other people knew more about what I needed than what I thought I needed to round out my career. I thought my career was slowly beginning to wind down. Once you go over twenty years, why, you know you're on the downhill side, and everything after that is just gravy, because the train's already run its course on the track, and you're just reaping the benefits of your first twenty years.
>
> When I got to MAG-36 I found out that it was the largest aircraft group that the Marine Corps had (and may have ever had) because we had over 3000 Marines in the group. My responsibility there was just like any other sergeant major's job: just try to keep things running smoothly in the group itself and assist my group commander wherever possible. I made the assignment of all the squadron sergeants major, and tried to keep things in harmony where they were concerned.

One of his squadron sergeants major was Robert Cleary, and, like the others, his fitness reports came to Massaro for review. These evaluations were consistently outstanding. The strongly favorable impression that he made led Massaro later on to assist him in his career assignments, leading eventually to the very top.

Massaro went on to define some of the specifics of his work:

> I spent as much time as I could away from Futema. I made two or three trips down to Vietnam and over to Thailand, and those areas down there where we had troops. We also had troops scattered throughout Okinawa, and I tried to visit them on a regular basis. I was responsible for the billeting of the staff NCOs that reported in to the group. In addition, I was the senior member of the Meritorious Promotion Board. So my duties there were somewhat consistent with the duties that I had in other places.
>
> I won't say that I had a free hand, but I had the ability to function without too much real guidance while I was there at Futema—just so it was consistent with the group commander's policies and his desires. His men had not made a very good showing in a previous visit by the inspector general as far as the physical fitness test [PFT] was concerned. After I outlined a policy that I thought would turn this around and presented it to the group

commander, he approved it. We implemented the policy and in a couple of months we only had about ten staff NCOs in the whole group that couldn't pass the PFT, and most of those were because of inherent physical reasons.

While physical fitness was part of official doctrine, the real implementation of an aggressive Corps-wide policy would come to the fore three years later under Sergeant Major Henry Black and General Louis Wilson. The Futema program was a direct consequence of Massaro's personal rugged pattern of "recon" conditioning. Anything that he expected of his men, he expected of himself—and maybe a little bit more. Another squadron sergeant major at Futema, George Rogers, never forgot Massaro's drive to keep in shape:

> I think the one thing that I can remember about him, as much as anything, was that we all used to run quite a bit around the perimeter road. John was the only one I ever knew that always ran with combat boots on. Everybody else wore tennis shoes or running shoes. I would be out there running along the perimeter road with my mind wandering, and from a distance I would start hearing the clump of combat boots, and I'd think, "Well, here comes Sergeant Major Massaro," and here he'd come and usually pass me and keep going; always a smile, always a wave, combat boots a-going, and away he'd run.

It was time to move again in August, 1973, and although there were "indications" that he might become the post sergeant major at Parris Island, what happened in reality was quite different. He had had a wide range of billets over the years, but now the old "recon man" was headed for a wholly new experience: staff duty at Headquarters Marine Corps. There he moved in as the sergeant major of the Inspection Division. He later outlined his function:

> My job was to provide the inspector general [IG] (who in turn provided the Commandant) with as much input as I possibly could on the Marines in the field...with the pulse beat of the Marine Corps. During that two years I spent with the IG, I visited every major command in the Marine Corps at least once and some of them twice. The Marine Corps in those days was in a transition state from Vietnam combat back to peace time, and different units had made greater progress than others in achieving a peace time environment where they had good, sound disciplinary programs and good, sound training programs. Some units were outstanding, where others were found to be unsatisfactory in certain areas.

> Oftentimes I'd have not only first sergeants and sergeants major give me their comments, but also lower ranking Marines would come up and say, "Sergeant Major, I think that this is something somebody needs to know." And they'd tell you the things that they thought were right or wrong, or the things that they thought needed to be brought to someone's attention for action.

It was during his tour with the Inspection Division that Massaro was able to influence favorably the future careers of two other senior NCOs, both of whom would go on to be Sergeant Major of the Marine Corps. The reports he wrote, and, when requested, the advice he gave bore great weight. One such laudatory inspection report praised the record of Henry Black who was then the wing sergeant major of the 1st MAW. On another occasion, a colonel, whom Massaro had known as a lieutenant on the drill field at San Diego, asked him for his recommendation for a topnotch man to take over as the sergeant major of the Marine Security Guard Battalion. Massaro named Robert Cleary as his first choice and he got the job. In future years, they would see a lot of each other....

May of 1975 was an emotional month of transition for Massaro. Henry Black was about to come aboard as the new Sergeant Major of the Marine Corps, and Massaro was forced to do some serious soul-searching:

> We had comparable time in the Corps and I really felt that, with his selection, there went the last opportunity that I would ever have to fill that particular billet. About the same time I happened to be in the monitor's office and I saw that he had an opening to go to the recruiting station in Salt Lake City. I thought that, with twenty-seven years in the Corps, I might as well end it right there. I personally didn't think it was the best place to go, but I felt it would be for my family.

> And I also felt that, in view of the fact that I would probably not have another opportunity to be the Sergeant Major of the Marine Corps, it would be kind of selfish on my part to go to Camp Pendleton or somewhere like that and fill a major billet that somebody else could be filling who would have a shot at it. So I told the monitor that I'd greatly appreciate that assignment and he subsequently made it.

> Right after that, my old friend, Clint Puckett, who had not as yet retired as Sergeant Major of the Marine Corps, found out about my recruiting assignment. He called me in and he said, "You don't want to do that. Change your mind. You'll get another chance."

Massaro really did not think so, and, against Puckett's advice, he executed the orders to Salt Lake in July, 1975. With his prior knowledge of recruiting duty, it was easy to slip into the billet there. Salt Lake, however, was not making its quota; it was having a very difficult time with an area that covered Utah, Idaho, and Montana. The first road trip Massaro made with the officer in charge covered 2,200 miles in nine days. He later analyzed the problem:

> A month later, I made the same trip by myself. The thought occurred to me that I was wasting my time, that I really wasn't able to help the local recruiters the way that I wanted to, because I didn't have enough time to spend with them. So, when I got back to Salt Lake, I recommended to the officer in charge that our recruiting station be closed down; that they divide our area up: give Utah to Sacramento, give Idaho to Portland, and give Montana to Seattle. He forwarded my recommendation to the next higher echelon but they said, "No, we could never do that."

> The next month, while I was on the road again, a colonel came out from Headquarters Marine Corps, and my officer in charge told him the

same thing. He replied, "We'd dearly love to close this place down, but we can't do it." About a month later, however, recruiting appropriations were cut for all the armed forces, and so our higher echelon took my suggestion and closed down the Salt Lake station.

Massaro then received a set of orders in April, 1976, to return once more to the familiar San Diego recruit depot where, with his seniority, he expected to serve as the depot sergeant major. Out of the blue, those orders were superseded by new ones sending him to the 1st Division at Camp Pendleton. Reporting in, he was assigned as the division sergeant major. This naturally brought him into frequent contact with its commander, Major General Edward Wilcox. As Massaro later pictured their relationship:

> He was a very personable individual who spent a great deal of time reviewing every detail of every facet of a Marine's case when it came to disciplinary action. What would happen is that the division inspector would prepare a brief, and then he'd give it to me and I would brief the general. After the general was briefed, I'd make arrangements for the Marine who was requesting a hearing to come before the general. So it wasn't unusual for me to spend lengthy periods of time talking to the general, both in a formal and an informal manner, with regards to these cases that we had pending within the division itself.
>
> One afternoon in January, 1977, the general's aide came to me and said, "Sergeant Major, the general would like to see you tomorrow morning in his office at 0900." This wasn't an unusual occurrence. Frequently the aide would set these appointments up, and it would work the other way too. I'd just go see the aide and say, "Captain, I need to see the general," and at the first available opportunity, I was in there. On this occasion I said, "Fine, sir," and I thought no more of it.
>
> The next morning, at the predesignated time, I went in to the aide, and he indicated that the general was ready to see me. Immediately upon walking into the general's office, he handed me a phone and he said, "The Commandant of the Marine Corps would like to speak to you." It was General Wilson himself, and he informed me that he had chosen me to be the next Sergeant Major of the Marine Corps!

It had been the traditional multi-stage screening process which had brought Massaro's name to the top. Back in November of 1976, the Commandant's Enlisted Performance Board had started evaluating the records of 180 sergeants major, including women. They then passed along twenty-eight names to a general's board, and five names emerged from there to reach the Commandant. Wilson next consulted with his assistant commandant, his chief of staff, and his director of personnel. There was also an informal, off-the-record supportive recommendation from his retiring sergeant major, Henry Black. No personal interviews were conducted, but these discussions produced "a joint conclusion," as Wilson termed it, "There was a general consensus, which I liked to have, even though I had not known Massaro previously."

When the 1st Division runs field exercises at Camp Pendleton early in 1977, the division sergeant major is there with his troops.

General Wilcox says, "Sergeant Major, there's a phone call for you. I think you'd better take it." Massaro gets the big news from the Commandant at Camp Pendleton in January, 1977. Note addition of Scuba Diver insignia.

During the two months that followed the Commandant's phone call, Massaro arranged for the transfer of his responsibilities in the 1st Division. One of the personnel matters he handled was the assignment of an incoming man to be a regimental sergeant major; that man was Leland Crawford, who would later come to Headquarters, following Massaro's trail.

March 31, 1977, saw the Post and Relief ceremonies at the Washington Barracks. Wilson presented the Sword of Office to Massaro, repeating the time-honored words of Pate twenty years earlier, "I hereby give into your charge the Sword of Office of the Sergeant Major of the United States Marine Corps, symbolizing the proud traditions which distinguish the Sergeants Major of the Corps." Massaro's appearance and comments on that memorable day were captured by a reporter:

> At age 47, Massaro's face is like leather. What is left of his hair is crop-ped so close it is like a shadow on his head. He has honest blue eyes without a flicker of meanness in them.
>
> At six foot, 175 pounds, Massaro is taller and heavier than the five foot ten, 140 pounds, he was when he joined the Marines twenty-nine years ago, but in no worse shape. In his latest physical fitness test, he scored 278 out of 300. He said if he ever falls below 225, a first-class score for a Marine 17 to 25 years old, he will retire. Four days a week, Massaro runs five miles....
>
> Massaro said, "When I was a young Marine nearly all the Marines were riflemen. In the Korean War, there are authenticated instances in Marine history where cooks and bakers and motor transport men actually had to pick up a rifle and join Marines in rifle squads and infantry platoons.
>
> "It's no longer a truism that every Marine is a rifleman.... Many of our fields are so advanced, so technical...computer operators, key punch operators...without that much emphasis on being a rifleman. Electronics firms are standing in line to capture these people who are discharged from the Marine Corps.... I have no skills. I have no technology. My heart lies with the young Marine in the fire team and in the squad, in the infantry company."
>
> There are almost 4,000 women in the Marines today. Some say there will be 10,000 before long. Will the day come when women Marines will be in the front lines in combat? I wouldn't say that; I don't foresee this is going to happen. To be honest with you, if it gets to that point, I would have to say the United States of America is going to be in a pretty sad state of affairs. When we can't recruit enough young men to do our fighting for us and we have to rely on women, I feel, as a society, we've reached the bottom of the barrel.

In a job as complex and demanding as that of the Sergeant Major of the Marine Corps, a smooth transition from one incumbent to the next is highly desirable. As Massaro observed:

> Sergeant Major Black had everything laid out for me. He showed me the things that he had done or was working on, and covered a few things that he had hoped to accomplish and hadn't been able to do, which he

The Commandant, General Wilson (left), marks the occasion of a March 31, 1977, change of command. Black (center) will be turning over his Sword of Office to the incoming Sergeant Major of the Marine Corps, John Massaro (right).

Official portrait in June, 1977. Massaro proudly wears the Scuba and Parachute insignia of a "recon man" above his ribbons, with his rifle and pistol qualification badges below.

At the Post and Relief of the Sergeant Major of the Marine Corps. Black retires, Massaro comes aboard, and two other top enlisted men attend the ceremony. From left to right: Master Chief Petty Officer of the Coast Guard Phillip Smith; Black; Massaro; and Chief Master Sergeant of the Air Force, T. N. Barnes.

thought that I might be interested in looking into. Probably the thing that made the transition as easy as it was, was the office personnel that we had.

The staff sergeant there had worked for Sergeant Major Puckett and Sergeant Major Black and had an extremely thorough knowledge of the office procedures. There was also a very good gunnery sergeant who took care of all my orders (going and coming), passports, even my eyeglasses. I couldn't even begin to recount the things that he did on a day-to-day basis that, had he not done them, I would have had to take time away from something else more important to do these things.

There was another senior staff NCO there with whom Massaro would have a lot of contact. The personnel sergeant major was now Bob Cleary, and a few years later he, too, would move into Massaro's office.

Massaro's first priority, however, was his new boss. He quickly found out that Wilson wanted to continue the relationships and procedures that he had previously developed with Henry Black. There were, of course, the inevitable inspection trips:

On the trips themselves, I generally spent a certain amount of time with General Wilson. If he gave a speech or a talk I would always attend. Oftentimes Marines would have questions that they would ask, and I would write these questions down. Then when we got back to Headquarters they would be researched, and a reply would be provided to the Marine.

In addition to that, there would be portions of the time devoted to my going out into the field and talking to Marines, going to the various organizations and trying to get a feel, or an input, from the enlisted standpoint, so that I might better help the Commandant make a decision on training or something else that he might have to consider later on. When we would get back to Headquarters, I would prepare a written report and submit this to the Commandant. Frequently he would write notes on the side of my report of things that he was desirous that I would do, things that needed follow-up.

Early on in the job, I learned that it was a very sensitive position that I had, and it required the cooperation of many of the other branches within Headquarters to keep things running smoothly. Often I would try quickly to resolve questions through them. Then, when I'd submit my report to the Commandant, it would already have been taken care of.

On trips within the continental United States, NeDean would sometimes accompany her husband. The Commandant, well aware of the impact of family matters on enlisted morale, always encouraged Massaro to discuss any such issues with her.

Given the diversity of the personnel in the Corps, the sergeant major was required to demonstrate great flexibility on his trips:

At different places I went I did different things. Sometimes at the end of the day, after we got our day's work out of the way, why, another sergeant major and I would go for a nice, long run. This was always a good way to end a day and get the cobwebs out of your head. Each visit had its own individual character because every place you went there were different people and varying situations.

There were good things about all of them. Often they'd have a happy hour at the NCO Club, which would give you an opportunity to meet old acquaintances whom you hadn't seen for a long time, or who didn't happen to be in the units that you'd visited during the day.

There were two concepts of the Commandant's which Massaro had repeated occasions to discuss with the troops. One was physical fitness—a permanent passion for someone whose career had focused on being a "recon man"—and this involved a continuation of Black's efforts to weed out fat men. As he later evaluated it:

The Marine Corps had a standard of physical fitness. My own personal feelings were that every Marine ought to be able at least to pass all, or most of that test, and do it to the best of his ability. I fully realized that there were Marines who just didn't have the physical capabilities that the good Lord had given me, but I also knew that these things don't always come naturally. You've got to work at it and you've got to keep working at it. So I tried to maintain a program where I could achieve a test score above and beyond what was expected of the youngest Marine in the Corps.

I really don't think that I was as hard on overweight Marines, probably, as Sergeant Major Black had been. Being the first sergeant major to work for General Wilson, he really took the brunt of trying to get rid of that fat man image. By the time I got there, there were only a few whom I had to lean on (or cause to be leaned on), by having a letter written from Head-quarters Marine Corps to the Marine through his command. So it really wasn't that big a thing for me.

Wilson's other concept touched a very sensitive area in the psyche of the Corps, the role of the D.I. Having served on the drill field for three separate tours, Massaro paid close attention when the Commandant expressed his views:

> There is a fraternity among drill instructors, not only current but past, in which they feel that they have a mission in life to prepare a man for combat. That's not true at all! Their mission in life is to take that ten weeks and find out if this young man is capable of being a Marine. Then, if he's capable of being a Marine, he has many people between the time that he finishes boot camp and he goes to combat to teach him how to be a Marine in battle.
>
> There is a fine line there. What we have to do is to make recruit train-ing difficult and an abrupt transition from civilian life to military life which one will never forget. And we Marines are superior at that, obviously. No Marine ever forgets his drill instructor! That man has an emphasis and a responsibility toward seventy-five young men that no one ever has had for those seventy-five individuals before.

Massaro naturally understood these feelings of Wilson's, since the official Marine Corps Drill Instructors Code set forth standards and goals which he had personally lived by, "These are my recruits. I will train them to the best of my ability. I will develop them into smartly disciplined, physically fit, basically train-ed Marines, thoroughly indoctrinated in love of God, country, and Corps. I will demand of them, and demonstrate by my own example, the highest stan-dards of personal conduct, morality, and professional skill."

Another subject which was the focus of Massaro's attention proved to be a sticky wicket. As one of his peers, Sergeant Major "Mack" McKinney, later commented:

> Some of the Reserve sergeants major on "extended active duty" were in competition for promotion with the rest of the regular sergeants major. However, they were almost all assigned to one individual place, and were not available to be transferred overseas or any other place.
>
> To my knowledge, none of them were actually performing a real sergeant major's duty. They were in billets like NCO in a recruiting district. The result of John's analysis of this problem was that the Marine Corps came out with the order that no longer were these people to be sergeants major; they now had to go up the master sergeant/master gunnery sergeant route. John did that. I give him credit for taking hold of that and taking the heat that followed.
>
> There was, in particular, one female sergeant major up in Philadelphia. She fought this thing tooth and nail down the road. Fortunately John held

On an inspection trip to Okinawa with the Commandant in October, 1977, Massaro (left) and Wilson (right) check over a terrain situation model on the 4th Marines parade field.

Grand finale: the Commandant, General Barrow, pins the Legion of Merit on Massaro shortly before his retirement in the summer of 1979.

his position and never wavered one iota. He was quiet, but effective, just tremendous...probably the smartest, the most intelligent of all the Sergeants Major of the Marine Corps.

Besides the "big issues," there were the little things that Massaro did on trips which shed a flash of light on his character. There was, for example, another sergeant major, George Rogers, whom he had previously served with and who now had recruiting duty in Pennsylvania. As Rogers later remarked:

I was having a meeting of recruiters in Allentown. I really needed to boost their morale. Things were pretty tough going there in the late '70s for recruiting. So I called up John and I asked him if he would come up and talk to my recruiters. I said, "They really need a shot in the arm. I know it's not much for the Sergeant Major of the Marine Corps to come up and talk to a few staff NCOs." He answered, "Absolutely no problem. I'd be delighted to."

When he showed up I was talking to the recruiters myself in a room with a door and a glass window. I looked out and I saw John standing outside. I finished what I was saying and he was still standing outside. So I went out, and I asked, "Why didn't you come in?" He replied, "I didn't want to interrupt you when you were talking to your Marines." This is the type of thoughtful guy that John Massaro was. Then he came in and I introduced him, and he really gave my Marines a good shot in the arm.

And what was really impressive was that, just to come up there and talk to probably forty or fifty Marines, he had obviously spent a great deal of time researching the subject. He had gone over to see a general at Headquarters to find out what the recruiting statistics were, and what we were doing. He had all of that right on the tip of his tongue when he was talking to us; he was as well prepared as if he was talking to an assembled division somewhere.

He really epitomized what the Sergeant Major of the Marine Corps should be. The man was impressive looking. I never saw him with a uniform that was less than perfect. He was not only a good talker, but he was a good listener.

Back at Headquarters, Massaro found his time filled to overflowing with other responsibilities, such as sitting on the Uniform Board and the Augmentation Board (selecting enlisted personnel for transfer from Reserve to regular status), and overseeing the college degree program. As Massaro explained the last, "The Marine Corps had a college degree program whereby enlisted people could go to a college and achieve certain things in the way of educational advancement. There were specific guidelines, and each year, when the order came out, it would have slightly different guidelines of what they were looking for as far as rank, and time in service, and that type of thing. Our board would then select them, and they would go to a college."

Carrying on the start that Black had made, Massaro organized a Sergeants Major Symposium in 1978, with the resulting batch of recommendations that funnelled to the various staff sections of Headquarters for evaluation and for action.

A broadening of the role of the Sergeant Major of the Marine Corps took place during Massaro's tenure. He was the first one in that billet (with the senior enlisted men of the other services) to give Congressional testimony on a range of issues directly affecting enlisted personnel. On a more limited issue, one past injustice was rectified in December, 1978. After Clint Puckett had made the initial effort some four years earlier, a bill was finally passed which authorized extra retirement pay for three of his predecessors—Bestwick, Rauber, and McHugh.

There were, of course, the continuous demands on the Sergeant Major of the Marine Corps to articulate publicly, lucidly, and effectively his views on every aspect of the enlisted personnel. On a 1979 trip to Quantico, for instance, he was asked to summarize the role of a staff NCO. He replied:

> It is two-fold. His primary responsibility remains, as it has through the ages, to train his troops. It's his responsibility to train them so that, regardless of the type of mission, the troops are equipped to execute and accomplish the mission.
>
> In addition, the staff NCO has a responsibility to the young officer. He has a wealth of practical experience acquired over a number of years. If this is presented to a young officer, in a fashion the officer is receptive to hearing, he has a range of knowledge that can be drawn from to assist in the accomplishment of his mission.
>
> However many staff NCOs believe they have lost a lot of the prestige and responsibility they had before the Vietnam War. There are a few areas that must be looked at to explain the loss of prestige that many felt happened during the Vietnam conflict.

Massaro went on to point out that, at one time, 5,000 of the finest staff NCOs had been commissioned, and another 2,000-3,000 commissioned a short while later. This, he felt, had in essence taken the heart out of the staff NCO corps. And the young NCOs who had to step up and fill the vacated billets really didn't have the time in grade to acquire the practical knowledge needed to advise adequately their platoon commanders.

Then Massaro continued in a happier tone:

> This process now is reversing itself as the number of peacetime years increase and the promotions slow down. In talking with officers today I find that their respect and confidence is growing rapidly. Staff NCOs are getting the practical experience and technical knowledge to handle the pre-Vietnam position again.
>
> The Marine Corps itself has done much to increase the knowledge of the young staff NCO, by providing instruction in leadership and other areas that budding staff sergeants should know. We're working to increase the knowledge of not only the young staff NCO but also the senior ones, and to make them all better Marines.
>
> The greatest things for the young ones are the Staff NCO Academies at Quantico, Lejeune, and El Toro.

Approximately one year ago, they were directed to teach the same program of instruction so that, regardless of the academy attended, the students would get the same course. For those who don't attend one of the academies, there is the Staff NCO Extension Course, as well as other courses. Then there is a course for the seniors to help in their career development.

Early in 1979, Wilson's term as Commandant was drawing to a close. Massaro knew it would be the end of his active duty also, particularly since he felt that he "shouldn't violate the Corps' policy of little or no service beyond thirty years." The new Commandant was General Robert Barrow, who assumed office on July 1. Massaro stayed on for six weeks, while his successor, Sergeant Major Leland Crawford, was getting ready to take over, and on August 14, he had his own retirement ceremony at the Washington Barracks.

At his request, this parade was comprised exclusively of enlisted men, the first time this had ever been done on such an occasion at the barracks. The high point came when Barrow pinned on him a Legion of Merit. The citation from the Secretary of the Navy read in part:

>...Sergeant Major Massaro's performance was exemplary in every respect. His concern for the morale and welfare of Marines was demonstrated by his efforts to avail himself of every opportunity to meet with them and provide counsel. Sergeant Major Massaro travelled thousands of miles, and visited every major Marine Corps command and many of the smaller commands, and, as a result, was able to provide the Commandant with logical and thoughtful advice on all pertinent matters.
>
>He served as an able ambassador for the Marine Corps, and he was eagerly sought as a guest speaker by many organizations. Sergeant Major Massaro's thirty-one years of distinguished service to the Marine Corps in war and peace, at home and abroad, served as a noteworthy example of outstanding and meritorious service to all Marines....

The Commandant then added a few words of his own, "He has truly been an outstanding sergeant major. Wherever you have been, whatever you have done, you have set an example for young men to follow." It had been *some* thirty-one years for an "uncommon man!"

With their home in Utah, NeDean and he naturally wanted to head back there. The "sergeant major network" now swung into action. Henry Black, now with the Veterans Administration (VA), was able to talk to the right people, and Massaro got an opening in the VA office in Salt Lake City. After two and a half years there, the VA wanted to move him to Portland, Oregon, but the local ties were too strong. Besides, he had already moved eighteen times in his three decades of active duty. After a six-month leave of absence, Massaro declined the offer.

Now it was a real retirement: "Since that time I just pretty much did what I wanted to do." In the summer time, he kept busy with meticulous attention to his yard and his garden. In addition, he periodically took two or three days to go over to a farm run by the Mormon Church. There he worked on the irrigation of the farm and handled the tractor and the spraying for the crops. When winter came, it was travel time. He spoke with enthusiasm:

> Retirement is not as good as being in the Marine Corps, but it's as good as it can be if you're not a Marine. We've really enjoyed joining the Good Sam Club. When I retired from the VA we bought a travel trailer and, the first year that we were gone from here, we went for fifty-one days down into southern Utah, Nevada, Arizona, and over into California and back. Then each successive year, after the middle of October, we went on the road anywhere from four and half to five months through the winter. We've got a son that lives down in St. George, Utah, and one that lives down near Las Vegas, and wherever the sun's at in the winter time, that's just kind of where we went.

They frequently stopped at military camp grounds, and arranged a trip now and then so Massaro could be the guest speaker at a Marine Corps Birthday Ball. Their travels enabled them to keep in close touch with their six children. They comprised four girls and two boys, born over a twenty-year span from 1946 to 1966. Now, of course, they are grown and married, school teachers and nurses, scattered nearby in Utah and neighboring states. Massaro's parents are dead, with his father, John, going in 1972, and his mother, Dorothy, going in 1981. As compensation, NeDean counted up proudly, "We claim twenty-seven grandchildren, and we had two more who died. That's twenty-nine!"

The picture of the man emerged clearly: wife, children, home, and church—pretty solid foundations for a very solid man. In retirement he was still the same six foot, 180 pound person with the alert blue eyes (with glasses now) and the "whitewall" haircut. He was still a man who knew the value of the supportive role that others had played in his career, "I feel and believe, even more deeply than I ever did before, that I owe a great debt of gratitude to all of the officers and enlisted Marines that I had the pleasure and privilege of serving with and enjoying for over thirty-one years of my life. Had it not been for these remarkable individuals my career would not have been possible."

And he was still vivid in the minds of those who knew him through the years. Robert Cleary put it this way, "He was the one whom I looked up to from the young days when I was on the drill field. He was a leader and very articulate. He was another one who pushed physical fitness. I thank God that he did, because I think that when he was in the office he kind of turned it around, when a lot of men were trying to go in another direction. We were letting people put weight on, and they didn't look like Marines, and there were a lot of lackadaisical situations. He cleared a lot of that up for the next sergeant major."

It was his successor, Leland Crawford, who felt that "Massaro was probably, of all the Sergeants Major of the Marine Corps, the best one. He was a beautiful family man. John didn't drink (even coffee); he didn't curse; he didn't smoke; he didn't swear (although I had heard stories from back in his younger days that he did). But as he matured he was just a perfect gentleman, very religious. He didn't get excited: kind of quiet, but always on top of things. I guess I had boundless admiration for John Massaro."

Then there were his predecessors. Henry Black saw him as "a picture Marine: rugged, big, good physical shape. John ran four or five miles a day, even in retirement. He used to be a hellraiser, he told me, when he was younger. You could never believe it later. He was a tremendous person; just a tremendous Marine." And Joe Dailey was equally impressed, "Sharp, a real Marine, 100 percent. He was a 'recon man,' and he was just one of those Marines that you always took to.... Always slim, trim, alert, that type of guy."

The stories that cast Massaro in a different light in his younger days were true. He had grown up as a rough-and-tumble kid. "If we had any real trouble with someone then, we'd go behind the school building and settle it with our fists." In his mid-teens, there were the usual pre-occupations of girls and beer. The system was to slip a few dollars to someone of legal age, who would then go into the bar, buy the beer, and bring it out to the youngsters. Once in the Corps, Massaro became a regular amongst the serious beer drinkers in the local slopchute (enlisted man's club or nearby bar). This led, on one occasion, to an unfortunate encounter with the California Highway Patrol. As his service time lengthened and he rose in rank, he began to question the pattern of his drinking. Finally, after Christmas Mass at Iwakuni in 1959, he made up his mind and gave it up—forever.

This same tour in Japan marked a turning point in another important personal aspect of Massaro's life. He had always been a committed Roman Catholic, while NeDean was an ardent member of the Mormon Church. When he returned from Japan after fifteen months there, he found that his children were now accustomed to attending LDS services, so he went alone to Mass. Ten years later, he started to join them from time to time, and slowly a pattern developed in which he would go more and more with them. Massaro retained affiliation with the Roman Catholic Church until a couple of years into his retirement. By then, however, the prevailing Mormon pattern in Utah caused him to make a final decision to change. In October, 1981, he joined the LDS Church.

For a final evaluation of the man, there are the words of a former Commandant, General Paul X. Kelley: "John Massaro I've known for a long, long time. I went to jump school with him in 1957, and I would put him in a class of those whom I can count on one hand in my thirty-seven years of service, about whom I would say, 'These are the finest staff noncommissioned officers I have ever known.' He would be one of those individuals: extremely capable, forceful, physical, yet with a lot of smarts and a lot of savvy. I think just a darn good Marine—a 'recon' Marine all the way."

So that's what a "recon man" is really like!

Chapter 10

THE COAL MINER WHO MADE GOOD

Sergeant Major Leland D. Crawford

The start was certainly inauspicious for the life of the young man. Leland Crawford was born in Sharon, West Virginia, on February 16, 1930, amidst the bad times of the Great Depression. One of seven children, he saw his mother dead when he was five years old, followed, but not replaced, by the arrival of a stepmother a few years later. This led him to quit high school to work on the railroad at age fifteen. He recalled, "When I wrecked a caboose, the inspectors came, and, when they found out that I was fifteen, they fired me."

His father had worked in the coal mines since he was nine years old, so Crawford headed there and put in five years of hard work as a miner himself. It was during this time that his father drilled into him a maxim that he would carry with him for the rest of his life: "If you are going to dig a ditch, dig it well, because you'll never climb out of a poorly dug one!"

Crawford had made an abortive attempt to join the Marine Corps when he was eighteen; then, with the advent of the Korean War, he saw several relatives and friends, who had previously been Marines, reenlist. His patriotic sense was further kindled by the exciting combat stories his uncle, a Marine gunnery sergeant in World War II, had told him. Thus it was that, on September 26, 1951, Crawford went to South Charleston, West Virginia, to enlist in what he felt was "the world's finest."

He followed the traditional path to boot camp at Parris Island. Later on he admitted, "I had been searching for something that I didn't find until I got to Parris Island: for travel and adventure; for feeling good whenever I accomplished something; to be congratulated when I did a good job, and to get constructive criticism when I didn't." Acknowledging he was "kind of a hell raiser" when he arrived, he found that it did not take long for boot camp to instill in him the discipline which he never had had before. Graduation from recruit training left an indelible impression. Long after, he still remembered, "I kind of had a tear in my eye, because it was the first time in my twenty-one years that I'd really had the comradery, and the esprit de corps, and the togetherness that we, as a group of seventy-five people, actually had. To be honest about it, I think I found a home then."

December of 1951 found Crawford assigned to the Infantry Training School at Camp Pendleton. Four months later he was in a rotation draft, on his way to Korea. There he served first as an infantryman in the 7th Marines, and then as an artilleryman in the 11th Marines. It was here he first encountered a man whom he came to admire "more than anyone I've ever met in the Marine Corps, an old first sergeant named Glenn Morgan. He was kind of like the father that I didn't have," and it was Morgan who talked Crawford into reenlisting when his time was up. (Some years later, in Vietnam, he would again persuade Crawford to extend his tour of duty.)

In Korea Crawford had his first experience with the infamous "Category 4," recruits in the lowest mental and educational category. "I had Marines in my squad who could not read or write. I had to write letters home for them. That was a shame."

Not long after making sergeant, he was transferred back to the United States to join the 10th Marines, 2d Marine Division, at Camp Lejeune in July of 1953. Serving as a section chief, he was again promoted in October, 1955, this time to staff sergeant.

Another move came in June, 1956, to Parris Island. There he attended Drill Instructors School, and, upon graduation, became a drill instructor with the 5th Recruit Training Regiment. That occurred shortly after a drill instructor had caused the drowning of several recruits on a night march. In the house cleaning that quickly followed, numerous drill instructors were relieved of duty, and the Commandant, General Randolph Pate, combed the NCO ranks of the Corps for top-notch men to replace them. In addition, a new commanding general of the recruit depot, Brigadier General Wallace Greene, assembled some 400 drill instructors (including Crawford) in the post theater, and laid it on the line to them. He spoke bluntly of the trouble the Corps was in, and asked for their support in getting it back on the right track. Those drill instructors responded enthusiastically. "We did one hell of a job there in getting our Corps regrouped," was Crawford's feeling.

Looking back on this experience in later years, he evaluated its impact, "Drill instructor duty was the growing stage of my career. It instilled the maturity and leadership traits essential to every Marine."

October, 1958, brought Crawford to the 1st Marine Brigade at Kaneohe Bay on Hawaii's Oahu Island. Running field exercises, Crawford felt that (outside of drill instructor or combat duty) "that was probably the best tour of duty that I'd ever had because of the caliber of men whom we had at that time in our Corps." One of those outstanding men was Tom McHugh, who was his regimental sergeant major, soon to assume the duties of Sergeant Major of the Marine Corps. Another pleasant aspect was the implementation of a reorganization of the Marine NCO structure, which meant that, while remaining a staff sergeant, Crawford moved up a notch in pay.

Then it was back to the drill field in San Diego in October of 1961. Upon arrival, he found to his dismay that he was slated to go through Drill Instructors School. Along with other former Parris Island drill instructors, he went to see the chief instructor, to see if they all could be excused from that six weeks of schooling. The answer was a resounding, "No! Here in San Diego we do things differently." And that was that—even though Crawford found during his tour that things really were not any different, "I graduated just as fine recruits at San Diego as I had at Parris Island. It's not where a recruit graduates; the big thing is who he is."

There was another staff sergeant whom Crawford got to know on the drill field. His name was Robert Cleary, and he was destined to go a long way in the Corps. They established a good rapport with each other; as Crawford explained, "We kind of thought the same, and that was Marine."

Selection as gunnery sergeant came at this time, and this was a landmark for Crawford. Since enlisting as a private, he had always felt that "there was nothing more impressive than a professional staff NCO. I always looked forward to becoming a company gunny." There was a freeze on all promotions at that time, so it was eleven months later, after moving to the base at Twenty-nine Palms, California, in February, 1964, before his promotion took effect. There he rejoined his old outfit, the 11th Marines, as a battery gunnery sergeant. Field exercises and artillery training were interrupted when Crawford was sent to a special school in Coronado, California, for training in firing nuclear rounds. Upon graduation, he applied for duty with a nuclear ordnance platoon.

Shortly thereafter occurred one of the more colorful episodes in Crawford's action-filled career. It remained vivid in his memory:

> Over one Labor Day, we had a field exercise going on for the entire division, and when we stood down [finished] they granted us a little liberty. Three of us gunnery sergeants went to town. We started drinking a few

beers, and we went into this one establishment. I ran into one of my young Marines in there, drinking beer and shooting pool. Just two weeks prior to that we had taken up a collection in our outfit to bail him out of jail, because he was caught drinking under age. And here he was, in there drinking again!

So we ran him out of there, and in doing so the owner of the place wanted to know why. I told that individual, "That young man's not twenty-one years of age; he has no business being in here drinking alcoholic beverages." So at the end of it someone made a wrong move or took a wrong swing at one of us, and I guess the guy's bar was kind of leveled out there. Before it was over with, I think we were all in San Bernadino county jail, and I had lost my security clearance for nuclear ordnance, and was given two years' probation by the police.

Less than a year later, in February, 1965, he went overseas to a battery of the 3d Marine Division in Okinawa. Almost immediately it headed for combat. On March 8, Crawford landed at Da Nang in Vietnam as a part of the first 155mm artillery battery of the Marine Corps to serve there. Based on Hill 327, southwest of Da Nang, they fired in support of the 3d Marine Regiment.

Promoted to first sergeant, he returned after a year to serve in the headquarters company of Force Troops at Twentynine Palms. It was a divisive time for the country and for the Marine Corps, as Crawford recalled years later:

> That was probably the hardest job I ever had in the Marine Corps. It was the year of 1966. The Marine Corps was building, and we activated portions of our 5th Marine Division: the 26th Marines, the 27th Marines, the 13th Marines, the 11th Motor Transport, and some of the other separate battalions. All of the rejects at that time came to Twentynine Palms. And I mean *rejects*: homosexuals, flag-burners, the hippies, the yippies, the "we" generation, the people who didn't want to go to Vietnam, the deserters.
>
> The biggest majority of the troops were already in Vietnam, and all we had there were skeleton outfits. I had over 800 troops on my company roster, but I could only muster about 100. I had 700 deserters! One of my jobs was to get seat-fillers for the planes going to Vietnam—getting these people back from desertion, getting them outfitted in their uniforms, getting them court-martialed, getting them their sentences, and then sending them to the brig at Camp Pendleton.

After their time was up, Crawford had to arrange their release from the brig and see that they received their pre-deployment training. Then he had to get them on buses, have them taken down to the El Toro air base, accompanied by guards with loaded shotguns, and then have them escorted to the planes going to Okinawa. That was the only way he was able to get them over there. He continued:

> We were always court-martialing them. One day an individual would be a prison chaser, and he would chase [escort] another individual to the court martial. (That's when we did a court-martial on the battalion level.

We didn't have the legal officers involved in it as we do today.) We would give that individual a six months' sentence. This guy would chase him to the prison, and then the next day we would court-martial the chaser, because I had no good guys there!

Fortunately I had a company commander, Captain Peter Rowe, who was a very dynamic individual. I think he and I were the only two sane ones in the entire company. As a matter of fact, my administrative chief was a deserter. My clerks were deserters. It was just one horrible company. It was worse than some of those old casual companies that we had after Korea.

That painful period lasted until June, 1967, when he returned to Vietnam as a company first sergeant in the 4th Marines. Crawford considered that tour to be one of the highlights of his career, because of the superb quality of the men with whom he worked. Somehow he escaped the "seat-fillers" and found fine young Marines, top-notch NCOs, and outstanding company commanders (including one, Captain Keith Thompson, who had been a recruit under Crawford at Parris Island). The exigencies of war brought him opportunities to function in a variety of roles: "I held every job in the company from first sergeant to gunny to platoon commander to company commander on two different occasions."

The first time was in June, 1968. Crawford's company was then touching on the border of Laos, and they were sent out to look for the bamboo fords that the enemy would build right beneath the surface of a river for their supply routes. The company found several and blew them up, after which it pulled back to the battalion position on Hill 500. Crawford detailed the story of a wild night:

> We'd been in their back yard, so they started mortaring us quite heavily. I can recall we had a chaplain who was over at our company area having a cup of coffee with myself, Captain Richard Manla, and the company gunny. It was just dusk. Boy, all of a sudden I heard that tubing, and when you hear tubing you know what it is. Here came the 81mm mortar shells!
>
> As the first sergeant of that company I had always selected the command post [CP] and told the company commander, "Here's where the CP's going to be." But my captain had it moved this time. He said, "First Sergeant, why did you select this site here?" I replied, "Well, Captain, I've been selecting the CP sites for eleven months now. I just assumed that this was where you wanted the CP to be, where we can best control our three platoons." He answered, "Well, I think we ought to move it right back up here." That kind of upset me a little bit, because we had already dug all the damn fox holes.
>
> Anyway, he's the captain, so I said, "Okay, Skipper, we'll move the son of a bitch." We moved that bear back up there, and we dug about three new fighting holes for him and me and the radio operator, and we set in. Then, bigger than hell, when we got mortared, we got two or three guys, including the captain and myself, wounded there right in the CP

(which brought me a Purple Heart). But in the area I had previously selected there wasn't even a round which hit near it! So when they pulled the captain back, I took charge until they sent a First Lieutenant Walter Jones up later to assume the position of company commander.

There was more action the following month. Close by Landing Zone Stud and Hill 715 near Ca Lu in Quang Tri Province, his company was on a "search and destroy" mission. Another company had been in action one night, and had been forced to leave some of its dead on the scene before withdrawing. Crawford long remembered what followed:

> Our company was assigned to go out and retrieve the other company's dead. In doing so, our skipper, Captain Banks, took us down from the 700-foot contour line to about the 400-foot contour line, and we came right into the area where we felt that the wounded or dead were. We grounded our packs and our flak jackets, and we went in to search.
>
> The enemy had some command-detonated claymore mines in there. Our company commander was up in the front of the column trying to get information from one of the young lieutenants who had just joined the company. Then one of those command-detonated claymore mines just took the top of his head off—killed him. The North Vietnamese had concealed a rope to pull and fire that damn thing just when you got in that little area.
>
> Darkness was coming on; we were in heavy canopy; we had a lot of young troops, new troops to Vietnam. We had three brand new second lieutenants and a couple of old seasoned staff sergeants. I immediately took charge when our battalion commander, Lieutenant Colonel Edward Deptula, told me to take over. He said, "Brother Crawford, you command that company and get them out of there." Well, I did; we reorganized and we got out all our wounded and our dead and the dead from the other company. We finally got back to a secure area in a bomb crater, and we set up a defense there.
>
> I gave thanks right there for the good training that the Marine Corps had given me over all those years. Because of cross-training (communications, map reading, adjustment of artillery fire and so forth), I always thought that I brought that company out of there with no more casualties. Finally we regrouped with the rest of our battalion back on Hill 715.

For his dramatic leadership in this bloody encounter, Crawford was recommended for a Silver Star Medal. However, someone in the division rear altered the award to a Bronze Star.

By October, 1968, his Vietnam tour was over, and, at its conclusion, Crawford was awarded a second Bronze Star. While he had gone out on forty-six combat patrols and served in every possible leadership position in his company, he downplayed this particular award, "It was kind of like an end-of-tour award for meritorious service, and I never did believe in those."

Transferred back to Camp Lejeune, he reported in to none other than Tom McHugh, who was now the sergeant major of Force Troops there. Crawford thought that McHugh was going to assign him to the force reconnaissance troops, and perhaps with the idea of planting that seed, played golf with the old sergeant major on the weekend that he arrived. It didn't quite work out that way, for on Monday morning McHugh told him that he was sending him to a company in the communications battalion that had not passed an inspection in six months, "You go down there and get that goddamn outfit squared away!" Crawford found that "their administration was completely screwed up! I just don't think anybody was in charge." However, a forceful new major, Robin Cobble, arrived, and Crawford dug into the mess with him.

Shortly thereafter, orders came through transferring Crawford to Washington, but he telephoned Headquarters and asked for a postponement in order to finish successfully his work with his company. A delay was granted and, when the commanding general's inspection took place, the revitalized company passed with flying colors.

With that accomplished, he moved up to Washington in March, 1969. There he served as first sergeant of the ceremonial guard company, a part of the battalion at Washington Barracks at 8th and I Streets, although his office was two blocks away in the Navy Yard. When he reported in to Major Frank Breth, who was to be his commanding officer, he was greeted with, "First Sergeant, I've never met you, but I needed a first sergeant. I screened about twenty record books, and I selected you to come here to be my first sergeant." Crawford said, "Well, I appreciate that. What got that?" He answered, "First of all, you're over six foot two. I want a tall first sergeant out there. Plus, you've got a good background of troop handling and you're a former drill instructor."

Taking over the ceremonial guard company, Crawford found a congenial environment. The Commandant had, a short while before, laid down a policy of "only Vietnam veterans" at the barracks, and the new first sergeant found that he had "some of the finest Marines I've ever met in my life: young NCOs, several of them highly decorated, who have since gone on to be sergeants major and commissioned officers today." And they learned a lot from Joe Dailey, then the Sergeant Major of the Marine Corps, who used to visit the barracks from time to time just to talk to the troops.

The company had a wide range of duties. There were three regular drill platoons and a silent drill platoon that put on the famous Friday Evening Parade at the barracks. There was regular guard duty at the barracks. There was the responsibility to provide Presidential security at Camp David. There were many funeral details for the burial of every Marine who came from the metropolitan Washington area and had been killed in Vietnam. There were the assignments to provide color guards throughout the Marine Corps (when the Washington parade season was over). This last duty took Crawford, the ceremonial guard company, the silent drill platoon, and the drum and bugle corps to ceremonies at bases all over the United States, as well as to Canada and England.

For wide-ranging duties such as these, not just any staff NCO would do. To find men with the proper qualifications, Crawford and his next CO, Major James Cooligan, would step over to see the personnel sergeant major at Headquarters, Clint Puckett, who later recollected, "He also used to come over with his sergeant major whom I had known since Korea days. My office was so small that they couldn't sit down. Of course, Crawford's so big, I don't think he could have gotten through the door!"

Recalling his own role, Crawford outlined the situation:

> My job as the first sergeant there was coordinating a lot of the ceremonies: the funerals, the arrivals, the many different types of ceremonies. I worked directly with the section chief of the body bearers. I can remember not one time when we ever missed a ceremony—all because of the dedication of the young NCOs that we had working there. What I really enjoyed were the two commanders that I had; they gave us staff NCOs a special trust and confidence to do our job, without breathing down our necks.
>
> Prior to my getting there, the headquarters unit of the company was not ceremonial. They were the clerks, the cooks, the bakers, the candlestick makers, the barber, the PX guy, and so forth. So, one of my first jobs was that I got all these guys trained for ceremonial duties. I put it to them straight, "If you're going to be in this company, you're going to be ceremonial."

Crawford had two young sergeants and they started training the men in how to do the manual of arms, be body bearers, use the ceremonial sword, and perform all the other formal ceremonies, cross-trained so they could do anything. His story went on:

> That was right during the height of that big operation we had in Vietnam, Dewey Canyon. We were burying a lot of Marines at Arlington Cemetery! One time we selected this one burial detail to go out to a town in Virginia, and I sent a bus out with this young sergeant in charge of the body bearers and firing party. As he was going out the bus was wrecked. That sergeant ran across an open field, while he had his spleen injured and a couple of his ribs broken. You talk about dedication and loyalty! He ran across this open field, when he should have waited there until the ambulance came and took him to the hospital. But he got on the phone and called me and panted, "We're going to be late for that funeral."
>
> I, in turn, got all this Bridge-on-the-River-Kwai bunch, as I referred to them (the cats and dogs in my headquarters), and I gave them a notice and within 10 minutes they were out of there in full dress blue uniforms. They arrived just five minutes late for the funeral. So that's just the type of Marines that I had there in the ceremonial guard company.

One final tour in Vietnam lay ahead, and in December of 1970 Crawford went over to serve as a company first sergeant in the 1st Marine Regiment. Working in an area near Hill 65, his rifle company covered the careful withdrawal of the rest of the division as it prepared to leave Vietnam. There was a pattern of constant patrolling, "running around in the small hamlets," and operations in conjunction with the Marine combined action units.

It proved to be a very short tour of duty, for in May, 1971, he was ordered back to Camp Pendleton. Transferred there to a different battalion in the regiment, he achieved part of his final objective: he became an acting sergeant major in September. Three months later, his goal was formally realized when his battalion commander, Lieutenant Colonel Edward Deptula, gave him a field promotion to sergeant major. He was forty-one years old, and twenty of those years had been devoted to the Marine Corps.

Along the way he had picked up the nick-name "Crow" (not "Craw"). There may have been some other names applied to him after two episodes at Camp Pendleton. The commanding general of the Fleet Marine Force, Pacific, came aboard to give a talk at the camp theater to a large number of troops. Reflecting the civilian attitude of the early seventies, there was one young Marine who thought that he was a real "wise guy." He peppered the general with rude questions, harassing him, and trying to show him up. Then he ran full tilt out the door. Crawford had stationed himself there, and his oaken arm was held straight out, motionless. The kid ran right into it, with a big "clunk" of his Adam's apple. After that "clothes-lining," he gave no more trouble.

A somewhat similar incident occurred later on in the gymnasium. There was a formal retirement ceremony to say goodbye to a respected sergeant major, with the entire battalion and visiting dignitaries assembled. All of a sudden, while the National Anthem was being played, through a side door burst two Marines. They were clad in KKK-style white sheets with red fluorescent road marker cones on their heads! Calling out through bull horns, they started to disrupt the ceremony. Crawford jumped up and ran across the floor. Let him describe what came next:

> The first one, I could look at just about where his eyes were. And I hit that son of a bitch, and I sent him clear over there. The other one came around and I took a swing at him, but I missed him. It was so slippery in there that my feet went straight up into the air. The crazy thing about it was that they were in there protesting the sergeant major retiring. When we dragged those two guys out the side door, there were two blacks, a Samoan, and me: all sergeants major. So you couldn't holler racial prejudice at that time!
>
> There was a reporter out there from a local paper with a camera, and he was taking a film of all this. Those two Marines had called that reporter up, and he came in there and he was taking TV pictures of it. We took that damned camera away from him—myself and another sergeant major— and we emptied all of it right there on the deck and we ran him off the base.

Two years later came a brutal opportunity to find out what kind of physical shape he really was in—and how his endurance stacked up against the young Marines, twenty-five years his junior, in the battalion. With his commanding officer, Lieutenant Colonel Orlo ("O.K.") Steele, he took the troops to Bridgeport, California, for a period of "round robin" training. This was a program in which a company would rotate its activities: a week out in the woods honing infantry tactics; then a week of mountain climbing; then a week on the suspension traverse, doing vertical hauling, and practicing river crossings.

After finishing that gruelling workout, they all marched fifty-one miles to Nevada with full packs and all the weapons of an infantry battalion. With

Staff Sergeant Crawford with his old-fashioned campaign hat as a symbol of his status as a DI in San Diego in 1961 (above). Looking older and even more serious (right), Sergeant Major Crawford returns to San Diego 13 years later to supervise a recruit training battalion in 1974.

the sergeant major and lieutenant colonel (both in their forties) leading the way, they covered those fifty-one miles in seventeen hours and two minutes. Arriving at their destination, Steele asked Crawford how many men had been previously listed as needing remedial physical training (PT). When he replied that there were about twelve, and that all of them had made it all the way on the march, the lieutenant colonel growled, "Well you take them off the damn remedial PT. If they performed this they don't need remedial PT!" It was a very tired body of men that lay down for the night to await transportation back the next day. Crawford never forgot that night:

> As my colonel and I laid down there on our poncho liners he said, "Crow, what time are we getting up?" I said, "Zero four hundred." He answered, "Let's get up at zero three-thirty." Then I asked, "What are we getting up a half an hour early for? Hell, I need my zees as much as those young troops do!" He replied, "You'll find out tomorrow morning."
>
> I found out then why he got us up a half an hour early! Rigor mortis had done set in on my legs; I could hardly walk after humping that fifty-one miles. I've always said that the old-timers can do as much as any young kid can but, see, we can't bounce back like they can. It took me a good twenty minutes before I could walk around there. My legs were so stoved up, I could understand why he made us get up a half an hour early. I've always respected him for doing that.

In April, 1974, Crawford received orders to return once more to San Diego as sergeant major of a recruit training battalion. The Marine Corps was changing radically in those post-Vietnam years. The drug addicts and the trouble makers had been thrown out. While his new assignment was one for which Crawford was superbly prepared by his past experiences, he described the real challenge he nevertheless faced:

> I had been a successful drill instructor on two previous tours of duty. The Marine Corps was just coming out of the tedious years (as I refer to them) with the Category 4s and McNamara's Project 100,000 [when the Marine Corps had been forced to accept recruits in the lowest mental quartile]. Now we were no longer taking them, and we were getting good quality people. I think 1974 really started the Corps in rebuilding. When they came in with the all voluntary force in '72, they finally put it into force in '73, and about '74 was probably our first good year; and we've had better years thereafter.
>
> On the drill field, prior to that—I'm not saying there was a lot of maltreatment going on there—but a lot of drill instructors were getting in trouble for violating the Standard Operating Procedure [SOP]. I felt, and I still feel today, that that's where you need the old sergeant major, because he can get out there and he's already been through what these young drill instructors haven't been through. That's exactly what he is; he's an advisor to his commander and he's also a father to his drill instructors. He's a person that they should be able to come to if they've got a problem.

Crawford sought to change their procedures so they followed the SOP—just by talking to them. In the two years that he was there in that battalion, it did not have one court-martial. And the other battalions were having at least seven to eight courts-martial a month. He felt that the key requirement was close supervision by the sergeants major and the chief drill instructors. Explaining this crucial point, he went on to specify that "close" did not mean over-supervising, did not mean micro-management and doing their jobs for the drill instructors. It meant being there with them, and cutting potential problems off in the bud before they became serious. That could not be done by going to work at seven in the morning and going home at four in the evening. The sergeant major had to be there at night, and early in the morning, and he had to sit there and talk to those drill instructors, and if they had a problem, he had to find out what their problem was. He recalled one particular night:

> I can recall going on deck one night about 2300. [Going on deck is going into the barracks.] And here was every drill instructor in that series in there. Now damn it, drill instructors work seven days a week, 15 hours a day. I can recall in my younger days as a drill instructor, the biggest majority of us were either separated, or we were getting a divorce, because of the hours that we had to perform. I've been married two times myself. My first tour at Parris Island as a DI wasn't successful at home and we had problems. When I got transferred to San Diego, that did it.
>
> So I tried to prevent that from ever happening in my battalion again. Well, that night there was the series gunny and all four senior drill instructors and their juniors in there, at 2300. This was an hour after taps! I said, "What the hell are you people doing in here?" "Well, the lieutenant is punishing us because the squad bay wasn't clean this morning." I'll tell you right now, I went out of my damn tree! I shouted, "Who's the goddamn idiot lieutenant?" Then I said, "Gunny, you get these drill instructors and you get them home right now, and you get them a good night's sleep. If that lieutenant's got anything to say about it, you tell him to come and see me right now."
>
> At this point the lieutenant came up there, and he said, "What's going on?" I shot back, "I'm sending these drill instructors home. If you don't like it, you be in the battalion commander's office tomorrow morning at 7:00. We'll discuss this real quick." It's things like that right there that causes drill instructors to violate SOPs. It causes them to maltreat recruits.
>
> So I can say that it was our supervision and our attention to duty that prevented a lot of drill instructors from taking that first step to put his hand on a recruit.

As always, the period on San Diego's familiar terrain came to an end, and his new orders took Crawford to strange duty in January, 1976. He was transferred to become the group sergeant major of Marine Aircraft Control Group 18 on Okinawa. He was not pleased. First, however, there was a parade at the recruit depot, honoring his service, with all the drill instructors and his wife Fayette present, while the battalion commander praised the job he had done there.

Looking ahead with dismay, Crawford worked until the last possible moment, and then he "dragged [his] feet all the way to the airplane." His resentment sprang from a strong desire to go to an infantry or artillery regiment—not aviation. But Okinawa it was, and when he arrived he started learning. The air group there told him that "they control the sky," and that they were the people who ran the radar, the communications, and exercised tactical air control for fighter planes. There were four squadrons in the control group, as well as Red Eye missiles, so Crawford was a busy man.

His attitude toward aviation began to change quickly. He found that the two successive commanding officers under whom he served, Colonel John Knope and Colonel Ronald Proudfoot, were "super dynamic, real professionals, totally committed to their work." As for the enlisted men, he was impressed when the inspector general came out from Headquarters, and every staff NCO passed his physical fitness test and his personal appearance rating. It was now clear to Crawford that "these aviator people were just as much Marines as we were in the ground forces. They were some dedicated people over there. But you also have the old sergeant major putting the boot to their butts!"

Crawford supplied his own motivation for a long-delayed step forward in his personal life in 1976. The man who, as a youth, had left high school for the coal mines enrolled in a local school in Okinawa and proudly earned his degree as a graduate of Kubisaki High.

In January, 1977, he headed stateside, once more bound for the 1st Division at Camp Pendleton. Upon reporting in to the division sergeant major, he found the office jammed with well-wishers, for John Massaro there had just been selected as Sergeant Major of the Marine Corps that very day. Crawford's hope was for the 5th Marines, because he had already served in every other regiment of the division (the 1st, the 7th, and the 11th). It was not to be. Since choice of duty for sergeants major is heavily influenced by seniority, a senior man was moved up from the 11th Marines to serve as division sergeant major, and Crawford inherited his job in that regiment. The 11th Marines, as part of the 5th Marine Expeditionary Brigade, became heavily involved in a combined arms exercise at Twentynine Palms. That brought double duty for Crawford as brigade sergeant major and regimental sergeant major.

Another career step came in May, 1979, when he moved up to become division sergeant major. Two months later, he took the division colors to a 1st Division reunion in Washington, D.C. The new Commandant, General Robert Barrow, was the speaker. Since they were both together at the head table, the two men had a chance to get acquainted. Shortly thereafter, back at Camp Pendleton, Crawford was out on a five-mile training run when a jeep pulled alongside, and the driver told him to call Headquarters "real quick." Going back to his office, he asked, "What in the world do they want me to call Headquarters for?" Dialing the number given him, he remembered, "It was the sergeants major monitor, who said, 'You sitting down?' I answered, 'Hell no, I'm not sitting down!' He said, 'Well, sit down!' I asked, 'What in the hell is going on, a death in the family or what?' He replied, 'No, the Commandant wants to see you back here the day after tomorrow for an interview.'"

Recovering from the shock, before getting on the plane to fly east, Crawford started putting the pieces of the puzzle together: the nice conversation at the reunion with the Commandant, the previous request to send in a photograph, the fact that he was well up on the seniority list, his overall career track record....

It was "interview time"—the first time the Commandant had seen face-to-face all ten candidates for Sergeant Major of the Marine Corps. The memory remained etched in Crawford's mind:

> I was the sixth one. I walked into the Commandant's office and he asked me the "wrong" questions, questions about Marine Corps recruit depots. Hell, I knew them. So we had a lengthy little chat there of about forty-five minutes, and I really enjoyed that. But I didn't really think that I was going to get the job for one simple reason: I don't say I was a bad Marine, but I was kind of a "liberty risk" sometimes in my younger days.
>
> In addition, my wife was gainfully employed at that time, and she and I had discussed this. She had said, "Crow, if you go back there, I can't go with you because I can't get a leave of absence." And my wife made pretty good money. That job, at that time, would have paid me $351 more. I thought, "Is that worth it? Is the prestige worth it? Or what? I don't know." I'd already fulfilled my ambition—to be a gunnery sergeant.
>
> So I explained about my wife to General Barrow, and, in his mysterious way, he just nodded his head, "Yes. Yes." Then a good friend of mine was brought in shortly thereafter. Next I think two other gentlemen went in. As a matter of fact, Bob Cleary was considered at that time.
>
> Well, the general didn't tell me anything at that moment, but afterwards one of the Headquarters colonels called to me, saying he wanted to speak to my wife. I said, "Colonel, if you've got anything to say, you can speak to me. You don't need to talk to my wife." He grunted, "You're kind of hard-headed aren't you, Sergeant Major?" Anyway, I heard later that he got ahold of my wife's employer and talked to her; he told her about the job, and he discussed a two-year leave of absence for my wife.

On that note Crawford headed back to the west coast, awaiting the Commandant's selection. A few days later, Crawford was presenting the commanding general of the 1st Division, Major General Charles Cooper, with the division colors in a formal parade ceremony. The general leaned over and, in a low voice, confided, "I hate to tell you, but you are being transferred back to Washington, and you're going to be the Sergeant Major of the Marine Corps." Crawford replied, "General, you are really testing my presence of mind. I could drop these colors right at your damned feet!"

The Commandant, for his part, had followed the traditional procedure of having a board of general officers winnow a list of sergeants major for the top job. The finalists were passed on to Barrow, and, after the personal interviews, he picked Crawford:

> There was something about Crawford that made him my favorite; and therefore while the others, I believe, were fully qualified, it was not a decision over which I had to agonize or worry whether I was making the right

choice. I focused on him during these interviews, and he became my choice.

I had not known him previously which is a little unusual. You would have thought that, somewhere along the way, our paths would have crossed. I didn't really look at his record in any great detail. I wanted to see what he was like as a man, and the kind of answers he gave to my questions, and sort of get a feel for him as an individual.

In the selection of the Sergeant Major of the Marine Corps, there's so much visibility there that you should, to the maximum extent, reduce the uncertainties. When it's *the* Sergeant Major, it is such a high visibility job that you really want to make it right, get the right one, because it would be very bad to get one and find out that you weren't working well together, and that he should move on. If that happened after three or four months it would be very shocking.

Thus, on August 15, 1979, Crawford took over from Massaro as *the* senior enlisted man of the Corps. From the start, the chemistry of his relationship with the Commandant was good, and this, in a way, was very surprising. They really seemed to be "the odd couple." Barrow was the epitome of a very sophisticated, highly educated, quietly understated Southern gentleman. Crawford was totally different. He came from the other side of the tracks, a coal miner with very little formal education, brash, rough-hewn, outspoken, with a penchant for four-letter words.

Yet there was a certain curious similarity beneath their diverse exteriors and styles. Barrow had a basic understanding of the enlisted man, for he had been one for a year. He had left Louisiana State University to enlist as a private, and had made corporal as an assistant drill instructor in San Diego before gaining entrance to an officers candidate class. He even had a nickname then, "Louisiana," as Crawford would later be called "Crow." And they each wore multiple medals for distinguished combat records.

More fundamental in their understanding of each other, however, was the fact that they had both come up to the very top against heavy numerical odds. When Crawford earned his staff sergeant stripes in 1955, he was only one of 10,000 with that rank amidst the 186,750 enlisted Marines on active duty. It was a long way to the top from there, and the competition would grow increasingly stiff on the way. In 1979, when the time came to select a new Sergeant Major of the Marine Corps, there were 1,250 very senior NCOs in the top rank of E-9, sergeants major and master gunnery sergeants. Only one would be chosen. The same pressure was present for Barrow in his climb through the officer ranks. When a man pins on the four stars of the Commandant of the Marine Corps, he has been subject to the most intensive scrutiny and competition over three decades of service, and he has proven himself among an elite group of his peers. Thus the two men, despite their apparent dissimilarities, recognized and respected what the other had accomplished in his long climb: twenty-eight years of service for Crawford and thirty-six years as a commissioned officer for Barrow.

Crawford's official portrait as Sergeant Major of the Marine Corps, with his decorations headed at that time by two Bronze Stars.

Now they went to work as a team. Generally the two of them would meet about three times a week for a discussion of Crawford's trips to various Marine locations around the country. Sometimes Barrow would suggest a base that he wanted Crawford to visit and report back on. Then there were the Commandant's regular morning staff meetings, which the sergeant major would attend "if he had something to say."

In November, 1980, Crawford convened a sergeants major symposium at Headquarters: forty-four of them were present, as well as two master gunnery sergeants. They spent a week discussing eighty-one different subjects, with thirty-four final recommendations eventually being sent to the staff sections there for further study and perhaps implementation. The range of issues was enormous: pay (as always), proficiency and tactical tests, uniform regulations, promotion warrants, overseas orders, and even "ingrown beards."

Whenever Barrow made a trip to a Marine base, Crawford always accompanied him there, but on arrival, they would split up. As Crawford described it:

> When we would go to a base, I never went behind him. He went one way; I went the other. I would have a completely separate itinerary there, for I would have the sergeant major of the base have that worked out prior to my arrival. He would forward it in advance for me to approve it. I always ensured that, if the Commandant talked to the enlisted in a group, in a theater or wherever, or to a mixed group of officers and staff NCOs, I was always present for one simple reason: no surprises. And I could handle the staff NCOs' questions which they directed towards the Commandant.
>
> In addition, I made quite a few trips by myself. I visited every continental Marine recruiting station with the exception of Houston, Texas, as well as the ones in Hawaii and Guam. I also visited every Marine barracks in the Corps except Marine Barracks, London.

On one occasion Crawford had a great change of pace from the routine of these inspections. He slipped away for a trip to the national convention of the Non-Commissioned Officers Association, in Las Vegas. Naturally he was included in the speakers panel, which consisted of current and former senior sergeants. Clint Puckett was also there, brightening his retirement with reunions with old friends. Thinking back to that convention, Puckett later commented, "I called the Commandant's office and asked them to pass the word to the Commandant that I had seen Crow Crawford, and that he was loud, crude, inclined to be profane, and the troops just loved him! And I'm not talking about just the Marines or former Marines, I'm talking about all of them. He was the star of Las Vegas, take my word for it."

An additional first-hand evaluation of his trips is in the account of another sergeant major, George Rogers, who also saw Crawford in action:

> One was when I had the recruiting station in Harrisburg. He had been invited up to speak to the NROTC unit at State College. Since the Sergeant Major of the Marine Corps was going to be in my territory, I made it a point to be there myself. With his style, I was kind of leery. I was really wonder-

Checking out a "Huskie," Crawford (right) is in the driver's "seat" on a 1981 visit to Cam Lejeune.

Crawford photo

ing how he was going to go over with a group of college students, since Crow is kind of a diamond in the rough. It was fantastic! The man got up there—he murdered the English language like he always does—and yet by the time he was done, those kids were in love with him. They thought he was the greatest thing they had ever seen. They asked him a lot of questions, and it was really a good visit.

The strong impact that Crawford had on other people was further illustrated by another memory of Rogers:

I had another personal experience which well illustrated Crow's force of personality. I had planned to retire, and I submitted my letter of intent to do so in the summer of '83. About two weeks later, I got a phone call from the Sergeant Major of the Marine Corps, Leland D. Crawford. He said, "What in the hell do you think you're doing? You damn well aren't going to retire! I've got you slated to go down and take over FMFLant." I mumbled, "Well, I...." You didn't argue too much with that guy, you know! I started to say, "Well, my plans are made. I'm already...." He interrupted, "I'm not going to put up with that! You aren't going to retire. You're going to go down and take over FMFLant." So we talked some more and finally I said, "Well, I'll think about it for a while." He concluded, "Well, you sure as hell better do that." So I did; I went home and talked it over with my wife and thought about it a little bit. About a week later I called him back and said, "Okay, you win." He replied, "All right. I've already withdrawn your letter of resignation anyway." And that was how I ended up down there in FMFLant instead of being retired.

Besides these dealings and visits on his own, Crawford, of course, made many other trips with the Commandant. Barrow outlined them:

Typically, if we went to the western Pacific, we would talk, probably, in the aircraft on the way, maybe more than once, sharing thoughts about what we might find, and what we should be looking for, and discussing when we were there last and what we saw then. It was sort of an informal preparation, feeding off one another, "Now, Sergeant Major, don't forget, I would like for you to go down to such-and-such a place and really check them out there. I'm so busy I'm not going to be able to look in on some of the things that interest me. As you know I'm not going to be able to see the brig, so you drop in on them (probably best unannounced). They should always be ready in the brig, because that's twenty-four-hour-a-day work. So just drop in on them, and let me know what you find out."

When we arrived someplace, he was never made captive by the local sergeants major: like, "Well Sergeant Major, we're glad to have you out here. Let's go over to the Staff NCO Club and meet some of the people and have a little bite to eat." Not Crawford! He hit the ground running. If they hadn't already been told what he wanted to see and do, he would soon tell them.

He might talk eight or ten times to a theater full of sergeants and below. He knew how to talk to them in a way that they liked. He would ask them, "Do you have any questions?" and some would obviously fudge around and he would say, "What's your name, Private? See me right after this." In other words, the kid maybe had a thing so personal that he didn't want to ask it in the theater. Or some youngster would ask a question the answer to which everyone should know, a policy thing that clearly this command didn't understand. He would explain it. He could talk authoritatively, intelligently, effectively on just about any subject that would interest a young Marine.

How did Crawford come across to these Marines all over the world? Barrow put it this way in summarizing his sergeant major's style:

To begin with, he was an impressive man physically. He was about six foot four, and he stood very straight. He had a very manly demeanor about him. He looked you straight in the eye when he talked to you, and had no hesitation or lack of confidence in himself. When he spoke, he would not only answer any questions without equivocation, but he would also offer his thoughts on anything that he wanted to offer them on—which I found to be a pleasure....

Crawford evoked instant respect from those who would see him by his demeanor, his self-assured manner. That grew if you heard him talk or involve himself in some project. I used to say to my wife (and maybe to an aide or two) that, if Crawford had had the education and experience, for example, that I had had and others had, then *he* could have been the Commandant of the Marine Corps.

Barrow went on to underscore his sergeant major's instincts: whether about a private, another sergeant major, or even officers, noting that Crawford sometimes, most discreetly, usually after the general had asked him a question, would express his concern about some officer situation. This was based, the Commandant felt, on native intelligence, with innate perceptiveness and an ability to understand things. This was a most senior NCO who did not "have any hang-ups which would get in the way, such as a big ego or any insecurities. He was a man unburdened by any psychological, personal burdens. He was smart, and he was interested in people, and he had a lot of experience. He'd been around the Marine Corps so long that he had seen everything that one could expect to see, probably several times. He and I had this great rapport." This rapport was well illustrated in the way the two men would work together after returning from a trip. As Barrow described it:

> He would come back from a trip with a pocket full of names on paper notes that he was going to check on when he came back to Washington. Each name had a different problem. He was not one who would say, "General, I've got about thirty-five to forty names here who...." He wouldn't do that; he'd just go on about his business, and deal with those problems himself on his return.

> If I felt the need for me to take some sort of action, I had to be mindful not to compromise him. I never wrote a letter or made a phone call back to a command from which we just came and said, "My sergeant major tells me that...." Knowing that, he had confidence in talking to me, certain that I wasn't going to get him in hot water with someone. I might add, he didn't do that often.

> I think all Marines, irrespective of rank or how long they had been in the service, have a certain awe and respect for the Commandant. They want to see him; they want to meet him; they'd like to hear him talk. That would be true of, say, a theater full of sergeants and below. But they may be more tuned in to the sergeant major than to the Commandant *if* that sergeant major is effective.

> For, among other things, they see him as one of themselves. They might think that, if they stayed around long enough and had the breaks, they might end up being Commandant. (General Gray, our former Commandant, is a classic example.) Or, "If I stayed around long enough and really worked at it, I might be Sergeant Major of the Marine Corps." So that sergeant major brings with him a certain image, a certain set of achievements that young Marines and staff NCOs and a lot of officers have a high respect for.

Inevitably, problems would surface during those trips, and sometimes Barrow would assign Crawford to a special task force to deal with a particularly knotty or far-reaching one. In 1980, for example, some twenty-five percent of all Marines were not getting paid the proper amount of money, due to computer foul-ups in the reporting system generated out of the Marine Corps Finance Center in Kansas City. To better understand the problem, Crawford, representing the needs of enlisted Marines, and Colonel Donald Morris, representing the technical skills of the manpower division, went to every major command in the continental U.S. and in the Fleet Marine Force, Pacific and Atlantic. They found that, among other problems, the Reserves were going to monthly meetings, but not being paid for three or four months. This led to a series of recommendations to the Commandant which were instrumental in clearing up the failures in six months.

Until 1980, it had been Marine Corps policy to have unaccompanied overseas tours in the western Pacific: you went out and your family stayed home. Barrow saw from his trips the negative effect this had on morale. It was peacetime; more young Marines were married and had families. They had different personal expectations from those who had served in Vietnam combat. So the Commandant decided to change things. Again, Crawford and Colonel Morris hit the road. It was out to Okinawa for twenty-one days, back in the U.S. for five days, and then right back to Okinawa again. Their report proposed a set of guidelines, which were approved by Barrow, outlining which family members could accompany a Marine overseas on certain assignments, and what should be done about housing them there.

Amidst the continuous pressure of his job, a major personal crisis now arose for Crawford, presenting him with an agonizing career decision. Barrow explained the situation:

> Mrs. Crawford was a very lovely lady, and had had a very fine job on the west coast. Knowing that it was important that he have his wife with him in Washington while he was my sergeant major, she came east to be with him. They set up housekeeping with the understanding, of course, that historically it had been a two-year tour of duty. So she got a two-year leave of absence from the company she worked for. Then, when that ended, they would go back to the west coast, retired.
>
> Well, I leaned on him to stay; and he, like a good Marine, responded.... He was not the kind of man who would have said, "Well, General, I thank you for asking me, but I think I'd like to hang it up." That's not the way he was. When he did stay, that meant Mrs. Crawford went back to California to resume her job. So he had what amounted to a two-year unaccompanied tour in Washington, D.C. I must confess that I feel now that I abused him, his marriage, and his wife.
>
> That's not to say that they didn't get together ever. He would go to the west coast, either with me or sometimes on his own, and she made some trips back here. On one of my western Pacific trips, I made sure that she would be able to get off work and come with us. So she accompanied us on our swing around to Japan, Korea, Okinawa, and the Philippines, which I think she enjoyed.

Admitting this separation was "hard" for him, Crawford nevertheless plunged into the next two years with determination. The trips all over the world continued unabated. When his sergeant major would come into his office, Barrow remembered, "Routinely he came in to go over whatever he'd been doing, and whatever he'd picked up in the way of information. You see, a sergeant major, to be most effective, needs to be the eyes and ears extension of the Commandant. I see the room; he sees the corners and underneath the chairs.... And you'd better find some way to determine if a policy is really well transmitted so that it has reached everybody. Most importantly, is it being properly understood?''

A case in point was Barrow's edict in January, 1982, clamping down hard on drug usage. Crawford felt that "at least seventy percent of our people were either using drugs or had used them at that time." The policy was crystal clear: substance abuse was to stop immediately. Soon Crawford's phone rang. It was an old sergeant major, Igor Cowan, at a Marine air base, "Crow, it's the best damn thing the Commandant ever came out with! Goddamn, we've got the druggies chasing for their helmets and flak jackets!''

Of course, the crucial requirement was mass personal communication to make sure the policy was clearly understood and thoroughly implemented. So it was on the road again, as Crawford recalled the story:

> General Barrow and I went out throughout the whole Corps, and he talked to officers while I talked to staff NCOs. And he and I both talked to the enlisted about helping us in the endeavor of cleaning up these drugs within our Corps. Once I was down at Albany, Georgia, with him, and naturally the Commandant got the theater with the officers. I had the church with the staff NCOs and also the enlisted.
>
> And as I was talking, I was looking around. I explained, "You know, I'm here to ask the staff NCOs' support in enforcing the Commandant's rules and regulations on illegal substances. I'm asking you to assist us in this. But, goddamn, as I look around here, you slobs are not even supporting him in grooming regulations!" So I stormed out of the church right in the middle of my appeal. I know they didn't like it, but the hell with them! I told the Old Man as soon as we got on the airplane, and he replied, "Good for you!''

Working their way systematically across the country, the two men addressed meeting after meeting. Crawford later estimated that he spoke to 60,000 Marines on the east coast alone. Unit commanders and NCOs alike made substance abuse (both drugs and alcohol) a priority. This kind of leadership, combined with drugsniffing dogs, urinalysis kits, regular testing of everyone, and rehabilitation counseling, paid off. In one month there was a reduction of seventy percent in marijuana use.

Back at Headquarters, an endless variety of problems arose day after day. The letters poured in and out of the sergeant major's office; the phone calls poured in and out. Always there were issues which seemed unimportant in the big picture, but were central to the lives of the individuals who contacted Crawford. Barrow gave some examples:

> I knew a young officer who had a rifle platoon; he had a young private first class who had been moved several times, and I think had taken out a couple of family allotments. In any case, the things he'd done had created

opportunities for his pay record to get screwed up, and it did. And he didn't get any pay. That young officer exhausted all possible channels and persons in the command—it was a rifle platoon so the major command was a division—and he got nowhere: pay masters, sergeants major, commanding officers, what have you. So the young officer, knowing that Crawford was someone who would get things done (it's funny how you acquire this reputation), called him on the telephone. Within, literally, hours, that young man had his pay.

Another typical case might be when he'd get a letter from some private first class someplace, who felt comfortable enough to write to the sergeant major, "Dear Sergeant Major, I would like to know why I am now into my second month of mess duty? I thought we were only supposed to do thirty days. I feel that someone is visiting a little punishment on me or something, because now I'm back in the mess hall for another thirty days."

Well, he wouldn't write back to the private first class. He'd call the sergeant major of that man's battalion. "Sergeant Major," I can hear him now and the sergeant major on the other end of the line is probably scared to death, and feels like he could almost hear him without the telephone, "What's Jones doing down there on mess duty over thirty days?" Gulp, "I don't know, Sergeant Major." "Well, goddamn it, find out and call me back! You know my number!" "Yes, sir!" Not only would he call back with an answer, but if the young man was still inappropriately on mess duty, he would say, "Sergeant Major, he's no longer on mess duty." So Crawford was on the phone all the time.

Now some of the absolute purists about command channels and chain of command and all that would say, "He shouldn't be doing that. If that young man had a problem, he should express it through the chain of command and let them try to resolve it." Some others would say, "If the sergeant major got a letter like that, he ought to put a 'Forwarded for Your Action' endorsement on it and send it back into the channels." Yes, maybe so.

But, damn it, the way things so often work, it would usually take one hell of a long time for it to get done, and there'd be a lot of discussion and paper shuffling— particularly if some fellow had stepped out of the chain of command. They might visit a little vindictiveness on him: "What the hell do you mean, writing to the Sergeant Major of the Marine Corps?" But I approve of that procedure, for these are not major things, these are not policy things, these are personnel action things. And Crawford was very good about that.

It wasn't just the problems of the junior enlisted; even more frequent were dealings with staff NCOs, and Crawford was just as hard-nosed here. When a really serious deficiency came to his attention, he would work in conjunction with the personnel sergeant major and the sergeants major monitor:

If it was staff NCOs, very seldom did I ever discuss that with the Commandant. I took care of that on my own level, and he knew I did. We either had that gentleman seek employment somewhere else, politely putting it, or we'd give him a set of goddamn orders to Adak, Alaska!

If I thought an officer out there was not supporting what the Commandant said, then I would run that through the Commandant. You had to use a little tact on it. And I'll add another thing: you had to have your ducks lined up all in a row, too. You didn't go in to see him half-cocked. But it was very seldom I ever had to do that.

Any Corps-wide policy is bound to have unfortunate side effects on certain individuals in certain circumstances. Crawford was deeply involved in one such situation, which evolved when the Marine Corps was forced to create "geographic bachelors." That upset Crawford, even though it was for the needs of the Corps. He gave, as an example, a master gunnery sergeant who had just returned from Okinawa in one of the Corps' critical Military Occupational Specialties (MOS). That man could be required, because of a shortage in his MOS, to report in to El Toro, California, while his family remained at Cherry Point, North Carolina, where he had a home. Since his MOS was needed at El Toro, he would receive a permanent change of station to there. He would not like it, but, as a Marine, he would go there, while his family remained in North Carolina.

Crawford went on to point out that turning the Marine into a "geographic bachelor" did several different things—all bad. He was separated from his family and thus didn't have regular family quarters. He only had sub-standard quarters, and meanwhile he was a master gunnery sergeant who "lived like a bum there at El Toro!" They also took his commuted rations allowance away from him. With things like that, one problem just compounded into another problem, and so there were a lot of bitter people in the Corps. Crawford worked hard, if he ran into an individual like that, to get him transferred close to his family. He was a man of direct action, "I think I got the word out throughout the Corps that, if that happened, for them to get hold of me, and let me try to handle that on my level at Headquarters. Several times, if I felt that maybe I couldn't work with the staff people making the assignments to get this individual the assignment that he really needed, then I would just go to the Commandant, and he would approve it—sometimes."

On one memorable occasion, Crawford had to try to help a senior NCO whom he knew very well, a master gunnery sergeant, Richard Allen, stationed at Norfolk, Virginia. That man had a handicapped child who had multiple sclerosis and required special medical care. Crawford knew that the monitor section had looked at that NCO and seen that he hadn't been to the Fleet Marine Force (FMF) for several years. Since he had two years left to do in the Marine Corps, they were going to transfer him out of Norfolk to an infantry regiment in Camp Lejeune. The family would be split because North Carolina would not give medical treatment until a year's residency had elapsed. Crawford described what happened next:

So the old master gunny came up to me, and he had a little tear in his eye. I said to him, "Goddamn it, Allen, that's not the real Marine Corps doing this."

So I went up to the assignments branch and talked to the staff NCO about it. He answered, "Sergeant Major, there isn't anything I can do on that. The major over there is the one who signed off on that." Then I went over to talk to the major, and he burst out, really loudly, "Sergeant Major, I run this damn shop!" or words to that effect. In other words, get out of here, I've made the final decision. Well, all the typewriters were stopped. I happened to be the Sergeant Major of the Marine Corps, and he shouldn't have talked to me like that. I didn't say anything to him; I just replied, "Thank you, Major," and left.

But I went down to General Barrow, and I showed him the whole package and explained it to him, and (I'm serious) a tear came to his eye. He asked, "What do you want me to do, Sergeant Major?" I said, "Just sign it right there. I'll take care of it." Then he went on, "Do you want me to handle this?" I answered, "No, sir, Let me do it. I've got my face to save, as the Japanese say. He embarrassed me up there a little while ago. You let me handle this." So he just wrote on there, "Do it! B."

I took that request for assistance back up on the fourth deck. I walked into that little cubicle where all the assignment staff was, and all the typewriters stopped again. I walked over to the major's desk and I told him in a very clear voice, "I just left the Commandant's office, and I explained it all to him and it says down there, 'Do it! B.' Now if you want to disagree with that, you go down and talk to him." He wasn't about to go down there....

On Crawford's repeated field trips, he encountered the inevitable interview by a local newspaper or TV reporter. One of his favorite memories of an interview was one which took place in Australia. He and the Commandant had gone to Perth to watch the joint exercise of a Marine squadron, which had just flown in from Japan, with a Marine amphibious unit which had just come in from the Indian Ocean. It was the first test of a brand new concept: the unloading of a Maritime Prepositioned Ship combined with a practice landing of the Marines. The officers later gathered on the top deck of one of the ships to hear the Commandant's comments, while Crawford went down to the lower deck to speak to several hundred of the young enlisted Marines. At this point a crew from Australian TV came on board to record the proceedings.

That evening, in his hotel, Barrow turned on the TV news. The commentator came on in dramatic tones, "And now the man in charge of all the Marines gathers his men about him to tell it like it is." Barrow awaited his picture, but there was Crawford, front and center in the camera's lens. Barrow afterward observed, "He did a great job. It was kind of a no-nonsense speech, 'Your country's proud of you being out here doing what you're doing; but by God when you go on liberty....' that sort of thing. It was a mixed speech of admonition and admiration. Anyway, I laughed and said to my wife, 'You know, that doesn't bother me one bit, because he looks like he could very well be in charge of all the Marines.'"

This, then, was Crawford's style. Even after a day's work normally would be over, he kept busy. Barrow was keenly aware of this:

At night he may have appeared to be pleasuring himself, but he was still (underneath that) all business. So he would go to the various clubs, drop in on the Enlisted Club or the Staff NCO club, and yes, he'd have a beer or something. The troops would gather around, and he sponged up all kinds of information. He was kind of always on duty. He didn't leave the day's work and go off with two or three cronies to a restaurant or someplace. He went where there were people to be met, people to listen to, and people to talk to in small groups.

So it went for four crowded years. As the Commandant's term was ending, Crawford prepared to clean out his own office. The walls were blanketed with plaques, awards, souvenirs, and pictures stretching back through years of memories: the 11th Marines, the drill field, the far-off places...It would seem strange to split up from the general with whom he'd shared so many experiences. It was curious: here were two strong-minded men who had, over all that time and amidst all those activities, never had a difference of opinion. Crawford was emphatic about it:

> I never did go in there and have him say, "Sergeant Major, that's it! Get out of here." Never! With other commanders, yes, but with General Barrow, never. I remember one day on one of his telephone conference calls he asked, "Isn't that right, Sergeant Major?" And I disagreed with him, "No sir." He said, "Well, if you want to find out the straight scoop, I guess you ask the sergeant major." I had such a warm relationship with him. What I liked about him: he let me operate on my own. And I think he gave me that special trust because he knew that I was going to do the right thing and not embarrass him. But then I never gave him any surprises either....
>
> I served almost thirty-two years in the Corps, and in all that time there were probably only two other men— officers or enlisted—that I respected as much as General Barrow. Words really cannot express my feeling toward him: a superb gentleman.
>
> What I particularly admired was his genuine interest in young Marines. That was a key reason that we got along so well together. I remember so vividly our trip to Beirut in May, 1983. This was shortly after our embassy there had suffered that huge explosion. When the general got with our young Marines there, he seemed to be no longer a sixty-one-year-old four-star general, but rather a thirty-year-old captain who fitted right in with those men.

The final day was June 27, 1983. At the retirement ceremony, Barrow had the pleasure of awarding Crawford the Navy Distinguished Service Medal, the first time this had ever been given to an enlisted Marine. Clearly, he was an "uncommon man." The citation from the Secretary of the Navy read in part:

> ...As the Commandant's principal advisor on matters pertaining to enlisted Marines, Sergeant Major Crawford's perceptive analytic ability enabled him to provide the Commandant with thoughtful and timely advice concerning Marines and Marine Corps policies. His concern for the morale and

welfare of the individual Marine was evident in his counsel with the Commandant, with other commanders, and with young Marines around the world.

An exemplary leader in his own right, Sergeant Major Crawford sought to improve the quality of leadership and professionalism of senior staff noncommissioned officers throughout the Marine Corps. In order to foster a free flow of professional knowledge among these key personnel, he instituted an annual symposium for sergeants major and master gunnery sergeants. He was also instrumental in the creation of an advanced course at the Staff Noncommissioned Officers Academy at Quantico....

Starting a strange new life after thirty-two years of active service, Crawford sold his car, piled everything in a pick-up truck and headed back to his roots. Saying he was "going to work in the corn field," he and his wife went to West Virginia. It was, however, only a brief visit with relatives, and then they drove on. There had been twenty-two "changes of station" for him over the years, and now they wanted to settle down permanently. The next stop was San Antonio, Texas. There he met with the president of the Non-Commissioned Officers Association (NCOA), and they made a deal for Crawford's employment. Towing the car leased to him by the NCOA, they finally reached their destination, the suburbs of San Diego.

His wife, Fayette, came from that area. They had first met when he was a drill instructor at the San Diego recruit depot in 1963. It happened that he was with a group of sergeants off duty, having a beer, of course. A crisis arose when the proprietor ran out of their favorite brand, but he made a quick phone call, and his supplier sent over a fresh batch. It was brought by a pretty girl; Crawford was much taken with her; there were initial refusals, then dates, and a spark was struck.

Life in the Marine Corps took him away, but they kept in touch. Then, when he returned in 1971 from Vietnam for duty at Camp Pendleton, things became really serious. Years had passed since his first marriage had ended, and now he felt that he had found the right person. They were married in May, 1972, and bought a California-style ranch house outside San Diego.

After his retirement they settled in it for good. It was "old home week" for both of them, with a string of parties renewing former local friendships. Then came a trip for the two of them to the NCOA convention in Las Vegas. There Crawford was host to his successor as Sergeant Major of the Marine Corps, Robert Cleary. Each year they kept traveling, cruising the highways for four-month trips all over the country in their mammoth RV motor home (which enabled him to broaden the scope of his public relations work for the NCOA). Visits with old friends and attendance at Marine Corps events kept familiar contacts alive: Crawford was the featured guest speaker at six different Marine Birthday Balls in 1987.

The mass of mementos now hung on the walls of their living room. One side was dominated by a huge gun cabinet which held, at one time, some of his seventy-one weapons of all types. Several of these received good usage, for hunting trips in the mountains were a regular diversion. One special prize was a Springfield Model 1903 rifle, used by Marines up to the early days of World War II; it was a present from Henry Black. The phone would ring with news of the children, Mark and Joyce (who, while her father was Sergeant Major of the Marine Corps, graduated from high school in the town were he had first enlisted, Charleston, West Virginia). Golf continued to be a strong interest, with memories crowding in of games he had played with the Commandant and old NCO friends.

Keeping in shape was also part of the retirement agenda. Maybe not the daily four-mile runs of yesteryear, but he continued to look good with regular long walks. The 240 pounds fitted well on the 6 feet, 4 inches, with size 13 shoes supporting it all. The blue eyes could still throw off electric sparks beneath the close-cropped brownish-grey hair, grown a little thinner. The adjectives from old interviews hadn't lost their accuracy: "facial features like a rock slide," "weathered look," "a gaze that could pierce steel." And the voice! It still boomed out with the impact and authority of an old sergeant major.

Chapter 11

THE WORLD TRAVELER

Sergeant Major Robert E. Cleary

It was a grim day in the history of the Marine Corps. It was October 23, 1983. A speeding nineteen-ton truck, driven by a suicidal terrorist and crammed with high explosives equal to six tons of TNT, smashed into a building at Beirut International Airport which was the temporary headquarters for a Marine Battalion Landing Team. There was a cataclysmic explosion. Death and desolation were everywhere; 241 Marines, soldiers, and sailors were killed.

Shortly after he heard the news, the Commandant, General Paul X. Kelley, received a phone call from the Commander-in-Chief, President Ronald Reagan, who was in Augusta, Georgia. He told Kelley that he was returning to Washington, and asked Kelley to meet him that morning in the White House. After two meetings of the National Security Council that day, President Reagan asked the Commandant to go to Beirut as his personal representative. Shortly thereafter, the phone rang on the desk of the Sergeant Major of the Marine Corps, Robert Cleary: "Pack your gear—we're leaving for Lebanon in the morning."

Air Force Two raced across the Atlantic to Frankfurt, Germany, and then the group hurried to the hospital in Wiesbaden, dreading the agony which they knew awaited them. As they entered, a doctor spoke quietly to Cleary, "Some of these Marines came into this hospital last night, and I didn't think they were going to make it. I don't know what you Marines are made of that makes you anything special." It was a time of high tension, and Cleary drew back angrily at the apparent sarcasm.

But the doctor quickly gave his own answer: "I'll tell you what makes Marines special—three ingredients. These Marines who came in here, who had been blown way up into the air, had three things going for them. First, they were young; that helps anybody. Then, they're physical studs, every one of them was a physical specimen from PT. But the third, and most important, fact is that they were Marines, and they refused to die." At this point there were tears in the eyes of all those who heard.

Rejoining the Commandant, Cleary picked up a number of Purple Heart medals to award the patients. Together they approached the bed of a desperately wounded lance corporal in the intensive care ward—his life hanging in the balance. Temporarily blinded by dust and powder from the explosion, with his lips fused together, he could not believe that this really was the Commandant when Kelley bent over him and introduced himself. Slowly, hesitantly, his hand reached up to feel the four stars on the collar of the general's camouflage uniform. Then he beckoned awkwardly for a pencil and paper and, with a great deal of effort, scrawled two almost indecipherable words. They were "Semper Fi," the Marines' contraction of their time-honored motto, "Semper Fidelis," "Always Faithful." No one moved...there was total silence in the room.... (The young man later recovered, and Kelley presented him with those same four stars, beautifully mounted in a shadow box.)

Three other hospitals were visited, and they found the same high morale. In Naples, for instance, Cleary had told the walking wounded men in advance, "Don't try to stand when the Commandant comes in to award your Purple Hearts." When Kelley walked into the ward, as a man, they all were on their feet, snapped to rigid attention. Then Cleary would ask a man how he was, and his reply would be to ask about somebody else, "Did my buddy make it?"

The trip to Beirut itself was one of the most painful legs of their journey; they were grim with anguish and concern for what lay ahead. General Kelley later described the scene:

> At the time we arrived they were still digging out bodies. There were people who were still buried alive within the building. There was a great deal of emotion that was running high, and Sergeant Major Cleary showed a very cool and deliberate form of leadership in talking with the senior noncommissioned officers who needed a bucking up.
>
> It's always fine to be a handsome-looking sergeant major who can walk around in a parade-ground atmosphere, but it's another thing to be a guy who has "smelled a dirty infantryman." Cleary had done that; he knew what they were; he knew what made them tick, and he was a tremendous

General Kelley (left) and Cleary (right) in Beirut In October, 1983. Note their full battle dress and the sandbags in the background.
Cleary photo

As personnel sergeant major at Headquarters in 1978.

LEATHERNECK photo

shot in the arm. We literally had senior NCOs with tears in their eyes over this great tragedy, but to see this fine figure of the Sergeant Major of the Marine Corps giving them his moral and physical support had a lot to do with building back their self-confidence and esteem.

Cleary's modest recollection of this extraordinary visit spoke of:

...being in Beirut under combat conditions, seeing our troops, and letting them know that somebody from the "head house" (as they call Headquarters) was there and was concerned about them—not just "somebody" but the Commandant and the senior enlisted man of the whole Marine Corps. I thought the world of those troops. They had been placed under the most trying of all conditions, being fired upon by a faceless enemy and not being able to return fire, because the "rules of engagement" didn't permit it. If you want to test discipline, here was the ultimate test! After seeing combat in Korea and then three tours of duty in Vietnam, I felt that they were the best disciplined troops I'd ever seen in my thirty-six years of experience.

From dramatic experiences such as these, it was a long way back to the prosaic beginnings of Cleary's career. Born in Tewksbury, Massachusetts, on June 2, 1931, he graduated from Holyoke Trade High School in May, 1949. Two years later, on October 24, 1951, he enlisted in the Marine Corps in Hartford, Connecticut. Admitting that he was "kind of a wild guy, feeling my oats in those days, a pretty tough guy," he later explained, "I wanted to be in the finest fighting outfit in the world, and several of my idols were Marines."

Graduating from the Parris Island recruit depot, he was assigned to a demolition specialist course at Camp Lejeune, and then to the 7th Engineer Battalion at Camp Pendleton, where he served until April, 1953.

With the Marines heavily engaged in combat in Korea, Cleary joined the flow of replacements going to the 1st Division there. Upon arrival, he quickly found out that war requires versatility: he was put on a caterpillar tractor and told, "Never mind demolitions; now you're a cat-skinner!" He could hear firing on the front lines, but there he was, grading roads. Racing through his mind was the recurring feeling, "I'm over here to be a Marine and get up there and see some action." The opportunity soon came. One night the Chinese overran some exposed positions and volunteers were called for. Cleary quickly stepped forward and was soon in a truck crossing the Imjin River bridge, headed for an outpost called The Hook. No sooner had they arrived nearby than one of the other men shouted, "Incoming!" As Cleary scrambled to get out of the truck, an artillery shell ripped the whole top off of it in a blinding flash. Scared but unhurt, he jumped into a ditch. There was a jumble of scrambling and yelling all around in the dark of the night. Soon a lieutenant materialized in the blackness and shouted, "Corporal, grab your rifle and I'll show you your sector." Taking Cleary to a ridge, he pointed out the Marine positions and had a nearby private show him where their sector of fire should be. Cleary was now on his own. The first thing he did was to check the positions of the men around him. As he later remembered it, "They never asked me who I was. They could see I was a corporal because I was in charge. I didn't know who they were. All I knew was that they were Marines. Before going to Korea as an engineer, I had bitched about infantry training; I thought I didn't need it. Well, now I thanked God that I'd had that training, because it had prepared me to be a small unit leader and take charge. We got along fine."

This wild night crystallized in Cleary's mind his determination to transfer from his designation as an "engineer" to that of "infantryman," and he did. In early April, 1954, he received a "meritorious promotion" to sergeant and later that month orders came through sending him back to the United States. After a tour in his home territory with the reserve training center in Springfield, Massachusetts, he returned to Camp Pendleton in the early part of 1958. There he was assigned duty as a military policeman and promoted to staff sergeant in May. That entailed a variety of responsibilities: foot and motor patrol, desk sergeant, and cross-country "chaser" escorting prisoners to different locations. It was a demanding job because "we had some pretty tough Marines" to handle. (Since the Corps reflects a broad cross-section of Americans, there are always, even in peacetime, a small percentage who are court-martialed.)

Another major shift occurred in April, 1961, with a move down the coast to San Diego. Here he took over as a drill instructor at the recruit depot: long, long hours turning civilians into fighting men, but "a bunch of very dedicated Marines," he felt.

It was in these early days of Cleary's career that some friends used to call him "Rocky," derived from his addiction to physical fitness. He led his recruits in getting well prepared for the physical readiness test: putting your pack on, crossing ravines, climbing ropes, and the like. Then, when they would later pass the physical fitness test, "You're ready to go over wherever we're going!" And Cleary was ready, for, after two years as a D.I., he finished up as an instructor in hand-to-hand combat.

Next, in April, 1963, Cleary moved back up the coast to Camp Pendleton, and joined the 5th Regiment, 1st Division, first as a section leader and then as a platoon sergeant in an 81mm mortar platoon.

In February, 1964, he was transferred again, this time to the 3d Division on Okinawa, where he served as platoon sergeant and platoon commander of an anti-assault platoon equipped with flame-throwers, 106mm recoilless rifles, 3.5" rocket launchers, and demolition high explosives. Moving next to the 1st Regiment of the 3d Division as a platoon sergeant and platoon commander, he was promoted to gunnery sergeant and went to Vietnam in 1965— the first of three such combat tours.

There his battalion was initially in a "float phase," moving up and down off the coast of Vietnam. Battalion operations involved making company landings and vertical helicopter envelopments (where the Marine "choppers" would carry troops to land behind the enemy forces). There soon came a move ashore to the Marine base at Phu Bai. Then, during Operation New York, he was wounded in combat by a fragmentation grenade and received his first Purple Heart medal.

Next came Operation Jay in June of 1966, a major sweep against the enemy in the countryside. Cleary recalled afterwards, "We received small arms fire from a village. Upon penetrating it, we set up our own base of fire. We found we were up against a 'hard core' battalion. 'Hard core' meant well-trained, well-disciplined North Vietnamese regulars who had been to boot camp, not just guys who fire at you and leave. They were there to stay! We lost nearly half of a platoon of our Marines out of one company, and we came under intense small arms and mortar fire. Calling in air strikes for support, we stayed there for a couple of days." With officers killed or wounded, Cleary stepped in as a platoon commander. He was not only wounded again (for his second Purple Heart), but his combat leadership was so outstanding that he was awarded the Silver Star medal.

His citation from the Commanding General, Fleet Marine Force, Pacific (FMFPac), read in part:

> ...On 25 June, 1966, during Operation Jay, Gunnery Sergeant Cleary and his platoon came into heavy contact with a well-entrenched Viet Cong battalion located in a tree line near the village of Ap My Phu. Upon making contact with the enemy, he launched his platoon into the assault and, with complete disregard for his own safety, moved among his men shouting instructions and words of encouragement.
>
> At one point in the assault he spotted four automatic weapons and one sixty millimeter mortar that were delivering a deadly hail of fire into his advancing platoon. Immediately, he moved along the tree line and through the vicious hostile fire to direct one of his squads in destroying the Viet Cong emplacements. Although wounded, he refused to be evacuated in order to maintain the impetus of his platoon's assault....

There was still more combat for Cleary after that remarkable feat. In all, he participated in fourteen major operations as a "grunt" (the name given to infantry foot-sloggers). After many months, life took on an almost surrealistic tinge—particularly when Cleary's company fought in areas which had been blasted by air raids. A war correspondent there wrote of the men who "marched past craters left by our B-52 bombers that made the countryside look like the Valley of the Moon. For hundreds of feet around each crater the trees were flattened and bits of jungle animals and Viet Cong bodies were strewn around like so many abandoned Christmas toys."

Finally, after Operation Hastings at "The Rockpile," Cleary was flown out to be debriefed by his battalion intelligence officer. His new orders were to return to Camp Pendleton. There, in August, 1966, he was assigned as a company gunnery sergeant in the newly formed 27th Marines. It was almost fifteen years since he had enlisted as a private.

A year later he returned to San Diego once more for a short tour as a drill instructor and, while there, was selected for promotion to first sergeant. This brought a transfer back to Camp Pendleton and the 27th Regiment again.

Stateside duty was not to last, however, for combat-wise staff NCOs were badly needed in Vietnam, so in March, 1968, he returned there. His second tour was with a battery of the 1st Light Anti-Aircraft Missile Battalion. Recalling those days, Cleary commented:

> I had never known what a missile battalion was, and never had any interest in being the senior enlisted man in one. But I found that this was a unique situation and I really enjoyed it.
>
> We were positioned on Hill 225 near Da Nang. A demanding test of the basic training of my Marines took place one night when enemy action in our area was extremely high. Our intelligence sources had placed Hill 225 at the top of the target list. Sure enough, Viet Cong sappers hit several outfits located at the bottom of our hill. They got under the barbed wire and blew up the munitions dump there.
>
> This was the main dump for the whole Da Nang area, and all hell broke loose: aircraft ordnance, artillery shells, and every type of high explosive filled the air with a shattering roar. Our hill received tremendous shock waves that caused massive clouds of heat, combined with flying dirt and shrapnel. Destroyed or damaged were some of our missile sites, our radar and other high tech equipment, as well as our living area.

Cleary and his officers mustered their men immediately, moved to the back slope of the hill, set up a perimeter defense, and prepared for any eventuality. No one knew what might happen next, for there was incoming small arms fire. The night passed safely, though, and at daybreak the men of the battery moved back to their original site. The overall damage proved not to be as bad as had been expected. Thanks to a lot of fast-thinking Marines, lives had been saved and most of the equipment was only damaged rather than completely destroyed. Cleary continued:

> A few nights later, the Viet Cong breached the wire on our inner perimeter. They got into our compound, destroyed and damaged some missile equipment, and wounded some of my Marines before we drove them out.
>
> So the tour that I served with this battery was a real experience to say the least! I was proud of these men; they were there as missile technicians, but, when the chips were down, they had handled themselves just as well as any full-time infantry ground unit. This was true in spite of the fact that we experienced our share of racial tensions and some drug usage, plus a few Marines (including some senior ones) who were marginal at best.

For his superior performance of duty, Cleary was awarded the Navy Commendation Medal with Combat "V" by the Commanding General, FMFPac, with this citation, which said in part:

> ...Throughout this period, First Sergeant Cleary performed his duties in an exemplary and highly professional manner. Skillfully coordinating and supervising the activities of his noncommissioned officers, he provided consistently outstanding support to his unit. Working tirelessly and with meticulous attention to detail, he implemented sound management procedures, monitored all reports and logistic matters, and provided guidance and assistance to all who sought his aid.

In addition, First Sergeant Cleary initiated numerous improvements in living and recreational facilities, and rendered valuable assistance in organizing the perimeter defensive fires. On one occasion, he organized and led several reconnaissance patrols to observe hostile activity in the vicinity of the base camp, and gathered intelligence data which subsequently resulted in the seizure of 191 Viet Cong suspects. As a result of his diligent and resourceful efforts, the operational effectiveness of his unit was greatly enhanced....

Once more he returned to Camp Pendleton for service—this time with the 28th Marines, soon redesignated the 7th Marines. Now the focus was on long conditioning hikes with packs heavy with full combat gear: "Our battalion was one of the very first to complete a fifty-mile march. It was the best thing in the world for us. Later on, when I was Sergeant Major of the Marine Corps, I pushed for that type of training, because I remembered how much it helped me when I got into combat. The more you sweat in training, the less you bleed in combat!"

After this grind, Cleary returned for his third tour in Vietnam. This was, again, a wholly new type of duty. Now promoted to sergeant major, he was assigned to Marine Medium Helicopter Squadron 165. As an infantryman at heart, Cleary initially resented this, but he later observed:

The challenge was there and I carried out my orders. Once on duty with the squadron, I came to feel that this was one of the best assignments that I ever had—being able to qualify as a .50 caliber machine gunner, and fly combat missions with some of the world's best pilots, and serve along with the crew chiefs who were totally dedicated Marines proved to me how important the team effort is in our Corps. I came away with a new appreciation of the tremendous talent we had in Marine aviation.

We hit some hot zones with heavy flak and some areas in landings supporting the Vietnamese Marines. I got 180 missions as an aerial gunner, and I did everything, as sergeant major, that the troops did. We were among the last combat Marines out of Vietnam, when we finished our missions in December, 1972.

As a qualified aircrewman and gunner, Cleary now added three Air Medals to his awards and was able to wear Combat Wings with three stars, which meant that he had received three strike/flight awards.

While Cleary was serving as squadron sergeant major, John Massaro was his group sergeant major. Cleary's fitness reports passed by Massaro's eagle eye, and he later remembered, "Cleary's fitness reports were just super, and his squadron commander was extremely well pleased with the job he was doing." When it came time for him to rotate back to the United States, Cleary had a week's layover at Futema on Okinawa where he again saw Massaro, and that additional contact consolidated Massaro's opinion of Cleary, "He really made a tremendous impression on me as far as being the type of Marine who could get the job done."

The comparatively small size of the Marine Corps has meant through the years that the most senior NCOs have usually served together and know each other well—including strengths and weaknesses. Thus Massaro's high opinion of Cleary's abilities would soon influence his career.

But first Cleary headed back to the States, and in May, 1973, he took over as sergeant major of Marine Fighter Squadron 223 in Yuma, Arizona. A few months later, however, he was transferred to the 2d Light Anti-Aircraft Missile Battalion there. One day the Commandant and his sergeant major (Clint Puckett) flew in for an inspection. Puckett's experienced eye quickly registered his impressions, "While I was not super impressed at this time (as I was later), I definitely remember a sharp, good-looking Marine, the battalion sergeant major, who pushed the first sergeants there to answer our questions."

After a little over a year of Yuma duty came still another move to still another widely different assignment. This came about in the following typical Marine Corps way. Massaro had now come back to the inspection division at Headquarters. Colonel Frank Koethe, commanding the Marine Security Guard Battalion (the embassy Marines) had, when he was a lieutenant in charge of the drill instructors school in San Diego, known Massaro and respected his judgement. One day, when he saw Massaro, he said, "Sergeant Major, have you got a little time?" "Yes, sir, Colonel." "Then come on over to my office. I need to talk to you." When they got in his office he told Massaro, "I need another sergeant major. This guy here now is just not hacking it. I've got to get somebody who can get out and get with these young Marines, and present an outstanding appearance and everything. Give me three names in preference if you were to select them yourself."

Massaro put Cleary as number one on his list, taking into account his past impressions and the fact that at this time Cleary was unmarried—an important asset for a job that required extensive travel all over the world. The upshot was that in September, 1974, Puckett called Cleary to tell him that he was going to fill the now vacant billet as the Marine Security Guard Battalion Sergeant Major in Washington. Cleary pleaded for time to make family arrangements, because his mother was living with him and would have to return to his brother's house in Massachusetts. Furthermore, he had just bought his home in Yuma, and would now need to make arrangements to sell it. Puckett's reply was crisp, "You've got two weeks—no more."

Naturally, in two weeks Cleary was on deck in Washington to start work with the Marine Security Guard. This consisted of companies located at 118 United States diplomatic posts throughout the world, with regional Marine headquarters in places such as Panama, Nairobi, Morocco, and Frankfurt. As the senior enlisted advisor, Cleary made the rounds with the battalion's commanding officer.

They travelled to all of the security companies individually, or else visited their regional headquarters, in a little over a year of global inspections. Exotic place names like Yaounde, Tegucigalpa, and Mogadishu became commonplace for them. Cleary remembered:

"We did fifteen to twenty, sometimes twenty-five, within a period of thirty or forty days—two-day visits, in and out. The motto of our security battalion was "In every clime and place," and they could support that motto! At each embassy or legation, we visited the Marine Security Guard. While the colonel talked to the diplomatic staff there, such as the regional security officer, I would check up on the Marines—how were their living quarters, how were they treated, how was their morale and discipline, were they being treated as well as their State Department counterparts, etc.

The visit would last a day and a half, sometimes two days, and then we were on the road again. For instance, when we went out to Africa from Frankfurt, we would travel on a weekend so that we could be there Monday morning, ready to start a new cycle. The Marines really appreciated our visits. In some places they were treated as second-class citizens, but our men knew that our last stop, without fail, was the ambassador. We would go in there and sit down, and it was really a great feeling because he'd never ignore our colonel. Then he'd ask me, "Sergeant Major, how do my Marines look? Are they being treated well?" And I would tell him, believe me I would!

After more than a year of this frenetic pace as a world traveler, there was well-earned recognition for Cleary in the form of an official Certificate of Commendation from the chief of staff at Headquarters.

Then the tempo changed again for Cleary, shifting him late in 1975 to a desk job in Washington. He was selected to be the personnel sergeant major at Headquarters Marine Corps. There he worked with several generals, dealing with the welfare of the enlisted men, manpower management, transfers, and promotions. His assignment was one of great power, for it controlled the most sensitive issues in the lives of all enlisted personnel worldwide. There were delicate shadings, nonetheless, in his relationship with the Sergeant Major of the Marine Corps. When Henry Black was in that billet, he commented later, "I never sent my work load over to him. When they addressed a letter to the Sergeant Major of the Marine Corps, I told him that it was mine, and I didn't care what it was about: it was my responsibility." Nevertheless, Cleary was able to help frequently by rounding up information which Black needed for his correspondence.

Working in conjunction with the Sergeant Major of the Marine Corps, Cleary sat on the Commandant's Enlisted Performance Board, the Augmentation Board, and the Education Board.

The performance board met every two weeks (sixteen officers and the two senior noncommissioned officers) to evaluate individuals all the way up to sergeants major and master gunnery sergeants. They would consider anyone who wanted to stay in the Corps who had problems—deficiencies in performance or personal problems such as weight or appearance. All eighteen would then vote on a recommendation, which bore a great deal of weight when it went to the Commandant for a final decision: retain or out.

For Reserve Marines who wanted to augment (continue) their career in the

Corps, the Augmentation Board considered each case individually. This board consisted of three senior sergeants major at Headquarters (the inspector general's sergeant major, the personnel sergeant major, and the Sergeant Major of the Marine Corps) and four or five officers, including Reserve officers. Meeting irregularly, at most twice a year, the board members had searching personal questions about quality, motivation, education, appearance, and family status. That evaluation also went to the Commandant, who could make one of several decisions: discharge, retain for a six-month or a two-year extension, or refer to a field command for more information on the individual.

During that period, the close linkage between Massaro and Cleary continued. Massaro had now become the Sergeant Major of the Marine Corps, and he later recalled, "Cleary was of invaluable assistance to me. It's always good to know the personnel sergeant major well, because then you can short-circuit a lot of problems. Normally it might take a lot of paperwork to resolve something, but often all I had to do was pick up the phone and call Cleary. I'd say, 'What about this or that?' Within a day he always had an answer for me." This high level of efficient cooperation extended downward and outward. If there was a question about a sergeant major in one of the field units or the various bases of the Marine Corps, "I'd get an answer just like that."

In addition, Cleary was able to help Massaro in a different way. There are many demands, obviously, on the Sergeant Major of the Marine Corps to attend meetings, preside at ceremonial occasions, make speeches, and perform a wide variety of public functions. When Massaro could not fulfill one of those obligations—because he was away on one of his frequent trips, for instance—he would ask Cleary to stand in for him, "All I had to do was call Cleary; he would go and he was just super."

Sergeants major in the field commands received the same cooperation. One of them summarized the way he avoided the bureaucratic quagmires of Headquarters:

> When he was the personnel sergeant major, I dealt with him a lot. He was a very helpful individual in dealing with personnel problems. If I needed background information on somebody, or some help at Headquarters, he was normally the guy I would talk to, rather than the Sergeant Major of the Marine Corps, because he was usually there, and the Sergeant Major of the Corps was, more often than not, on the road somewhere.
>
> If you needed some immediate boost at Headquarters, a little bit of a nudge to some department or some section, Bob Cleary was the guy to talk to, because he knew his way around. He could tell you just about anything about how things worked at that level. Unfortunately, sometimes he talked so much about it that, by the time he got done, you weren't sure what he'd said. But, there was no doubt about it: he was a very knowledgeable individual, as far as working with the staff officers and that sort of thing at Headquarters.

In July, 1979, Cleary received orders to take over as sergeant major of the 3d Division in Okinawa. It was while he was there that a curious administrative error occurred in Washington. In October, 1979, Cleary's term of enlistment expired, and normally there would have been an extension of only two years, bringing him to the decisive thirty-year retirement mark in October, 1981. Someone in the Personnel Division of Headquarters overlooked that traditional deadline and wrote up the papers for a routine four-year re-enlistment.

In any event, crisis events halfway around the world cut short his Okinawa tour of duty. After only a year there, he was brought back once more to the Marine Security Guard, now in Quantico, Virginia. It was unusual to re-assign a sergeant major to this job, but, with the incendiary hostage situation in Iran (where Moslem fanatics had stormed the U.S. Embassy in Teheran and were holding fifty-two Americans, including nine Marines), the Corps wanted an "old hand" with a world traveler's experience in the security guard post. His knowledge and skill brought Cleary his second Navy Commendation Medal. The Secretary of the Navy's citation read in part:

> ...Displaying inspirational leadership, desire to excel, and devotion to duty, Sergeant Major Cleary accompanied the commander to every detachment worldwide, and ascertained problems that could adversely affect the unit and program. He monitored instruction provided at the Marine Security Guard School, and compared the theoretical instruction with the actual conditions he observed in the field.
>
> Deeply committed to the support of the Marines, he assisted in the content and quality of instruction provided to new noncommissioned officers in charge, counselled those afield, and advised the battalion commander on the specific response required to generate optimal performance from the disparate personalities at detachments worldwide. His keen advice on every facet of the command and his counselling proved to be invaluable.
>
> In addition, he occupied a crucial niche in the Marine Security Guard organizational framework, providing the advice and impetus required to keep the organized unit operating as a dynamic, responsive, and viable organization. As a result of his diligence and seemingly unlimited resourcefulness, he gained the respect and admiration of all who observed him, and contributed significantly to the accomplishment of his unit's mission....

After a year and a half of embassies, plane trips, and inspections, Cleary was selected for a new billet in January, 1982: sergeant major of the Marine Corps Development and Education Command in Quantico. Working with the generals there, he dealt intensively with the enlisted men in the various commands, such as the Education Center, the Basic School, and the Officers Candidate School. Based on a regular pattern of briefing the commanding general, Cleary was able to play an active role in starting a program to designate a "Noncommissioned Officer of the Month": "We had some real quality-type young NCOs whom I didn't think were being properly recognized, so we also convened promotion boards." He also took a strong hand in starting up a senior staff NCO course and upgrading the Staff NCO Academy there in Quantico. In addition, he helped to develop well-organized programs for athletics and anti-drug education.

Cleary spent most of his time "on the street, out in the various commands every day: talking, watching, being there with the troops, finding out, being a sounding board." Usually in the evening the commanding general would ask about this, and he would typically reply, "They're doing well in that command, but they need some more sergeants," or "The sergeants there aren't being used the way they should be."

That latter problem was a continuing concern of Cleary's. He saw young corporals promoted to sergeant and then guaranteed a particular duty location, just because they were re-enlisting and staying in the Corps. He later recalled:

> This upset me and a lot of the other senior NCOs. These men didn't have the hands-on experience, but that was happening primarily because the Corps was hurting for NCOs, and it was trying to keep those people. Then they would send them to us at Quantico to teach young men at the Officers Candidate School. They were also running courses there with such things as five sergeants in a demonstration squad at the Basic School. They weren't doing what a sergeant gets paid for. We corrected that and other examples of misuse of NCOs....

While not as glamorous as combat, his assignment to the Development and Education Command nevertheless played a crucial part in the training of future Marine leaders, both enlisted and commissioned. Cleary's "superb performance, sound judgement, and total devotion to duty" were recognized by the award of a Navy Achievement Medal.

After seventeen months in Quantico, a bolt of lightning struck Cleary's career; the word came through in May, 1983, from Headquarters in Washington: he was selected as the Sergeant Major of the Marine Corps. As Cleary later described the moment:

> I received a phone call while I was out of the office. In fact, I was attending our morning Colors Formation. When I got back, I was told that our next Commandant, General Paul X. Kelley, had called and asked that I return his call. My first reaction was, "What the hell did I do wrong?" A personal call from a new Commandant is not part of your daily routine! Nevertheless, I had an idea what he wanted to talk about, but it still came as a bit of a shock. I never did get to sleep that night.
>
> Later I got a call from Crow Crawford, who was then serving as the Sergeant Major of the Marine Corps. He told me that he was flying to Beirut at 18,000 feet in the Commandant's aircraft, and didn't want to wait to land before congratulating me. I told him I was flying at 19,000 feet and my feet hadn't left the ground.

But he was, of course, really well prepared: as a sergeant major, he had served in a total of nine different commands under eight generals.

General Kelley later gave the background on how Cleary was picked:

> I had been on the selection board for this billet in 1977. At that time Sergeant Major Cleary was one of the leading contenders, but, because

of his younger age and the fact that he had so many years left in service, we picked another man [Massaro]. Thus he had come to the fore even during that earlier period of time.

Now we went through the normal screening process whereby a board of colonels pruned the sergeants major down to about twenty-five. Then a board of three general officers, headed by a lieutenant general, looked at their records and narrowed the list to three men. Amongst those three, I had known Cleary by reputation, including the fine job he had done in combat. Also, I knew him previously when he was the personnel sergeant major at Headquarters, which is not an enviable job—trying to keep everybody happy. He did it very, very well. Furthermore, I liked his leadership style; he was down there with the troops, and I was well aware of his performance of duty in Quantico.

I think that, if you look at the full spectrum of characteristics and you go write down what would you want in the Sergeant Major of the Marine Corps, first of all, you'd want one who was most representative; then one who was athletic, who was trim, who was forceful; and I think Cleary certainly filled those requirements to a pre-eminent degree. He was very, very articulate and very forceful, as I found later, in expressing his views. He had a very good background as an infantryman; had a Silver Star, and was well decorated in combat as an enlisted man. Thus he had all of those qualities one would have to have to give him credibility with the young enlisted troops of the Marine Corps.

From the three recommended men Kelley had to pick one. He consulted with the assistant commandant to make sure that he had no objections whatsoever, and they both agreed that Cleary was an "uncommon man," the best qualified for the job. The generals were not alone in this assessment. As a former Sergeant Major of the Marine Corps, Clint Puckett, looking at the diversity of Cleary's career since he had first met him, felt that he was "better grounded than any of us" to assume these new responsibilities.

Thus the tenth Sergeant Major of the Marine Corps took office on June 28, 1983, to serve with the new Commandant, General Kelley. With his earlier four-year re-enlistment, it was just short of thirty-two years since he had joined up as a private. He had travelled the world over and, even for a senior Marine NCO, had had an extraordinary range of duties and experiences.

Indoctrination into his new job began for Cleary as soon as he checked into Headquarters. The memory was still vivid to him afterwards:

The first few days were like a revolving door—out of one office and into another. The briefings dealt with promotions, assignments, career planning, fitness reports and many other areas of interest. One nice thing about the briefings was that I had the chance to meet the Marines who were doing those jobs. If I had a question, say on promotions, I knew whom to talk to.

My briefing period was designed to take advantage of a "contact relief" with retiring Sergeant Major Crow Crawford. He was a big help in bringing me up to speed on what was currently happening, and what changes were in the mill. I had a chance to learn from him, and I picked up some of the valuable knowledge he had gained over the past four years.

The official portrait of Cleary as Sergeant Major of the Marine Corps, 1983, complete with 21 service ribbons (to which the Distinguished Service Medal was later added), the Combat Air wings with three stars, and the inevitable Rifle and Pistol Expert Markmanship Badges.

During his initial briefing with Kelly, he received his marching orders. The Commandant wanted him to be a "major player," and they set up a pattern to meet at least once a day—and often twice—so each would know what the other was doing. There was not, however, any special set of instructions or definition of precise duties. The official Marine Corps Order simply stated that the sergeant major was "to advise the Commandant on all matters pertaining to the welfare, morale, and performance of enlisted Marines." Then it concluded with that typical military catch-all, "and performs whatever other duties the Commandant may direct." Kelley put it this way, "I want you to be my eyes and ears for the welfare and morale of the troops."

Obviously this was a broad and generalized job description, and it was up to Cleary to put it into practical application. This is where the many years of experience told. He became the Commandant's chief advisor in establishing new policies that affected enlisted personnel, in reviewing enlisted policies that were already in effect, and in evaluating how they were impacting upon the morale of the troops. As an example, Kelley recalled:

> The sergeant major came to me and told me there had been a pattern of foot-dragging on the prospects of turning over the Staff Noncommissioned Officer Academies [one in Quantico for the east and one at the El Toro air base in California for the west] to the senior leadership in the enlisted ranks for them to run, as opposed to having officers run them. There was a reluctance on the part of officers to give up something which they had had for so many years. Finally, Cleary convinced me that it was the right thing to do. I merely directed that it happen and gave a terminal date for it to happen.
>
> I don't think that I've ever known a sergeant major who was more attuned to the requirements for training and education. It was during my tenure as Commandant that we started the Platoon Sergeants School at the Camp Pendleton School of Infantry for staff NCOs. That was really a result of a lot of pressure levied on me by Cleary. He had a keen sense of what it took to be an effective NCO or staff NCO, and he was very forceful in expressing his opinions; he would never be classified as a shrinking violet!
>
> He also encouraged me to address every graduating class of the Quantico Staff NCO Academy, as another example. They would come to Washington for a tour of Headquarters Marine Corps, and then I would sit down for about a one-to two-hour bull session with the staff NCO classes. This was kind of informal; I'd sit up front on a chair, and we'd just talk about the Corps.

Cleary also played a significant role in communications with Marines in the field. He urged the Commandant to set up a pattern of small, give-and-take meetings when they made their frequent trips together to bases all over the world. These were half-hour sessions they would have with groups of twenty: one with privates, privates first class, and lance corporals; another with corporals and sergeants, and still another with senior noncommissioned officers. As Kelley described it:

We would sit down with these groups (much to the chagrin of some commanders on the scene). They were young Marines out there of all ranks, and we were trying to get the pulse of the Corps. It was a free-for-all. We'd make a few opening remarks—Cleary and I—and then ask, "What's on your mind? What are we doing right? What are we doing wrong?" The sergeant major was the one who really encouraged me to do that, to get the feedback from the troops. You *never* get that when you have everybody commingled in all ranks.

One of the pressing issues that always came up on those field trips was the personal life of the individual Marine. It was at that juncture in the long history of the Corps that statistics showed more Marines were married than were single. This meant a radical change from the "old days," for it raised to a priority level family concerns about transfers, finances, and health care. As Kelley summarized it, "If there's any one thing that will destroy the morale or drive a Marine out faster, I don't know what it is other than the fact that you are not taking care of his family."

Cleary was the right man to deal with this need. Now a devoted family man with a lovely wife and fine children, his standards of conduct were impeccable. Thus, at every base, he would be involved in Marines' problems about family housing, dependent schooling, and financial arrangements.

His wife, June, always accompanied him. It was the Commandant's wish: "When I got off the airplane with my wife, I wanted the Sergeant Major of the Marine Corps to get off the plane with his wife. In that context, he was an equal—the titular head of the enlisted." So June Cleary played her part too. She met with the enlisted wives, checked on child care centers, and counselled with pregnant, single women Marines. Her warm, articulate personality, Kelley felt, "encouraged an openness that probably no other person could have gotten except the sergeant major's wife."

These concerns about quality of life led Cleary to a broader stage. Three times he testified before Congressional committees, and twice he met with the Secretary of Defense about such issues, as well as the retirement system. During one of the Congressional hearings he was asked if he thought that proficiency pay would be useful in the Marine Corps. Without batting an eyelash, he replied that, if the legislators were going to give proficiency pay to the Marines, they'd have to give it to all 198,000 of them! At social functions he would be asked by Congressmen how proposed bills would affect enlisted personnel, their recruitment, or their retention in the Corps. Clarity, knowledge, tact, and conviction were essential requirements for the Sergeant Major of the Marine Corps.

Another crucial factor in the life of every Marine was—and is—promotion to a higher rank. Every day letters or phone calls would come to Cleary when he was at Headquarters, citing some omission or injustice, real or imagined. At every base he would visit, similar questions would always arise. When you get your chance to button-hole the man with the ear of both the Commandant and the personnel sergeant major, you seize the opportunity!

A typical occurrence—Cleary, as Sergeant Major of the Marine Corps, on a trip to the Marine Barracks, Pearl Harbor, with the Commandant in October, 1985. He is at the head table, "giving the word" over a microphone to a large gathering of senior NCOs.

On a visit to Camp Pendleton in February, 1985, Cleary (right) makes a point.
Cleary photo

Beyond individual cases, however, lay the deeper, complex problem of the Corps' overall promotion policies. Again, Kelley gave an insight into Cleary's active nature:

> In the Marine Corps, if you are a buck sergeant and you have not made staff sergeant by the time you have twelve years of service, chances are you won't stay in. In many cases, it was not your fault because the "military occupational specialty" [MOS] you had was frozen, and it had been the policy that we couldn't give promotions there. So we had some absolutely superb young Marines who were being asked to leave the Corps after twelve years, through no fault of their own. Had they had a different MOS (with vacancies) they would have been promoted. Cleary was absolutely relentless in trying to get me to change that policy because of the impact on morale.

Some modification was finally obtained for those sergeants stuck in over-populated MOS categories. On an individual basis they were permitted to serve past the twelve year mark, so they could compete for selection to staff sergeant. (There was also consideration of moving these sergeants to a different MOS category, but it became clear that this would have caused too many problems: over-populating the new MOS and shifting senior people who would not know their new field as well as the personnel whom they would then be directing.)

Another field in which Cleary took the lead was the bi-annual Sergeant Major's Symposium. Many senior officers felt that the suggestions from it in the past had been trivial, or could not be implemented, or were even silly. Cleary turned this around to bring forth some really substantive recommendations from the symposium. These ranged the whole gamut from uniforms to tactics, from professional schools to dependents, and—always—promotion opportunities.

As a case in point, the 1984 symposium was attended by forty-eight of the Corps' most senior NCOs—mostly sergeants major, but with a few master gunnery sergeants representing technical fields. They brought to the meeting more than 180 recommendations. These were the result of mini-symposiums which had been held at the local level.

Some forty recommendations ended up being forwarded to the Commandant. One of these, for example, urged that Marines assigned to non-Fleet Marine Force units overseas should receive appropriate recognition for the hardships they endured and the duties they performed. It called for the authorization of a new Marine Corps Overseas Service Ribbon. (The decoration would be the counterpart of the Sea Service Deployment Ribbon awarded to Marines who served ninety consecutive days at sea.) The Commandant approved and petitioned the Secretary of the Navy, James Webb (a former Marine officer, highly decorated for combat in Vietnam), to establish such a ribbon. With his agreement, it was authorized for non-FMF Marines serving twelve months on foreign shores.

When asked to summarize his work at Headquarters as Sergeant Major of the Marine Corps, Cleary gave a comprehensive overview:

> I sat in on the Commandant's briefing held every morning in his office and, at this time, I had the opportunity to bring up issues pertaining to the enlisted side of the house. The military secretary also gave me a high priority on the Commandant's schedule along with the general's aides. My working relationship with General Kelley was similar to the working relationship between a platoon commander and his platoon sergeant, or a commanding officer and his sergeant major, only at a much higher level.
>
> I got outstanding support from the chief of staff's office and other branches of Headquarters, and needless to say this was very important.
>
> While I certainly didn't make policy, nor did I interpose myself in the chain of command, I also had the opportunity informally to impart to our Marines some of the time-tested standards and attitudes that have made us unique. In many, many ways, the Sergeant Major of the Marine Corps can make substantial contributions to the welfare, morale, and discipline of the Marine Corps without ever moving a piece of paper or signing his name.
>
> We had symposiums, formal conferences, and meetings of senior enlisted regularly, and they were very important. I think that the most important thing the sergeant major can do, however, is to provide this informal channel of communication from and into the Office of the Commandant.

Cleary accompanies the Commandant to the traditional Marine Corps birthday party cake cutting on November 10. This particular 1986 party was held in the Rose Garden of the White House with President Reagan and several of his senior Cabinet Officers as participants.

Here (below) Cleary smiles broadly as a proud father with his son, Michael, and daughter, Maribeth, and the then-Vice President and Mrs. Bush at a formal reception in the garden of the Commandant's House in June, 1987.

White House photos

Cleary was a member of several boards, such as the Permanent Marine Corps Uniform Board. Summarizing, he stated, "I was the enlisted conscience among the officers and duty-bound to speak out on behalf of all enlisted Marines on matters pertaining to their interests. The bottom line was that I tried to act independently as the principal enlisted assistant on all administration, technical, and tactical requirements of the Corps. I was restricted in the performance of my duties by two people: the Commandant and myself."

Besides those day-to-day dealings with the lives of active duty Marines, Cleary was very sensitive to the importance of retired personnel. A priority there, of course, would be thoughtfulness for any man who had preceded him as the Sergeant Major of the Marine Corps. Thus, when Frank Rauber (long ago retired) and his wife Kay would come to Washington, Cleary would see to it that they were well taken care of. The men would have a talk in the office at Headquarters, while a woman Marine would keep Kay company. There would be a car and driver to escort them, and VIP seats at the traditional Friday evening parade at the Marine Barracks. It was part of a long-cherished tradition of the Marine Corps to take care of its own.

Then there was also the responsibility of representing the Corps in a wide variety of outside situations. This led Cleary to such diverse occasions as speaker at the National Defense University and the Army's Sergeants Major Academy; reading the Epistle at the emotional memorial service which the Corps holds annually on its November birthday at the Washington National Cathedral; participation in the Armed Forces Week observances in San Antonio, Texas; and, surely the most pleasant of all, a return to his birthplace, Tewksbury, Massachusetts, as the Grand Marshall of a celebration of the town's 250th birthday: "Home town boy makes good in a big way!"

Since the U.S. Marine Corps has always operated on a global basis, the sergeant major and the Commandant continued the custom of keeping in touch with Marines in foreign military services. There was, for instance, a trip to England, a homecoming with a big welcome for Kelley, who had served on an exchange tour with the Royal Marines twenty years earlier. Cleary and the Commandant spent five days with them, moving about to their different stations and observing their training.

The most colorful insight into Cleary occurred during the "mess nights" when the Royal Marines, in a friendly way, would try to pour as much liquor as possible into an American Marine (just as they had twenty-five years earlier with Frank Rauber!), possibly hoping for a public downfall. Kelley reported, "Cleary upheld the highest traditions of the Corps in never allowing that to happen."

Perennial tension in the Middle East resulted in another five-day trip—this time to Israel to observe their training methods.

The most unique visit, however, was to mainland China. As a member of the Joint Chiefs of Staff, Kelley was the first Marine Commandant to make an official visit as a guest of the government. It was for four days, and the size of the delegation was severely limited, but Kelley insisted, "My senior enlisted man will be there."

Once there, they visited places no other American had seen in forty years. There was a demonstration by members of their fledgling Marine Corps (an "organization" which Cleary believed they had pulled together on the spur of the moment as an appropriate gesture to American Marine visitors). That exhibition consisted of men marching into a room in perfect cadence, seizing blocks of some material, and smashing them to pieces on their foreheads! Cleary was not impressed with this as a proof of military competence.

The presence of a sergeant major, with all those stripes on his uniform sleeve, but no insignia of rank on his shoulders as the officers had, was a source of vast puzzlement to the Chinese. They could not figure out who that man was to whom the senior general would frequently turn and ask, "What do you think of that, Sergeant Major?" Finally, they pressed the Commandant for an explanation. He gave it and concluded with the recommendation that they should institute a similar position. And so there is today a Sergeant Major of the Chinese Marine Corps because of that historic visit.

Kelley summarized Cleary's participation in the trip by saying, "He was viewed with the utmost awe and respect throughout our whole stay. I think that gives you the true measure of the man. He always conducted himself above reproach, impeccable in every way."

And so the four years went by with the unending flow of paperwork and meetings at Headquarters, the frequent rounds of inspection trips to Marine bases, the private meetings with the Commandant, and the global journeys, with Beirut and Wiesbaden burned indelibly into Cleary's mind. Now, with Kelley's tenure as Commandant ending, and thirty-six years of active duty for Cleary, it was time to go.

Theirs had been a productive relationship. As Kelley evaluated it, "I have watched other sergeants major and other Commandants, and I'm not, in any way, trying to say that our relationship was closer or better. What I'm really saying is that I don't believe any other Sergeant Major of the Marine Corps that I have ever seen (and I've seen them all) had as much open access to the Commandant's corner office as Cleary did. But he deserved that! He was not a man who suffered fools: he was a man who was very substantive in what he did."

Cleary's predecessor, Crow Crawford, summarized his career succinctly, "I've known Bob for probably twenty-five years, both in the 7th Marines and as a drill instructor. While he was a real hell-raiser in his younger days, like a lot of others, he kind of mellowed out after he got older. Sometimes Bob was kind of secretive. He wasn't very out-going in a lot of ways. But don't get me wrong: he was as strong as a bull; he was a good Marine; he had some good tours."

Now the good tours were over and the customary retirement parade at the Marine Barracks in Washington was planned, but the rains came in a torrential downpour, so the ceremony was shifted inside to the John Philip Sousa Band Hall. There the Commandant had the pleasure of pinning on the man who had served him—and the whole Marine Corps—so well the Navy Distinguished Service Medal. His official citation by the Secretary of the Navy read in part:

...Sergeant Major Cleary consistently displayed an ability to communicate with all Marines, positively influence them, and present their views to the Nation's leadership. As the Commandant's sounding board on enlisted matters, he provided constructive, insightful advice on matters involving the morale and welfare of Marines around the world. As a leader of Marines, Sergeant Major Cleary traveled extensively to posts and stations of the Corps to speak and listen to Marines.

His personal involvement in all matters pertaining to the quality-of-life of the individual Marines and their families directly affected improvements in these vital areas. Sergeant Major Cleary's strong interest in professional education resulted in enhanced educational opportunities for Marine noncommissioned and staff noncommissioned officers. Continued improvements in the conduct of the annual Sergeants Major Symposium greatly enhanced the benefits gleaned from the experience and knowledge possessed by the Corps' senior enlisted personnel....

Just to add a further nice note of recognition, there was a personal letter from President Reagan. It spoke of Cleary's "dedicated service" and commended him for his "critical role in the preservation of America's security and freedom."

Thus, on June 25, 1987, this "uncommon man" ended nearly thirty-six years of active duty and entered the strange world of retirement and civilian life. His hair was still cut close, and his build was still trim, but when any Marine NCO hits thirty years of service, he knows retirement is usually the next step. Cleary's selection as Sergeant Major of the Marine Corps had added an unexpected four years of active duty to his career. The demanding pressures of that job had so consumed him that he really never prepared for retirement.

When it came he found that he now had time to enjoy his family more. In 1975 he had married June Poole (after an earlier marriage had been broken up by the round-the-clock requirements of a drill instructor's life). June and he had then shared trips together with the Commandant and his wife, but now they could spend some real time together.

Then there were Cleary's three children, growing into their own careers: a son who was a captain in the U.S. Air Force and had been selected in a worldwide Air Force competition as "The Logistics Officer of the Year," a married daughter finishing college in Ohio, and another daughter in Massachusetts, proud of her newly-earned Masters degree.

Never one to be idle—retirement or not—Cleary was soon busy building a family home. While temporarily based in the suburbs of Washington, he would spend most of the week at the construction site in Virginia Beach, Virginia. It was a hard-driving job: up in the blackness before dawn and work until late at night. "I didn't have time to really think," he later confessed, "but in eight months I built that house! When we moved into it, I knew I would finally be able to enjoy retirement. But I still thought of the Corps all the time. I tried to keep in touch through my reading and seeing some of the other sergeants major from time to time."

And so Sergeant Major Robert Cleary, the world traveler who had participated in the high drama of Wiesbaden and Beirut, shifted gears to settle down to the quiet life of retirement.

Chapter 12

THE NEW, NEW BREED
Sergeant Major David W. Sommers

For a long time Marines have been familiar with the evocative phrase, "the Old Breed." It was coined by a famous Marine author, John W. Thomason, to describe the old-time professionals, the highly-trained regulars who formed the backbone of the historic Marine victories in France in World War I. Those who survived went on to be the hardened NCOs of the Caribbean expeditionary days of the 1920s and '30s—the "old Corps" known to Bill Bestwick and Frank Rauber. And when Pearl Harbor exploded, those later veterans were the core who infused their values and their savvy into the tidal wave of new recruits—a wave that would eventually roll bloodily across the Pacific, with McHugh, Sweet, Dailey, and Puckett.

A third of a century after Thomason's men marched to the killing ground of Belleau Wood, another Marine author, Andrew Geer, in writing about the Marines' dramatic campaigns in Korea, modified the traditional phrase to "the New Breed." They proved worthy of their predecessors, as Black, Massaro,

Crawford, and Cleary so amply demonstrated, both in Korea and Vietnam.

Now, some 40 years after the famous landing at Inchon, there is a "New, New Breed" in the Corps. Of course, the traditional elements of the Marine mystique are still there: the undying esprit de corps; the intimate sense of bonding and interdependence that stems from a brotherhood small in size; the proud heritage that every man is trained, first and foremost, to be a combat infantryman, regardless of his ultimate assignment; the centuries of experience that dictate, "If there's trouble anywhere, we'll be sent, so be battle-ready now!" There are still the senior NCOs and officers whose multiple rows of ribbons speak of decades of devoted service in war and in a vast variety of duty stations in every corner of the globe; still the drill instructors in boot camp who continue miraculously to mold raw civilians into the Marine pattern; still the aviators who practice ceaselessly the complex, infinitely delicate task of precise, close-in bombing runs in support of their ground troops. The list of the familiar elements that have always been part of the word "Marine," and still are, could go on and on.

But that summation would be an oversimplification, presenting only a partial view of the current Corps. The men who fought their way into legend in the volcanic ash of Iwo Jima and the frigid hills of "frozen Chosin" are now retired or dead. The roar overhead of the piston-powered, gull-wing Corsair plane is no more. Physical abuse of recruits in boot camp is long past. The tent camps and temporary buildings at the old infantry bases have been replaced with expanded, permanent brick structures. Professional education for enlisted personnel has grown from a hit-or-miss, learn-by-osmosis process to a tightly organized series of graduated training courses.

Recruitment has become a highly developed technique; gone are the simplistic posters of exotic locales and the typical enlistment of the unsophisticated farm boy with very little education. Today's recruiter is carefully trained, backed by professional television ads which stress the motivation and elite selectivity of "the few, the proud." Today's recruit is a person with a high school diploma who comes from a much more complex, sophisticated, and fragmented society than "the good old days." And that recruit may well be a woman or a black or a Hispanic who would not have been part of the Old Breed. Thus, the leaders of the New, New Breed must deal face to face with a wide variety of Marines, as well as with modern problems such as race relations and the threat of drugs brought in from the civilian world.

Besides the radical changes in the people, there are the revolutions in the world around them. Close at hand are enormous equipment differences from the past: in field uniforms, in rifles, in supporting weapons, in electronics, in light armored vehicles, air-cushioned landing craft, and vertical lift aircraft—all leading to different combat tactics.

Further from the immediate, individual concerns of the New, New Breed are equally important broad-scale changes in the world that directly affect them. There are the extraordinary developments in Russia and Eastern Europe, coupled with continuing tensions in the Middle East. There are the budget reductions that have resulted in a soul-searching evaluation in the Marine Corps: what actual funds will there be in the future for what weapons? In the reduction of its troops: who? where?

Beyond the questions of Europe and the Middle East, many people feel that the United States may well face situations in which our national interest must deal with a variety of "brushfire" emergencies, low-intensity conflicts, insurgencies, terrorist incidents, and unstable tensions threatening our citizens in a global range of Third World, underdeveloped areas. Where would this mean an encounter with modern, high-technology weapons such as missiles?

General Alfred Gray, Commandant as all those issues and questions converged upon the Corps, was most forceful in stating what these uncertainties meant to the Corps, "It must have the ability to win in combat.... It must have amphibious capability, and an expeditionary nature.... It is uniquely suited for maritime power projection.... It must be trained and ready for high-tempo, fluid, combined arms, maneuver-oriented conflict."

Thus the New, New Breed has had to evolve to meet the inexorable demands of new kinds of personnel, new kinds of equipment, and new kinds of international uncertainty. The responsibility for preparing the troops for such demands must rest heavily on today's NCOs. It is they, more than any commissioned officers, who are in the most intimate contact with the troops; it is they who must train and set the example for a future trimmed-down, lean and mean team in Marine green; it is they who must learn and teach the new weapons and high-tech equipment; it is they who must apply the tactics of all-out, full scale war, or, alternatively, of surgical ground strikes, surprise landings, fast-moving mobile units, raids, feints, ambushes, stealth, infiltration, night actions, and all the other critical elements of special operations capability. Above all, they must have the ability to improvise and provide the personal on-the-spot leadership that will be essential for successful action in the emergencies that are bound to lie ahead.

These burdens of modern Marine NCOs increase progressively as their rank rises, with demands on all sergeants major now that were not even dreamed of in Bill Bestwick's day back in the '30s. A senior NCO of today must apply the complex directives that emanate from Headquarters on training, education, personnel, and a dozen other policies.

There is one enlisted man, however, who has an even greater load to carry, for he must play a central role, both in the formulation of these policies and in seeing that they are implemented in the field. That man is, of course, the Sergeant Major of the Marine Corps. With the fundamental changes that have occurred in American society, in recruits, in the world situation, in weapons and tactics, and in the financial resources available, that most senior NCO, the "Enlisted Man's General," must himself represent the embodiment of the best qualities of the New, New Breed (and that, of course, includes an equal concern for women Marines who are such an integral part of today's Corps).

Different skills and different facets of character or style are appropriate and can be effective in different eras. The requirements of today are not necessarily for a Sergeant Major of the Marine Corps who is an outstanding combat hero with Navy Cross or Silver Star, nor for an imposing recruiting-poster build, nor for a charismatic, extroverted personality, nor for a limited administrative specialist. No, the leadership requirements now are more subtle, more diverse, more complicated. This is the story of how one David Sommers proved himself to be an "uncommon man" who could deal with those requirements.

Begin with some of the ways in which he saw himself, "I'm no John Wayne Marine—not a 'poster Marine.' I'll never be called 'the greatest Sergeant Major of the Corps.' I'm just a face in the crowd. What you see is what you get. Ask me any question, and I'll give you an honest answer. I'll give my assignment 100% effort. I don't look on myself as a 'manager'; organizational skills are only a part of an all-around leader. To me, the young Marine is my foremost priority."

Here was obviously a modest man, given to understatement and a low-key approach. Only five feet, six inches tall and slender at 150 pounds, he didn't present an overwhelming physical appearance. Yet, above all the other talented, experienced, highly qualified, more senior sergeants major, it was he who was chosen for the top billet. How did he perform and what did he do in this demanding assignment and those that preceded it? And what did his actions, and the comments of his Commandant, reveal about the true stature and abilities of this man, as he and his Corps faced the multiple challenges of the New, New Breed and a spinning world?

Sommers' first day as the Sergeant Major of the Marine Corps was June 26, 1987. His selection came as a surprise to him—and to a great many other sergeants major who were senior to him. He was, after all, only forty-four years old and had less than seven years service as a sergeant major. Even more irritating to a lot of old-timers, he was only ninety-sixth on the lineal list of rank. "There were some upset folks when I was selected because it was deemed that I was too junior," Sommers later admitted.

The only attitudes that really mattered, however, were those of the two selection boards and the new Commandant. First, a group of senior officers had screened the 150 most senior enlisted Marines and narrowed the field to twenty-five. Then a board of three generals had nominated five finalists for the Commandant's selection. These names were ranked, at Gray's request, from one to five, and Sommers came out as number one. Gray had known the quality of the sergeant major's work previously, and a review of his whole enlisted career (as detailed later in this chapter) convinced the Commandant to make Sommers his choice.

The two men were starting their tours simultaneously, both new faces in key billets. Gray was a special case himself. A "mustang" who had come up from the ranks as a sergeant, then commissioned an officer, he had been selected over three senior generals as Commandant. More at home in "cammies" (camouflaged utility uniform) with enlisted men and junior officers in the field than in dress blues in rarified Washington settings, he knew what he wanted the Corps to be, and he hit the ground running; new ideas, new policies, new procedures, and new terminology all came in a flood.

The new Commandant launched a Campaign Plan for Training to provide standardization throughout the Corps. The plan emphasized "Battle Skills Training" and "Basic Warrior Training": all Marines, regardless of their technical specialty, would receive instruction in combat fundamentals. Personnel and organizations dealing with training and education in both Quantico and Washington were consolidated to form the Marine Corps Combat Development Command in Quantico. A "Professional Military Education Program" for all staff NCOs was instituted, and a Marine Corps University was organized as a resource for the entire Corps.

The promulgation of a list of required reading strengthened an understanding of the lessons of military history. That list, with scores of books, new and old, comprised a series of titles allocated to ranks running from sergeant all the way to colonel. Some layers of bureaucracy at Headquarters were eliminated, and top priority in the allocation of personnel was given to units in the field who were trained to fight. Besides the three division bases at Camps Lejeune, Pendleton, and Butler on Okinawa, and their three supporting air wings, Gray's focus was on the distinctive role of the forward deployed Marine air-ground task force, ready at all times for intervention anywhere.

Those, then, were some of the swirling new currents that Sommers had to deal with after he took office. Fortunately, he had some helpful resources to draw on. He had known Gray earlier in two different assignments, so he had a feel for how the man thought and how he liked to work, "When we talked, I kind of knew the direction General Gray was going. I knew where he was coming from. I knew what he expected of a sergeant major. I knew what he expected of any Marine, and that was very simply: number one, you should not be afraid to make a decision; and, number two, you should do the very best thing you can for the Marine Corps and the country. As long as you have that as an end-goal, you're not going to have any problems."

His original marching orders from Gray, as Sommers described them, were succinct, "We'll go down the trail together on this thing, but I want to tell you one thing we're going to do. We're going to get around to see our Marines; we're going to take care of them; and we're going to have a good time doing it." That was it; there were no specific guidelines.

The Commandant knew his man and trusted him to proceed on a course that would carry out the new policies being enunciated. Gray sketched their beginning this way:

> I just said, "Look, we're going to continue to operate up here as we always have in the past; the tried-and-true leadership ideas and the things that we've grown to use and to learn and to love about our Corps are still as valuable as they ever were. So we're going to use those kinds of ideas. You're the Sergeant Major of the Marine Corps. You have an open gangway (as I would say) to do whatever you think you must do in the best interests of the Corps and the country.

1987 official picture of Sommers as Sergeant Major of the Marine Corps.

"You need to be a spokesman. You need to share the philosophy with everybody when you speak. You need to travel; you need to go with me whenever I go places where that's appropriate and where you can do something for your Marines. By the same token, you shouldn't go when you're just going to end up being a potted palm or something like that. I want you to have your own agenda and to press on."

Really, with someone of the caliber of Sergeant Major Sommers, as well as (I would add) the others that were in the finals for selection, with those kind of people, they don't need much in the way of marching orders. They know what must be done and they know how to go about doing it.

In addition, Sommers had had a thorough briefing on the traditional functioning of the billet from his predecessor, Bob Cleary. This was a wearing process, requiring repeated commuter trips from his previous station at Quantico, half a day there and half a day at Headquarters. Finally, he had, of course, his twenty-seven years of active duty experience as a resource to draw on.

Nevertheless, the new billet required a radical change in perspective. As Sommers later confessed, "It is really a culture shock when you first come into the assignment of Sergeant Major of the Marine Corps. Here you are: one day you've got a unit—each one of these Marines belongs to you, and you know about them, and you look after your own—and then, all of a sudden, you've got [at this time] 197,000 of them. Now, all of a sudden, you're concerned, in the same way you were about that battalion, with the entire Marine Corps and what goes on and what happens that night throughout the Corps, rather than just throughout a unit."

One of the very first things that Gray noticed, as the two men began to work together in the harness, was the illogical location of the office of his sergeant major. It was where Bob Cleary had been, several wings away in the Headquarters building, actually amidst the Navy personnel working there. The Commandant's teasing began, "Ask the 'Sergeant Major of the Navy' if he can make the trip over to my office for a talk." It was not long before everybody got Gray's message:

> I thought that the sergeant major was simply too far away from the nerve center here, and that was not the style that we hoped to use here at Headquarters. We wanted to keep communications open, and we wanted the sergeant major to have immediate access to the Commandant, to the chief of staff, or indeed to anyone else that he thought necessary. He then got that access, and he had that kind of authority. So I was needling him quite a bit originally about being "the Sergeant Major of the Navy," over there where the rugs are blue and all that kind of thing.

Within a few weeks, a location was "found" next to the assistant commandant's office; then that general moved and Sommers took over his space directly adjoining "the Big Corner Office." Now he was in a proximity which Gray felt was "fitting for the Sergeant Major of the Marine Corps." This physical closeness was given real significance by Gray's accessibility. As Sommers summarized it:

> He had an open-door policy. I could go in and see the general any time I wanted to, pretty near daily. I didn't need to set up an appointment or deal with his aide. If I had something I needed to talk to him about, I'd check his schedule and see when he was going to be in the office, and then I'd just walk on in and talk with him. But I didn't bother him unless I absolutely thought that it was necessary. He was extremely busy, and he didn't need me going in and making small talk, and he didn't need me going in and asking about something I should have been making a decision on in the first place.

The Commandant's concern about his sergeant major's office location carried over to the very personal issue of his living quarters. Sommers remembered:

> General Gray, when I first came into this billet, was extremely upset that there was no place for the Sergeant Major of the Marine Corps to live; so much so that he wanted me to move into Quarters Two at 8th and I [the Washington Barracks]. I didn't want to move in there, and that was our very first disagreement. He wanted me to take a house before he got one! He was scheduled to move into Quarters Two while the Commandant's House was being renovated, but he wanted my wife and me to take that house. We didn't do it, and the main reason was that we thought that it would be best for Kenneth, our son, to remain in his school in Quantico.

The end to this housing saga came over two years later, after endless hours and miles of commuting from Quantico. Gray kept pushing for permanent quarters that would always be assigned to the Sergeant Major of the Marine Corps. For years the achievement of this idea had proven elusive, despite many previous efforts. Now the other services joined in a joint push for quarters for their senior enlisted man. As Gray recalled, "We got a lot of support from the people on the Hill [Congress], and in the endorsement that we sent forward on this package, I was able to write in my own handwriting that 'I feel very strongly about this; so strongly that I offered the Sergeant Major of the Marine Corps a set of quarters at Marine Barracks, 8th and I.' We were fortunate that this program was approved." The happy conclusion was that Sommers (and his family) were able to move into the permanent quarters of the Sergeant Major of the Marine Corps in September, 1989.

Located within walking distance of Headquarters in Arlington, Virginia, it was a modest place, but a happy home for them. Finally, they had a house to settle down in after years of multiple, short-term moves. Kenneth, their son, was finally able to put down roots in one location. As his father analyzed it, "He had to bounce through schools, changing almost every year. I'm really proud of him because he made more sacrifices because of my assignments than many people would ever imagine. I mean he might have complained about it, but he packed up and moved again and came here from Quantico. Now he has enlisted in the Corps. He's done very, very well."

Yvette, the mother, took things with a pretty laid-back attitude:

It's been interesting. I'm used to the military. My father was in the Marines, and there were the years I was in the Corps. So I just go with the flow. Of course, when necessary, I do a lot of complaining, a lot of crying, kicking, screaming, and so on!

As for Dave, he's just down to earth; he's got a good sense of humor; he gets moody like everybody else, but he tries to make time for his family although he's not home very often. When he does get here, the first one who gets greeted is the dog (because she insists). He's not into television; he likes to fish when he has time. He likes yard work and playing golf, but he hasn't had much time for either.

Sommers paid due tribute to Yvette, "The wives of the Sergeant Major of the Marine Corps, all of them I'm sure, have gone through the same thing that Yvette has gone through: we move around and wheel and deal, and she's packing; she's moving; she's unpacking.... They have to put up with a lot. Now she's put together, with five other wives, a guide for enlisted men's wives. It has been published, and the title is *Roses and Thorns*.

Back at his Headquarters desk, Sommers soon found that, with the avalanche of change that characterized Gray's new policies, it was obvious that a steady pattern of field trips was essential in order to communicate accurately and clearly with the troops. New directives had to be understood; Marines spread across the globe had to be motivated; only then would the Corps as a whole move willingly to implement the spate of innovations and evolve to meet effectively the challenges of a radically new era.

So out they went, the two of them together. In the first two and a half years, Gray made 329 speeches, with 172 addressed to 78,000 of the military and 157 to over 60,000 civilians. (A clear index of the importance the Corps attaches to the support and understanding of the civilian world—not to mention 97 media interviews.) He piled up over 336,000 air miles, and visited 214 cities and 180 military bases. The pattern was simple: if there were enlisted Marines involved, Sommers was there working with him. If it was overseas, Sommers was there. Together they covered twenty-two countries ranging from Brazil and Panama in Latin America, to seven countries in Europe, to Bahrain and Oman in the Middle East, to Japan, Korea, and Okinawa in the Far East. It was grueling!

Sommers commented:

I really think every trip that we went on was a success, in my opinion. General Gray could be a bear in the office. I mean, he could really be a *bear* in the office, with all the things piling up in there! But you got him out of the office and got him around Marines, and he was just a different person. He was ready to go; he was fired up!

He would walk into an area with a group of Marines, and instantly they were motivated, and they wanted to hear the Commandant, and they wanted to see the Commandant, and they wanted to touch him; they wanted to shake hands with him; they wanted to have their picture taken. He was a very personable individual.

In fact, I can't think of any trips that we really didn't accomplish what we set out to do. We had some overseas trips, however, that were very trying ones. As an example, we had trips where the Commandant would exchange a visit to the British, or to the French, to the Brazilians. They really got their money's worth because they didn't give you any break.

That schedule was laid out to the point where you didn't have any time at all. You didn't even have time to make a head [bathroom] call! And they would zip you from one place to another, pass you from one group to another, and when you got back on the plane to come home, you were so tired that you were really ready to take a break. The plane was a refuge.

After every trip we got back together, and sometimes after every leg of a trip where we were going to hit different bases. We would talk about areas that I found and that he found, and we would compare notes. General Gray was very good when I would tell him things, and I would indicate to him that I'd like to take care of that myself. In turn, I would tell him if I knew something he should be aware of.

Just as in past years, the relationships with the personnel sergeant major and the first sergeant/sergeant major monitor at Headquarters were crucial to the skillful functioning of the Sergeant Major of the Marine Corps. Sommers gave full credit, "My right-hand man was the personnel sergeant major. He was of tremendous assistance to me because he was very knowledgeable about the Headquarters. He'd previously been the first sergeant/sergeant major monitor. I could call him from the plane; I could call him from Okinawa; I could call him from anywhere and have him look into something for me, and I would get the right answers and I got them very quickly."

Gray also noted the importance of these trips and his close working relationship with Sommers:

When we would go to the west coast or to the Far East or wherever Marines were, normally we would both address large groups of Marines. So the sergeant major and I probably talked to nearly all the Marines we had on active duty then, and we spent a great deal of time talking to those in the Selected Marine Corps Reserve as well.

The sergeant major would use his own judgment. He would be with me to watch the unit-type training and operations and observe things, and he'd comment on certain tactical thoughts. Or, he would go off separately depending on what he thought ought to be done. If he knew, for example, that I had to have a conference or meeting, then he'd make the choice of whether to go to that meeting, or he might have been out watching one of the other regiments, or over in the squadron, or down in the force service support group.

It was that way, for example, when we went to Brazil. In addition to watching their demonstration operation, we talked to just about all the Brazilian Marines that were involved in the demonstration. The sergeant major would, in each of the countries and places that we'd go, also visit the security guard detachment Marines at the embassy or consulate. He would frequently go over there to their quarters and spend an evening with them.

That same trip to Brazil produced a ludicrous situation. It is nearly impossible for foreign military services to comprehend fully the prestige and power status of the Sergeant Major of the U.S. Marine Corps, so they tend to lump him in with the unimportant "nobodies" when the Commandant pays a visit. While in Rio de Janeiro, Sommers naturally made contact with the Marine NCOs there. When it came time for the American visitors to travel to a meeting, the "three sergeants," as they were called by the Brazilians, were put in a wreck of an old car last in the official cavalcade. Halfway there, the car broke down completely.

It was quite a scene: the driver speaking no English, exclaiming volubly in Portuguese and gesticulating with his arms; the three sergeants in their "cammies," pushing the car and sweating in the hot sun; the rest of the cavalcade disappearing down the street; and the passers-by tossing off rude comments and gestures to the gringos. Finally, after an hour, Sommers was able to rejoin the official party. Sizing up the situation, Gray inquired deadpan, "Well, where have you been?"

In their trips around the United States, the two men naturally encountered a wide variety of situations, ranging from problems that required top-level correction to happy moments when they could compliment, reward, or give proper recognition to an individual or a unit. Gray recollected, "We were at Camp Lejeune, visiting the School of Infantry, and the sergeant major saw some things he didn't like with respect to the use of the noncommissioned officers in their instructional role. He went right back down there and had a session with everybody, including the sergeant major down there, and got it all straightened out." Sommers was more explicit in his recollection, "Some of the staff NCOs were goofing off on their jobs, and the sergeant major, who should have been supervising them, was very blase when I expressed my disgust. That sergeant major is no longer there."

Gray continued with another example of his sergeant major meeting a problem head-on:

> In a similar vein, we were at Parris Island. We had a good visit down there; it was a surprise visit. (By the way, a lot of our visits were surprises, no-notice type things, and that was good.) But he still had an instinct that some additional discussion should have been carried on with some of the drill instructors, regarding their attitude and that type of thing. Then, when we had an incident down there, he was on the plane the next morning and had an immediate session with all the drill instructors and the sergeant major again. He took great pride in the fact that he was a former drill instructor and he watched that area very closely.

What Sommers found was that the drill instructors had gotten so wrapped up in the immediate problems of the moment, in training their own particular recruits, that they had lost sight of the broader picture of the future capabilities and careers of those boots. They did not seem to be fully cognizant of the sensitivity of their assignment to mold young recruits properly. When Sommers finished his meeting with the DIs, then they understood!

One of the happy occasions was a visit Gray and his sergeant major made to the Interservice Rifle Match awards night. The Commandant noticed that one Marine buck sergeant (the lowest ranked sergeant, with the three chevrons above, but no "rocker" below on his arm insignia) had won a large number of awards. He mentioned this to Sommers, who, being the kind of man he was, then took it upon himself to do a little checking up. He discovered that the sergeant was going to have to get out of the Corps because he had never come up for promotion, and thus had not made staff sergeant in the allotted time span. When Sommers reported those facts, Gray gave the marksman a spot promotion to staff sergeant (with one "rocker") right then and there.

As a Commandant who preferred "cammies" to dress blues—and even his office coffee cup was a camouflage-covered field canteen cup, although it did have the four stars of his rank!—as a man of this temperament, it is not surprising that he did not want any formal, dress parade honors rendered to him when he arrived at a base for an inspection. When such an elaborate, red-carpet welcome was laid on at a visit to one base, with the tarmac crowded with ranks of senior officers, a fleet of cars, etc., Gray was *not* pleased. The door of the plane opened; a mass of hands were raised in expectant salute for the general; then Sommers stepped out first, briskly returned the salute of the gaping brass, and, with no Commandant evident at the moment, was driven off in the car brought for Gray.

This kind of easy, empathetic relationship between the two men was evident at many dinner gatherings and other meetings, where Gray, when he had finished his speech, would call out, "Sergeant Major, stand up!" And, pointing to Sommers, he would proclaim to the room, "That's the guy who really runs the Marine Corps!"

On the Commandant's plane, flying back to Headquarters from a trip, Sommers would often bring up a problem he had uncovered. Gray's reaction was two-fold: he would offer his help if the sergeant major wanted to handle the matter, and, at other times, he would telephone a command that he was sending Sommers to relay his (Gray's) particular current concern to the field.

Once Sommers returned from a trip, he followed a very careful, set routine, a procedure well known to any successful person with wide-ranging responsibilities. It is called, "Touch all the right bases." Accordingly, he explained:

> When I came back, the first thing I would do was get together with the monitor and the personnel sergeant major, and I would go over all the things that I had found on the trip. Maybe it was dealing with an individual, or trying to get a fitness report squared away, or maybe it was a promotion, or maybe it was permanent change of station [PCS] orders. Maybe someone was getting orders to someplace where he shouldn't have been going or else to where he should have been going. Then I would have to write an appropriate memo on it to send to the appropriate agency to get it squared away. But I have to admit that the personnel sergeant major took, probably, ninety percent of those questions and got them answered.

Sommers enjoyed a good relationship with both the monitor and the personnel sergeant major. Because he was doing major command assignments, the monitor assigned all the sergeants major and first sergeants except for those working for a general. Sommers handled the latter, giving the final 'okay' on them. But, before he did that, he brought in both the personnel sergeant major and the monitor and together they looked at all the assignments. This often involved a call to the FMFPac sergeant major, or the FMFLant sergeant major, or the man who was currently in the billet. Then the three men would assemble, and the other two would say, "Okay, this is what we think. This is who we ought to have." But then Sommers would say, "Convince me why this guy should have that assignment." There was one continuing problem he encountered in the assignment process:

> I refused to put a sergeant major into a command billet (that is, working for a general) just because he thought it was his turn. I tried to make sure that a sergeant major assigned to a command billet had at least two years left to do in the Corps. I believed that assigning them for eight months or eleven to twelve months was not the way to go because the unit suffered. You would just be doing a turnover.
>
> Then I tried to make sure that I matched up the sergeant major with the general, and I also asked to make sure that the general wanted that sergeant major, so that they would work well together. It was extremely important for any unit, whether it be division or brigade or base, that those two got along. If they didn't like each other, and he was only accepting that sergeant major because he'd been assigned there, you were not going to accomplish anything, and the Marines there were going to suffer. So I got into some heat over those assignments, but General Gray allowed me that flexibility.

Another problem Sommers had to deal with was a situation where there was a sergeant major who was very senior and nobody wanted him. A base or wing commanding general objected to him, but yet when Sommers looked at the fitness report this man had received when leaving a previous billet, he found that they had given him an outstanding fitness report. So the problem fell back on the Sergeant Major of the Marine Corps or the monitor, because the generals would ask, "Why are you sending this guy to us? Why is he going to get this billet?" And Sommers knew that sergeant major was really not going to do the job properly. He reflected sadly:

> Somehow, I think, when a man got to be senior they were less likely to tell it like it truly was. I found that many general officers would do that. They'd give a guy a good fitness report instead of flat out relieving him. The Headquarters element—the monitor, the personnel sergeant major or I, much like our predecessors—we couldn't do anything about that. We were enlisted Marines, and we had to carry out policy and enforce regulations. We didn't make those regulations. If they would just have called it like it was, it would have given us something we would have been able to work with.
>
> Then there were the senior men who were in a key billet and were simply not doing their job adequately. I made telephone calls to a certain

base, and I told the sergeant major there that I was getting a lot of reports that he was not doing what he was supposed to be doing, and that I thought it probably would be time for him to retire, because I was not going to assign him to another major command.

Say that he was then working for a two-star general, and I could have given him a set of orders to I&I duty up in Hoboken, New Jersey, or some place like that. Was that really fair to the Marines up there? I thought that these kinds of cases needed to be moved along, and I'd say that we were doing a better job of moving these people out.

Besides coordinating with the other enlisted power centers at Headquarters, Sommers was careful to touch base with the appropriate generals, "I would also, when I came back, go up and see the general who was the director of manpower or else his deputy chief of manpower. I'd talk to him and let him know what I had found out. I tried to give the general (the director) or the deputy chief of that particular agency as much 'heads-up' as I could on things that maybe I had picked up, things which the Commandant was kind of upset about. I'd go up and let them know, 'You're going to be getting some paper on this. The general's upset about it. We need to get some answers on it.'"

There were also, of course, the trips that Sommers took on his own. The Corps interfaces in a variety of ways with the civilian world, so there are always community events, organizations, or dinners at which the Sergeant Major of the Marine Corps is asked to speak. Add to those the solo visits to major Marine bases. The meetings with enlisted personnel on these trips required Sommers to be fully informed and completely up to date on current policies for dealing with a wide variety of problems. His talks ranged over leadership, professional education, combat training, male-female fraternization, family and child abuse, promotions, the drill field, drugs, required reading, among other issues. The enlisted feedback that he got from these meetings provided the foundation for Sommers' actions at Headquarters: "Will this be applicable or effective for the troops in the field?"

In addition, he made a special effort to keep in touch with recruiters. The Marine Corps has divided the nation into six districts, and Sommers met with each district sergeant major once a quarter. Together they spent three days making a swing around to all the recruiting substations. They found the recruiters were "hungry for news of what's going on in the Corps." Some of the men they met with had become, in effect, "career recruiters." They were excellent salesmen, but they hadn't been out in the field with a rifle unit in some time, and so were not fully informed on current life in the Corps. The Sergeant Major of the Marine Corps, more than anyone else, was superbly informed, and thus highly qualified to update them on policies and actions. Beyond this, however, Sommers' priority was to check up on the recruiters themselves— how they were personally and individually, and how their families were getting along.

The Commandant heard reports about these trips, too, and added a nice touch as a follow-up. He and Sommers had a policy of calling up recruiters who were doing really well and giving them "a little pat on the back." It's not hard to imagine the effect on morale when a recruiter isolated out in some small town received a congratulatory phone call direct from the most senior level of Headquarters.

The role of the sergeant major with a strong-minded Commandant who had inaugurated a massive wave of changes was an interesting challenge, to say the least. Proximity, both in offices and travel, helped. Mutual respect helped. An open door and an open mind by Gray both helped.

Sommers was an integral part of the top-level staff discussions as the new ideas were thrashed out. Gray was frank to say, "There were some real fire fights in Headquarters about matters of policy and what was needed to take care of our people. Every Marine leader worthy of the term is vitally interested in taking care of our people. It's the sergeant major on the enlisted side, along with the command structure, that's the focal point for making sure that we do this the very best that we know how."

To insure the input of his senior enlisted advisor, the Commandant had a warm pattern of always asking in these meetings, "Sergeant Major, what do you think?" Sommers' reply usually came, not in the form of submitting his own program, but in evaluating a given proposal as to how it would work in the field, what its practical effect would be on the enlisted personnel in a rifle company or fighter squadron.

One crucial area that they both labored long and hard on was professional military education. Gray was crystal clear:

> If our Marines do not have a life-long idea of learning, then they will not rise to the top of their profession, nor will they maintain the professional confidence that you need now and that's needed for tomorrow. I thought that we can always be more prepared, and we can always learn, and we can always train even better to meet the challenges of the future. Therefore, one of the things that I believed in strongly was a good, solid, institutionalized training and education program for all Marines, regardless of rank or grade.
>
> So what we moved to, with respect to the Training and Education Center at Quantico, was the idea that we would have an *overall* training and education plan, and a series of programs in the Marine Corps that would seek to standardize and institutionalize all of the noncommissioned officer schools, all of the staff noncommissioned officer academies, and all of the schools for officers no matter where they might be. That, of course, is now in place. The sergeant major played a big role in this evolution with respect to the enlisted schools.

General Gray also took the lead in creating a Warfighting Center at Quantico. He felt that the Marine Corps had to have a focus for a doctrine for combat, "for that's what we're really all about." And there were many other aspects of learning, as Gray explained:

> The Marine Corps University is the capstone university for all of these educational and related training programs. It focuses on education, officer

and enlisted. The non-resident portion, through the use of some advanced techniques in correspondence-type instruction, has a big role to play in our university. We also expanded the Marine Corps Institute's role with respect to enlisted education.

We added to the recruit training process, at both Parris Island and San Diego, about five extra days of what's known as "Basic Warrior Training." This is additional infantry-type training: patrolling and combat skills and the like. This is the first part of the "Marine Battle Skills Training Program."

The next phase is when they go to the School of Infantry. We established one of these on each coast, and brought back infantry training for everybody, regardless of their occupational field. Non-infantrymen go for twenty-eight days of advanced infantry training, and then they go on to logistics training, supply training, aviation, machinist, whatever it is. The infantryman stays another thirty-one days beyond that. So he gets a total of fifty-nine days of advanced infantry training, and really, now, by any measurement, he's a basic commando when he comes out of that program!

After this came phase three, advanced leadership training at all levels, and finally there was a "unit sustainment" phase which was conducted out in the field. That was designed to have the commanders of different kinds of units be the judges of what kind of training to do and when to do it, so as to fit it in best with their overall missions and tasks.

Summarizing the reasons for this massive overhaul, Gray said:

The underlying idea of all this is that warriors are going to fight better when they fight smarter, and when they learn, and when you provide the framework for them to be able to deal with uncertainty. It's the corporal and the young lieutenant who are on the point and in the crises. So we were working to provide a kind of framework where we were trying to increase their ability to use their thought processes, to really think. We were trying to institutionalize that so that people can grow up through the system within our Corps.

Sommers' involvement with the development of the "Professional Military Education Program" was continuous. The resulting guidelines and requirements for staff NCOs were minutely detailed and very demanding. There was a carefully defined progression of resident and non-resident courses, professional reading, seminars, and structured self-study for each rank, staff sergeant through sergeant major/master gunnery sergeant. Under the aegis of the Marine Corps University, there were four Staff NCO Academies brought into full operation at Camp Lejeune, Camp Pendleton, Quantico, and on Okinawa.

Every Marine who went through these courses was brought face to face, and then left, with a copy of the Staff NCO Creed:

I am a Staff Non-Commissioned Officer in the United States Marine Corps. As such, I am a member of the most unique group of professional military practitioners in the world. I am bound by duty to God, Country, and my fellow Marines to execute the demands of my position to and beyond what I believe to be the limits of my capabilities. I realize that I am the mainstay of Marine Corps discipline, and I carry myself with military grace, unbowed by the weight of command, unflinching in the execution of lawful orders, and unswerving in my dedication to the most complete success of my assigned mission.

Both my professional and personal demeanor shall be such that I may take pride if my juniors emulate me, and knowing perfection to lie beyond the grasp of any mortal hand, I shall yet strive to attain perfection, that I may ever be aware of my needs and capabilities to improve myself. I shall be fair in my personal relations, just in the enforcement of discipline, true to myself and my fellow Marines, and equitable in my dealings with every man.

The Staff NCO Academies were supplemented by courses for corporals and sergeants at Parris Island, Twentynine Palms in California, and Kaneohe Bay in Hawaii.

The NCOs of the Old Breed would be scratching their heads at all that educational organization. It is no longer the Corps they knew. And today's Sergeant Major of the Marine Corps is in the forefront of this wave of the future.

There was a subtle danger lurking in this intensive drive for professional military education. As NCOs and officers worked their way through their series of courses, it was (and still is) possible to fall prey to the curse of "careerism." This was a mind-set which really raised Gray's blood pressure:

It's extraordinarily difficult to get away from this because it's grown up in our society. These people who put themselves ahead of other things and are primarily interested in what can be done for them, that's almost become a way of life in a great part of our society. So, in a way, we're swimming upstream. But I'm very adamant about it: careerism has no place in the profession of arms.

I define careerism very simply as individuals who put themselves and 'getting ahead' at a higher priority than the people that they are privileged to serve with and lead. Now, wanting to get ahead, that's as American as apple pie; that's not really the issue. It's when you seek to take advantage to get ahead, to be more worried about yourself than you are about the people you serve with, then you're deep in the middle of careerism, and we have no room for that in the Marine Corps.

So that was another of the new messages that Sommers carried throughout the length and breadth of the Corps. Gray applauded, "He did this continuously. The sergeant major was a superb spokesman for our policies and for our philosophy. He was a part of developing it, and he believed in it. It was very easy for him to talk about it, and he did it, I think, extremely well."

Within the inner workings of Headquarters, Sommers, after advance discussion with the personnel sergeant major and the monitor, pushed for other changes. One tradition fell by the wayside, a victim of the budget crunch. There was no 1990 Sergeants Major Symposium. The 1988 symposium, however, had led to a massive review of past recommendations. Sommers later recounted the events:

As far as that symposium went, we had discussed a lot of issues. Then we had those issues forwarded to the Commandant, but he sent them back out to me. Every time something would come up—for instance, boots—I would say, "Well we talked about that at the symposium a couple of years ago." When I'd done this over a period of time, finally the general said, "Every time I say something, you tell me that you talked about that at the symposium. I want all the notes from all the symposiums from the time you ever started having them."

So he gave me all the 1988 notes back, and then we went through every record of all the past symposiums. For any items that we had in 1988 that had been talked about before, we did a comprehensive folder on those. We put this thing together and gave it to the Commandant, to the assistant commandant; it took a lot of staff work in the Headquarters and needed a lot of answers.

Promotions! Now that is a word which guarantees total attention from every Marine—and sometimes frustration and anger. One of the aspects of the enlisted promotion boards that quickly attracted Sommers' eye was the minimal representation of enlisted personnel in the composition of the boards. After an appropriate amount of jockeying, he was able to rectify that by getting top-level agreement for a major increase, so that there were eight enlisted members on every board.

There was an even more fundamental problem regarding promotions: stagnation. Good men (and women) who deserved to move up in rank, and could not, were leaving the Marine Corps. Their departure could have been on their own initiative, born of frustration, or it could have been because a hard and fast rule in the Corps forced it. That rule required that a corporal with eight years' service, or a sergeant with thirteen, must be promoted or must get out. Sommers faced the situation frankly:

There were a number of reasons why we had difficulty with promotions. All of it was self inflicted. If we previously had thought we needed more sergeants in a particular group, we would then authorize more sergeants. This went on for years until there was a terrible imbalance in a lot of occupational specialties. In some MOSs, we had more staff sergeants than we had sergeants. It didn't take a genius to figure out that you were not going to get promoted there if you were a sergeant. We tried to bring that in line by balancing our occupational specialties and the rank structure within those specialties.

The solution was slow and difficult, a program of "Enlisted Career Force Controls." They consisted of a series of steps to achieve a proper pyramidal rank structure and a proper number of personnel within any given MOS (e.g. fewer staff sergeants than sergeants). Sommers played a key role in the institution of an Enlisted Selective Retirement Board to be a part of that process. The board had the painful task of picking out Marines to be retired, not because they had performed poorly, but because their MOS was overcrowded with NCOs of their rank.

In a different initiative, one of his innovations paid off in greatly improved communications with a crucial, influential group, the sergeants major of the principal commands in the Corps. This was achieved by circulating to them on a regular basis the "Sergeant Major of the Marine Corps Memorandum." It relayed up-to-date information on a wide variety of subjects devoted to both the personal and the professional life of the troops—subsistence allowances, retired pay, required reading, tuition assistance, fitness reports, medical benefits, and many other issues.

Then there were the old problems that never really go away, and the Sergeant Major of the Marine Corps must continue to deal with them. He made this appeal on a subject very familiar to Black and Massaro:

> I encourage each of you to take a good look around your unit. Are you closing your eyes to the personnel who are overweight, or need to be placed on the personal appearance program? Are we allowing some to slide because of rank or the old standby, "The Marine does a good job" bit? I challenge each of you, no matter what their level, to look over your Marines and ensure you are following the Commandant's direction....

> We continue to send fat Marines to WestPac! I took a look at a list of overweight Marines that arrived in Okinawa. Unbelievable! The winner was a gunny who was fifty-five pounds overweight. The gunny must have had one helluva time on leave. How about jumping into the middle of this weight problem? It goes without saying that as leaders we take a good hard look at ourselves first!

Sommers used his memorandum to confront other problems head-on. The Corps, in its drive for excellence, had a formal "Substandard Performance Program." This pinpointed the precise numbers of NCOs who were failing in such noticeable areas as personal conduct, appearance, or leadership ability. They were the targets of his blunt pronouncement:

> I believe Marines that are on the program should strongly consider leaving the Corps. More than likely they have been given numerous opportunities to improve their performance and they have failed to do so. By remaining on active duty, these Marines are preventing more qualified Marines from being promoted. These Marines can do themselves and the Corps a good deed by leaving our ranks.

> By not doing what is required at their present ranks, they are guilty of misappropriation of government funds. Think it over. If the above is upsetting to those Marines, it is meant to be. It is meant to get them thinking about the damage they are doing. I will not give you the numbers of substandard performers by unit; it would be embarrassing for some. However, I am mailing the numbers to the applicable unit sergeants major.

It's easy to imagine the harsh conversation when the unit sergeant major called in that sub-standard Marine for a little heart-to-heart chat!

Race relations continued to be a subject Sommers always addressed when he met with the troops. Speaking of this issue, he observed:

Although I think we were doing well in that area, there were still problems that needed to be looked at. This was an issue where we put that
problem behind us in the '70s, and then we kind of let it lie dormant. We
hadn't paid a lot of attention to it, and there were little pockets of that sur-
facing all the time. So the race business was something you have to stay
on top of all the time. You got new Marines in. They came from society
at large, from varied places, so it was not something you should think you
can correct one time and it was going to be corrected forever.

Particularly in peacetime, family concerns loom large in the minds of all
military personnel. In the days of the Old Breed, most of the enlisted men were
bachelors, married in reality to their Corps. Not so today! As Sommers analyzed the situation:

The biggest problem with retention in my opinion was the factual or
perceived loss in different benefits—medical, commissary, post exchange,
pay—and I could go on and on. We had more dependents than we had
Marines, and if a young man couldn't support his family and give them
the things he knew they needed on the salary we were paying him, he was
going to take his training and skills to the civilian community. We're foolish
to think the military is just going to continually be able to support itself
with an all-volunteer force if we continue to cut back.

To proclaim that concern where it counted the most, Sommers was a regular
visitor to Capitol Hill. There he testified three or four times a year on "quality
of life" before the Senate or House Armed Services Committee. The senior
enlisted men from the other services were there also, and the litany had a
repeated ring of familiarity—cost-of-living adjustments, housing needs, dependent care, etc. The reasons for focusing on these issues were clear in Sommers' testimony:

In contrast to the past, today's Marines have different expectations of
the service. A good job and a family, which used to be long-term goals,
are important to many high school graduates during their first enlistment.

In the past three years, for the first time, the Marine Corps has had more
dependents than Marines. Today, more than forty-two percent of Marines
are married; two out of three families have children under the age of eleven;
over half of the spouses work outside the home; and one out of three
spouses is under the age of twenty-four. Thus family support cannot be
overlooked, if only for the sake of combat readiness.

The cost of maintaining two households, the separation of the family,
the burden of child care, and the increased stress brought on by more short-
term deployments to Okinawa, shipboard deployments, and deployments
away from their home base, are all detractors from readiness.

Quality of life issues directly impact on our warfighting capability. We
have recruited good people, prepared them for combat, and now, to keep
them effective and in uniform, we have to help them take care of their
families.

With these factors so crucial, the Marine Corps had opened "Family Service Centers," and Sommers continued his statement with a plea for funding two more of them. He then moved on to the central problem of pay, pointing out the harsh facts of family life in the Corps:

> Last year almost $400,000 was received in food stamps at Marine Corps commissaries. We can only speculate on how much Marines spent off-base in food stamps, or even more importantly, how many were eligible for the assistance but were too proud to ask. Only when our pay approaches, and stays in line with the civilian community, will we be able to assure our Marines that their reward for service will not be poverty.

This picture of Sommers testifying in front of a Congressional committee was a lucid example of the demands placed on him by the New, New Breed. He had to push insistently on the issues that were uppermost in the minds of "his" troops. This led to a spate of bureaucratic jargon that was familiar to the Congressmen, but seemed strange coming from a veteran Marine sergeant major: "early outs," "selective reenlistment bonus," "employment cost index," "comparability gap," "promotion pyramid," "geographic bachelors," "quality of life," "CHAMPUS reform initiative," "gerontology," "COLA adjustments," and other such arcane terminology.

Dealing with Washington power centers was all in a day's work for Sommers. Besides those trips to Capitol Hill, there were visits to the Pentagon. He was on his own, knowing the Commandant trusted him to handle himself in a way Marines could be proud of. He recounted an episode which occurred earlier in his tour as the Sergeant Major of the Marine Corps, "I walked in one morning, and I said, 'General, I've got to go see the Secretary of Defense. Is there anything that you want me to particularly talk about or not talk about?' He looked up over his glasses, and he replied, 'Sergeant Major, you know what's going on. Tell him like it is.' I never went back in and asked the Commandant another question about what I should say to the Senate Armed Services Committee, or the Congress, or anybody else I talk to."

Returning from those sessions to Headquarters quickly immersed Sommers in the enlisted personnel of the Corps, symbolized by the flood of correspondence that flowed unceasingly in and out. It touched every conceivable facet of Marine life:

* Sergeant Major in Georgia: "An injustice was done" in the failure to promote this staff sergeant.

* A casualty report on the death of a Marine on liberty in California.

* Lance Corporal in California: a suggestion to improve training of enlisted Marines. (Sommers sent this one on to the Commandant.)

* Gunnery Sergeant: commitment to improve his physical fitness.

* Private First Class in Virginia: suggestion for new type of equipment.

* Lance Corporal on a battleship: thanks for the help given to his father.

* Sergeant in Nevada: thanks for help in getting travel pay due him.

* Lance Corporal in helicopter squadron: urging refresher ground combat training for aviation technicians.

* Former recruit: thanking Sommers for the training he gave as a D.I. in boot camp before the man went to combat in Vietnam.

With the sudden invasion of Kuwait by Iraq in August, 1990, Sommers' previously stated goal of "success on the battlefield" instantly became a demanding reality. Whether at Headquarters or on repeated trips to the Persian Gulf area, he was deeply involved in the deployment of regulars, mobilization of Reserves, and support for "his troops" in the combat zone. He later described the situation he and Gray found in the early days over there:

> When we initially went over the first time, the Marines were scattered pretty thin. The conditions weren't very good, but they were working up to better living conditions. We traveled throughout the Marine areas, both by vehicle and by helicopter.
>
> For my part of it, I dealt with the sergeants major population we had there, as to what they needed. I was concerned about whether they had the number of personnel they needed. For instance, we would find out what units, if any, were missing people or had personnel problems. We would come back here; we were able to expedite getting those personnel assigned.

A top priority was to build up Marine Corps combat strength in the Gulf area, and Sommers glowed with pride:

> For the Corps, I think we did pretty well, in that we were kind of prepared to do whatever the President wanted us to do. It didn't require a whole lot of reorganization for us. Probably the most astounding thing for us was when we started to call up our Reserves. That hadn't been done since Korea, and there were some little glitches. But I believe that our show-up rate for our Reserves called was ninety-six percent. We were overwhelmed with the response....
>
> On a trip over there, we went up to the 1st Marine Division position; the Commandant wanted to talk to Major General James Myatt. I walked around with Sergeant Major Chuck Chamberlin, the division sergeant major. Chuck and I walked around his lines and talked to his people.
>
> I talked to young machine gunners out in the middle of the desert in holes where that sand kept falling in on them. Attitude was great. They didn't have anything but MREs [Meals, Ready to Eat] and water and ammunition, and they were happy. The Commandant asked one of them, "What do you need? What can I get for you? What do you need more of?" The Marine thought for a few seconds and looked up at the Commandant and said, "Well, I could use a little more ammo." I mean that's the kind of attitude that was prevalent throughout the force.

On his return from these on-site visits, Sommers would always go to see the appropriate senior staff at Headquarters:

For instance, Lieutenant General Norman Smith in manpower, I would go up and brief him on what I found. I'd try to give him "heads up" on areas that I knew were of concern to the Commandant. I would certainly bring in the personnel sergeant major [Jack Mooney] who played a big role in this Headquarters on things like personnel and promotions.

We would deal with the division sergeants major that were not over there yet. We knew we were probably going to see the 2d Division move quickly, so I would go down to Camp Lejeune. I tried to personally talk to sergeants major that were going to go over so that they had a good feel for what they were going to encounter, or things that they needed to take, or areas they needed to be cautious in with their personnel. You know, people to take: enough of this MOS, enough of that MOS.

In looking ahead to the forthcoming combat, Gray had one overriding personal worry, and Sommers felt it deeply:

General Gray was very, very concerned with the possibility of heavy casualties. Intelligence, everybody was pointing towards that. He was extremely concerned. As a result, we spent a lot of time going from one unit to another, and the general was literally holding school on our commanders. I sat in meetings with him continually. We would come out of the meetings and we would discuss what went on in the meeting, and it was always, "What do you think, Sergeant Major?" I would share my thoughts with him about what transpired in the meeting, about what he was doing.

I also often shared with him my worry for him personally.... He was so concerned that we were going to take heavy casualties that I was becoming increasingly concerned for his own health. I mean, the man didn't sleep, he didn't eat. He was constantly traveling, constantly working, constantly preaching that message of preparedness.

Naturally, Sommers and Gray had to work with the higher echelon, Central Command, in addition to the intensive visits to their own Marine units:

With the Central Command sergeant major, I talked about our personnel who were assigned to the Central Command. We had a lot of Marines assigned over there. When the Commandant went in with General Schwarzkopf, I would ask that Army sergeant major about our Marines there: if he needed more, if he needed less, if they were doing well, if he had any problems with any of our people. Not one time did he say anything but the highest of praise for our people. At one point he told me that he wished he could get more Marines. He felt that he would be able to get a little bit more done!

As 1990 drew to a close, Sommers had an idea. Why not have General Gray take some authorizations for meritorious promotions when the two men went to Saudi Arabia for Christmas with the troops? He later recalled the furor:

So I went in and recommended that we take meritorious promotions away from recruiting for that quarter and give them to the forces in southwest Asia. Boy, you talk about lighting off a torch! I was in a major battle with recruiting over this one. But I got through Lieutenant General Norman

Smith in manpower, and finally the Commandant said, "That sounds like a good idea. We're going to do it." Then I thought, well, that's kind of unfair because, if we do that, what about our corpsmen and our dental techs and religious personnel? Those guys are pretty good.

So I called the Master Chief of the Navy, Duane Bushey, and I said, "Duane, I've got a request. I don't know if you can make this happen for me, but I would really appreciate it. When we go to Saudi Arabia at Christmas, I'd like the Commandant to have some Navy promotions." Duane talked a little bit on the phone and then he said, "Well, we don't have a meritorious promotion like you guys have got, but let me see what I can do." So I told him, "The Master Chief of the Navy can do anything. I have confidence in you."

He came back later and we had fifteen meritorious promotions for the Navy. Then Jack Mooney, the personnel sergeant major, came in to me and said, "Hey Dave, that was good. But you left out the SeaBees."

So I had to go back down to the master chief with my hat in my hand and say, "You did a great job getting me those fifteen promotions, but can you get me three more? I mean, what about our SeaBees?" He did it.

We went over there and General Gray was able to promote not only our Marines meritoriously, but he was able to promote our sailors that serve with us. Out of all the things I look back on, that stands out, because I remember getting bloodied up pretty good with recruiting over that one, but I won that!

This Christmas period in Saudi Arabia was also a time of high tension and deep emotion, as Sommers later recounted the scene:

We ate dinner with them in the field, and you could feel the tension. You could feel the anticipation, because we knew we were getting close. It was a very, very emotional trip for the general and me. So when you walk the lines, and you talk to the young Marines, and you shake their hand, and you answer their questions, knowing full well that here, in a couple of weeks, that this young boy is going to be involved in some of the most intense combat that he ever dreamed possible, it's a very difficult, very emotional thing to do.

One of Sommers' habits provided a heart-warming example of his strong personal identification with "his troops" and their families:

Every trip over I carried a notebook, and as I travelled through I would ask the Marines continually, "Is there anybody you want me to talk to when I get back? Anybody you want me to call?" Well I would come home with notebooks full of names and numbers, and I would sit at home till all hours of the night, calling parents and saying, "I saw Jim over in Saudi Arabia. He's doing good. He looks healthy. He's doing this; his unit's doing this, that, and the other." I couldn't begin to tell you how many telephone calls I made to do that kind of thing.

As the date for initiating combat in Desert Storm drew near, Sommers' major preoccupation became the combat replacement companies. Working with the Headquarters personnel sergeant major and the monitor, Sommers reviewed their efforts:

> We did an awful lot of shuffling around. We had all our combat replace-
> ment companies in Saudi Arabia ready to go up and replace those MOSs
> that we anticipated taking heavy casualties. The Marines who were involv-
> ed in these companies were not happy, because they had thought that they
> were going to Saudi Arabia and join a combat unit and get up there on the
> front lines! Then they found that their reason was to be a replacement should
> we have casualties.
>
> We were extremely well prepared. We would go out of here from Head-
> quarters to the field units and say, "Okay, you've got fifteen sergeants ma-
> jor. You've got thirty first sergeants. We need this many from you to fill the
> combat replacement companies."

Following the participation of Marine aviation units in the intensive air assault on Iraq in January, 1991, Marine ground units jumped off in combat in February, in conjunction with Army and allied United Nations forces. These were hard days for the Sergeant Major of the Marine Corps and his Commandant, as Sommers later confessed:

> Probably the biggest and the most emotional for me was the feeling that
> this was happening and I wasn't right in the middle of it, being there to do
> whatever it was that I could do. It was very difficult for me and for the Com-
> mandant as well, knowing we had duties to fulfill here at Headquarters, so
> we couldn't be there.
>
> Every morning I was on the message board for the numbers of casualties
> and wounded. It was just difficult to have to sit and look at those numbers.
> When we finally punched through and got the upper hand on this thing,
> and saw that we were going to take a minimum of casualties, I could not
> tell you how elated we were. It was just a feeling that was difficult to describe!

The elation that Gray and Sommers felt was multi-faceted. Beyond the battle victory, with its limited casualties, they experienced a wave of justified pride.
The concepts, innovations, and programs which they had labored over so long
and so hard in the preceding three and a half years had borne remarkable results.
As Sommers later summarized it:

> We had focussed so hard on our capability, on training, on maneuver
> warfare, on all the things that we actually did in the liberation of Kuwait.
> To me that was a final examination. Does it work? Yes, it did work because
> this is what we did: our Marines went through that place like a knife through
> butter, and they did it because they were prepared.
>
> You saw young officers and young corporals and sergeants who, in the
> true sense of maneuver warfare, weren't afraid to turn right. If they had been
> told, "When you get in here you're going to turn left," then if they got in
> there and there was an obstacle, instead of turning left, they'd turn right.
> They didn't have to worry about getting authority from a higher command
> to do that. They understood the commander's intent, and that freed them
> to do what they had to do.

Another part of the advance training that brought good results in the Gulf crisis was the skillful integration of women in a wide variety of the Corps' functions. Sommers gave full credit to their performance in a desert combat environment:

> Our women Marines went over there quietly. They did what they were told to do. If they were part of the Force Service Support Group [FSSG], they went as a member of the FSSG. The wing went with the wing, division/division. They did the same jobs in Saudi Arabia that they did in their units back here.
>
> I didn't hear any complaints from the women. I didn't see any women that I felt were not productive, were not doing what they were supposed to be doing. I just was very proud of our women, especially when I watched some of the news and I saw some of the other women of the other forces talking about "my child is left at home and this is a problem, and I've got this difficulty with me being here and the living conditions...."

Amidst the combat preparation and later the jubilation, there had been a continuing problem which was seldom recognized by the press or the general public. But it was on Sommers' mind day and night:

> Where I was having the difficulty was with all the Marines who did not go physically to Saudi Arabia to Desert Storm. They felt that they were left out. They felt that we had two Marine Corps: those that went and those that didn't. They were worried. I got questions like, "Sergeant Major, I didn't get to go. Am I going to be left out of promotions because I didn't go to Saudi Arabia?"
>
> So I have spent a lot of time traveling around the Corps, sending the message to them that this was a total Corps effort. The young Marines that worked in Barstow eighteen-hour days, and Albany, Georgia, and Camp Pendleton, and Camp Lejeune—all these places were making Desert Storm/Desert Shield work. That operation would not have been a success if it wasn't for the people that had to remain behind to make the machine work. It's been a difficult message to get across, difficult for them to understand, but we cannot allow the Corps to be split in two....

The ability of the Marine Corps to put forth a maximum effort in a time of need was clearly demonstrated when Sommers pointed out that during Desert Shield/Desert Storm "we had 91 percent of our forces deployed around the world.... Much of it was done with Reservists. You know, you put our Reservists in an outfit, and you look and you can't tell whether they're Reservists or regular Marines." Sommers went on to give some details:

> We had 4,000 Marines in the Philippines. Throughout this evolution we went to Liberia; we went to Somalia; we had them in Korea; we got into Thailand with drug interdiction; we had Marines serving in Okinawa who are in the fourteenth and fifteenth month of a six-month tour of duty.
>
> The American public doesn't understand that, when we say "total force effort," if it was not for these Marines being extended another six months

While normal Marine Corps policy restricts the naming of installations to deceased Marines,
there was an exception made in the Middle East in 1991. "Camp D. W. Sommers" gave
recognition to the outstanding support the Sergeant Major of the Marine Corps gave to
Operation Provide Comfort. This was the humanitarian relief operation for Kurdish refugees
carried out by the 24th Marine Expeditionary Unit, Special Operations Capable. The unit
headquarters were in the camp, located in Zahko, northern Iraq.
Watercolor by Colonel P. M. Gish, U.S. Marine Corps Museums Art Collection

and past the year mark on these deployments elsewhere, that we wouldn't
have been able to rotate the forces around like we did in southwest Asia.

The massive public acclaim for the troops returning from the Gulf was symbolized by the introduction of a bill in Congress to issue separate ID cards just
to those who had been in southwest Asia (as the Gulf region was called). Given
the enormous effort he was expending to develop an understanding of "total
force effort" globally amongst all the Marines who were not part of Desert
Storm, Sommers was greatly upset at the proposal. On the first day he found
out about it, he fired off a blunt memorandum to his Commandant, "Sir, this
stinks! If this passes it will be a terrible blow to all who serve. We have traveled a lot of miles telling our Marines that Desert Storm was a total force effort.
Now, because of some merchants trying to cash in, we are driving a separation between those who went and those that did not. This is wrong!"

Sommers then rushed to see Brigadier General P. Drax Williams, who
handled Congressional liaison, to tell him that he, as Sergeant Major of the
Marine Corps, was going directly to the Congressman supporting the bill. And

he did. First by phone, and then by a strong follow-up letter, he made his point, "To separate these men and women into 'two categories' with such a bill is not fair to their families or to our Marines.... To pass [this bill] as it stands will send the wrong message...." In the end, the bill was not enacted.

While Sommers was necessarily focussed on the Middle East for about a seven-month span in 1990-91, there were fundamental, long-term issues that occupied him throughout his tenure as Sergeant Major of the Marine Corps. He was, for example, instrumental in a major improvement in the way people were selected for promotion. To cure a past pattern where there had been a promotion shortly followed by a retirement, "we changed that drastically, and now if you submit a letter of your intent to retire, you're not going to be considered for promotion. If you turn down a promotion, you will never be considered for promotion again.... You have to give us two years if you're going to get promoted."

In addition, Sommers went in to see the Commandant and told him, "I was tired of going to Recruiters School and to DI School and finding Marines who had dropped out of the school strictly because of attitude." He then asked for permission, if any Marine dropped out of either school, through his own fault or attitude ("I don't want to do this"), to flag their personnel file, and they would not be allowed to reenlist. "Now, that's a hard line, but this is it," he concluded.

Because of his deep concern for younger NCOs, Sommers reflected on a battle he fought on their behalf:

> I worked for four years to get corporals back on the drill field, because I felt we were making a distinction between our corporals and other NCOs. This term "senior NCO" or "senior staff NCO" really sticks in my craw, because if he's a corporal or a sergeant, he's an NCO. If he's a staff sergeant or a sergeant major, he's a staff noncommissioned officer. [When the] first corporal graduated from DI School at San Diego, I was just elated, because that had taken some doing. I even went down and visited the commanding generals of the recruit depots to lobby, I guess you would say, for this.

The disappointments and failures for Sommers were few, but, as his tour of duty drew towards a close, they continued to rankle in his mind:

> I'm not only disappointed, I'm almost embarrassed that we were not able to do more to open up the promotion system for our young Marines.
>
> The other area that bothers me, and that I wasn't able to fix, is our Staff Noncommissioned Officer Academy. We're still playing catch up there. We still have to shop for staff NCO instructors and good people to fill our academies.
>
> As an example, if I find somebody in the field that I want to send to Quantico to be one of the instructors, I can't order him into the academy. He's got to be ordered into Quantico and then, if we work it right, and if we get on it with the personnel officer and all that kind of thing, then the guy gets over there. And I feel that's wrong.

Furthermore, they are still taking our instructors out of our academy, those who have drill instructor experience, to supplement the Officers Candidate School during the summer months. I lost four instructors at the academy in the summer of 1991.

Sommers was no man to coast towards the end of his tour. In his final three months of duty, he managed to get to his home for only eight days.

Looking ahead to ease the start of his successor as Sergeant Major of the Marine Corps, he called General Carl Mundy, the Commandant-designate, and they had a detailed discussion of the five final nominees. Then Sommers went on, "I said to the general, 'You've got this long period to prepare to be the next Commandant. I sure would like my relief to have the same amount of time, not four days, like I had. I'd like to have a long time here to work with him.' So General Mundy made his choice, and I have been working with Sergeant Major Harold Overstreet ever since.... Similarly, Yvette has been in close touch with his wife."

As a further welcoming gesture, Sommers had prepared, for the very first time, a handsome, official warrant for the billet of Sergeant Major of the Marine Corps. It was signed by General Gray and presented as a surprise to Sergeant Major Overstreet. Then Sommers went a step further, had the name of each past Sergeant Major of the Marine Corps properly inscribed on one of the new warrants, and mailed it to each of his predecessors.

Looking back at his career, Sommers did something that came straight from his heart, "I wrote President Bush a letter for a selfish reason: to thank the country, through the Commander in Chief, for allowing me to have the opportunity to serve the country. Having done this for thirty-one years, everything that I have today, I owe to my country and to the Marine Corps."

His modesty was evident when he gave credit for the accomplishments of his tour of duty, "The reason why I feel that we've had a good four years is because of the tremendous cooperation that I've had from the staff noncommissioned officers in the field. My fellow sergeants major in the field are the ones that truly deserve the credit for the things that have happened. They've done a magnificent job. I'm just very proud to be a part of them."

Taking an overall view of his tenure in this billet, Sommers summarized:

> I found that, obviously, you're not your own person any longer. My time was taken; almost every waking hour usually dealt with something to do with the Corps. I also found that I had developed a growing closeness to Marines in *all* commands, where, as a sergeant major in the field, you're close to your own unit. It took, probably, a little bit of time because of the change in attitudes that had to be developed with this assignment.
>
> I found that, when I read the message traffic in the morning, if I had a Marine who was injured someplace, in Okinawa or maybe Camp Pendleton or anywhere, then right away I'd be on the phone trying to find out how he's doing. It was almost like you're the battalion sergeant major of the entire Marine Corps. You were doing the same things, but it took so much of your time to do them.

United States Marine Corps

Commandant of the Marine Corps

To all who shall see these presents,
Greeting:

Know Ye that reposing special Trust and Confidence
in the Patriotism, Fidelity, and Abilities of

_____

I do appoint him to serve as the _____

Sergeant Major of the Marine Corps

Given under my Hand at Headquarters
United States Marine Corps, this _____ *day*
of _____ *, in the year of*
our Lord One Thousand Nine Hundred and
_____ *, and in the* _____ *year*
of the Independence of the United States.

COMMANDANT OF THE MARINE CORPS

1991: Sommers creates a brand new warrant for the billet.

This kind of man, with these kinds of abilities, evoked a ready characterization from Gray:

> I think that Sergeant Major Sommers was just one of the greatest Marines I've ever had the privilege to serve with. He had, I believe, the unique ability to have superb interpersonal relationships with people of all ranks and grades, and not just within the Marine Corps but also within the other services.
>
> I found, in my travels around, that people had enormous respect for him. He was a straight shooter; he was a real gentleman but he could be tough; he was persuasive; and he was aided by a wonderful wife who traveled at various times with us, and who was very interested in the enlisted functions on the various bases, the clubs, the family support, and all that kind of thing.
>
> He also did his homework. He was low-key much of the time, but when he had to lean forward and be a little bit more forceful, he knew when to do that and he knew how to do that. I thought he did a super job here. He was a very talented person!
>
> As an individual, I saw him as a very, very bright, intelligent, hard-charging leader, who set the highest of example and standards for himself. And he lived by them. He had a tremendous interest in human beings, taking care of people, and all that. He went out of his way to help not only the Marines, but also people from the other services whom he came into contact with, dependent children and the like.
>
> He was first and foremost an infantryman, and very proud of that. He maintained his skills; he continued to go out and shoot and spend time in the field involved in their activities. He really had only one fault, and that was that he tried to do too much sometimes and got himself worn out, and then I had to slow him down a little bit. But, he got used to that. Between his wife and myself, we kept a pretty good rope around him!

Clearly Gray felt that Sommers was an "uncommon man." The two of them had begun their terms together, and they finished them together. Their four-year tours of duty came to a close with the sergeant major relieved on June 27, 1991, and Gray three days later. Awarded a Distinguished Service Medal at his retirement ceremonies, Sommers made the transition to civilian life, taking with him a citation from the Secretary of the Navy. It began with "exceptionally meritorious service" and concluded with "stalwart leader, imaginative thinker...exceptional ability, significant contributions, and total dedication to duty." In between came the specifics:

> As the Corps' senior enlisted Marine, Sergeant Major Sommers continually provided the Commandant with astute and timely advice across the entire spectrum of concerns involving enlisted Marines. Particularly sensitive to quality of life issues, he gathered much beneficial information from Marines and their families and skillfully elevated his concerns to the nation's civic leadership.

Sergeant Major Sommers also provided the impetus for numerous initiatives to the betterment of management and training within the Corps. He was instrumental in expanding participation of enlisted Marines on Staff Noncommissioned Officers Promotion Boards, establishing a professional reading program for staff NCOs and instituting the Basic Warrior Course. These changes provided both better methodologies and avenues for the professional growth of the enlisted Corps.

He began his terminal leave by moving to a house he and Yvette had bought in Pensacola, Florida. Still only forty-eight years old, he wanted to "relax in the sun," and then consider a civilian career—perhaps with the Non-Commissioned Officers Association. The only clear decision in his mind was that he "wanted to help our young people."

He had been a real gung-ho, multi-talented Marine in the most senior enlisted billet. How did Sommers come to this position? How did he hone these abilities? The answers lie, of course, in the cumulative effect of his earlier years. These years may, at first glance, seem to represent a stereotyped Marine career of countless changes of station and steady ascent of the ladder of rank, but in Sommers' case there was a crucial difference. The varied awards that were made to him over the years marked him as someone special.

Born in St. Louis, Missouri, on February 18, 1943, David Sommers began high school there. A family move out to the town of Lemay made travel to classes too difficult, so the young man left school after the eleventh grade. During those years he had been reading about the Marine Corps and had followed the news reports of its earlier exploits in Korea. Later on he recalled, "I had my sights set on joining the Marine Corps, and at that time, the big push by the recruiters was, 'Well, you can go in now and finish high school while you're in the Marine Corps.' So that's what I did."

His seventeenth birthday came in February, 1960, and, wasting no time, he enlisted on March 25. Flying on "a little, two-engine prop plane that stopped in every state, I think, between St. Louis and California," Sommers headed for boot camp in San Diego.

Seventeen-year-old Sommers finishes boot camp at San Diego in 1960.

LEATHERNECK photo

Memories of that were still with him, "When I look back on it, I don't think I was overly shocked at the things that happened to me in boot camp. I expected a hard time; I expected a lot of physical activity, and that's what we got. I thought recruit training would never end. In fact, once I got into it, it was kind of like I'd never been anywhere else."

The infantry training regiment at Camp Pendleton came next, and then in the fall of 1960, he was ordered to the 1st Marines there. His company gunnery sergeant had a profound effect on that very young Marine. As Sommers later recollected:

> My gunny was a big man. He must have been six-three or six-four, and probably tilted the scale at about 200-205; an old recon guy, always starched and pressed and spit-shined, always immaculate, always had an answer, always knew the right direction to go. He was a big influence on me during those early days, because he was my role model. During those days I figured that if I could, in x number of years or however long it took, just be a gunny, that's what I wanted to be. My goal was to be a company gunnery sergeant of infantry Marines, like him.

The tour of duty at Camp Pendleton brought Sommers a series of promotions: to PFC, then to lance corporal, and finally to corporal, while serving as a fire team leader and a squad leader. One unforgettable episode was his first experience under fire, "We were out at Twentynine Palms on a live fire exercise, dug in in a defensive position.... During the preparatory fires, the artillery battalion that was in support of us had the wrong data on their guns, I guess, for they started dropping shells in on our company. I lost the company mule [a small, four wheel drive, flatbed vehicle, often mounting a 106mm recoilless rifle]; they blew up the company jeep, destroyed our radios, but never hurt a man!"

In 1962, his battalion rotated as a unit to Okinawa, where it was redesignated part of the 9th Marines. During the year Sommers spent there, he had a perfect opportunity to develop his skills as a small-unit leader. As he later described it:

> During that time, I took my squad for the battalion and the 9th Regiment competitions. Today they build a squad out of the regiment to represent the regiment in the squad competition. During those days we took a squad within a platoon and we had competition all the way up the line, through the battalion, regiment, division.
>
> We were judged on our infantry skills: squad fire and maneuver, hits on target, ability to patrol, map reading, call for fire, all that sort of field work. The thing I think was unique about it was that it was my original squad. I won the battalion competition at Mount Fuji on one of the live-fire ranges up there, and then I took my squad for the competition at the regimental level. We did not win that competition, but we had a pretty good feeling when we walked away from there. We had done what we were supposed to do.

April, 1963, brought a big transition. Sommers was ordered to the Basic School (for officers) in Quantico. As he later remembered, "They found out that I had a 'Water Survival Instructor' classification. They had just finished a new exercise building with a swimming pool, so they were looking for Marines who had the swim qualification to go in there. Thus I went over and was one of the first guys to go there as an instructor. At that time one side was the swimming pool; the other side was just a gym with mats where we taught hand-to-hand combat to the lieutenants with both bayonet and K-bar knife.''

In those days NCOs had to take actual proficiency tests to qualify for promotion. Sommers was in one of the last groups to have to run this gauntlet for sergeant. As an infantryman he took a test in about everything that had anything to do with infantry, from the 106mm recoilless rifle to the flamethrower to mortars to the light machine guns. He passed and was promoted to sergeant in December, 1963.

In March of 1964, he reenlisted and forthwith a transfer came through: Hawaii. Now with the 4th Marines, Sommers later commented:

> I had a good tour in Kaneohe in that it was great training. We were always deployed. I got to spend some time aboard submarines and had a lot of rubber-boat training, as well as rappelling and all the different helicopter assaults.
>
> We had a stand-by battalion which was the "alert battalion." Any time they called for the "alert battalion," we'd have to assemble and lay out our gear on the ball field: all your skivvies [underwear] and your mess gear and sewing kits and razors and all that sort of thing. We continually looked at it as just a drill.
>
> We did that one day, laid all the gear out, then put it back in our packs, got aboard busses and went down to Pearl Harbor, got aboard ship, and never did come back to Hawaii. We went to Okinawa. We didn't know until we got there and started drawing our combat gear that we were going to Vietnam!

Arriving there in April, 1965, Sommers' battalion was hard on the heels of the first Marine combat units that had come in the preceding month. Even that early in the war, there was a recognition amongst the top Marine generals that, as Sommers phrased it:

> We weren't going to be successful in Vietnam just by assaulting the enemy; we also had to care for the people, and we had to be able to do both. I didn't know anything about this "combined action company" idea until I came in from an operation, and I got a call to report to the company commander, who told me about this special company they were forming. He said that they were looking for volunteers from each of the companies, and he felt that, out of all his squad leaders, I was one who should go from our company.
>
> I kind of evaluated it, and then I went with a group of Marines from my company who decided to join. We were the very, very first such platoon ever formed, the spearhead of that whole program as it later developed on a large scale.

The new platoon went out to a village off the northern end of the runway of the air strip at Phu Bai. There it met up with a Popular Forces (PF) platoon, "kind of a ragtag outfit that was already out there; they were the local militia." Sommers' job was to interlace his Marines amongst this unit. He put his fire team leaders in as squad leaders amongst that PF platoon, and then his other Marines were interlaced in each squad, thus forming a combined action platoon.

Sommers served as platoon commander with the Popular Forces platoon commander as his "partner." They lived in a village where their command post was located, but he also had three other hamlets he was responsible for, a population of about 3,000 people. As a combined action platoon, their mission was not only to do civic action projects during the day, but also to do the patrolling and protect the village officials. Sommers outlined their danger-filled lifestyle:

> We had our share of contact. Back during those days the Viet Cong, the guerrillas, were used to having free rein over the whole place, and now all of a sudden there's somebody in there telling them they're not going to be able to come in there any more! So we had a good number of contacts, both patrolling and ambushes.
>
> It was really a great learning experience for me, because now I was in a place where I couldn't use all the tactics I had been taught through the years. Now I had to improvise an awful lot. As an example, I learned that, as we patrolled through a village, the Viet Cong's big thing was to lay low until we went through, and then to kind of tag on to the end of us, a good ways behind us. Then they would go into where they wanted, because they knew we had already been through there.
>
> One night I figured, "Well I'm going to see if I can cash in on this." As we patrolled, I gave the order that as we went along, I wanted the patrol to lengthen slowly, to lengthen out to the point where we really looked like a long, long patrol. As we did that, I dropped off a killer team from my center which had remained very close together. Then as we continued to march on time (we did this all by the watch), I had my men close up until they got to be one tight patrol again. We were moving around and purposely making a lot of noise, except for the killer team we had dropped off. The very first night we tried this, we cleaned their clock on an ambush. The Viet Cong walked right into us!

Since Sommers' platoon didn't have a lot of the equipment that his battalion had, he had to improvise. As an example, when they would go out on patrol, they found that the noise of the local geese was "just terrible, better than a watch dog!" So Sommers went out, got a couple of farmers together, and bought geese. Then he put them out in different key locations, and plotted artillery targets near the geese. Then, if he could hear the geese squawking out there in a certain direction, he would call in 105mm artillery fire on that area.

Feeling that their function was misunderstood and inadequately supported, Sommers later noted, "As a combined action company, we were kind of looked at as sort of rogues, bandits. Nobody knew what we did. We had been taken out of the battalion; we were kind of looked on as people kicked back out to a village somewhere, while everybody else was really doing the patrolling. So our own battalion didn't think a whole lot of us."

It should be easy to understand the constant tension and pressure that fell unceasingly upon the men who volunteered for this duty—out in the bush, all alone, a few Marines in a world of Vietnamese faces. Who was friend and who was foe? What was that sound in the pitch black jungle near the patrol? A man could get hurt doing this! And Sommers did in June, 1965. Only a month after he joined the combined action company, he was wounded in an ambush. His platoon caught a lot of small arms fire and grenades, and he was "hit in the head and the shoulder, kind of all over, with shrapnel." And that brought him a Purple Heart medal.

This was followed soon after by the award of a Navy Commendation Medal with Combat "V." The citation from the Commanding General, FMFPac, Lieutenant General Victor Krulak, praised him for "demonstrating exceptional leadership ability and determination" and went on to say:

> When in close combat, particularly in night ambushes during which Sergeant Sommers demonstrated exceptional attention to detail, his squad consistently inflicted heavy casualties on the enemy and, largely through his aggressive leadership and skillful tactical planning, sustained minimal losses. Undaunted by the language barrier and adverse weather conditions of torrential rains and intense heat, Sergeant Sommers set a personal example which inspired and motivated all who served with him, to achieve goals which could not normally have been expected under existing combat conditions....

The Vietnam tour drew to a close in April, 1966, and after a brief reunion with his parents, Sommers reported in to Parris Island, where he was sent through D.I. School. The experiences that followed were weirdly memorable:

> That was during the time of McNamara's Project 100,000. This lowered the mental and physical standards for admission to the armed services, and, as a result, we had some real loony-toons coming through. We were getting some of these kids from the draft, and some of them were volunteers. Some of them were sent by judges. It was the old routine of "You either join up or you're going to jail." The intelligence level was very, very low, average-wise. You never knew what might happen.
>
> I was out on the parade deck one day and had two FBI agents come to haul off a recruit who was wanted in several states for murder and armed robbery. Another time we were getting ready for the examination, and one of the questions was "describe the American flag." This recruit made the comment to me that it had fifty stars and thirteen stripes, was red, white, and blue, but it was only colored on one side. I was really baffled as to why he would tell me that, and then he said that he never saw the other side when it was hanging in his school room! These are the kinds of answers that we used to get.
>
> On the old physical readiness test where we had to force-march the three miles, I had one of these recruits turn around and butt-stroke me with

his rifle. It caught me in the eyebrow, and I had to have some stitches taken. Then I had a kid come from the motivation platoon, and when he centered in my hatchway [door], he was at fixed bayonet and attempted to stick me with the damn bayonet. I used to have to lock the hatch at night, but the thing was that the old saying "you never let them see you sweat" was really apropos!

Those bizarre events were somewhat compensated for when Sommers' warrant for staff sergeant came through in July, 1966. By the summer of 1968, it was time to move on, and he received orders to return to Vietnam for a second tour. The trip over was an unusual one. "I went on an old-class Landing Ship, Tank (LST), a real flat-bottom bucket-nose. I had four Marines, motor transport types. It took us thirty-five days to get over to Da Nang, rocking and rolling all the way. The only mission in life I had was to make sure that each day these Marines started the trucks we had on board. I got off at Da Nang eager to hand to whomever was waiting for me all the documentation for those vehicles. That was the most miserable thirty-five days I've ever spent in my life!"

Once there, Sommers was confident that he would be assigned to his preferred duty, a rifle outfit:

When I reported in to the 7th Marines, it was to Sergeant Major Puckett. I figured that I'd be going out to one of the battalions in the field, but he told me I would be in the headquarters company. Then he added, to my astonishment, "You're going to be the career planner and also the company gunny. They're joint duties."

As a company gunny, I was responsible for the security of the regimental headquarters, and the patrolling, and all the defensive positions, and the fields of fires. But, during the day, along with those things, I was also looking at personnel attrition, who was getting out, and who was rotating, all the responsibilities that a career planner had. It was a very interesting tour of duty, but I hated every minute of it!

One of the good things, though, was serving under Sergeant Major Puckett. He became another role model for me. He was very, very calm, not excitable, never heard the man use one word of profanity, never in any situation.... He'd come down to our tent sometimes, want to go on patrol with one of the units, and then he would go out with them.... He was always an individual that you could go to and get a straight answer.

Puckett, in later years, well remembered Sommers as "an outstanding young staff sergeant then."

The headquarters company received plenty of incoming fire. As Sommers subsequently noted:

Hill 55 is where we were located, right at the corner of Dodge City, Arizona country. We were pretty well sitting ducks most of the time. It was kind of a standard thing...almost like a game: they (This was North Vietnamese now; this wasn't Viet Cong.) would probe the lines and see how close they could get. They were using a lot of the old "lob bombs" and 122mm rockets.

They would recover the bombs that we had dropped that didn't ignite, and they would use a detonating device on them, put them on a bamboo sled, and then they would use a charge to catapult these bombs back up the hill. They weren't good for a lot of long-range targets, but they were very effective on us! So we kind of named them "lob bombs." Always about the same time every night, they'd start throwing the rockets in.

I bunked with two guys and we were sitting in our "hooch" one night. It had been raining (typical Vietnam—had been raining and raining and raining), and we had all been on patrols, and we'd come back in. We're sitting there having a beer (a little "stand down" time) and we start taking incoming fire. Our first thought was, "Let's move!" Our little "hooch" was right up on the line. So we went out to jump in our protective bunker, but in our absence, it had filled up completely with water.

It was so dark, you couldn't see at all, and the three of us scrambled into this bunker. It was a deep one, and there we were, bouncing around, going down and then coming up for air. It was hilarious! And every time a rocket would hit, you could feel the impact in the water. It would vibrate your whole body. I don't know whether we were better off in the bunker or the "hooch"....

Then there was the executive officer [XO] of our regiment. Any time he wanted to go anywhere, we'd mount the jeep, and I'd put a machine gun on the back. Invariably, he would want to go right down the middle of Arizona country, and it would be the driver, the XO, and me on the back with a machine gun. The only fire we ever took, luckily for us, was sniper rounds. But we would go right down the middle; it was almost like a game to see if we could make it. The signature that you would leave going down that old, dusty road in a jeep could be seen for miles. Why we never hit a mine and why they never waxed [killed] us is beyond me. As I look back on it, it's a good thing I was young and carefree then!

Sommers' overall performance brought him his second Navy Commendation Medal from the Secretary of the Navy. The citation first noted that he "was instrumental in the regiment maintaining a high reenlistment rate," and went on to add:

Serving additionally as a platoon sergeant with the reaction force, he ably trained and rapidly molded his men into an effective fighting force. When the regiment was displaced to a new area of operation in August, 1968, Staff Sergeant Sommers ably supervised the expeditious construction of living and working areas and ensured the continuous efficiency of his command. As a result of his diligent and resourceful efforts, the operational effectiveness of his unit was greatly enhanced....

In May, 1969, Sommers rotated back to the States, headed for D.I. duty at Parris Island again. Passing the qualifying tests, both mental and physical, he started his work as a senior D.I. This gave him an opportunity which he quickly seized. "Every platoon that I worked I would either have one new D.I. or most of the time I'd have two new ones assigned to me. I enjoyed a very good reputation as a senior drill instructor, especially coming back my second time. I really seemed to do things a lot easier than I did the first time." That's what his superiors thought, too, and a Navy Achievement Medal was forthcoming, with a citation signed by the Commandant of the Marine Corps, General Leonard Chapman. It said in part:

> ...he contributed greatly to the effective and efficient operations of his company. His work as a drill instructor was characterized by enthusiasm, diligence, perseverance, conscientiousness, and dedication. He won every drill competition he participated in during his tour of duty, and received repeated outstanding evaluations on his performance with each platoon he had under his command. His recruits consistently displayed the highest order of military bearing and professional competence, and were completely prepared to assume their duties as Marines.
>
> In addition to his superior training of recruits, he was constantly used for training new drill instructors. His precise and proper military manner, and his impressively immaculate and poised appearance had a direct influence on all who associated with him, and made him a model the Marine Corps can well be proud of. Due to his superior qualities and his exceptional knowledge of recruit training, he was chosen above his peers to be an instructor at a Drill Instructors School....

During that time of total immersion in training recruits, Sommers came to know the third man who served as one of his role models. This was Major General Robert Barrow, the depot commander at Parris Island. What made an indelible impression on Sommers was that Barrow "always had a handle on things; he could get his point across and get the job done. You would do things for him because he was the kind of person you wanted to work for. He was an inspirational leader."

Something that the official records do not reveal for this tour of duty was a nickname that Sommers acquired: "Ambush." He must have been lying in wait for any wise guy who got out of line.... This was also a time for exciting developments in his personal life. A lively young lance corporal from Chicago named Yvette Valentine was serving then at Parris Island. Visiting a friend's home there, Sommers met her and the attraction was mutual. They were married on September 5, 1970. Two months later he made gunnery sergeant, and then Yvette left the Corps. "At that time you were not allowed to be pregnant and remain in the Marine Corps. Things sure have changed since then!" Yvette later reflected with a wry smile. Thus their only child, Kenneth, was born in June, 1971.

With Sommers' promotion he was assigned to the prestigious position of drill master of the D.I. School. While there, he wrote a manual of arms to be used with the M-16 rifle. "I did that jointly with my counterpart from San Diego, and that was kind of a neat way to do it. Headquarters Marine Corps sent us a big stack of pictures, and they said, 'Here's where we want the rifle to be. Write a manual to get it there.' So we did this jointly between San Diego and me, mailed a lot of correspondence back and forth."

Again he had performed in an outstanding manner, and another Navy Achievement Medal was awarded to him, enabling him to put a Gold Star on his ribbon for the first one:

> ...Gunnery Sergeant Sommers, an extremely competent and resourceful leader, was responsible for and directly supervised the successful training of over a thousand recruits while serving with the 2d Recruit Training Battalion. Because of his broad knowledge of recruit training and professional excellence, he was assigned to Drill Instructors School in November, 1970, where he instructed and later supervised the training of prospective drill instructors. A very versatile staff noncommissioned officer, he rapidly progressed from general military subjects instructor to drillmaster of the Drill Instructor School.
>
> Among his many accomplishments as drillmaster, he made significant contributions to Marine Corps efforts to develop a manual of arms for the M-16 rifle.... Additionally, he designed instructional materials to be used by the drill instructors of the recruit training regiment to prepare themselves to teach recruits the M-16 manual of arms....

A whole new world then opened up for the gunnery sergeant when he was ordered to Washington in December, 1973. There he was enrolled for two months in the Marine Security Guard School (then adjacent to Headquarters in the suburb of Arlington, Virginia). Completing the course of instruction, he was sent to be NCO In Charge (NCOIC) of the Marine Detachment at the American Embassy in Caracas, Venezuela. It was "like being a mini-battalion commander."

As NCOIC, Sommers was responsible for the living conditions of his Marines, for their diet, the mess hall, financial accounts, and the security—for everything dealing with the Marines and the security of the embassy. These were unsettled times in Venezuela:

> It was during the years when they were undergoing nationalization, and they were in the process of retaking back the claims of all the American oil companies that were down there. There was also a third political party coming on line during those years, so there were enough problems in Venezuela, political problems, that made duty interesting. As an example, we had our Marine vehicle pipe bombed one night. And we had the embassy strafed, had numerous demonstrations. They would ride by with automatic weapons and crank off a few rounds at the embassy and that sort of thing, just enough to keep you on your toes!

Yvette accompanied her husband on this tour, and her comment on Venezuela focused on a little family battle, "He has a terrible taste in civilian clothing; I tried to get him into something a little more modern in style, but it was a long time before I could get rid of those old suits." Sommers took it casually, "I never had to worry about it; I always had a uniform to wear."

August, 1975, brought a return to the Marine Security Guard School in Arlington, and also his promotion to master sergeant. Sommers immediately applied for redesignation as a first sergeant. That warrant came through in 1976, although he lost his time in grade seniority, and had to start all over with the new date of rank.

Life at home with Yvette was too good to last, and orders for an unaccompanied transfer overseas arrived in August, 1977. A family dialogue ensued: "I've got to go overseas. Where do you want to live?" "Well, I don't want to live here, I'd like to go to South Dakota or North Dakota, but it's cold. Arizona's nice and hot. My sister lives there. That's a good place." So off to Tucson she went, and off to Okinawa he went.

Reporting in, he was assigned to an outfit with the unwieldy title of first sergeant, Headquarters and Service Company, 9th Engineer Support Battalion, 3d Force Service Support Group. As Sommers described it:

> We had the combat engineers, who have all the light equipment, and they're the guys who breach the mine fields, and lay the mine fields and the barbed wire, and that sort of thing. Then we had the force engineers who had all the heavy junk, all the tractors and the big road-graders. In my battalion, we could do just about anything. We could make fresh water or we could put up a bridge. We could make a road; we could build a building; we did plumbing; we did electricity. We had the guys that could make everything happen that needs to happen to build a headquarters, or a bunker complex, or put in an airfield, or any of that sort of thing. Then we had a company which was all the carpenters. We used to call them the "wood-butchers."
>
> I went through three company commanders in a year. When I first got there I had one who rotated right out, and they didn't have a replacement for him. So they brought in a young lieutenant, an outstanding young guy who had, however, absolutely no background in the area of command and had very little idea of what a company CO was supposed to do. We talked a lot! I admired him because he knew that he needed help and was willing to listen to me. He learned quickly, and in a few months he became an effective CO.

Ordered back to Camp Pendleton in August, 1978, Sommers went to another unit with a highly distinctive name, the Marine Corps Tactical Systems Support Activity [MCTSSA]. There he began one more learning experience:

> I didn't know what the hell MCTSSA was; I'd never heard of it. I found that it was a research and development unit. I learned a lot in there; we did everything! I helped develop a new amphibious tractor program. We spent a lot of time working on that, developing all the fire suppression systems, and the turret for the .50 caliber machine gun, and all the things that it takes to put a new tractor together.
>
> We had a number of different units; a lot of civilian contractors belonged to MCTSSA. But my main job there was that of being a first sergeant. It was a unique outfit in that it had a lot of technicians: radio operators, radar guys, amtrackers. It was really a conglomeration of MOSs. There were very few privates and PFCs; most of them were NCOs. So it presented some

different and unique challenges; keeping everybody reminded that they were in the Marine Corps was a big challenge. As a first sergeant, my normal paperwork was non-judicial punishments, guard rosters, reports, unit diaries, and all that sort of thing. So I learned a little bit about the support side of things, and that there are Marines doing other things than those in infantry and engineers.

During this tour of duty, the brigadier general in charge of MCTSSA, Alfred Gray, was 3,000 miles away at the Development Center in Quantico. Like any good supervisor, he travelled out to California frequently to check up on his far-flung unit. And that's how Gray, the future Commandant, first became acquainted with David Sommers.

Promotion to sergeant major came in October, 1980, and Sommers knew exactly what he really wanted to do, "I called up Headquarters when I made sergeant major, to find out where I was going to go. I wanted to move over to the 1st Division. Unbeknownst to me, the regimental sergeant major at the recruit depot in San Diego (who had been on the drill field with me at Parris Island) had already talked to 'Crow' Crawford, and he had already talked to the monitor. So they already had my assignment set for San Diego. Those two rascals, between them, they tried to make me think it was my choice to go to San Diego, but they had that thing figured out before I even called!"

When he broke the news to Yvette, she "just gave him one of those looks that said 'not again?' " It was, however, an enjoyable tour of duty. He had begun his own career there 20 years earlier; this was his third time at a recruit depot, and he was superbly qualified to serve there. "I felt very well prepared."

Nevertheless it was not easy:

> I wound up really spending more hours on duty, and I learned very quickly that it's harder to keep drill instructors out of trouble and to keep track of them than it was the recruits. Recruits are very easy to control, but, as battalion sergeant major, all my attention was devoted to the drill instructors: not only their performance of duty, and the way they conducted themselves, but with their welfare as well. They were, for the most part, very young and full of energy. They had one goal in mind, and that was to make their recruit platoon the very best possible Marines they could. In doing that, sometimes they got a little over-zealous and—without even knowing it sometimes—could violate the Standard Operation Procedure [SOP].
>
> Part of the solution was to be around. I found that, rather than hold a lot of meetings, I'd go in very early in the morning; I'd be in the mess hall for breakfast. My battalion commander and I used to take turns. At least one night a week we'd stay very late or we'd stay there over night. That way we'd walk around and visit the D.I.s during the recruits' free time. Then, after Taps, we'd walk around and talk to them. We really got to know them better; they were able to talk to us, and it worked out well. I had a lot of good people in that battalion.

Whether it's Parris Island in 1970 (left) or San Diego in 1980 (right), Sommers is right at home in his D.I.'s campaign hat.

P.I. photo: Sommers

Again, the quality of his effort was recognized. There was a third award of a Navy Commendation Medal. That citation was signed on behalf of the Secretary of the Navy by an old acquaintance, General Barrow, now the Commandant of the Marine Corps. It praised Sommers for:

> Exhibiting genuine personal concern for the proper training and welfare of the Marines under his cognizance, he provided innovative resolutions to their problems, and contributed significantly to the successful accomplishment of his battalion's mission. Displaying superior leadership, professional ability, and initiative, he inspired all who observed him and was an example for others to emulate.
>
> Through his expertise, diligent efforts, and remarkable enthusiasm, he established a high degree of esprit and dedication within his unit. In addition, he was twice selected to be senior enlisted member on a Headquarters Marine Corps directed drill instructor screening team, and received a Letter of Appreciation from the regimental commander....

It was back to a field unit in June, 1982, when he was transferred to be a battalion sergeant major in the 10th Marines, 2d Division, at Camp Lejeune. One of that artillery regiment's batteries was sent to Lebanon, where the Marines faced a tense and volatile situation in Beirut. This gave Sommers a classic opportunity to apply the old Marine maxim, "A good NCO always takes care of his troops":

> Like so many times when we sent out a battery to join in a unit for a "float," [Marine units detached from their base and put aboard ships for flexible deployment, often in danger zones] they were sort of looked at as kind of bastard children. Nobody over there really laid claim to them except when they needed them; they didn't really get a whole lot of attention or all that great support.
>
> So one of the things I did while I was there in Lejeune was that I kept in very close contact with their first sergeant. I would do things like package up equipment they wanted; anything our battalion got back in the States, that battery got in Beirut. I cashed in a few markers from people I knew, and I got these things flown over to Beirut and delivered to the battery.
>
> General Gray was my division commander, and I also knew, through experience, how the meritorious promotion system worked and how the numbers system worked. So I made sure our battery over in Beirut got their share of meritorious promotions (and it probably wasn't done as legally as it should have been done).

Besides these special priorities, Sommers naturally carried on his normal daily duties, "My battalion commanders allowed me to do all the enlisted assignments. I literally got to run the enlisted Marines. I took care of it completely."

"Taking care," in his nature, meant concern for and involvement in the pressing problems of any of his enlisted personnel. "Crow" Crawford later sketched an example of this fundamental trait of Sommers, "He was kind of a quiet guy; he reminded me of a person who, if he's in a room with 100 people, you'd never know that he's in there. But very proficient. What I liked about him was the way he took care of his Marines. Yes he did! I can recall a request where he really gave such strong support to this one individual." Sommers continued the story:

> This was a corporal, a really good Marine, and he had been diagnosed as having epilepsy. They put him in front of a Medical Board, and they said the standard thing, "Okay, you're going out." The kid didn't want to go out. He was really a fine, young, hard-charging Marine, with a wife and baby.
>
> I kept meeting a dead end. So I got on the hook, and I called Crow. I said, "I need your help here. This guy is worth fighting for. He's worth salvaging." Crow answered, "Let me see what I can do." I don't know whose idea it was, but I wound up by sending him to Washington to see Crow. He reported in there and Crow walked him around and built up his case. The bottom line was, after all the homework was done, we put the kid in front of another board, and they retained him. They changed his MOS to photographer, and he went to the 2d Division, a staff sergeant doing one hell of a fine job.

By that time his senior commanding officers seemed to be almost in a rhythm of recommending Sommers for an award on every tour of duty. Now Gray took the initiative (which he would remember three and a half years later as Commandant) to have him awarded a Meritorious Service Medal. The citation, on behalf of the President, referred to:

...his dogged determination in matters pertaining to troop welfare and morale, and his unyielding demand for excellence, helped hone the enlisted Marines of the battalion to a professional level that was second to none.

His demonstrated leadership, professional competence, and vast expertise contributed to the successful conduct of four separate deployments and gained the admiration and respect of all who served with him....

Tucked into Sommers' citation was one very illuminating phrase, "four separate deployments." Here was a clear confirmation of what it meant to be battle-ready in the New, New Breed. In a single fifteen-month span, his outfit had deployed four times from Camp Lejeune for combat exercises. Upon his return in November, 1983, from the last of these, where his battalion had participated in NATO maneuvers in Denmark, England, and Germany, Sommers received a phone call from Robert Cleary, then Sergeant Major of the Marine Corps.

It proved to be another blow to any dream he and Yvette might have had to settle down for a long while in one home. He was to go to Quantico as soon as possible, Cleary told him. When Sommers reported the news to his wife, she was distressed, and he observed:

That was kind of an interesting development. Her perspective was much different, for we had just bought this home. She had lived in it about eleven months; I had, through deployments, lived in it off and on, but not very much. When we had bought the house, we figured that nobody ever leaves a division under three years, so "We're good for at least three years here." But in about fifteen months, I got the new orders, and Cleary wanted me in Quantico before Christmas. But after all the rushing around I did to get to the Basic School, everybody there was gone on Christmas leave. I turned right around and drove back home and stayed there for another two weeks.

When he went back to Quantico, he had been told by Cleary that he was going to be there for six months, and the powers that be were going to decide whether they really wanted or needed a sergeant major at the Basic School. Sommers continued:

Nobody could tell me a whole lot about what I was supposed to be doing. When you are a sergeant major, you usually have enlisted Marines. I found that I had nothing but lieutenants. The general told me, "These lieutenants are now your troops." So I start teaching, twenty-three hours per student company. I taught all the drill and ceremony myself, physically got up and taught it, including the sword manual.

I also got involved with the chief of tactics, and thus I would be out in the field whenever I could. I'd go to the "Three-Day War," as we called it, and act as the sergeant major of the battalion under the chief of tactics as the battalion commander. In order for the lieutenants to get the right ideas, I did everything from patrol the lines—walk to check machine gun emplacements, check fighting holes, check patrol routes—to everything else that you would do as a battalion sergeant major.

Quantico, 1984: The sergeant major with lieutenants graduating from the Basic School.
LEATHERNECK *photo*

Sommers was also responsible for classroom work. For the first fifteen minutes of every drill class he used to teach leadership, saying, "Okay, Lieutenants, today I'm going to tell you a little bit about Request Mast. You know about it in the way they told you in your previous classrooms. Now let me tell you a little bit about Request Mast when you actually go to a platoon, and you've got to deal with your first sergeant and your battalion sergeant major and your battalion commander."

It was a familiar story at the end of this tour of duty: another Meritorious Service Medal from another Commandant, General Paul X. Kelley:

> ...As the primary drill and ceremonies instructor, he instructed eighteen student companies, devoting many personal hours coordinating parades and ceremonies. He single-handedly designed and supervised the renovation of the School's parade deck, and initiated the acquisition of a complete set of state flags for display. He enhanced the officer students' understanding of the staff noncommissioned officer/officer relationship, through the development of a leadership discussion panel and numerous training exercises....

New orders arrived in July, 1985, giving Sommers another complex designation—sergeant major of the Marine Corps Air-Ground Combat Center and the 7th Marine Amphibious Brigade (MAB) at Twentynine Palms, California. He later described that billet with a happy smile:

> That was a great tour of duty for me. In fact, I have to say that it kind of culminated all the things that I had learned over the years, because now, on one side, I'm the base sergeant major of the Combat Center; my other hat is the sergeant major of the 7th Amphibious Brigade. I had all the

The sergeant major amidst the desert rocks and sands at Twentynine Palms in 1986.
Sommers photo

responsibility for all the house-keeping chores of a base sergeant major: dealing with housing, traffic court, family problems, club systems, Special Services problems, Request Mast to the commanding general, etc. On the other side, I had all the operational commitments that a division sergeant major would have when it comes to operations, deployments, getting units ready, habitability inspections: all the things of a tactical nature.

I worked for two superb generals. One of them was General Ernie Cook [Major General Ernest Cook] who wrote me up for the Legion of Merit. I'd have to say that he was probably one of the finest men I've ever met. For working with him and for him, I should have paid him to learn the things that I absorbed from him! I was really set back when I got that Legion of Merit. Knowing that General Cook, a man of his caliber, felt that my performance rated that, I was just really taken aback.

The Legion of Merit, very rarely awarded to enlisted personnel, came with this citation from the Secretary of the Navy, James Webb, himself a highly decorated former Marine officer in Vietnam:

> ...Responsible for the general welfare, morale, and readiness of over 8,500 sailors and Marines, and their over 5,000 dependents living in a remote area, Sergeant Major Sommers' initiative, ingenuity, and untiring selflessness established a new and higher standard of excellence for sergeants major. He displayed exceptional judgement, insight, and devotion in caring for military members and their families, and gave generously of his off-duty time as a volunteer counsellor at the Family Services Center.
>
> Focusing on the vital need for noncommissioned officers' training, he spearheaded the revitalization and expansion of the Marine Corps Air Ground Combat Center and 7th Marine Amphibious Brigade Noncommissioned Officers School. Not only active in garrison, Sergeant Major Sommers participated in eight MAB-sized exercises and Exercise Gallant Eagle 86. In austere conditions, often involving intense heat and personal discomfort, he was ever-present in the field among his sailors and Marines, inspiring them by his example and ensuring their general welfare....

Once more, it was time to move, and Sommers was assigned back to Quantico to become the first enlisted director of the Staff NCO Academy there in June, 1987. This was not his first choice:

> I did not want to go. I had, once again, only been on a tour (at the Combat Center) for approximately eighteen months. We had just gotten settled in. Cleary and I really had some heated conversations over my going to be the director of that academy. I didn't want to go because I finally had a tactical unit. I was in an amphibious brigade, and I was doing the deployments. We were a "fly-away" brigade. If there was going to be something happening, then we were going to be there, as the Maritime Prepositioned Shipping [MPS] brigade.
>
> I thought that the idea of this academy was great; it was a long time overdue, and a lot of effort had gone into making it happen. But I did not want to go, because I had worked so hard to get back to an infantry unit. Now I was there, and now I was having to leave. Plus, there was the family aspect. I looked at the number of times that we had moved, every two years since 1973, and our last three moves had been under eighteen months. Financially we were devastated. We lost our house; we lost our savings; our kid had been bounced back and forth; Yvette had lost jobs because of my frequent transfers.

These frank reactions pinpoint a harsh fact of life for many Marine families: severe financial pressures. Sommers' case was hardly unique, and he spelled out the circumstances with a touching poignancy:

> We had to pay to sell our former house in Jacksonville by Camp Lejeune. Then there was the amount of money that it had taken for us to move and to reestablish a household in California. We figured that we would

finally recover from it in about three years. After that we'd be kind of ready to do it again. But we didn't have a chance to recover from it.

We couldn't sell the house in Jacksonville, because there were so many people getting orders to leave there, and the housing market was flooded. So we tried to rent it for quite a while, but we had to rent it with a negative cash flow. These are just some of the obvious reasons why I did not want to go. They were very selfish reasons but, having been bounced around under eighteen months for the last few stations, we just didn't have time to recover financially.

But, as a Marine, he went where he was ordered, with Yvette and Kenneth also pulling up stakes once again. In Quantico, Sommers started to dig in to learn his new assignment. A class from the Selected Marine Corps Reserve (the "Ready Reserves") was there for their annual training duty, while the new director was "still in the process of checking in. I really didn't have a chance to get my feet on the ground." This was because his phone rang on June 18, 1987:

It was General Gray. He made a lot of small talk about how the classes were going. I said, "They're doing fine." He went on, "You know I'm going to be the Commandant." I answered, "Yes, sir. I think it's just fantastic." Then he kind of laid it on me; he announced, "Well, you're going to be my sergeant major. I'll see you tomorrow morning." I was sitting there in this room, having just received the call, and still having a very clouded head from just arriving in Quantico to begin with.

We had just gone through all the pomp and circumstance about passing the flag, and about the first time an enlisted man was now the director and all the attendant publicity. My head was still ringing from all that, and now General Gray had told me that I'm going to be his sergeant major and be the Sergeant Major of the Marine Corps. I just completely lost it; I was speechless!

And that was the way that all of the training, all of the awards, and all of the personal abilities finally brought Dave Sommers to be the "Uncommon Man" of the New, New Breed.

Chapter 13

CONCLUSION

Eleven men, spanning a third of a century—they were remarkable men with striking similarities yet with individual differences.

Perhaps the most obvious similarity was their ability to rise above their contemporaries to the pinnacle of enlisted rank. Some 600,000 Marines served in World War II, and out of that huge number, just six men went on to be the Sergeant Major of the Marine Corps. Another 400,000 Marines served in Korea and 800,000 in Vietnam, and from them just five men emerged to climb to the peak. That achievement was a confirmation of the outstanding talent, total dedication, and inner drive that characterized those men.

Not one of these men went past high school, and several never even finished that. They came from modest backgrounds, often from small towns, and were frequently rough characters in their youth. Thus their achievements were due solely to the individual personal abilities which they developed over the years.

Another common thread was their capacity throughout their careers for dealing skillfully and effectively with people—people of all types: an unruly recruit in boot camp, a bumbling private, a staff sergeant with a family problem,

In a reunion at FMFLant, Norfolk, Virginia in November, 1991, five Sergeants Major of the Marine Corps totalled up their 157 years of active duty. Left to right: Crawford, Sommers, Overstreet, Cleary, and McHugh.

Photo by Gayle Earley

salty old-time sergeants major, young college-graduate lieutenants, and bevies of senior generals. These diverse relationships molded all of them, so that they developed a sixth sense of when to push and when to lay back, when to come down hard on someone and when to listen sympathetically and act supportively.

Those eleven men, of course, gave the principal part of their lives as career Marines. This meant that all of them had seen service "in every clime and place" (as the Marine Corps Hymn says), whether in garrison duty or combat, and this had developed far-reaching relationships with wide cross-sections of both enlisted and commissioned Marines. It may be surprising to outsiders to realize how often the paths of these men intersected, "I served under him," "I knew him when he was a sharp young NCO on his way up," "We always used to hear stories about...." It's one of the crucial benefits of being around for thirty years in a military organization that is small compared to the other services.

Once they reached the top, those eleven "uncommon men" all evinced an ability to adapt. When they arrived at Headquarters, it was a new world of board meetings, policy directives, generals everywhere, and non-stop phone calls, letters, and trips. They more than survived in this rarified atmosphere. They demonstrated that they had grown through the years, broadened their talents, and developed their personalities. Thus they were able to maintain a pattern of representing forcefully at that level the interests of their enlisted personnel.

Their continuing effectiveness was due to three fundamental factors. First, they were all exceptionally able men. Second, they had accumulated decades of experience in knowing whom to talk to, how to get things done, and how to get them done right. Third, they benefited from a critical element which was more highly developed and broadly recognized in the Corps than in the other services. Following the Marine lead, each military service established "The Senior Enlisted Man" position, but his status in the Corps was truly special.

The incumbent's incessant trips bring him into personal contact with enormous numbers of enlisted personnel of all ranks in every corner of the globe. His long career has built a widespread network of friends, contacts, and peer relationships. His record in war and peace, as symbolized by the galaxy of ribbons on his uniform, is plain for all to see, and commands respect.

Most important of all, probably, is the intimate association with the Commandant. It is truly a unique relationship. When he sees someone who is doing a poor job, or something which is going well, he only has to step into the Commandant's office for a comment, or mention it to him on a plane trip, and things happen.

There have been other similar elements in the sergeants major. In a world where military life has become increasingly diversified and technically specialized, the heart of the Corps remains the basic infantryman. It is no coincidence that the men the Commandants have chosen have all served with distinction in combat and have remained infantrymen at heart. Most of them had served as drill instructors, and every one had been a rifleman.

Another asset has been the deep attachment the sergeants major have felt for particular men (and the units) with whom they have served. There are precise memories of names and dates and places which they can call up with extraordinary clarity and, sometimes, deep emotion.

One final similarity must be noted. The success of all these men, the praises heaped upon them, the superior qualities attributed to them—may seem out of balance, a fanciful dream of improbable, indiscriminate hero worship. The facts, however, fully support this admiration. Their records of accomplishment are there for all to see. Others knew them in every conceivable circumstance, and their affection and respect are evident.

Most compelling are the views of their Commandants. Here are men with thirty-five years of active duty who have served with literally hundreds of NCOs, and who know first-hand the challenge of leading a Corps of several hundred thousand heterogeneous people. From an outstanding group, each Commandant chose the one man he felt was the best. Those commanding generals do not mince words, shade the truth, or undeservedly compliment anyone. Yet they too are unanimous. The sergeant major was (and is), in spirit and in influence, the "Enlisted Man's General."

Any overall evaluation of the Sergeants Major of the Marine Corps must inevitably look at the differences between them. One difference is the length of their tour of duty in that billet. The recent practice has been for the man to come aboard with a new Commandant, serve with him for his four-year term, and then retire with him, as Crow Crawford, Bob Cleary, and Dave Sommers did. From Frank Rauber to John Massaro (except for Clint Puckett) the sergeants major served with two different Commandants. The shortest tour was Henry Black's, less than two years.

There has been an evolution in base pay over the years, but the scale of this change is unexpected. Bill Bestwick drew $319.80 a month, while Dave Sommers received $3280.50, a 10-fold increase. And the gap would be still wider if "subsistence allowance" (for food) and "quarters allowance" (for housing) were added in.

In another area there have been radical alterations in enlisted professional education. Whether it is D.I. School or First Sergeants School, Bill Bestwick's successors have had training opportunities far beyond those available in the "Old Corps."

The fundamental differences in the sergeants major have naturally been in their temperaments and styles. As the preceding chapters have indicated, they all had the requisite talent and motivation, but these qualities were applied in widely varying ways. A few were administrators or organizational managers. Some were exceptionally quiet, modest, and restrained; others were gregarious, outgoing, colorful, and articulate. One or two were studious; the others were not. Some were hard-nosed and direct, while others adopted a softer approach. Their physical appearances varied as widely as their personalities, from big, tall, and impressive to ordinary looking.

The role of the sergeant major evolved over the years. It was natural that everything was tentative when Bill Bestwick took over as the pioneer. After all, no such function had ever existed before in the American military. Originally the billet was placed in the Office of the Chief of Staff; later it was transferred to the Office of the Commandant. It is unclear how close Bestwick's personal relationship was to the Commandant. Travel has increased; speeches have multiplied; the phone calls and letters have grown exponentially. So has the individual authority of the Sergeant Major of the Marine Corps. He now makes his own decisions, without reference to the Commandant or any other officer at Headquarters, on a variety of matters which are far beyond the scope of his earliest predecessors.

The attitude of the Commandant has been crucial to the role of his sergeant major. Although the eleven men and their functions have varied, the results have been productive because all the Commandants, with minute exceptions, have had a supportive view of the importance of the billet.

General Wallace Greene (1964-1967): "I think it was a very wise and good action when General Pate decided to set this billet up. I think from the moment it was filled, all through the years, the individual in the billet did a great deal, a tremendous amount, of good things for the Marine Corps. I think it was a very fine billet, a very good idea, and I would certainly credit General Pate and his staff for setting it up."

General Leonard Chapman (1968-1971): "Well, I think it's priceless. Yes, it is good. It's a tremendous advantage to the Marine Corps to have the top enlisted man right there, advising the Commandant. That's what he does, he makes recommendations, gives advice, carries out policies."

General Louis Wilson (1975-1979): "I think it's a great idea; a tremendous idea, one which we should never give up as the top of the pyramid of enlisted personnel. How the sergeant major is used, I think, is simply up to each Commandant. No Commandant can be constricted by set rules as to how he's going to use anybody. Therefore it comes down to being a matter of judgement." Wilson went on to elaborate:

> I think we have to be careful in selecting an NCO who is known as an iconoclast: that is, an NCO who is "different." You've got to be careful about that, because people have a tendency to follow a direction in which they think a future for their promotion lies. We have to be careful about this, because we don't want a group in which every individual sets out to be "different": "Maybe I can be selected because I did such and such."
>
> This is not to say that in war he shouldn't be a leader. Obviously he should have combat decorations. Nevertheless, don't be "different." You've got to fit sort of within the mold, I think. You want a typical NCO, known as representing the whole Marine Corps, to be the sergeant major, and, therefore, to be a role model for young Marines everywhere.
>
> This is one reason that I did not want a personal selection by the Commandant to override what would, in effect, be a board to select from overall commands. In other words, if the word went out that, in order to be Sergeant

Major of the Marine Corps you had to work previously for the Commandant, I did not want that.

If I really were tasked to write a job description for the sergeant major today, I would have to say, basically, his job is to do what the Commandant wants him to do. It has to be a personal relationship, one in which the Commandant has to feel confident that, to the rest of the command, the sergeant major is regarded as knowledgeable. Because once the command feels he's a spy, he loses (I think) his effectiveness.

In summary, Wilson felt that the Sergeant Major of the Marine Corps was a job to which all enlisted Marines should aspire, very much as officers should to be the Commandant. Anyone who did not aim for that in his earlier years was not a real professional. Wilson concluded that once a man was chosen for that billet, it was up to the Commandant to make sure that it was a job with dignity and prestige, where it was recognized that the man was indeed the senior enlisted man in the Corps.

General Robert Barrow (1979-1983):

"I believe that the relationship of any sergeant major with his commanding officer or commanding general must necessarily be a close and personal one. They must be in harmony; they must be able to almost read one another's thoughts; there has to be a very high degree of mutual respect and, hopefully, mutual admiration. If it's like that, it is a great and good thing to see in action. You can never predict with any certainty at all, that you, in fact, will have that kind of relationship when you pick one. Not everyone even gets a chance to pick one; a lot of commanding officers get one assigned."

General Paul X. Kelley (1983-1987):

"I think the overall usefulness will depend entirely upon the importance that the Commandant himself puts on it. I must admit that I have seen a very spotty performance in this area. I have seen Commandants who didn't pay a lot of attention, didn't give easy access to their sergeants major. It may have been personalities, or it may have been just their styles. My comments are that the best, most effective sergeants major I have seen are the ones who have had easy access to their boss, unimpeded access. Cleary had that with me. I'm sure the other successful ones did too, and there were a lot of them who were very successful."

Kelley added that the key requirement for the two men was "rapport" and "making sure that everybody understands that he's part of your team." This meant "making sure that the staff NCOs understand that he does have access to you, that they do have a pipeline, and that we together participate whenever possible in their activities." There was a proviso, however, for Kelley made clear that the Sergeant Major of the Marine Corps could just "sit down there and answer gripes from staff NCOs, but that's really not what he's there for. He is there to provide the Commandant, and only the Commandant, with recommendations on how best to preserve the morale and the esprit and the other things dealing with our Corps."

General Alfred Gray (1987-1991) made this comment:

> I think the billet of the Sergeant Major of the Marine Corps, within the structure of our Corps, is a crucial billet. I think that it really facilitates doing what must be done: providing the proper kind of guidance and leadership to the Corps. It's a great channel of communication for the Commandant. It's a channel for getting things done. It's something that provides a focal point which other young Marines can look to and aspire to. I think it's an extraordinarily prestigious billet; being the Sergeant Major of the U.S. Marine Corps is probably the most prestigious enlisted billet of any of the armed forces around the world.
>
> In fact, when we travel, in many of the other countries they don't understand the billet of the Sergeant Major of our Marine Corps. They don't understand why he's with me sometimes and does this and that. Occasionally we get into some little international "social list" challenges, but it's only the protocol side. When you're traveling, some of these organizations are not used to having a senior enlisted representative traveling with the Commandant. So the protocol, as such, is set up just for officers only, that type of thing. However, it's never any major problem.
>
> What I'm saying is that the Sergeant Major of the Marine Corps, I think, commands a unique respect within his Corps of Marines, to include all the general officers. It goes beyond what you'll see in other services and other countries.

Thus the Sergeant Major of the Marine Corps fills a unique billet. And those eleven men did it in a way that clearly demonstrated, time after time, that a man can raise himself from humble beginnings to the most respected enlisted position in one of the world's most famous military services. Dedication, sweat, blood, tireless effort, and innate ability brought to fruition have earned them the right to be called "Uncommon Men."

Appendix A

DECORATIONS

Sergeant Major Wilbur Bestwick

Letter of Commendation with Commendation Ribbon and Combat "V"
The Navy Unit Commendation
The Good Conduct Medal, 8th award
The American Defense Service Medal
The American Campaign Medal
The National Defense Service Medal
The Asiatic-Pacific Campaign Medal with four bronze stars
The World War II Victory Medal
The Korean Service Medal with three bronze stars
The Korean Presidential Unit Citation
The United Nations Service Medal

Sergeant Major Francis D. Rauber

The Good Conduct Medal, 7th award
The Marine Corps Expeditionary Medal (Haiti)
The China Service Medal
The American Campaign Medal
The World War II Victory Medal
The National Defense Service Medal

Sergeant Major Thomas J. McHugh

The Navy Commendation Medal with Combat "V"
The Navy Achievement Medal
The Purple Heart Medal
The Presidential Unit Citation with four bronze stars (in lieu of second
through fifth awards)
The Good Conduct Medal, 9th award
The American Defense Service Medal
The American Campaign Medal
The Asiatic-Pacific Campaign Medal with one silver star
(indicative of second through sixth awards)
The World War II Victory Medal
The Navy Occupation Service Medal with European clasp
The National Defense Service Medal
The Korean Service Medal with four bronze stars
The Vietnam Service Medal with three bronze stars
The Korean Presidential Unit Citation with three bronze stars
The Republic of Vietnam Cross of Gallantry with Palm
The Republic of Vietnam Meritorious Unit Citation, Civil Actions Color
The United Nations Service Medal
Letter of Commendation

Sergeant Major Herbert J. Sweet

The Legion of Merit
The Bronze Star Medal with Combat "V"
The Purple Heart Medal, four awards
The Navy Commendation Medal with Combat "V"
The Secretary of the Navy Commendation for Achievement Medal
The Presidential Unit Citation with three bronze stars
The Navy Unit Commendation
The Good Conduct Medal, 9th award
The American Defense Service Medal with one bronze star
The American Campaign Medal
The Asiatic-Pacific Campaign Medal with three bronze stars
The World War II Victory Medal
The National Defense Service Medal
The Korean Service Medal with one star
The Korean Presidential Unit Citation
The United Nations Service Medal

Sergeant Major Joseph W. Dailey

The Navy Cross
The Silver Star Medal
The Legion of Merit
The Bronze Star Medal with Combat "V"
The Purple Heart Medal
The Navy Commendation Medal with Combat "V"
The Combat Action Ribbon
The Presidential Unit Citation with two bronze stars
The Navy Unit Commendation
The Good Conduct Medal, 8th award
The Marine Corps Expeditionary Medal
The China Service Medal
The American Campaign Medal
The Asiatic-Pacific Campaign Medal with four bronze stars
The World War II Victory Medal
The Navy Occupation Service Medal
The National Defense Service Medal with one bronze star
The Armed Forces Expeditionary Medal
The Vietnam Service Medal with one silver star
The Korean Presidential Unit Citation
The Wharang Medal with one gold star
The Vietnamese Cross of Gallantry with two silver stars
The Republic of Vietnam Armed Forces Service Honor Medal 2d Class
The Republic of Vietnam Cross of Gallantry with Palm
The Republic of Vietnam Staff Service Medal, 2d Class
The Republic of Vietnam Campaign Medal
The United Nations Service Medal

Sergeant Major Clinton A. Puckett

The Navy Cross
The Legion of Merit
The Bronze Star Medal with Combat "V"
The Purple Heart Medal
The Navy Commendation Medal with Combat "V"
The Combat Action Ribbon
The Presidential Unit Citation with two bronze stars
The Navy Unit Commendation
The Good Conduct Medal, 9th award
The Asiatic-Pacific Campaign Medal with bronze star
The American Campaign Medal
The World War II Victory Medal

The Navy Occupation Service Medal with European clasp
The National Defense Service Medal with one bronze star
The Korean Service Medal with three bronze stars
The Vietnam Service Medal with one silver star and one bronze star
   (6 awards)
The Korean Presidential Unit Citation
The Vietnam Presidential Unit Citation
The United Nations Service Medal
The Republic of Vietnam Campaign Medal

Sergeant Major Henry H. Black

The Silver Star Medal
The Legion of Merit
The Bronze Star Medal with Combat "V" and two gold stars (in lieu
   of second and third awards)
The Purple Heart Medal
The Navy Achievement Medal
The Presidential Unit Citation with four bronze stars
The Good Conduct Medal, 8th award
The Navy Occupation Service Medal with European clasp
The National Defense Service Medal
The Armed Forces Expeditionary Medal
The Korean Service Medal with four bronze stars
The Vietnam Service Medal with four bronze stars
The Korean Presidential Unit Citation
The United Nations Service Medal
The Republic of Vietnam Campaign Medal

Sergeant Major John R. Massaro

The Legion of Merit
The Navy Commendation Medal with Combat "V" and gold star
   (in lieu of second award)
The Combat Action Ribbon
The Navy Unit Commendation
The Meritorious Unit Commendation with one bronze star
The Good Conduct Medal, 9th award
The National Defense Service Medal with one bronze star
The Korean Service Medal with three bronze stars
The Vietnam Service Medal with silver star (5 awards)
The Korean Presidential Unit Citation

The Republic of Vietnam Cross of Gallantry with Palm
The United Nations Service Medal
The Republic of Vietnam Campaign Medal with device
Marine Corps Parachutist Insignia
Marine Corps Scuba Divers Insignia

Sergeant Major Leland D. Crawford

The Navy Distinguished Service Medal
The Bronze Star Medal with Combat "V" and gold star (in lieu
of second award)
The Purple Heart Medal
The Combat Action Ribbon
The Presidential Unit Citation with two bronze stars
The Navy Unit Commendation with two bronze stars
The Meritorious Unit Commendation with two bronze stars
The Good Conduct Medal, 9th award
The National Defense Service Medal with two bronze stars
The Armed Forces Expeditionary Medal
The Korean Service Medal with three bronze stars
The Vietnam Service Medal with one silver and three bronze stars
(8 awards)
The Sea Service Deployment Ribbon
The Korean Presidential Unit Citation
The Vietnamese Cross of Gallantry with silver star and bronze star
The Vietnamese Honor Medal, 2d Class
The Republic of Vietnam Unit Cross of Gallantry with Palm
The Vietnamese Meritorious Unit Citation, Civil Actions Color,
with Palm
The United Nations Service Medal
The Republic of Vietnam Campaign Medal with device

Sergeant Major Robert E. Cleary

The Navy Distinguished Service Medal
The Silver Star Medal
The Purple Heart Medal, 2d award
The Air Medal, 3d award
The Navy Commendation Medal with Combat "V" and gold star
(in lieu of second award)
The Navy Achievement Medal
The Combat Action Ribbon
The Presidential Unit Citation with bronze star

The Navy Unit Commendation
The Meritorious Unit Commendation
The Good Conduct Medal, 8th award
The National Defense Service Medal with bronze star
The Korean Service Medal with two bronze stars
The Vietnam Service Medal
The Sea Service Deployment Ribbon
The Philippine Presidential Unit Citation
The Korean Presidential Unit Citation
The Vietnam Presidential Unit Citation
The Republic of Vietnam Meritorious Unit Citation, Gallantry
    Cross Color
The Vietnamese Meritorious Unit Citation, Civil Actions Color
The United Nations Service Medal
The Republic of Vietnam Campaign Medal with device
Combat Aircrew Insignia with three stars

Sergeant Major David W. Sommers

The Navy Distinguished Service Medal
The Legion of Merit
The Purple Heart
The Meritorious Service Medal with gold star (in lieu of second award)
The Navy Commendation Medal with Combat "V" and two gold stars
    (in lieu of second and third awards)
The Navy Achievement Medal with gold star (in lieu of second award)
The Combat Action Ribbon
The Presidential Unit Citation with bronze star
The Navy Unit Commendation
The Meritorious Unit Commendation
The Good Conduct Medal, 8th award
The Vietnam Service Medal
The Sea Service Deployment Ribbon
The Vietnam Presidential Unit Citation
The Vietnamese Meritorious Unit Citation, Civil Actions Color
The Republic of Vietnam Campaign Medal with device

Appendix B

TOURS OF DUTY
THE SERGEANTS MAJOR
OF THE MARINE CORPS

Sergeant Major Wilbur Bestwick	23 May, 1957 - 31 Aug, 1959
Sergeant Major Francis D. Rauber	1 Sep, 1959 - 28 Jun, 1962
Sergeant Major Thomas J. McHugh	29 Jun, 1962 - 16 Jul, 1965
Sergeant Major Herbert J. Sweet	17 Jul, 1965 - 31 Jul, 1969
Sergeant Major Joseph W. Dailey	1 Aug, 1969 - 31 Jan, 1973
Sergeant Major Clinton A. Puckett	1 Feb, 1973 - 31 May, 1975
Sergeant Major Henry H. Black	1 Jun, 1975 - 31 Mar, 1977
Sergeant Major John R. Massaro	1 Apr, 1977 - 14 Aug, 1979
Sergeant Major Leland D. Crawford	15 Aug, 1979 - 27 Jun, 1983
Sergeant Major Robert E. Cleary	28 Jun, 1983 - 25 Jun, 1987
Sergeant Major David W. Sommers	26 Jun, 1987 - 27 Jun, 1991

Appendix C

LEATHERNECK, MAY 66: SWEET

"A day with the sergeant major starts at his office, located in the chief of staff's section at Headquarters and next door to the Commandant. Sometimes it begins with a meeting of the Enlisted Performance Board, which also includes meritorious promotions and approval for reenlistment beyond 20 years.

"The sergeant major takes his place at the end of the conference table, next to the Personnel Sergeant Major and the only other enlisted member of the board. The rest of the membership is made up of majors and lieutenant colonels with a full colonel, the Head of the Promotion Branch, as senior officer.

"Sweet lights up a cigar that glows when the lights go off and a chart is projected on the wall. The chart reflects the performance of the Marine under discussion. It shows his weaknesses, his problems, and his career. Sweet studies the chart intently, puffing hard on the cigar. The man's record is not good, but he wants to reenlist for six more years which could give him 23 years of active duty. The board recommends only a three-year enlistment. Sweet agrees.

"Another chart is projected and it reflects the service career of a gunnery sergeant who has 26 years in the Corps. He wants to reenlist for four. His record is good but not outstanding. He's been in grade for 13 years, with each promotion board passing him by. The board asks for recommendations. There are two. One recommends a two-year enlistment, and the other is a 'thumbs down.' Sweet swivels around in his chair to face the other members. He thinks the lack of promotions needs explanation and discussion. 'This man is in a mighty rough field in which to get promoted,' he says. He asks the Personnel representative how many were promoted to master sergeant in that particular MOS field.

The answer is that only token promotions have been made for several years, since there is no shortage in that MOS.

"A recommendation is then made that the man be permitted to reenlist for the number of years he requested. It is approved. Sweet wins the round.

"He continues to study the charts and to vote—not always with the majority of the board. Like most enlisted men, he is more critical and expects better performance from staff NCOs. He does, however, support to the end a Marine with a good record who has not been promoted.

"The Meritorious Promotion Board has a recommendation for a meritorious promotion to sergeant. It concerns a corporal who has been an acting platoon sergeant for more than a year, and his commanding officer wants him promoted. The board is opposed to the recommendation, but Sweet points out that the man must be better than others or the billet would have been filled. He thinks the corporal should be promoted. The board disapproves the recommendation, because it is felt that the corporal would be promoted through normal channels before the board's decision reached the field. The sergeant major loses a round.

"After the two-hour board meeting, Sweet returns to his office. A huge stack of mail awaits him. The letters he receives are interesting, and some of them bring back memories of the past. Some are from old friends he hasn't seen for 20 years; others are from Marines he has not met—but who think the Sergeant Major of the Marine Corps has the power to get them anything from a promotion to duty in Paris.

"A gunnery sergeant wants a transfer to the duty station of his choice. Another wants to know when he can expect a transfer. Someone else wants to know when he can expect some more personnel. Sweet answers them all methodically and impartially. He pulls their records to familiarize himself with their cases. He then visits the appropriate monitor, and politely asks what's in the mill. His answer to the writer is the same answer he gets from the monitor.

"Another letter is from an old buddy of pre-World War II days, who reminds him of the good times and the liberty they pulled in the late '30s.

"He opens another letter. He studies it intently for a few minutes. It is from a doctor who congratulates him on being named Sergeant Major of the Marine Corps, and reminds him that it was he who cut a bullet out of Sweet on Guam. Sweet remembers him well. 'He had a tent set up on the side of a hill, and was about the busiest person in the combat area at the time.'

"The next correspondence is from a major, recently selected for 'light' colonel. It reads: 'I wish to extend my congratulations upon your selection as Sergeant Major of the Marine Corps....' It is in response to a congratulatory letter the sergeant major has sent him.

" 'You know,' the sergeant major reminisced, 'this man was a PFC in my outfit when I was a first sergeant of a ship's detachment. He caught me at a very busy moment one time, and requested permission to apply for Officers Candidate School. I practically threw him out of my office. Later, I found time to talk with him about the possibilities. My recommendation and confidence in him were well founded.'

"There was not much time for reflection. The sergeant major was preparing for a trip to the Western Pacific with the Commandant. Before leaving, he wanted to stop by and talk with the people in the Personnel Programs Branch. They might have some hot scoop he could pass on to the troops in the field. In an hour, he was fortified with statistics for promotion opportunities and personnel planning.

" 'This is one of the things I enjoy most about this job,' he said. 'I've got 'the word' for the troops. They all ask me about promotions and then they hit me with, 'When can we get to Vietnam?'

"Sweet explains the promotion system, and tells them that the Commandant wants them to complete their normal tours on station; that the Commandant appreciates their desire to get in the fighting; and that they will probably get their chance.

"When requests come in by letter, his answers start off with, 'This is in reply to your letter of 24 February instant.' It may end with a 'Sweet-ism'— 'May your life be as abundant as the crabgrass on the suburban lawn,' or, 'May you always have fair winds and a following sea...'

"The phone rings. The call is from a Marine in Norfolk. Friendly conversation...then an impossible request. Sweet's answer: 'Look, you know I can't do that for you.' His voice is crisp. It is evident that the position of Corps Sergeant Major will not be used to someone's personal advantage. The caller from Norfolk gets the message. He hangs up g-e-n-t-l-y.....

"The door opens. It's an officer from Quantico completing a staff study on the billets of sergeants major in the Marine Corps. He has come to see the right man.

"Sweet sums up his viewpoints. It's experience talking: 'There's too much aloofness on the part of some sergeants major. They should work closely, not only with the commanding officer, but the executive officer and adjutant as well. They should get out from behind their desks and circulate—feel the pulse of their units. They should keep their COs informed, be the voice of the enlisted Marines. They should concern themselves only with enlisted matters, and they should hold informal meetings with the first sergeants and troops as often as possible. They should set the example by appearance, mannerisms, and knowledge....'

"It is time for chow and the sergeant major heads across the street to the Henderson Hall mess hall. He goes through the cafeteria-style chow line, and parks his tray at a table with several other senior enlisted men. They swap sea stories, parry questions about each other's jobs, and speculate on the future of the Marine Corps. There is no mention of retirement.

"After chow, Sweet may be scheduled for a meeting of the Permanent Uniform Board, of which he is a member. There he listens to recommendations from the field on various items of uniform and participates in the discussions.

"His next stop may be the Naval Hospital in Bethesda, Maryland, to visit the sick or wounded Marines. He does this weekly when he's in Washington.

He says he finds no bitterness in the attitude of the wounded Marines, 'No one feeling sorry for himself—and many asking what are their chances of going back to Vietnam.'

"The sergeant major goes on most trips with General Greene, the Commandant, as a member of his personal staff. Sweet always finds time to talk with the enlisted Marines on these trips, and he keeps the Commandant informed on their feelings and problems."

Appendix D

(Reference Notebook Item IIH10a DFB5,
Approved by CMC 25 Mar 69)

POSITION

The Office of the Sergeant Major of the Marine Corps is the Senior Enlisted Marine in the Marine Corps. He is assigned to the Office of the Commandant of the Marine Corps.

RESPONSIBILITIES

The Sergeant Major of the Marine Corps advises the Commandant in matters pertaining to the enlisted personnel, and assists the Commandant in the performance of his duties.

DUTIES

The Sergeant Major of the Marine Corps is assigned the following duties:

a. Member of the Commandant's Enlisted Performance Board.

b. Member of the Permanent Marine Corps Uniform Board.

c. Member of the Commandant's Party on all visits and inspection trips to Marine Corps installations when enlisted personnel are involved.

d. Available, when directed by the Commandant, to assist staff agencies in any matters pertaining to enlisted personnel.

e. He is the Commandant's representative at the Staff Noncommissioned Officers Symposium.

ADDITIONAL DUTIES

The Sergeant Major of the Marine Corps receives many letters from the field. These letters are in the form of requests for information, status on promotion, suggestions, ideas, and recommendations. These letters, if need be, are processed through the various staff agencies and a reply is returned to the sender. This is an important source of communication with the field.

SELECTION AND APPOINTMENT

The Sergeant Major of the Marine Corps is selected for this billet by a board of General Officers, and is appointed by the Commandant.

TOUR OF DUTY

There is no fixed term of office for the incumbent. The Sergeant Major of the Marine Corps serves at the pleasure of the Commandant.

PREREQUISITES FOR SELECTION

The minimum prerequisites for selection to the position of Sergeant Major of the Marine Corps are:

a. Be serving on active duty in the rank of Sergeant Major.

b. Have served at least 20 years of active service.

c. Be of outstanding physical appearance and military bearing.

d. Be capable of expressing himself well both orally and in writing.

e. Has participated in at least one major campaign in which the Marine Corps was involved in combat.

BACKGROUND

The billet of Sergeant Major of the Marine Corps was established by administrative action in 1957....

PAY

Executive Order 11414, dated 11 June, 1968, established the basic pay of the Sergeant Major of the Marine Corps at $902.40.

Appendix E

NOTES ON SOURCES

Dedication

This quotation is from page 276 of a small book of Marine stories by Maj Hubert G. Duncan, USMC, Retired, and Capt William T. Moore, Jr., USMC, Retired, entitled *Green Side Out*. West Palm Beach: Gayle Publishers, 1982. Used by permission.

Chapter 1

The information on the early days of the rank is drawn from a variety of sources in the Marine Corps Historical Center (MCHC), Washington Navy Yard, Washington, D.C., particularly the library, the files in the Reference Section, and the Art Collection. LtCol Charles H. Cureton, USMCR, made helpful comments. A Marine Corps Historical Reference Pamphlet, *United States Marine Corps Ranks and Grades 1775-1969*, published in 1970 by the Historical Division of Headquarters Marine Corps, has valuable information. There is also useful material in *Leatherneck*, Jul 75, Nov 81, and Dec 87. The initial discussion of the origin of the billet is taken from the author's phone conversations with Simpson and Schatzel.

Chapter 2

Since Bestwick and his wife are dead and had no children, and because General Pate and many of Bestwick's contemporary NCOs are also dead, the major source for information was necessarily Bestwick's personnel file. This was supplemented by some material in the Marine Corps Historical Center files, and in *Leatherneck*, Dec 62 and Jul 75, and in *Marine Corps Gazette*, Nov 57. The quotation on how Bestwick "smoothed out some of the real problems" is from an interview with SgtMaj Floyd Stocks, USMC, Retired. Maj Duncan's descriptions are from pages 156-59 in *Green Side Out*. The quotes about "his general" and "uniform of a full Marine colonel" are from an interview with Maj Richard T. Spooner, USMC, Retired, whose mother was a very close friend of Bestwick.

Chapter 3

This chapter is based on quotations from the author's personal interviews with Rauber, his wife, Puckett, and Stocks, as well as correspondence from Sister Remigia. The quotation about Shoup, "Marines are inclined," is from *The American Weekly*, 14 May 61, page 14. The quotation on transfer policy is from *Marine Corps Gazette*, Jan 60.

Chapter 4

This chapter is based on quotations from the author's personal interview with McHugh, who was originally so modest he was reluctant to discuss his life. Some additional particulars come from the author's interviews with Greene, Chapman, Hugel, Crawford, Carson, Puckett, Kay Rauber, and letters from his daughters. Shoup died before he could be interviewed. The "hard but fair" quotation is from *Seattle Post-Intelligencer*, 11 May 65.

Chapter 5

This chapter is based on the author's personal interviews with Sweet and his wife, Greene, Chapman, Black, Puckett, and SgtMaj C. A. McKinney. News release number 495-70 from HQ, Force Logistic Command, in Da Nang has details on Sweet's return to Vietnam with the V.A. Totals of trips come from *New York Times*, 1 Aug 69. The "take my saber off" quote is from *Kansas City Times*, 17 Aug 67. The message "To sergeants major and first sergeants," the quotes about "big holes were left" and "lit a candle" are all from HQMC news release KTW-83-69. The "podium" quote is from the Washington *Evening Star*, 26 Mar 67.

Chapter 6

This chapter is based on the author's interviews with an elusive Dailey, Chapman, Massaro, Cleary, and Rogers, as well as letters from Dailey's daughters. General Cushman died before he could be interviewed. The Da Nang press interview is from III MAF news release 1817/SW. The "3100 letters" information is from *Navy Times*, 26 Jul 72. Chapman's speech at Dailey's posting is from HQMC news release CMC 147-69.

Chapter 7

This chapter is based on the author's personal interviews with Puckett, his wife, Massaro, Crawford, McKinney, Cleary, Sommers, and Black. Details on the burial of the "Unknown American" on 30 May 58 are from a "service information release" from HQMC. The information on "24 college-level correspondence courses" is from *Leatherneck*, Mar 73. "The Enlisted [Man's] General" is quoted from the *Washington Post* in *Leatherneck*, Jul 75. Cushman's quote about "accelerated the pace" is from HQMC news release DLS-160-75.

Chapter 8

This chapter is based on the author's personal interviews with Black, Cleary, Crawford, Puckett, Wilson, and Rogers. The quote about "majority of the mail," is from Black's column in *Leatherneck*, Jun 76. The retirement quotes, "I came into the Corps," and "For those who have fought," are from the Fredericksburg *Free-Lance Star*, 1 Apr 77. The specifics on the selection process for Sergeant Major of the Marine Corps are from HQMC news release CAB-158-75. Cushman's revised selection criteria are from HQMC news release CAB-62-75. Numerical data on Commandant's trips furnished by his aide.

Chapter 9

This chapter is based on the author's personal interviews with Massaro and his wife, Wilson, Kelley, Rogers, McKinney, Dailey, Crawford, Black, Puckett, and Cleary. The "face is like leather" quotation is from *Cleveland Plain Dealer*, 2 Apr 77. The "It is two fold" quotation is from *Navy Times*, 4 Jun 79.

Chapter 10

This chapter is based on the author's personal interviews with Crawford and his wife, Barrow, and Rogers. The quote, "I had been searching..." is from an interview of Crawford by *Wisconsin State Journal*, 25 Feb 82, as is the statement about a 70 percent reduction in marijuana use. The details of the sergeants major symposium are from USMC news release SJ-227-80, 21 Nov 80. The quote "could have dropped those colors" is from *Navy Times*, 20 Aug 79. The quotes, "if you are going to dig a ditch," "drill instructor duty was the growing stage," and "a gaze that could pierce steel" are all from *Leatherneck*, Nov 79. The quote "facial features like a rock slide" is from *Navy Times*, 1 Oct 79. Claim that DSM is "first awarded to an enlisted Marine" is confirmed by the Military Awards Branch of Headquarters.

Chapter 11

This chapter is based on the author's personal interviews with Cleary, Kelley, Puckett, Black, Massaro, and Crawford. The quote from President Reagan is from a letter on 18 Jun 87. Other background material is from *Marine Corps Gazette*, Sep 85. The quote about "proficiency pay" is from *Marines*, Jan 87.

Chapter 12

This chapter is based on the author's personal interviews with Sommers, his wife, Gray, and Crawford. The "always had a handle" quote about Barrow is from *Leatherneck*, Dec. 87. The "Ambush" nickname came from a plaque on the wall of Sommers' office. The details on Enlisted Career Force Controls are in Marine Corps Bulletin 5313, 19 Jun 89. The Sergeant Major of the Marine Corps Memorandum on substandard performance is the Dec89/Jan90 issue. The details of the Professional Military Education Program are in ALMAR 176/89 of Sep 89. The "$400,000 in food stamps," quote is from *Marines*, Mar 89. Yvette Sommers' 132 page book, *Roses and Thorns*, was published in 1990 by the Marine Corps Association in Quantico, Virginia.

Appendix F

NOTES ON ENLISTED RANK
1946 - 1992

The structure of enlisted ranks when Bestwick became the first Sergeant Major of the Marine Corps was based on a massive consolidation of titles that took effect on 1 December 1946. At that time eight former ranks, including sergeants major and first sergeants, were designated master sergeants; gunnery sergeants became technical sergeants; platoon sergeants were renamed staff sergeants. Subsequent developments are best summarized in the 1970 Marine Corps Historical Reference Pamphlet, *United States Marine Corps Ranks and Grades, 1775-1969*:

> The Marine Corps announced in December 1954 the establishment of two additional titles within grade E-7. The rank of sergeant major was to take precedence over the newly resurrected first sergeant, who, in turn, was placed above the master sergeant. This last change was made to give recognition to noncommissioned officers acting in these important billets; the job of first sergeant or sergeant major was too important to be classed merely as an administrative specialty.

> This re-emphasis on the role of the senior noncommissioned officers was followed by a sweeping revision of the enlisted ranks and grades of the Marine Corps in 1958, after Congress amended the Career Compensation Act of 1949 and authorized two new pay grades, E-8 and E-9. This revision was designed to relieve the crowding at the E-7 grade, caused by the rapid World War II output of noncommissioned officers and, since then, by the moving up—appropriately enough— of the specifically skilled men which every service was requiring more and more. The end result, however,

was an unbalanced structure, too heavy at the top.

By 1958, the proportion of NCOs in the Marine Corps had climbed to fifty-eight percent of the total enlisted strength, a startling figure when compared to the twenty-five percent of 1941. It is even more startling when one considers that the Marine Corps from its founding until World War I never had a proportion higher than 18.8 percent, with the usual percentage ranging between thirteen and fifteen percent....

This compression at the top, fifty-eight percent in 1958, led to rank imbalance and confusion. There were E-7s supervising other E-7s, while some corporals continued doing the same job after promotion as they did before. In short, the prestige of the NCO, traditional and necessary to any military service, was declining at the very time when it should be increased.

The solution to this imbalance, plus other desirable changes, was ordered by the Commandant on 25 November 1958, to be effective 1 January 1959.... In this revision of 1958, the ranks of corporal through master sergeant were upgraded one pay grade each, making room for an additional private rank. The sergeant major/first sergeant program was retained, with its historic command prestige, but a new technical leadership was introduced into the top NCO levels, in recognition of the ever-increasing complexity of waging modern warfare, by permitting E-8 and E-9 billets to be filled also by occupational specialists. Since technical adeptness was now required of quite a few others besides the technical sergeant, this title ceased to have value and it was deleted. Marines holding that rank were designated acting gunnery sergeants.

The rank of corporal was placed in pay grade E-4 in order to preserve his status as the junior NCO in the Marine Corps. The rank of sergeant with three stripes, formerly E-4, was selected to replace the rank of staff sergeant at E-5, in order to have two ranks of NCOs and to remove one rank from the ranks of staff NCOs which would start at staff sergeant in pay grade E-6. Personnel holding the rank of staff sergeant would carry the title of acting staff sergeant until promoted.

The occasion also enabled the Marine Corps to reapply its colorful history to the grade structure. The title of lance corporal, first used by the Marines in the Indian Wars of 1830s was revived. Now, for the first time, it was a permanent rank. In addition, the memorable "Gunny"—the gunnery sergeant and the master gunnery sergeant—was exhumed.

In E-7, the gunnery sergeant was used in place of the master sergeant, partly to restore the traditional rank and to move the title "master sergeant" from pay grade E-7 to E-8. As for the first sergeant, no change was involved except to raise the rank from E-7 to E-8. The rank of master gunnery sergeant, revived to provide leadership in occupational fields, was put at the top in E-9, alongside the sergeant major, raised from E-7 to E-9 and still the senior NCO.

Viewed in its entirety, the new enlisted structure enhanced career attractiveness which, for more than a century, had drawn volunteers to the Marine Corps. There was full acknowledgement of the modern military picture, yet no Marine could sadly say that "things aren't like they were in the old Corps." Also, the first year under the revised structure, fiscal year 1959, saw a new proportion of NCOs—a more logical 37.4 percent....

These modifications to the enlisted ranks proved so successful that they are still in effect a third of a century later. Thus the 1992 enlisted grade structure is as follows:

Grade	Pay Grade
Sergeant Major	E-9
Master Gunnery Sergeant	
First Sergeant	E-8
Master Sergeant	
Gunnery Sergeant	E-7
Staff Sergeant	E-6
Sergeant	E-5
Corporal	E-4
Lance Corporal	E-3
Private First Class	E-2
Private	E-1

Index